Karl Marx

Significant Figures in World History

Charles Darwin: A Reference Guide to His Life and Works,
by J. David Archibald, 2019.

Leonardo da Vinci: A Reference Guide to His Life and Works,
by Allison Lee Palmer, 2019.

Michelangelo: A Reference Guide to His Life and Works,
by Lilian H. Zirpolo, 2020.

Robert E. Lee: A Reference Guide to His Life and Works,
by James I. Robertson Jr., 2019.

John F. Kennedy: A Reference Guide to His Life and Works,
by Ian James Bickerton, 2019.

Florence Nightingale: A Reference Guide to Her Life and Works,
by Lynn McDonald, 2020.

Napoléon Bonaparte: A Reference Guide to His Life and Works,
by Joshua Meeks, 2020.

Nelson Mandela: A Reference Guide to His Life and Works,
by Aran S. MacKinnon, 2020.

Winston Churchill: A Reference Guide to His Life and Works,
by Christopher Catherwood, 2020.

Catherine the Great: A Reference Guide to Her Life and Works,
by Alexander Kamenskii, 2020.

Karl Marx

A Reference Guide to His Life and Works

Frank W. Elwell, Brian N. Andrews,
and Kenneth S. Hicks

ROWMAN & LITTLEFIELD
Lanham • Boulder • New York • London

Published by Rowman & Littlefield
An imprint of The Rowman & Littlefield Publishing Group, Inc.
4501 Forbes Boulevard, Suite 200, Lanham, Maryland 20706
www.rowman.com

6 Tinworth Street, London, SE11 5AL, United Kingdom

British Library Cataloguing in Publication Information Available

Library of Congress Control Number: 2020945798

ISBN 978-1-5381-2289-1 (cloth: alk. paper)
ISBN 978-1-5381-2290-7 (electronic)

♾™ The paper used in this publication meets the minimum requirements of American National Standard for Information Sciences—Permanence of Paper for Printed Library Materials, ANSI/NISO Z39.48-1992.

Karl Marx as Icon, mixed media on paper by Steven Rosser, professor of Art, Rogers State University, 2020.

Contents

Preface

Karl Marx (1818–1883) played multiple roles during his lifetime. He was a philosopher, a crusading journalist, as well as a political organizer and activist advocating democratic reforms, working-class political organizations, and the establishment of a socialist political order. As a journalist, propagandist, and political actor, Marx wrote to inspire men and women to immediate action. As a prophet, he forecast the eventual revolution of the working class, the overthrow of capitalism, and the establishment of a stateless, socialist society. Jon Elster (1986) argues that too many have merged the two figures of Engels and Marx into one entity. Even scholars often use Engels's statements in interpreting Marx. Marx was a genius, a profound thinker. Engels was not. While they collaborated over the course of some 40 years, both engaged in separate projects as well. While Marx read some of Engels's manuscripts without much objection, the views expressed are Engels's, not Marx's. Much of what Engels wrote, especially after Marx's death, contributed to the myths surrounding Marx's theories. "He began the tradition of codifying Marx's thought into a total system that promises answers to all questions in philosophy, the natural sciences, and the social sciences" (Elster 1986, 11). Marx is indeed a genius, but his theory is not the unified field theory that explains all social phenomena that Engels asserted.

Neither is Marx's genius in his analyses of the structure and dynamics of socialist or communist societies. The socialist aftermath of the revolution is a woefully underdeveloped topic in his texts. He did little writing on this future society, and what he did write consists of vague generalities. In "A Critique of the German Ideology" (1845–1846), for example, Marx writes in glowing terms of a society in which there is no division of labor. Where one can "do one thing today and another tomorrow, to hunt in the morning, fish in the afternoon, rear cattle in the evening, criticize after dinner, just as I have a mind, without ever becoming hunter, fisherman, shepherd or critic" (9). How this vision accords with Marx's later economic analysis on the necessity of capital's development of productive forces as a foundation for socialism is problematic. His imaginings in the quote above are more suitable to a preindustrial mode of production.

Marx's later assertion of a "dictatorship of the proletariat," which was supposed to aid in the transition to communism, is also challenging. Although the term may be analogous to the capitalist's control of the state (the "dictatorship of the bourgeoisie"), contemporaries like Mikhail Bakunin recognized that such unchecked power would lead to abuse. In sum, his posited transition between the two modes of production is hugely problematic. His writings on socialism and communism are neither extensive nor very convincing. There are far better advocates of socialism, far better descriptions of how it would work in an industrial setting. But, putting aside his predictions of the inevitability of socialism and how such an economy would work, there is still much of value in Marx. His most important contributions are as a political economist, a social scientist analyzing the origin, structure, and evolutionary trajectory of capitalism. Marx's real genius lies in his analysis of capitalism as a sociocultural system.

Marx developed the perspective of historical materialism that puts primary emphasis on the methods by which a society exploits its environment to provide the necessary resources for its population. His focus is on how these forces of production determine the relations of production and how both interact with the rest of the sociocultural system. The way in which the individual relates to these forces of production determines their position in society, their social power, prestige, and life chances.

As a social theorist, Marx's writings have had an enormous impact on all of the social sciences. His most significant contribution is in establishing a conflict model of social systems. Rather than conceiving of society as being based on consensus, Marx's theory posits the domination of a powerful class over a subordinate class. However, this domination is never long uncontested. It is the fundamental antagonism of the classes that produces class struggle that ultimately transforms sociocultural systems. "The history of all hitherto existing societies is the history of class struggles" (Marx and Engels 1848/2012, 1). The engine of sociocultural change, according to Marx, is class struggle. Social conflict is at the core of the historical process.

A second significant contribution is that Marx locates the origin of social power in the ownership or control of the forces of production. Marx contended that the production of economic goods—what is produced, how it is produced, and how it is exchanged—has a profound effect on the rest of the society. For Marx, how men and women relate to one another in the continuous struggle to secure needed resources from nature forms the basis of the entire sociocultural system.

A third contribution to the social sciences lies in Marx's analysis of capitalism and its effects on workers, capitalists themselves, and entire sociocultural systems. Capitalism as an historical entity was an emerging and rapidly evolving economic-political system. Marx brilliantly grasped its origin, structure,

and workings. He then predicted with an astonishing degree of accuracy its immediate evolutionary path. One need not take Marx's whole cloth—that is, to accept the inevitability of revolution and socialism—to integrate these insights into a coherent worldview. Understanding the structure and dynamics of capitalism is essential in understanding contemporary sociocultural systems and, thus, human behavior.

"The first historical act is," Marx (1845) writes, "the production of material life itself. This is indeed a historical act, a fundamental condition of all of history" (10). Humanity's needs for food, shelter, housing, and energy are central to understanding the sociocultural system. Unless men and women successfully fulfill this act, there would be no other. All social life is dependent on fulfilling this quest for a sufficiency of eating and drinking, for habitation and clothing. This is as true today as it was in prehistory. Do not be fooled, Marx is telling us: we are as dependent on nature as ever. The quest to meet basic needs was man's primary goal then and remains central when we attempt to analyze the complexities of modern life. However, men and women are perpetually dissatisfied animals. Our struggle against nature does not cease when we gratify these primary needs. The production of "secondary needs" evolve, when we find means to satisfy our primary needs. To meet these primary and secondary needs, Marx argued, men and women form societies. The first of these societies, communal in nature, were based on a minimal division of labor. These classless societies in which men hunted and women and children gathered vegetables, tubers, and grains were egalitarian. With the domestication of plants and animals, the division of labor begins to emerge in human societies. The division of labor, or increasing specialization of roles and crafts, eventually gives people differential access to resources, skills, and interests. This division eventually leads to the formation of antagonistic classes, the prime actors in human history. From this point on, humans engage in antagonistic cooperation to meet their primary and secondary needs. "By thus acting on the external world and changing it, he at the same time changes his own nature" (Marx 1867/1976, 127).

All social institutions are dependent on the economic base, and a thorough analysis of sociocultural systems will always reveal this underlying economic arrangement. The way a society is organized to meet material needs will profoundly affect all other social structures, including government, family, education, and religious institutions. "Legal relations as well as the form of the state are to be grasped neither from themselves nor from the so-called development of the human mind, but have their roots in the material conditions of life. . . . The anatomy of civil society is to be sought in political economy" (Marx 1859, 1). The mode of production is the most potent factor influencing the rest of the social system. Like all the great macro social theorists, Marx regarded society as a structurally integrated system. Consequently, any aspect of that whole, whether it be legal codes, systems of education, art, or religion, could not be understood by itself. Instead, he believed that we must examine the parts in relation to one another and to the whole.

In his masterful three-volume work *Capital*, Marx described in detail the origins, structure, and dynamics of capital circulation and growth. Writing in the early stages of capital development, he grasped the essence of its political economy. He forecast ever-increasing productivity through technological innovation, mechanization, chemical engineering, and the detailed division of labor applied to extraction, manufacturing, communication, and transportation industries. Marx saw these same techniques used as well in the industrialization of agriculture, thus removing millions from their livelihoods and making them available for exploitation by the captains of industry. He foresaw this agricultural industry, poisoning the land and draining it of nutrients, as well as the devastation of the urban environment. He saw the centralization and enlargement of industry, the frantic rise and fall of commerce, and the resulting churning of employment.

Along with this enlargement and centralization, he pointed to the rise of credit mechanisms such as banks and joint-stock companies (corporations). Because they are playing with other people's money and have limited liability, Marx asserted, they are not as risk averse. As the economy centralized and competition eliminated many former capitalists, the more successful would become money capitalists, many of whom would no longer have direct management responsibilities. He saw a continuous growth of the proletariat, a class that had nothing to sell but their labor. As part of this class, he wrote of an increase in the number of skilled managerial workers who would enjoy only slightly better treatment from the capitalist system, though he may have underestimated their numbers as well as their rewards in an advanced capitalist society.

Marx asserted that a large surplus population of unemployed and semiemployed workers was necessary to keep the wages of workers down so that this surplus pool would be available for work in times of hyperactivity. This pool of surplus labor was critical because Marx asserted that the internal contradictions of capital subjected the economy to periods of boom and bust. He claimed that it is in times of hyperactivity that wages rise and profits decline. Capitalists respond with further mechanization that results in increased production. Automation makes many jobs obsolete, stripping other jobs of skills and growing alienation of the workers who remain. Thousands of firms acting to preserve or grow their market share and their bottom line, thus producing more commodities than can be sold in the market. This overproduction leads to an economic recession, throwing millions out of work for extended periods.

In addition, Marx asserted that the capitalist class controlled the nation-state in their interests, establishing laws, taxes, regulations, and foreign policy to favor accumulating further capital. Because capitalism is a process continually seeking new markets and workers to exploit, he asserted that capitalism would eventually expand to encompass the world. He predicted a growing inequality within and between societies because capitalism seeks to increase profits by expropriating the surplus produced by the workers. Indeed, his analysis of the capitalist system's evolution in the 140 years or so after his death is remarkable.

Finally, because capitalism is a system for private gain rather than the social good, he asserted that there is an ongoing class struggle between capitalists and the proletariat. Thus, we come to his theory of crisis and the proletarian revolution. Marx ties this theory to the development of capitalism, producing periodic economic crises. He posited that through these crises, the proletariat would develop revolutionary consciousness. Workers would gradually recognize that capitalists structure the mode of production and thus the entire superstructure of society for their benefit alone, that the system cannot meet the needs of the masses because of the capitalist's need for profit. In some future crisis, Marx predicts, this consciousness would lead to revolt. However, while the periodic economic crises are real, there is little evidence of the widespread development of revolutionary consciousness among the working class in advanced capitalist societies.

Marx's prediction of a socialist revolution was always dependent on class action; it was never to be automatic, as some later Marxists claim in their theories of economic collapse with socialism rising from the ashes. Marx's reliance on a proletarian revolution may have missed some crosscurrents to working-class consciousness, such as nationalism, ethnic identity, cultural values, or status positions in an advanced industrial economy; such divisions serve to divide the working classes.

Perhaps the major flaw in his analysis is that he underestimated capitalism's power to control social reality through the forces of government, including its police powers, as well as the establishment of a welfare state. Additionally, he may not have anticipated the development of new communication and surveillance technologies, improved social technologies of propaganda and advertising, and the proliferation of inexpensive, mass-produced creature comforts and entertainments. However, another possibility is that the economic crises are not yet severe enough to break through capitalist control and consumer complacency and that the revolution is yet to come.

The three of us were very happy to be asked to work on this project, and over the two years we have worked on it, we have learned much. We thank Jon Woronoff and April Snider for their aid and comfort in the writing process and hope we did not give them too much heartburn. We appreciate Dimitri Bologna for the detailed labor he did on the manuscript. We are also appreciative of Rogers State University and the people of Oklahoma, who, in return for teaching their students, allow us the freedom to study history and the social sciences.

As in all the books in the series of *Significant Figures in World History*, we have made extensive cross-references in the entries. Within each entry, boldface type is used for terms that have their own entries, and other terms that are related are indicated by "*See also*" at the end of the entry.

Chronology

1600 Historians mark the slow emergence of capitalism starting in the 15th century, beginning with the city-states of Renaissance Italy.

1760–1820 The first phase of the English Industrial Revolution.

1770 Birth of German philosopher Georg Wilhelm Friedrich Hegel.

1777 Birth of Heinrich Marx, future father of Karl Marx, in Trier in what is now southwestern Germany.

1788 Birth of Henriette Presburg, the future mother of Karl Marx, in the Netherlands.

1789 The storming of the Bastille signals the beginning of the French Revolution.

1797 France annexes Trier into its empire.

1804 Birth of German philosopher Ludwig Feuerbach.

1805 Birth of French radical anarchist Louis-August Blanqui.

1809 Birth of French "mutualist" socialist Pierre Proudhon.

1812 Prussia issues its "Edict of Emancipation for Jews," effectively barring Jews from government service or the private practice of law. In Russia, the birth of writer and philosopher Aleksandr Herzen.

1813 The Battle of Leipzig, and Napoleon Bonaparte's abdication and exile to Elba.

1814 Marriage of Heinrich Marx and Henriette Presburg. Heinrich begins a law practice. Birth of Jenny Westphalen, future wife of Karl Marx. Birth of Russian anarchist socialist Mikhail Bakunin.

1815 The Congress of Vienna establishes a reactionary European political order.

1816–1819 Heinrich Marx converts to Protestantism in order to continue to practice law.

1818 Birth of Karl Marx on 5 May, the second of nine children.

1820 Birth of Friedrich Engels to Friedrich and Elisabeth, a wealthy family of textile manufacturers in Barmen, in the Rhine Province.

1825 Birth of German lawyer and socialist Ferdinand Lassalle.

1826 Birth of German socialist politician Wilhelm Liebknecht.

1830–1835 Karl Marx attends the lyceum in Trier.

1831 Death of German philosopher Georg Wilhelm Friedrich Hegel.

1835–1836 Karl Marx enters the University of Bonn to study law, picking up the nickname "The Moor" for his dark complexion.

1836 Foundation of the League of the Just in London.

1836–1841 Karl Marx transfers to the University of Berlin, studying law, languages, and philosophy; while there, he has his first encounter with the Young Hegelians. At the end of his studies at the University of Berlin, Marx submits his dissertation on Epicurus to the University of Jena.

1838 Death of Heinrich Marx. The status of his inheritance becomes a long-term source of conflict between Karl and his mother.

1840 Birth of German socialist politician August Babel.

1842 Karl Marx earns his doctorate in philosophy from the University of Jena. Denied the opportunity of an academic post, he accepts a position writing for *Rheinische Zeitung (Rhenish Newspaper)*, Marx's first experience with professional journalism. In Russia, the birth of anarchist socialist Peter Kropotkin.

1843 Prussian censors shut down *Rheinische Zeitung*. Marx marries Jenny Westphalen, and they move to Paris. Marx writes two of his initial works: *On the Jewish Question* and *Contribution to the Critique of Hegel's Philosophy of Right*.

1844 Marx begins an intensive study of political economy. While still in Paris, Marx encounters Pierre Proudhon and Mikhail Bakunin. Marx begins close collaboration with Friedrich Engels, the first being *The Holy Family*. His wife gives birth to his first child, Jenny.

1845 Under pressure from the Prussian government, the French government expels Marx from Paris, relocating to Brussels.

While there, Marx writes *Theses on Feuerbach*. Meanwhile, in Leipzig, Engels writes *The Condition of the Working Class in England*. Birth of Marx's second child, Laura. Helene Demuth enters service as a housekeeper in the Marx household.

1845–1846 Marx and Engels collaborate on *The German Ideology*, the first clear articulation of historical materialism.

1846 Marx and Engels help to found the Communist Correspondence Committee in Belgium.

1847 Marx publishes *The Poverty of Philosophy*, a critique of Pierre Proudhon's *System of Economic Contradictions*. Marx also delivers a series of lectures in Brussels, later published as *Wage Labour and Capital*. In London, the Communist Correspondence Committee and the League of the Just merge to form the Communist League. The new organization commissions Marx and Engels to write *The Communist Manifesto*. Marx's first son, Edgar, is born.

1848 Publication of *The Communist Manifesto*. The subsequent revolutions of 1848 roil much of Europe. Prussia demands the expulsion of Marx from Brussels, and he briefly relocates to Paris. He then moves to Cologne, where he assumes editorship of the *Neue Rheinische Zeitung*, using his position to advocate for revolutionary change.

1848–1850 Marx works on *The Class Struggles in France, 1848–1850*, published in serialized form in the *Neue Rheinische Zeitung*.

1849 Prussian authorities accuse Marx of fomenting insurrection, ordering his expulsion. After briefly relocating to Paris and receiving an order to leave from French authorities, Marx and his family take up residence in London, where he would remain for the rest of his life. Engels follows Marx to England, taking up a position overseeing a factory partially owned by his family. Marx's second son, Heinrich Guido, is born.

1850 Marx begins an intensive study of political economy at the British Museum, beginning work on *The Class Struggles in France, 1848–1850*. Marx's second son, Heinrich Guido, dies on 19 November. Birth of German socialist Eduard Bernstein.

1851 Marx begins episodic work as a journalist for the *New York Tribune*. In Cologne, the Prussian government begins the trial of Herman Becker and ten other members of the Communist League on allegations of plotting the government's overthrow. On 28 March, Marx's third daughter, Franziska, is born. On 23 June, Helene Demuth gives birth to Henry Frederick Demuth, and Friedrich Engels claims paternity.

1852 The Communist League disbands. Marx publishes *The Eighteenth Brumaire of Louis Bonaparte*, a scathing critique of Bonaparte's dictatorship as a manifestation of bourgeois counterrevolution. Marx's daughter, Franziska, dies on 14 April.

1854 Birth of German Marxist theorist Karl Kautsky.

1855 Birth of Marx's youngest daughter, Eleanor, on 16 January. On 6 April, the death of Marx's eight-year-old son, Edgar, devastates Marx.

1856 Birth in Russia of Georgi Plekhanov, the first Russian Marxist.

1857–1858 Marx begins writing a manuscript, later published in the early 20th century as "The Grundrisse." Birth of German Marxist Clara Zetkin.

1859 Publication of Marx's *A Contribution to the Critique of Political Economy* in Berlin, offering the clearest summary of his materialist conception of history. Publication of Charles Darwin's *On the Origin of Species*, which Marx studied and would cite favorably in *Capital: Volume I*.

1861–1863 Marx works on a manuscript for *Theories of Surplus Value*.

1862 The end of Marx's employment at the *New York Tribune*, further worsening his family's financial fortunes.

1863 Participation of Marx and Engels in the formation of the International Workingmen's Association (also known as the First International) at a conference held in London. Marx wrote the charter and delivered the inaugural address and would remain an active participant although often behind the scenes.

1864 Death of Ferdinand Lassalle from wounds suffered in a duel.

1865 Death of French "mutualist" socialist Pierre Proudhon.

1866 At the Congress of the First International held in Geneva, members approved a resolution for an eight-hour workday. The defeat of the Austrian Empire in the Austro-Prussian War leads to a surge of nationalist sentiment among the German states.

1867 Publication of Marx's *Capital: Volume I*, in Hamburg, Germany. His definitive work on economics, including his theory of value and his critique of the capitalist system's exploitation of workers. Engels promotes the publication by writing several favorable reviews.

1867–1880 Marx begins rewriting his economic manuscripts written before 1865, continuing that work until shortly before his death. These unfinished works comprise the material used by Engels for *Capital: Volumes II and III*.

1868 The Brussels Congress of the First International passes a resolution recommending to all workingmen the close study of Marx's *Capital*. Marx's second daughter, Laura, marries the French socialist Paul Lafargue.

1869 The Congress of the First International held in Basel, Switzerland, leads to a significant schism on the issue of landownership between "mutualist" followers of Proudhon and "collectivists" following Marx and the Russian anarchist socialist Mikhail Bakunin.

The collectivist position prevailed. Formation of the Social Democratic Workers' Party of Germany (SDAP). The SDAP affiliates with the First International. Engels begins supplementing Marx's income.

1870 The rapid defeat of France in the Franco-Prussian War consolidates the unification of the German Confederation into the German Empire under the leadership of the Prussian Hohenzollern dynasty. Germany imposes harsh surrender conditions, including territorial concessions and reparations. The abdication of Louis Napoleon leads to the establishment of the Paris Commune, formed in opposition to the Prussian peace and calling for a radical socialist government in France. The Commune's brutal suppression by French provisional authorities inspires Marx to write *The Civil War in France*, one of the most widely read works in his lifetime. At the London Congress of the First International held in London, Marx and Engels successfully advocate calls for active revolutionary struggle and the establishment of independent proletarian parties in each country. Death of Russian writer and philosopher Aleksandr Herzen.

1871 In Russia, Vladimir Ilyich Ulyanov—later known as Lenin—is born. In Poland, Rosa Luxemburg is born. In Germany, Karl Liebknecht and Friedrich Ebert are born.

1872 The Congress of the First International held in The Hague, reaffirming the principal resolutions of the previous Congress. Conflict emerges between the anarchist faction led by Mikhail Bakunin and the Marxist faction, with Bakunin's followers accusing Marx of authoritarian intentions. The Congress expels Bakunin's faction. Marx's oldest daughter, Jenny, marries the French socialist Charles Longuet.

1875 The Gotha Congress results in the merger of the two major German socialist parties into the Socialist Workers' Party of Germany. Marx, given an early draft of the party's platform, rapidly pens a scathingly critical review; this review is later published as *Critique of the Gotha Program*.

1876 Dissolution of the First International resulting from internal conflict among anarchist and Marxist interpretations of socialism. Death of Russian anarchist socialist Mikhail Bakunin.

1878 Publication by Engels of *Anti-Duhring*, a critical reply to a rival German socialist, defending what Engels characterized as "scientific socialism."

1880–1882 Marx begins reading and taking notes on the works of prominent anthropologists, particularly a recent book by American Lewis Henry Morgan. These *Ethnological Notebooks* were published in 1972.

1881 Formation of the Democratic Federation, the first British political party to advance a Marxist political platform at a conference in London. On 2 December, the death of Jenny von Westphalen in Paris, following a long illness.

1883 On 11 January, Marx's eldest daughter, Jenny, dies of cancer in Paris. On 14 March, Karl Marx dies of pneumonia and is buried at Highgate Cemetery. On 17 March, Engels delivers his eulogy.

1884 Engels writes the manuscript for *Origin of the Family, Private Property and the State*, drawing heavily on the American anthropologists Henry Lewis Morgan's *Ancient Society* and Marx's *Ethnological Notebooks*. The Democratic Federation changes its name to the Social Democratic Federation.

1885 Engels brings to publication Marx's *Capital: Volume II*, drawing heavily on Marx's rewritten economic notebooks. Formation in England of the Socialist League, a splinter group from the Social Democratic Federation.

1886 Marx's daughter Eleanor travels with her partner Edward Aveling to the United States, promoting the anarchist platform of the Socialist League.

1887 Publication of the first English edition of Marx's *Capital: Volume I*. Drawing heavily on the third German edition, Engels edited the volume, which was translated by Samuel Moore and Edward Aveling.

1888 Publication of Engels's *Ludwig Feuerbach and the End of Classical German Philosophy*, which includes in an appendix Marx's 1844 essay *Theses on Feuerbach*, its first appearance in print.

1889 The Founding Congress of the Second International is held in Paris, barring anarchist socialist groups from its membership.

1890 Merger of the Socialist Workers' Party of Germany with other socialist parties into the Social Democratic Party of Germany, the largest and most influential socialist party in the world.

1891 Meetings of the Second Congress of the Second International held in Brussels, Belgium. Resolutions include designation of 1 May as "May Day" in support of its campaign for a universal eight-hour workday. Adoption of the Social Democratic Party of Germany of the Erfurt Program, which follows Marx's critical diagnosis of capitalism but advances a platform of protecting workers' rights rather than calling for revolution.

1894 Publication of Marx's *Capital: Volume III*, heavily edited by Engels, in Germany.

1895 Death of Friedrich Engels in London. He is cremated, and his ashes are scattered in southeastern coastal England at Beachy Head.

1898 Marx's youngest surviving daughter, Eleanor, dies by her own hand.

1899 German socialist Eduard Bernstein publishes *Evolutionary Socialism: A Criticism and Affirmation*, and his "revisionist" version of Marxism exerts considerable influence among the leadership of the Social Democratic Party of Germany. Rosa Luxemburg publishes a scathing critique of Bernstein's revisionism, becoming a leading advocate of revolutionary socialism.

1900 Death of German socialist politician Wilhelm Liebknecht.

1901 Dissolution of the Socialist League.

1911 Marx's second daughter, Laura, commits suicide alongside her husband, the French socialist Paul Lafargue.

1913 Death of German socialist politician August Babel.

1918 Death of Georgi Plekhanov, the first Russian Marxist.

1919 Formation of the Spartacus League in Germany. It was later renamed the Communist Party of Germany as an offshoot of younger and more radical members of the Social Democratic Party of Germany (SPD). Rosa Luxemburg and Karl Liebknecht reluctantly support the Spartacist Uprising. The German provisional government, led by SPD leader and provisional president Friedrich Ebert, brutally suppresses the uprising. Freikorps units capture, torture, and execute both Luxemburg and Liebknecht.

1921 Death of Russian anarchist socialist Peter Kropotkin.

1925 Death of Friedrich Ebert, leader of the Social Democratic Party of Germany and the first president of the Weimar Republic.

1932 Death of German socialist Eduard Bernstein.

1933 Death of German Marxist Clara Zetkin.

1938 Death of German Marxist theorist Karl Kautsky.

Introduction

Writing or lecturing about Karl Marx (1818–1883) can be difficult. Much of the problem is that he has become a significant figure in history itself. He has inspired social movements and individual revolutionaries—some of whom have been faithful to his work, while many more have misused his name and writings. Governments in the 20th and 21st centuries have ruled tyrannically, citing Marx as their inspiration. Even today, Western professors teaching about Marx and his theories must deal with the Cold War and anti-communist attitudes that students often bring to class. Many students have common misconceptions of Marx's thought and theory, equating it with the communist parties of the old Soviet Union and other totalitarian societies. They are actively hostile to learning anything about it. Since the end of the Cold War, students are usually not active anticommunists, but they still tend to equate Marx with Soviet-style communism. Many assumed that scholars have thoroughly rejected his theories and relegated them to the dustbin of history.

In this introduction, we will not deal with the issue of nation-states ruled by supposed "communist" dictators. Marx died well before the revolution in Russia and other totalitarian systems of the 20th century. While he inspired many of the revolutionaries, he bears little of the responsibility for the totalitarian regimes that emerged (to explain the Soviet government, look to the czarist regimes). Marx is neither Lenin nor Stalin. While he often gets both credit and blame for the communist revolution in Russia, it was very much counter to his theory of historical materialism. Marx asserted that before a socialist revolution could occur, capitalism must first develop the means of production to the fullest extent possible under its rule. Throughout this development, capitalism would suffer periodic crises growing more severe over time. It is through their experience with these crises that the proletariat attains revolutionary consciousness. They gradually come to realize that the mode of production is developing to serve the interests of capitalists against the interests of workers. Only then, according to Marx, would the revolution occur, establishing socialism under the "dictatorship of the proletariat." This dictatorship would create a socialist society that would prepare man for the transition to communism. At the time of its 1917 revolution, Russia was a feudal society. It was a backward land, with little industrial development and only a small working class, not at all consistent with Marx's theory. A vanguard party led its revolution. While he may have inspired some of the revolutionaries and they selectively borrowed from his writings to justify their actions, he bears little of the responsibility for their crimes.

THE YOUNG MARX

Karl Marx was born on 5 May 1818 in Trier in southwestern Germany in the German Confederation. Karl was the second of eight children born to Henriette Marx (née Pressburg, 1788–1863) and Heinrich Marx (1777–1838). While some believe that Marx came from a long line of rabbis, it is not entirely true. What is true is that his grandfather on his father's side was a rabbi, and his uncle Samuel was a rabbi in Trier. Karl's father, Heinrich, studied law when Trier was part of Napoleon's empire; however, in 1815, it became a province of the Kingdom of Prussia. Around the time of Karl's birth, Heinrich converted to the Christian Evangelical Church of Prussia. The conversion was probably for reasons of his career—the Prussian government prohibited Jews from practicing law or working for the government. Perhaps another reason for his conversion, biographers speculate, were his Enlightenment beliefs. Heinrich's Enlightenment ideas played an active role in his son's values: respect for reason as the source of authority as well as an understanding of science, progress, and religious tolerance. The Evangelical Church baptized Karl at the age of six, and his mother followed about a year later. The evidence is that Karl was very close to his father.

Karl's relationship with his mother, Henriette, was very different. About 11 years younger than Heinrich, she was from a Jewish family that originated in Hungary but settled in the Netherlands in the 18th century and became successful merchants. She brought a substantial dowry to the marriage, allowing Heinrich to establish his law practice.

Rather than attending elementary school, Karl was probably tutored at home. He entered the Trier Gymnasium in 1830 at the age of 12. There he studied Latin and Greek in preparation for university studies. The director of the gymnasium, Johann Wyttenbach, was a man steeped in Enlightenment ideas, ideas that Karl exhibited in his graduation essay. A former official under French rule, the Prussian government was long suspicious of Wyttenbach's "radicalism." Toward the end of Karl's studies at the gymnasium, the government appointed a codirector more in line with Prussian sensibilities. Before leaving the school, Karl made it a point of snubbing the new man. Heinrich later made excuses for his son's behavior to the codirector.

THE COLLEGE YEARS

Karl left Trier for the University of Bonn in November 1835 to study law. However, he quickly got caught up in student life outside the classroom, frequenting taverns and engaging in brawls and reportedly even a duel. It was in Bonn that he picked up the nickname of "The Moor" because of his dark complexion. His father, Heinrich, insisted that he focus more on his studies and transfer to the University of Berlin. Karl was already engaged to Jenny Westphalen by the time he came to Berlin in 1836. Jenny was a girl some four years his senior and friend to his sister. While Karl was attending the university, his father died in 1838, and Karl struggled financially, borrowing money from his mother and friends to continue his studies. He abandoned his study of law and focused on philosophy. It is in Berlin that he took up with the Young Hegelians, especially Bruno Bauer, who became his mentor. At the end of his four years of study, Karl submitted his dissertation on Epicurus to the University of Jena. In addition to the thesis, the university required a compendium of all courses attended as well as certificates of competence in Latin for awarding a doctorate. Karl hoped to begin a teaching career with his mentor, Bruno Bauer, at the University of Bonn. However, the Prussian state terminated Bauer before Marx could gain the position. It was then that Karl turned to journalism.

COLOGNE

Writing a commentary on current events became Marx's primary way of making a living for the 20 years following his university studies. In 1842, after his prospects as an academic evaporated, Karl began as a writer for the *Rhineland News*, a newly founded paper headquartered in Cologne. The paper favored liberal reforms of the Prussian government, such as guarantees of civil liberties, a constitutional monarchy, and an elected legislature. His articles for the paper were very much in line with the liberal investors. Marx wrote two long essays in the summer and fall of 1842. The first essay was in defense of freedom of the press, criticizing the Prussian state as authoritarian and wedded to the past. Karl linked press freedoms to broader civil liberties and human rights. The second essay was in defense of the Young Hegelians.

Toward the end of 1842, the Prussian government was increasingly censoring the newspaper and looking for ways to close it down. In mid-October, investors hired Marx as part of the editorial board in hopes that he would moderate the paper in ways that would be more acceptable to the government and the liberal investors. Karl then moved to Cologne and was very active on the editorial staff. He worked to tone down the Young Hegelians who were writing for the paper, recruiting liberal writers to argue for reform of municipal government and advocating for free trade and an end to protectionism. Shortly after moving to Cologne, Marx joined a reading group headed by Moses Hess that often discussed socialist ideas. Nevertheless, he did not become an advocate for socialism in his journalism when writing about social issues. In writing of the debates in the Provincial Diet regarding laws about wood theft and the plight of the lower classes in Germany, for example, Karl blamed government policies rather than capitalists.

As the Prussian government continued to make its displeasure with the paper known, Karl's tone regarding the government and its officials became ever more mocking and sarcastic. While circulation boomed under Karl's editorial contributions, the Prussian government was not amused. In January 1843, the government ordered the *Rhineland News* to stop publication by April. Stockholders protested, even promising to dismiss Marx. People in Cologne sent a petition to the king, pleading with him to allow the newspaper to keep publishing. All such protest was to no avail. Marx became known to the Prussian governments as a dissident. However, he also made a name for himself with liberal members of Cologne's middle classes, who would continue to offer support over the next decade.

PARIS

Karl's experience with the government convinced him that he would have to leave Prussia to avoid censorship and repression. Arnold Ruge was coming to the same conclusion. He proposed to Karl in the spring of 1843 that he become a coeditor with Ruge on a new journal called the *German-French Annals.* They planned to publish the journal in Paris. The salaried position allowed Marx to marry Jenny on 19 June 1843 after a seven-year engagement. There were two ceremonies: one civil and one in the Protestant church. In the autumn of 1843, they moved to Paris.

In the 1840s, France was a constitutional monarchy with freedom of political expression and fundamental civil liberties far more liberal than those of the Prussian state. While living in Paris, Marx interacted with exiles across the political spectrum, from communists to capitalists, monarchists to democrats, and even anarchists. Marx immediately set to work trying to recruit French writers for the journal but had limited success. Most French socialists visualized communism as the fulfillment of Christian ideals in communal settings rather than the subversive political action of atheistic Germans (Sperber 2013, 120). The journal failed after only one double issue in February 1844 in which Marx had contributed two articles: "Introduction to the Critique of Hegel's Philosophy of Law" and "On the Jewish Question." Ruge could pay Marx only part of what he was due for his work. However, his supporters in Cologne were so impressed with his work that they raised a substantial sum of money so that he could continue his writing and his studies.

After the failure of the journal, Marx continued for some months in Paris, socializing with socialists, anarchists, and other radicals from across the continent. It is in Paris on 23 August 1844 that Karl first met Friedrich Engels. Engels had served in the Prussian army and associated with the Young Hegelians while stationed in Berlin. Shortly after his service, he became acquainted with communism through Moses Hess while visiting Cologne. His father, to separate the young man from his radical friends, sent him to Manchester, England, to work and learn the family textile business in 1842. Engels's radicalism grew as he learned about the conditions of the proletariat working in the textile mills. He sent pieces to the *Rhineland News* while Marx was an editor and wrote an article for the *German-French Annals*. Engels included much of this research in *The Condition of the Working Class in England* (published in German in 1845). Having fulfilled his family obligation of working in England, Engels was on his way home and stopped off in Paris to meet Marx. Engels ended up staying with Karl for 10 days (Jenny and child were visiting her mother in Trier). While there, the two laid plans for future writing projects and met with other European radicals.

After the failure of the *German-French Annals*, Marx wrote for left-wing German newspapers and began writing the "Economic and Philosophical Manuscripts" while still living in Paris. This work was unpublished in his lifetime and became widely translated and known only after World War II. It was in this work that Marx first delved deeply into political economy, writing in the tradition of classical economists such as David Ricardo and Adam Smith. It is here, too, that Marx wrote extensively on the alienation of labor, the historical task of the proletariat, and communism. These unpublished manuscripts allowed Marx to work out his initial thoughts on these and other topics and are the beginnings of his extensive critique of capitalism.

In his writings, Karl was extremely critical of the authoritarian Prussian government and its repression of speech and other civil liberties. The Prussian government took notice, and he became a marked man. In late 1844, the Prussian government pressured the French government to expel several German émigrés for anti-Prussian writings. Marx and Ruge were among those deported. In January 1845, the French government gave Marx one week to leave France, leaving Jenny and his daughter briefly behind to settle family business. Karl left for Brussels. Over the next five years, Karl

was committed to both anti-Prussian and anti-capitalist revolutionary activity.

BRUSSELS

Marx and his family spent three years in the capital of Belgium. While there, Karl continued to write and associate with other European radicals. To avoid further trouble with the Prussian government, he renounced his Prussian citizenship. At the same time, he assured Belgian authorities that he would not engage in political activities—a promise he would not keep. His second daughter, Laura, was born in October 1845, and his son Edgar was born in February 1847. The family lived in genteel poverty, living on money that Marx could earn from his writings, occasional journal pieces, and loans. It was during their time in Brussels that Jenny's mother arranged for a live-in servant for the Marx household. Helene (Lenchen) Demuth would help with the children and do the housework, a position she would hold for the rest of Karl's life.

It was while living in Brussels that Karl's hypercriticism of those who differed from him politically became more pronounced, even if the differences were slight. He took such differences personally and attacked perceived rivals bitterly both in print and in person. His intolerance and insistence on his views would be a hindrance in his attempts at organizing political groups.

In the summer of 1845, Marx and Engels took a trip to England to research political economy. Visiting London for a couple of weeks, Engels introduced Marx to members of the League of the Just. The League was a secret society of several hundred German exiles who also sponsored a more open German Workers' Educational Association. Karl Schapper, a "professional revolutionary," was one of the leading members of the League. In addition to meeting with German radicals, Marx and Engels met with English Chartists who were in the process of forming the Fraternal Democrats, an organization that intended to unite leftists across the continent.

On their return to Brussels, Marx and Engels founded the Communist Committee of

Correspondence, which was to serve as a clearinghouse for propaganda on communist theory, political economy, and news of activities of the various socialist groups around the European continent. In June 1847, the London League of the Just reorganized itself as the Communist League and developed a political program to further the cause of communism through propaganda and education. Marx became the head of the Brussels Congregation of the Communist League shortly after its formation. The League charged the congregations with establishing a Workers' Educational Association as its educational arm. In addition to Brussels, the League had congregations in Paris (where Engels played a prominent role) and two in Cologne. Toward the end of 1847, Karl also joined the Brussels Democratic Association. The Association sponsored regular public meetings promoting democratic reforms, free trade, and liberal positions on international affairs.

At the Communist League's Second Congress in London in November 1847, delegates adopted Marx's political goals—the overthrow of capitalism and the rule of the proletariat—whole cloth. The League also commissioned Marx to write up its revised declaration of political goals and policy. By January 1848, Marx had produced his masterpiece and most widely read work: *The Communist Manifesto*. It begins with this sentence: "A spectre is haunting Europe—the spectre of communism."

Across the European continent, many were losing faith in the old regimes. In 1847, there was severe economic recession brought on, in part, by harvest failures. Paris was in turmoil, with public meetings held in opposition to the constitutional monarchy and calling for democratic reforms. In Prussia, Austria, and other eastern European states, liberals called for a constitution to limit the absolute power of kings. Revolution was in the air; a specter was indeed haunting Europe—the specter of democracy. In February 1848, barricades went up in Paris, the monarchy was overthrown, and the French Republic was declared. Belgium, fearing that the Brussels Democratic Association might follow suit, took the opportunity on 3 March to give Marx

24 hours to leave the country. Not waiting, the police arrested him that afternoon and sent him off to jail, with Jenny soon detained as well. Released the next day, they had to leave the country immediately. Fortunately, the new provisional government of France welcomed fellow radicals to Paris. There, along with other German members of the Communist League, Marx and Engels laid plans to return to Germany to pursue their revolutionary goals.

COLOGNE II

Karl's revolutionary plan was twofold: to agitate for a democratic revolution and the establishment of a German republic and to organize and educate workers. The democratic revolution was necessary, in Marx's theory, to establish the rule of capitalists and thus the development of the industrial infrastructure of the German states. The second stage would establish workers' associations that would prepare the proletariat for their role in the evolution of the social order. Marx was not trying to foment a communist revolution at this time. The German states were hardly industrial societies, having a small working class. A communist revolution at this stage of development was counter to Marx's theory, as stated in the *Manifesto*, and later much elaborated on in *Capital*. The immediate goal was the establishment of a bourgeois society and such liberal reforms as freedom of the press, speech, and assembly. In most of his revolutionary activities in Cologne, Marx focused on this immediate goal. He found that highlighting class hostilities was counterproductive to rallying all classes to pursue democratic aims.

Andreas Gottschalk was the communist leader in Cologne. He was a True Socialist and formed the Workers' Association shortly after Marx arrived in the city. Gottschalk was a well-known charity physician and dynamic speaker who condemned Marx's two-pronged strategy. He considered Karl's insistence on the necessity of a bourgeois revolution to be a betrayal of the working class. The ongoing conflict with Gottschalk and other communist leaders resulted in Karl resigning his position in the Communist League in mid-1848.

To achieve his goals, Marx established a newspaper in Cologne: the *New Rhineland News*. Such a radical newspaper was now feasible because the Prussian government, in an attempt at liberalization, was allowing some press freedom. To fund the paper, Marx and his followers sold stock, mainly to his longtime patrons in Cologne. Marx joined the Democratic Society of Cologne, a radical political club federated with similar organizations across Europe and seeking democratic reforms of governments. Through the position of editor-in-chief of his newspaper and involvement in democratic organizations, Karl became a leading radical across the German provinces.

Marx's editorials were pointedly anti-Prussian. He slammed the Prussian royal house, heaped contempt on Prussian bureaucracy, and castigated the newly formed Prussian and Frankfort assemblies. The state had created these assemblies to liberalize imperial rule. Early on, Marx was denouncing them in his paper for incompetence and for not going far enough with democratic reforms. While remaining committed to his communist ideals, Marx purposely softened his advocacy of class struggle and attacks on capitalism. This moderation was part of his effort to reach a broad audience in opposition to Prussian rule and support for a German republic.

In September 1848, two Danish provinces, Schleswig and Holstein, demanded that they be allowed to join the German Confederation. While the Prussian government initially supported the move, under pressure from the czar of Russia, they abandoned the cause. The German National Assembly protested the capitulation, and nationalists as well as anti-Prussians were furious with the Prussian government. To make matters worse, drunken Prussian soldiers marched through the streets of Cologne, smashing windows and assaulting citizens. At public meetings, Engels and others called for confrontation with the Prussian soldiers and the establishment of a Red Republic. Rioting, barricades, and rebellion took hold of the city, and the government declared martial law. The government briefly suppressed the *New Rhineland News*, the Democratic Society, and the Workers' Association, and Engels had to flee the country.

In November of that year, the Prussian king, Friedrich Wilhelm IV, sent his army to dissolve the Prussian Constituent Assembly. Before the troops arrived, the defiant deputies called on citizens to boycott paying taxes until the king reinstated the legislature. Marx supported the call, changed the masthead of the paper to read "No more Taxes," and mobilized tax boycotts and even armed resistance through the democratic clubs. The government put down the rebellion in December of that year, and Prussia charged Karl with incitement to rebellion and resistance to government authorities. In his February 1849 trial, he argued that in supporting the Assembly's call for a tax boycott, he was defending a legally constituted body against the arbitrary dissolution decree. The jury acquitted Marx and his codefendants.

However, other crises were brewing. The paper was continually running short of money, creditors, and typesetters. Correspondents were clamoring for their money. More important, on 27 March, the German National Assembly in Frankfort proposed a new constitution with the king of Prussia becoming the emperor of a united Germany. Friedrich Wilhelm IV rejected the crown and refused to ratify the constitution. However, mass meetings occurred throughout the German states, many endorsing the proposal. Marx and other radical democrats were lukewarm regarding the proposed constitution, considering it a compromise with the most reactionary elements of the old regime. The *New Rhineland News* did little to add to the revolutionary ferment. However, the Prussian government seized on the moment to trump up charges that Marx was planning a revolt and expelled him as an undesirable alien in May 1849. Karl then tried to raise money to restart his newspaper in another German province. He was unsuccessful. He then headed to Paris, where conservative reaction had set in and Louis Napoleon had come to power. Not welcomed there, Karl and Jenny decided to move the family to London, where the government had a more liberal policy toward political refugees. The 1848 revolutions across Europe soon ended.

LONDON

Marx arrived in London in late August 1849; his family, now a wife, two daughters, and a son followed a few weeks later. Marx's meager income, combined with a growing family and the high cost of living in London's SoHo slums, would keep the family in poverty for most of their lives. SoHo was especially annoying, as they had been relatively affluent when Karl was the editor of the paper in Cologne. Karl, too proud to accept charity, would borrow from friends, run up tabs with landlords and grocery shops, and intermittently ask his mother for an advance on his inheritance. Marx's second son, Heinrich Guido, was born in November 1849, and his daughter Franziska was born in March 1851. Heinrich would die within days of his first birthday and Franziska within a year of her birth. To add to the family's misery, their eight-year-old son Edgar died in 1855. The deaths, particularly Edgar's, left the family devastated. The family's last child, Eleanor, was born in 1855, and she and her two older sisters were the only children of Jenny and Karl's to live to adulthood.

Over the next couple of years, thousands of political exiles joined Karl from the continent. By the summer of 1851, virtually all surviving members of the *New Rhineland News*, including Engels, were in London. Shortly after arriving in London, Karl reactivated the Communist League and formed a refugee committee to help political exiles. The committee appealed for funds from contributors as far away as the United States and issued support for hundreds of refugees in crisis. This aid proved to be not only an act of charity but an astute political act as well.

Marx also started the *New Rhineland News: Review of Political Economy*, a German-language journal edited in England but printed and distributed in Germany. Plagued by printing, sales, and distribution problems from the beginning, the journal was short lived, the last issue appearing in December 1850. In the journal, Marx's essay *The Class Struggles in France, 1848–1850* appeared in the first three issues. The journal also included attacks on Marx's political rivals.

While Marx's essays were moderate in tone, his Address of the Central Committee to the Communist League in March 1850 espoused extreme radicalism. In that speech, Karl anticipated an imminent revival of the revolution on the continent and the establishment of a republic in Germany. Nevertheless, rather than cooperate with the petit bourgeois democrats in these revolutions as he had advocated in the past, he supported different tactics. He now urged communists to independently organize and continue to push reluctant democrats to address proletariat interests, using force and revolutionary violence if necessary.

In September 1850, the League split over Marx's insistence on treating the democrats as political enemies rather than potential allies as well as over the timing of the coming communist revolution. August Willich and Karl Schapper, two rival communist leaders, insisted that the revolution was imminent and that communists should seize power with the revolution. Marx, on the other hand, saw the coming revolution as a process lasting many years, with the bourgeois first establishing a state and intensifying the mode of production. It was within this capitalist state that the workers would continuously press to change conditions and to make themselves ready to exercise power. Most of the German communists in London sided with Willich and Schapper; Marx and Engels still had their Cologne supporters but only half a dozen followers in London.

The conflicts that Marx had with his rivals in the communist movement were bitter and angry. They often consumed him, taking up most of his time and energy and taking him away from serious writing. Much of the conflict was due to personalities, for both Marx and Engels were arrogant and intolerant of dissenting opinions. Some disputes were undoubtedly due to their bourgeois as opposed to working-class backgrounds, which alienated workers. However, there were some real theoretical differences as well, as Marx continued to refine his theory of proletarian revolution. Capitalism must first intensify the forces of production to the greatest extent possible. The proletariat had to grow in both number and the awareness of their class position before a socialist revolution could be successful and eventually lead to a communist society. The 20th-century revolutions in Russia and China were far more in line with Willich and Schapper's vision of immediate and violent revolution.

It is during his early days in London that Marx makes the explicit connection between economic crisis and revolution. In the last issue of the *New Rhineland News: Review of Political Economy* (December 1850), Karl wrote, "A new revolution is only possible in the wake of a new crisis. The former, however, is just as certain as the latter" (quoted in Sperber 2013, 274). The connection between economic crisis and revolution would become central in Marx's theory. Note, however, that some followers took this to extremes. The *zusammenbruchstheorie* (theories of collapse) began in the 1890s and are still popular among those influenced by Marxist theory today. These theories posit that the contradictions between the forces and relations of production themselves would eventually cause the system to collapse, and only then would socialism rise from the ashes. Capitalism's eventual collapse is not a part of Marx's original theory. According to Marx, it would take a proletarian revolution to bring capitalism to an end.

In the fall of 1850, Engels, long cut off from his family and living in poverty in London, wrote to his father that he was no longer a communist. He asked his father to let him represent the family at the Ermen-Engels Mill in Manchester. His father accepted the offer, and Engels became a capitalist, using part of his salary to help Marx and his family. At the beginning of his employment, this was enough to keep Marx's creditors at bay.

In May 1851, Prussia arrested a member of the Communist League in Cologne. Over the next few weeks, the government arrested and charged 11 members of the League with conspiracy to overthrow the government. Happening more than a year later, the Prussian government intended the show trial to cast the 1848 revolution as the work of radical conspirators. Following Marx's advice, several of the defendants distinguished the Communist League with the more revolutionary ideology of Willich and Schapper. It was Willich and Schapper who advocated immediate revolution against the Prussian government. The Cologne League, following Marx and Engels, were opponents of the future bourgeois government rather than the existing monarchy! The court was not impressed with this argument. The machinations of the secret police producing forged documents and perjured testimony sealed the fate of seven of the 11 defendants. The court sentenced them to three to six years in prison.

The trial revealed that Willich had been in close association with the Prussian secret police. His popularity among the German émigrés collapsed, and the Willich-Schapper Communist League dissolved. At about the same time, Marx dissolved his Communist League as well, believing that all viable political action ended with the arrest and conviction of his Cologne followers. Marx would turn to his scholarship and writing as both a commentator on current affairs and a political economist.

Marx spent the better part of the 1850s, an age of reaction and repression in Europe, researching political economy and current events in the library of the British Museum. At the same time, he was dealing with the death of his children, his poor health, and depression and was scrambling for money to support his family. He became a freelance journalist, becoming a foreign correspondent for the *New York Tribune* and contributing pieces to several different newspapers and periodicals throughout the decade. By 1856, Marx was making enough from his journalism (with subsidies from Engels) to be able to move the family out of the slums of SoHo to a new home in Kentish Town. However, his finances remained tight. Unfortunately, with the advent of the Civil War in America, Karl's work for the *Tribune*, his chief source of income, was suspended.

During the 1850s, Marx completely withdrew from political organizing, instead waiting for the next economic crisis that would bring on the revolution. The 1857 worldwide financial crisis lifted his spirits considerably, and he once again began taking an active interest in politics. In 1858, Prince Wilhelm of Prussia succeeded his brother, Friedrich Wilhelm IV. He immediately dismissed the remaining reactionary ministers; the age of repression seemed to be at an end. As in the 1848 revolution, Marx's goals remained the same: opposing authoritarian rule and organizing the working class for the eventual establishment of socialism. He began negotiating with Ferdinand Lassalle for a proposal for him to return to Germany in a new newspaper enterprise. However, for reasons of family ties to London, his relationship with Engels, problems of regaining his Prussian citizenship, and distrust of Lassalle, Marx decided to stay in London.

Karl's financial situation was somewhat improved in 1863 with the death of his mother and inheriting money from her estate as well as the estate of a close friend. The money could not replace the lack of a steady income for long, but it did provide some relief. However, at the same time, his health took a turn for the worse. Marx suffered from painful and disfiguring growths—what he called carbuncles—on his body. Treatment was painful, difficult, harmful, and ineffective. The skin disease would incapacitate him sometimes for weeks.

In September 1864, Marx became one of the founding members of the International Workingmen's Association (IWA) (often called the "First International") and drafted the "Address to the Working Class" (or "Inaugural Address"), which set the goals of the new organization. Rather than an international socialist party, the IWMA was a loose federation of English labor unions as well as workers' mutual benefit and educational societies on the continent. The first convention in Geneva in 1866 was very much in line with the demands of working-class unions. The platform called for an eight-hour workday, some restrictions on juvenile and women's labor, an international inquiry into working conditions, and an endorsement of trade unions. Over the years, the IWMA raised funds in support of striking workers in several European countries and supported democratic reforms that would increase workers' representation in the British Parliament. Marx was leading the group behind the scenes, drafting documents and

making proposals, and holding meetings at his house in London.

Throughout the 1860s, Marx worked on his political-economic notebooks. From this work, he published *Capital: Volume 1* in 1867 in the German language. After its publication, Engels wrote several reviews in the press to promote the book. Marx continued working on his economic notebooks in anticipation of future volumes, work that he would never complete.

As the corresponding secretary to Germany for the IWMA, Marx had a particular interest in German working-class parties. As before in 1848, there was a tension between his strategy of uniting anti-Prussian and anticapitalist radicals. The two approaches became manifest in the two independent labor parties in Germany. The Lassalleans of the General German Workers' Association focused on organizing the working class but supported the conservative Prussian government in the unification of German states. In contrast, the People's Party, where even though many in the leadership were socialists, focused on establishing democracy and overthrowing Prussian rule rather than labor issues.

With the defeat of the Austrian Empire in the Austro-Prussian War in 1866, Otto von Bismarck began the process of German unification. Many former 1848 German revolutionaries and democratic liberals, swept away by nationalistic fervor, supported the chancellor. Marx and Engels were more reserved than other revolutionaries were, but with the establishment of the new German state and its Reichstag, they encouraged their German allies to participate in elections. Two of Marx's associates, Wilhelm Liebknecht and August Bebel, were elected to the Reichstag as members of the People's Party. In August 1869, Liebknecht and Bebel led a group that broke with the People's Party, formed the Social Democratic Workers' Party of Germany, and affiliated with the IWMA.

Marx was still struggling financially as the 1860s ended. With no steady income, he had run through the inheritances he had received several years earlier. Engels had been sending him money throughout the decade whenever possible. However, Marx still found it necessary to go to pawnshops, borrow money, or run up accounts at local businesses. Engels became a full partner in the firm in 1864, and in 1869, he sold his interest in the firm to the Ermen brothers. From this, Engels was able to retire and eventually move to London, devoting himself to the labor movement. In addition, he was able to settle Marx's debts and provide the family with a 350-pound annual income.

Marx and Engels initially supported Prussia in the Franco-Prussian War of 1870–1871, believing that France was responsible for initiating the conflict. However, as the war progressed, their allegiance shifted to France. Nevertheless, German victories were both quick and decisive. The Prussian army captured the French emperor Napoleon III at the Battle of Sedan on 2 September 1870. The emperor's government collapsed, the new French Republic was declared, and the war continued. Paris came under a siege that lasted four months, and famine and disease spread through the city. The national government signed a cease-fire and concluded a peace treaty with Bismarck. However, the concessions to the Prussians were so severe that many leftists and socialists demanded a return to war. Open rebellion against the national government soon broke out, demanding independence for Paris. Citizens of Paris elected a municipal council, called the Paris Commune. The Commune took control over the city, passing degrees such as separation of church and state, establishing worker production associations, and planning for communes throughout France. The national government crushed the Commune in "Bloody Week." It is estimated that more than 10,000 people were killed, and many more were executed or deported after the uprising. Marx detailed the Paris Commune and its meaning in a speech to the General Council of the IWMA, which he later wrote as a pamphlet, *The Civil War in France*. This work praises the Paris Commune as a first attempt at establishing a worker's state, a precursor of a future communist society. The publication sold thousands of copies, and Marx became a well-known communist theorist throughout Europe.

Marx and the IWMA faced two issues in the 1870s that would have long-term consequences. The first was the hostility between ethnic groups within the labor movement. The expansion of the franchise in Great Britain did not produce greater representation in Parliament for labor, Marx concluded, because of the hostility between British and Irish workers. Ethnic tensions and conflict would continue as wedge issues among workers (many of these wedges driven by members of the upper classes) to the present day.

The second issue that bedeviled the IWA was between the rivalry of Marx and Mikhail Bakunin for control of the organization. Bakunin, an anarchist, argued for the violent overthrow of the state with little to no regard for its economic foundations. Marx argued that such a revolution would accomplish little. The other issue between Bakunin and Marx concerned secret societies. Bakunin was a proponent; Marx wanted to keep them out of the IWA.

The political maneuvering between Bakunin and Marx continued for years. It finally broke out in denunciations in 1872. At the IWA Congress in The Hague in September, Marx had outmaneuvered Bakunin. Karl manipulated the representation of the delegation by first selecting a city close to his base of support in Germany and England. Second, he urged his supporters to attend or send him their proxies. Finally, he challenged the credentials of supporters of Bakunin and kept many of them out of the proceedings. In its closing days, the Congress voted to expel Bakunin and his right-hand man, James Guillaume, and move the seat of the General Council to New York. The anarchists held a rival Congress, many terminating their association with the IWMA. Marx had essentially neutered the IWMA to keep the organization out of the control of the anarchists. The organization soon became irrelevant and ceased to exist.

With the unification of Germany under Bismarck and the demise in the influence of the IWMA, Marx's German followers faced an increasingly hostile Prussian government. Marx's supporters in the Social Democratic Workers' Party sought to unify with the Lasallian General

German Workers' Association to present a united socialist voice. Representatives of the two parties met and wrote a preliminary program for a unity congress in Gotha in 1875. They did not consult Marx, who had heard about it through newspaper accounts. The draft contained a critique of capitalism as well as standard socialist calls for universal suffrage, shorter workdays, workplace safety, and freedom of association. However, this did not satisfy Marx, so he wrote a scathing response known as the *Critique of the Gotha Program.* His main objection was that the proposed program compromised too much with the Lasallian position. It appeared to advocate reform through an alliance with Bismarck's authoritarian state rather than the revolutionary action of the proletariat. The program called for support for state-sponsored producers' cooperatives, opposition to trade unions, and a focus on socialism within the context of the nation-state rather than an international movement, all of which were objectionable to Marx. Such a program, he believed, may lead to some mitigation of the worst abuses of capitalism, but it would only serve to prop up the capitalist state. Leaving the capitalist mode of production intact, Marx believed, necessarily leads to the grossly unequal distribution of goods and property. Despite the criticism, the Unity Congress adopted the original program with only minor changes. The merged group would later become the Social Democratic Party of Germany.

Marx's health continued to decline through much of the 1870s, forcing him to cut back on his writing and his active political involvement. He spent time with his grandchildren as well as taking care of his wife Jenny, who was also growing steadily more ill toward the end of the decade. Together, they took extended rest and recovery at German spas. In addition to tending to family matters, Karl translated *Capital* into French and continued work on his economic notebooks but unfortunately never finished the task. It is from these notebooks that Engels edited the remaining two volumes of *Capital* after Marx's death. Toward the end of his life, Marx was a widely known socialist and revolutionary throughout Europe. This was due mainly to the success of his pamphlet *The Civil War in France.* Leftists from all over the continent sought his advice, and he was the subject of newspaper interviews and profiles.

Karl's wife, Jenny, died on 2 December 1881. Karl was to outlive her by a little more than a year. During that time, his health declined rapidly; he developed a severe chronic cough, difficulty breathing and swallowing, and trouble speaking. Karl traveled for his health—to the Isle of Wight, Monaco, Algiers, and southern France (to visit his daughter Laura, her husband Paul Lafargue, and grandchildren) always in search of better climes for his health. On returning to the Isle of Wight, he received news of the death of his daughter Jenny Caroline on 11 January 1883. Shaken, he returned to London. On the afternoon of 14 March, Engels came to visit his friend and found him dead in his study.

A

ABSOLUTE SURPLUS VALUE. The term refers to the value produced by a worker in a **commodity** over and above the wages paid for that work. Lengthening the working day beyond which the worker produces the equivalent of his wages will increase absolute value. If the worker takes seven hours to create a commodity equivalent to his wages, then by lengthening the working day beyond those seven hours, the capitalist will increase absolute surplus value. In early **capitalism**, extending the working day was the primary way of growing **surplus value** for the capitalist. However, the successive **British Factory Acts** put ever more restrictive limits on such practices. These acts, along with **competition**, stimulated the development of **machinery** and the ever more **detailed division of labor**, thus increasing the **productivity** of workers so that they could reproduce their labor costs in a shorter period. *See also* RELATIVE SURPLUS VALUE.

ABSTRACT SOCIAL LABOR. According to Marx, the amount of human labor necessary for its production determines the **exchange value** of a **commodity**. Abstract labor is a concept developed by Marx that combines all types of work (skilled and unskilled) into a single measure of the duration of labor time expended in production. The measure reflects the average socially necessary labor time for the production of a commodity. Note that this is the *average* labor time, not the actual labor time to make the product. The **productivity** of the workforce determines average labor time

in a given society at that point in time. Marx uses the measure in determining exchange value. This value reflects the magnitude of the useful labor materialized in the object.

Although composed of numerous individuals with different skills, aptitudes, and working under various conditions, labor time is measured in homogeneous units, each unit being the same as all the others. Each unit represents **socially necessary labor time** that is required to produce any commodity under the "prevailing conditions of production" in that society with workers of average skill and working with average intensity (Marx 1867/1976, 129). For example, Marx suggests that the introduction of the power loom to **England** reduced by about one-half the labor time required to convert a given quantity of yarn into woven fabric. This increase in productivity changes the conditions of production. Those that continued to use the hand loom still needed an hour of labor time to convert the given quantity of yarn into woven fabric. Nevertheless, the labor time invested in his product now only represents only a half hour of socially necessary labor time, thus reducing the exchange value of his woven product by half. *See also* LAW OF VALUE, PRODUCTIVITY, RELATIVE SURPLUS VALUE, SOCIALLY NECESSARY LABOR TIME, WAGE GOODS.

ACADEMIC MARXISM. A variant of **Western Marxism** emerged in Western universities in the 1930s. Most prominent was the Frankfurt School, a group of scholars associated with the Institute for Social Research, at Goethe

University, Frankfurt. These scholars drew on elements of Marx, Immanuel Kant, Sigmund Freud, Max Weber, and select Western Marxists like **Lukács** and **Gramsci** to elaborate theories of social change. Among the key figures of the Frankfurt School are Theodor Adorno, Jürgen Habermas, Max Horkheimer, and Herbert Marcuse. Adorno and others of the Frankfurt School produced the classic sociological study *The Authoritarian Personality* (1950), an attempt to identify and categorize key personality traits contributing to the formation of anti-Semitic and authoritarian beliefs.

Marcuse's *One-Dimensional Man* (1964) illustrates the concerns motivating Western Marxism. The book offered an extended critique of both Western **capitalism** and **Soviet communism** as two sides of the same coin. Marcuse condemns Western capitalism for creating an elaborate and artificial system of social control in the form of consumerism, which serves as a form of "soft totalitarianism" masquerading as democracy. The never-ending demand for "new" products and the careless disposal of "old" products subverts human beings into unidimensional "**tools**," fueling dubious social purposes. The process flattens humanity, and the individual's critical capacities atrophy and wither away in favor of technical skill. Marcuse advocated a "great refusal" to accept the "hard" totalitarianism of Soviet-style communism and the "soft" totalitarianism of Western capitalism. It was a forlorn call for the recurrence of humanity's creative capacities. Contemporary academic Marxists would include **Immanuel Wallerstein**, **Harry Braverman**, and **John Bellamy Foster**.

ACCUMULATION OF CAPITAL. The accumulation of capital is the whole point of **capitalism**. The capitalist realizes this accumulation through an initial investment of **money** used to purchase **fixed capital** (**tools**, **factories**, **machinery**) and **variable capital** (**labor power**) to produce a **commodity**. The capitalist then sells this commodity for its original cost plus a **profit**. This profit is from the **surplus value** that the capitalist **expropriates** from labor, as the cost of labor is less than the value that they contribute to the commodity.

The capitalist uses profit in two ways. A portion goes to the capitalist for the consumption of essential goods and services (as well as **luxury goods**). The capitalist invests the other part in intensifying production in producing more surplus value. *See also* CIRCUIT OF CAPITAL, LABOR THEORY OF VALUE.

ACTIVE LABOR ARMY. Marx's term for the employed workforce. "Modern Industry has converted the little workshop of the patriarchal master into the great factory of the industrial capitalist. Masses of **labourers** crowded into the **factory**, are organised like soldiers. As privates of the industrial army, they are placed under the command of a perfect hierarchy of officers and sergeants. Not only are they **slaves** of the **bourgeois** class, and the bourgeois State; they are daily and hourly enslaved by the **machine**, by the overlooker, and, above all, by the individual bourgeois manufacturer himself. The more openly this despotism proclaims gain to be its end and aim, the more petty, the more hateful and the more embittering it is" (Marx and Engels 1848, 32). The capitalist can expand or reduce this active workforce in response to **economic expansions and contractions** through the exploitation of three different groups. First is the "floating **population**," which consists of the temporarily **unemployed**, those who are between jobs or who have been thrown out of work due to recession or industrial **innovation**. A second group ripe for exploitation Marx calls the "latent," who have not yet been integrated into the wage-labor system. Historically, this group would include peasants or **petite bourgeoisie** who have lost out to the **competition** for markets. More recently, the latent workforce consists of farmers who moved off the land due to agricultural concentration and women increasingly integrated into the wage-labor system. Finally, Marx notes a third category of the relative **surplus population** that he calls the "stagnant." "This forms a part of the active labour army but with extremely irregular employment. Hence, it offers capital an inexhaustible reservoir of disposable **labour-power**. Its conditions of life sink below the average normal level of the working class, and it is precisely this which makes it a broad foundation for special branches of capitalist exploitation" (Marx, 1867/1976, 796). *See also* INDUSTRIAL RESERVE ARMY, LUMPEN-PROLETARIAT, PAUPERS, PROLETARIAT.

ADDRESS TO THE CENTRAL COMMITTEE OF THE COMMUNIST LEAGUE. In 1850, Karl anticipated the imminent revival of the **revolution** on the European continent and the establishment of a republic in Germany. However, rather than cooperate with the **petit bourgeois** democrats in these revolutions as he had advocated in the past, Marx changed tactics. He now urged communists to independently organize and continue to push reluctant democrats to address **proletarian** interests, using force and revolutionary violence if necessary. "If, for instance, the petty bourgeoisie propose the purchase of the railways and factories, the workers must demand that these railways and factories simply be confiscated by the state without compensation as the property of reactionaries. If the democrats propose a proportional tax, then the workers must demand a progressive tax; if the democrats themselves propose a moderate progressive tax, then the workers must insist on a tax whose rates rise so steeply that big capital is ruined by it." Above all, Marx exclaimed, the democratic petite bourgeoisie are misleading workers; they are using the workers for bourgeois class interests. The proletariat must independently organize, "Their battle-cry must be: The Permanent Revolution." *See also* COLOGNE.

AGRARIAN QUESTION. A central tenet of Marx's vision held that the industrialized **proletariat** would ultimately instigate and guide the **socialist revolution**. In other words, **industrialization** and **capitalism** are prerequisites for the ultimate Marxist goal of revolution and the establishment of socialist systems. This necessity posed a series of both theoretical and practical problems, collectively known as the "agrarian question." The questions deal with the role of the **peasantry** in the **social evolutionary** process. What is the nature of the transformation of precapitalist economic systems into a capitalist economy? What is the

political role and allegiance of the peasantry in radical social and economic change? What of the fate of nonindustrial agriculturalists in the postrevolution socialist system? These issues were prominent for later Marxists,—particularly for **Lenin** (Akram-Lodhi, Haroon, and Kay 2010; Hammen 1972; Lenin 1972), and **Marxists** interested in revolutionary action in the Global South (Amin 2006; Harris 1978). For Marx himself, however, the problem was ultimately minor. He argued that the logical allegiance of the peasantry would necessarily be to the proletariat. Given the exploitative nature of capitalist systems, as the agricultural peasantry were increasingly subject to the forces of capitalism (including the **industrialization of agriculture**), they would join forces with the proletariat. *See also* CAPITALIST AGRICULTURE, *CRITIQUE OF THE GOTHA PROGRAMME.*

ALCHEMISTS OF REVOLUTION. A phrase deployed by Karl Marx in a series of pamphlets likely written in 1850 during internal socialist debates. Rival socialists **Karl Schapper** and **August Willich**, following the views of French socialist **Auguste Blanqui**, rejected popular revolutionary action in favor of small-scale revolts designed to seize the state and redistribute wealth. Marx believed that such a conspiratorial uprising would impede the development within the **proletariat** of **revolutionary class consciousness**. The phrase "alchemists of revolution" emanated from these internal debates over the future direction of the socialist movement (if it ever was a unitary movement).

An extensive quote from the 1850 *New Rhineland News* article, cited by Shlomo Avineri (1968), offers insight into the nature of the disagreement:

It is self-evident that these *conspirateurs* do not limit themselves to the mere task of organising the proletariat; not at all. Their business lies precisely in trying to preempt the developing revolutionary process, drive it artificially to crisis, to create a revolution *ex nihilo* [out of nothing], to make a revolution without the conditions of a revolution. For them, the only necessary condition for a revolution is an adequate organization of their conspiracy. They are the alchemists of revolution, and they share all the woolly-mindedness, follies and *idées fixes* [obsession that dominates the mind] of the former alchemists. They throw themselves on discoveries which should work revolutionary wonders: incendiary bombs, hell-**machines** of magical impact, émeutes [seditious tumult] which ought to be the more wonder-making and sudden the less they have any rational ground. Always busy and preoccupied with such absurd planning and conniving, they see no other end than the next toppling-over of the existing government. Hence their deepest disdain for the more theoretical **enlightenment** of the workers about their class-interests. Hence their not proletarian, but rather plebeian, anger at those gentlemen in black coats (*habits noirs*), the more or less educated people, who represent this side of the movement, and from whom they never manage to free themselves wholly as the official representatives of the party. (201)

Rubenstein (1987) notes that Marx's opposition of the **Blanquists** after 1848 and later of the **socialist anarchists** after the **Paris Commune** marks his intent on fostering a social revolution rather than a "*mere coup d'état.*" "Terrorism might kill a despot, or perhaps even force a ruling clique from power, but only mass violence could overthrow a social class" (157). *See also* WILLICH-SCHAPPER GROUP.

ALIENATION. The term "alienation" refers to "estrangement." The term has both legal and theological origins. When someone takes property away from a person, that person becomes alienated from his property. Many theologians interpret Adam and Eve's expulsion from the Garden of Eden as a kind of alienation from God. Marx's usage of the concept owes much to **Hegel** and the "Left Hegelian" **Ludwig Feuerbach**. Marx follows Hegel in acknowledging that human beings progress through acts of differentiation. As an infant, they are initially

incapable of seeing the distinction between themselves and their mothers. Gradually, the child comes to a recognition of their unique, separate identity. Marx draws on Feuerbach to reverse the polarity of alienation. Rather than an act of self-realization, Marx views alienation as a manifestation of the working class's oppression under **capitalism**. In Marx's theory, this would produce a **revolutionary class consciousness**, an essential element of Marx's prediction that capitalism would eventually succumb to a **proletarian revolution**.

Marx contends that alienation oppresses workers in four distinct ways. First, capitalist organization of work estranges laborers from the product of their **labor**; in other words, workers labor to produce **commodities** that they cannot own. Second, the organization of work insulates workers from the creative process itself. This organization forces the worker to engage in repetitive tasks that contribute to but do not culminate in the finished product. The **laborer** is engaged in endless drudgery without the reward. Third, the organization of work estranges the laborer from humanity itself, which Marx describes as a "**species being**," a defining feature of which is a yearning for creative expression. Fourth, workers are isolated from other workers by the **division of labor**. The very **competitiveness** of capitalism creates incentives for the **bourgeoisie** to extract the maximum amount of profit from labor, which necessitates rules inhibiting mutual interactions among workers.

Marx understood alienation through his approach to **dialectical materialism**, which was an essential part of his "turning Hegel on his head" and focusing on **material** conditions rather than on the power of ideas in shaping reality. Hegel viewed alienation as a state of self-consciousness encountering the external world, experiencing "estrangement" as unknown objects appear. According to Shlomo Avineri (1968), the Hegelian view of alienation is that "the final goal of consciousness is to arrive at this recognition: in Hegel's language, consciousness returns to itself" (97). Consequently, while Hegel rejects atomistic individualism, much of his approach to alienation and consciousness took place within individual consciousness.

Hegel's "Master and Slave" parable in *The Phenomenology of Mind* illustrates his dialectical approach to alienation. Both master and slave require one another; the master must subdue the slave to become master, while the slave must be subdued and accept that his or her life is subservient to their master. The slave might initially feel indebted to the master for sparing them and recognize that the master retains the power of life or death over them. The slave might also internalize a sense of inferiority for their physical subjugation. At the same time, the master experiences a sense of self-aggrandizement owing to their domination of another being. However, the relationship is dynamic and, over time, subject to change. The slave yearns for freedom, while the master requires the slave's continued debasement to maintain his or her sense of superiority. Eventually, they both demand what the other cannot give: for the slave, the master's acknowledgment of dignity and self-worth and, for the master, the slave's continued recognition of the master's dominance. While the master holds a **monopoly** on coercion, the slave—in recognition that death holds no fear for them in comparison to continued enslavement—reveals the master's vulnerability in their need for recognition. Mutual recognition of their "particularity" in occupying essentially "alienating" roles leads to joint emancipation as free and equal beings.

Marx criticized Hegel's view of alienation as reductionist and viewing what is important about humanity as taking place within individual consciousness. For Marx, human self-development and self-creation are inevitably linked to material **modes of production** within which historical persons find themselves (e.g., **feudalism** or capitalism). Marx's dialectical materialism emphasizes the relationship of workers with the material world and with other members of their class within the **relations of production** (e.g., bourgeoisie and proletariat). In contrast to Hegel, Marx contended that alienation emerges as the proletariat finds themselves increasingly **immiserated** by the bourgeoisie, whose self-interested pursuit of **profit** leads them to impose increasingly inhumane conditions on the proletariat.

The seemingly reciprocal relationship—wages in exchange for labor—is, in reality, "**wage slavery,**" as the bourgeoisie ruthlessly **expropriate** "**surplus value**" from labor.

For Marx, alienation is the philosophical irritant that is the motivating force for historical change. Alienation forms an essential component of Marx's prediction of how the proletarian revolutionary sequence will unfold; as the bourgeoisie increasingly squeeze the proletariat in a self-interested pursuit of profit, **class antagonisms** intensify as the proletariat become increasingly immiserated. The achievement of revolutionary class consciousness is the recognition of the essential injustice of the capitalist system. An essential aspect of Marxism is that the subsequent proletarian revolution would not replace one class system with another but would result in the proletariat seizing the government and creating a **dictatorship of the proletariat** dedicated to the destruction of class distinction. A **classless society** would have no need or use for a state, and the result would be **communism**, an open, democratic, and coercionless society in which human beings were free to explore and develop their creative capacities.

ANARCHISM. Anarchism represents a broad spectrum of belief regarding the fundamental illegitimacy of the **state** and a rejection of any form of coercion as a means of pursuing collective action. Some contend that anarchism is not a stand-alone ideology but is instead a kind of ideological modifier that expresses an extreme manifestation of the **Enlightenment** ideologies of liberalism and **socialism**. Anarchists generally share the belief that human beings are sufficiently capable of self-governance as to form spontaneous political associations, not requiring the coercive power of the state.

William Godwin's (1756–1836) *Enquiry concerning Political Justice and Its Influence on General Virtue and Happiness* (1793) offered an early modern articulation of anarchism. Written at the time of the **French Revolution**, Godwin expressed confidence that human perfectibility would culminate in the abolition of the state. Building his argument around eight logical precepts, Godwin contended, among other things, that human fallibilities are the product of mistaken beliefs and that, while society was an unalloyed good, government was always a source of evil.

Marx was critical of a variety of **anarcho-socialist** writers, ranging from **Pierre Proudhon** (1809–1865) to **Louis-Auguste Blanqui** (1805–1881) to **Mikhail Bakunin** (1814–1876) and **Peter Kropotkin** (1842–1921), among the more prominent. In some instances, the ideas with which Marx engaged were primarily theoretical; in other instances, particularly in Blanqui's and Bakunin's cases, Marx was engaging with rivals competing for influence within the broader world of **revolutionary socialism**. These controversies within the socialist movement evolved both in extensive writings and in actual revolutionary events, including the widespread **Revolutions of 1848** and the failed **Paris Commune** of 1871.

Anarcho-socialists expressed a wide range of disagreement over the method by which the state would be destroyed or abolished. Some agreed with Marx that the dominant **class** would never voluntarily surrender the coercive power of the state, that the coercive and manipulative capacities of the state necessitated **revolution**. Some, notably the more pacifistic and theoretically minded, like Kropotkin, accepted the need for revolution but rejected violence as a means that would necessarily corrupt the ends.

Anarcho-socialists tended to espouse a somewhat unsystematic application of violence as the vehicle for revolution. Supporters of Blanqui, for example, believed that a small, disciplined, conspiratorial cadre of revolutionaries could successfully seize individual states one at a time and rapidly consolidate power using dictatorial means. The charismatic Bakunin was inherently suspicious of structured thought, believing that only acts of violence could throw off the shackles of oppression. Whether committed to a vanguard approach or individual acts of violence, anarcho-socialists were innately skeptical. Anarchists within the socialist movement were opposed to Marx's conviction that the overthrow of capitalism must lead to a "**dictatorship of the proletariat**," which would use the power of the state

to establish a society without class distinctions. Anarcho-socialists believed that such a dictatorship would quickly lose its proletarian character and devolve into a ruling elite dedicated to preserving their power and authority. Bakunin, in particular, believed that such a dictatorship would be proletarian in name only, that those workers who seized the commanding heights of government would quickly discard their loyalty to the working class and assert for themselves elite status. Anarcho-socialists, in general, expressed skepticism that **revolutionary class consciousness** was achievable or that class loyalties were as deep as Marx believed.

ANARCHO-COLLECTIVISM, ANARCHO-COMMUNISM, ANARCHO-SOCIALISM. *See* SOCIAL ANARCHISM.

ANCIENT MODE OF PRODUCTION. Marx proposed that societies evolved due to changes in the **mode of production**. City-state political structures characterized the ancient mode of production. Urban organizations (as opposed to familial or tribal organizations) became the norm, and organized constitutional-based systems of law replaced earlier, less formal systems of law and justice. Animal-assisted agriculture is the primary **force of production** in this mode, though mining and craft specialization are also important. This mode of production differs from the previous mode by larger-scale political organization and the inclusion of the ownership of individual human beings (**slavery**), a characteristic that led some scholars to refer to this mode of production as a "**slave society**." Unlike earlier forms, this mode of production often justifies rule through some degree of popular participation in politics. Classical Greek and Roman societies exemplify this ancient mode of production. *See also* ASIATIC MODE OF PRODUCTION, *CONTRIBUTION TO THE CRITIQUE OF POLITICAL ECONOMY, PREFACE, THE,* TRIBAL MODE OF PRODUCTION.

ANCIENT SOCIETY (1877). *Ancient Society, or Researches in the Lines of Human Progress From Savagery through Barbarism* to *Civilization*, was an influential book by American anthropologist **Lewis Henry Morgan** (1818–1881), first published in 1877. In it, Morgan detailed his evolutionary framework for change and development in human societies throughout both prehistoric and historic human history. Morgan's theory of **social evolution** held that as changes in the **technological** capacity of energy acquisition progressed, there were simultaneous changes in family and **social relations**, property ownership and relations, and overall social, political, and economic structure. Morgan categorized these changes into three main stages of development: savagery, barbarism, and civilization. Marx first read *Ancient Society* in 1881 and saw it as further evidence that his materialist-based theory of social and economic change was correct. He began his work based primarily on the ideas presented in *Ancient Society* but died before finishing it. This work was published posthumously as *The Ethnological Notebooks of Karl Marx*. *Ancient Society* was also very influential on **Friedrich Engels**, whose work *The Origin of the Family, Private Property, and the State* drew heavily on the work of Morgan and Marx's notes on *Ancient Society*. *See also* PREFACE, THE.

ANTI-DÜHRING (1878). A book by **Engels** defending Marx's and Engels's brand of **scientific socialism** from Eugen Dühring's *Revolution in Science*, which was sharply critical of Marx. The socialist press of Germany was favorably reviewing Dühring's books. In 1875, **Wilhelm Liebknecht** encouraged Engels to respond to Dühring's critiques, and in 1876, Engels began the task of writing articles and pamphlets that attacked Dühring head-on. He combined these works in book form in 1878, which consists of three distinct parts: philosophy, **political economy**, and **socialism**. Engels defines political economy:

> Political economy, in the widest sense, is the science of the laws governing the **production** and **exchange** of the material means of subsistence in human society. Production and exchange are two different functions. Production may occur without

exchange, but exchange—being necessarily an exchange of products—can not occur without production. Each of these two social functions is subject to the action of external influences which to a great extent are peculiar to it and for this reason each has, also to a great extent, its own special laws. But on the other hand, they constantly determine and influence each other to such an extent that they might be termed the abscissa and ordinate of the economic curve. (Engels 1877, Part II: Political Economy, para. 1)

At the request of **Paul Lafargue**, Engels extracted the three chapters on **socialism** from *Anti-Dühring* and created the socialist pamphlet *Socialism: Utopian and Scientific* published in 1880.

ANTI-SOCIALIST LAWS OF GERMANY (1878). A series of acts passed by the German Reichstag at the instigation of **Otto von Bismarck** aimed at suppressing the **Social Democratic Party of Germany (SPD)**. The laws were renewed and extended four times. There had been two failed attempts to assassinate the Kaiser, and the last attack severely injured the Kaiser. Bismarck blamed the SPD for influencing the assassins. He then called for new elections to the Reichstag, coordinated a "rabidly" antisocialist campaign, and achieved a house much more amenable to his will. The new laws banned Social Democratic organizations, meetings, and newspapers. However, the SPD devised various strategies to get around the laws. The regulations did not prohibit the party itself from the Reichstag, so socialists used that forum to continue to spread their causes. They set up underground presses, recreational clubs, and other clandestine means to spread socialist ideology. Despite these strategies, authorities arrested and imprisoned more than 1,500 people before the laws lapsed in 1890. The Anti-Socialist Laws contributed to the solidarity of socialists in Germany. For this reason, many scholars consider them a serious political miscalculation on the part of Bismarck (German History in Documents, 2003).

ASIATIC MODE OF PRODUCTION. Another of Marx's precapitalist **modes of production**, generally characterized by his historical interpretation of Asian countries where there is an absence of **private property** within the **mode of production**, a collectively organized despotic **ruling class**, and the collective organization of the **labor** class in small agrarian village communities. Empires like those found in precapitalist China, the Ottoman Empire (until the late 18th century), and India under Mongolian rule were all social and economic formations characterized by the Asiatic mode of production. A distinguishing factor of this mode of production is that the labor class, through village membership, collectively has direct possession of the land. The ruling class, in turn, can collectively appropriate **surplus labor** through a tribute tax paid to the **state** by agrarian villages. State power and authority stemmed from the highest-level ruler, who claims to represent or embody divine right and order. As long as local villages paid tribute taxes, they were, to some degree, autonomous. A bureaucracy of regional and local religious leaders connected these villages to the more extensive state apparatus. This bureaucracy maintained direct contact between villages and central state authorities.

Marx developed the concept of the Asiatic mode of production (as well as other precapitalist modes of production) in the 1850s while formulating the theoretical and historical analysis of the development of **capitalism** that he outlines in the *A Contribution to the Critique of Political Economy* and, later and more thoroughly, in *Capital*. He also discusses these "forms which precede capitalist production" extensively in *Grundrisse* (Marx 1857–1861, 397–405). For Marx, the Asiatic mode of production was primarily a means of explaining the historical "unchangeability of Asiatic societies" where the "structure of the fundamental economic elements of society remain untouched by the storms which blow up in the cloudy regions of politics" (Marx 1867/1976, 479). For later **Marxists** and communists, the idea proved more controversial. For example, the concept of an Asiatic mode of production does not fit within the strict unilineal scheme of **social evolution** as conceived by **Engels, Joseph Stalin,** and others. In this scheme, societies evolve through technical progress in the development of **productive forces** from four defined stages: **primitive communism, slave**-owning societies (or **ancient mode of production**), **feudalism,** and **capitalism.** After the death of Marx, the Asiatic mode of production faded from Marxist orthodoxy. A related controversial issue was more practical for revolutionary Marxists: in the Asiatic mode of production, there is a lack of legally defined private property. Despite the lack of private property, systems characterized by an Asiatic mode of production nonetheless have well-defined **class systems**, class power, and exploitation, suggesting that merely abolishing private property does not necessarily lead to the abolishment of class exploitation. *See also* PREFACE, THE.

ATHEISM. Perhaps one of the most oft paraphrased statements of Marx is "**Religion** is the opium of the people." The full quote, found in *A Contribution to the Critique of Hegel's Philosophy of Right*, is "Religion is the sigh of the oppressed creature, the heart of a heartless world, and the soul of soulless conditions. It is the opium of the people." The broader context of this famous quote is essentially an argument by Marx that "man makes religion, religion does not make man"—that is, religion is a product of human invention. For Marx, this meant that religion could be an instrument of oppression. As part of the development of **class consciousness**, Marx argued that the proletariat would come to see religion as a product of their oppressors and would ultimately abolish religion.

Marx was an atheist from a very young age and remained one for the rest of his life (Schuller 1975). His atheism was ultimately rooted in his **materialist** philosophical and theoretical understanding of the world. This emphasis on the material **base** as the foundation of society leaves no room for metaphysical explanation. Further, Marx's concept of **historical materialism** strongly suggests that the structure and dynamics of human society are rooted in material concerns. Religion, therefore, is simply a by-product of these same base material concerns that govern the entirety of human society (i.e., it is a part of the **superstructure**). Although later Marxists—particularly those that implemented **communism** in the Soviet Union—were openly hostile to religion, Marx himself never believed that forced abdication of religious belief was necessary or desirable. Instead, he argued that the loss of religion would be a natural consequence of **revolutionary** change. *See also* BAUER, BRUNO, FALSE CONSCIOUSNESS, FEUERBACH, LUDWIG.

AUSTRIAN EMPIRE. A central European power from 1804 to 1867 under the rule of the Habsburgs. The **Kingdom of Prussia** and the Austrian Empire were the two major powers that vied for leadership within the **German Confederation**. *See also* AUSTRO-PRUSSIAN WAR, BISMARCK, OTTO VON, FRANCO-PRUSSIAN WAR, NATIONALISM, WARS OF GERMAN UNIFICATION.

AUSTRO-PRUSSIAN WAR. Prussia defeated the **Austrian Empire** in the Austro-Prussian War in 1866, which intensified the process of German unification under Prussian dominance and the banner of German nationalism. **Bismarck** wanted to replace the **German Confederation** created by the **Congress of Vienna** and unify the small states into a single German nation-state. The war resulted in Bismarck incorporating many of the smaller German states into Prussia and bringing others into the **North German Confederation** under Prussian leadership. In the process, Bismarck established a German Reichstag (parliament) elected by universal manhood suffrage. Many **1848**

revolutionaries and other radicals, carried away by nationalism as well as these liberal reforms, supported Bismarck in these moves. Marx and **Engels** remained far more hostile and suspicious of Prussia. Bismarck accomplished the unification of most of the rest of Germany as a result of the **Franco-Prussian War**.

AVELING, EDWARD (1849–1898). In 1884, Aveling, along with **Samuel Moore** and **Friedrich Engels**, translated the third German edition of volume 1 of *Capital* into English. In addition to writing popular works of science on biology, botany, geology, and **political economy** (*A Student's Marx: An Introduction to the Study of Karl Marx's Capital*), Aveling wrote several popularizations of **Charles Darwin**'s evolutionary theories. For one of these works, he asked Darwin's permission to dedicate the work to Darwin; Darwin refused. The note of refusal was in Marx's papers after his death, and the myth grew that Karl had asked Darwin for permission to dedicate *Capital* to him and that Darwin refused.

Aveling was a lover for a time of **Eleanor Marx** and in 1886 traveled the United States with her promoting the **Socialist League**. He was very unpopular in the socialist movement for his habit of borrowing money from everybody; he became more unpopular still when he left Eleanor for another woman and came back to her only when struck with kidney disease. Sperber (2013) characterizes him as "a cad and bounder straight out of Victorian melodrama" who, as her last lover, drove Eleanor to suicide in 1898 (473). Aveling died several months later.

B

BAKUNIN, MIKHAIL (1814–1876). A Russian **anarchist** and practicing **revolutionary**, Bakunin was born into a minor Russian noble family. After a brief and unhappy experience in the Russian military, Bakunin sought to earn an advanced degree to obtain a university position. Fascinated by **Hegelian** philosophy, he traveled to **Berlin**, Switzerland, **France**, and **Belgium** in the early 1840s. In his travels, he encountered **Young Hegelians** like Karl Marx, and he became radicalized in his opposition to the political domination of eastern Europe by Russia.

Bakunin participated in the **Revolutions of 1848**, particularly in the Czech uprising against the **Austria-Hungarian Empire**. In 1849, he joined in one of the last revolts of that tumultuous period and was subsequently arrested and deported to **Russia**. There, he was tried and imprisoned for roughly six years and then sent into permanent internal exile in Siberia. Bakunin later escaped from his exile by ship, traveling to Japan and later to New York. He returned to Europe in 1862 and immediately returned to revolutionary activity, helping to form secret societies in a variety of European countries and particularly developing influence in Italy and Spain. For roughly a quarter of the century, Bakunin was an open and active political agitator, showing up wherever social unrest spilled over into actual violence in the hopes of leading a popular rebellion.

At **The Hague International** of 1872, the Marxist faction accused Bakunin of fostering a secret society within the **International Workingmen's Association (IWA)**. The International subsequently expelled Bakunin and his faction from the IWA, which marked one of the many schisms in European socialism, in this instance between **Marxist** socialists and **anarcho**-communists.

Bakunin wielded considerable sway among European anarcho-communists and attempted to use his influence to seize control of the IWA. Bakunin, while joining Marx in advocating the violent overthrow of the state, mistrusted Marx's advocacy for a "**dictatorship of the proletariat**" to ensure the transition to a **classless society**. Marx, in turn, criticized Bakunin's criticisms as "Schoolboy drivel," claiming that Bakunin knew nothing of social revolution and arguing that Bakunin simplistically believed that a European social revolution could occur on "the economic foundation of capitalist production" (Tucker 1978, 544). These disagreements over the ends of revolution had their origins in conflict over the nature of revolution itself. For Bakunin, revolution began and ended with the destruction of the **state**; for Marx, only a revolution that destroyed **class** divisions was worth pursuing. While Bakunin steadfastly believed in a "revolution from below," fed by the discontent of the oppressed yearning for personal liberty, Marx dismissed the Revolutions of 1848 and the **Paris Commune** of 1871 as misdirected, their sporadic nature lacking the kind of critical mass necessary for toppling a modern state. *See also CONSPECTUS OF BAKUNIN'S STATISM AND ANARCHY*, GUILLAUME, JAMES.

BANKS. It is through the banking system that all available monetary reserves—savings of workers and capitalists as well as accumulated **surplus value**—become functioning capital to loan to enterprises to invest in additional **factories, machinery,** and **workers.** This pool of **money** is far more than could be raised by most individual firms. Besides, such credit allows capital to increase "the number of productive cycles through which a single sum of money capital can pass" in a year. Such an increase allows for the additional accumulation of surplus value that a firm can extract from its workers "since the same amount of surplus-value is produced during each of these productive cycles, all other things remaining equal" (Mandel 1981, 54).

Along with **joint-stock companies,** banking systems are part of a **credit system** that facilitates the **growth** of capital, contributing to its **centralization and enlargement** and stimulating **technological** investment as well as the development of the **world market.** Marx applauds this progress, as it quickens capitalism's mission of creating the "material foundations for the new form of production" as well as hastening the dissolution of the capitalist system (Marx 1894/1991, 574). *See also* CAPITALIST CLASS, CIRCUIT OF CAPITAL, COOPERATIVE FACTORIES, WORKERS' COOPERATIVE FACTORY.

BASE. In an analysis of society based on Marx's **historical materialism,** there are two linked theoretical components of society: the base (sometimes known as the structure or infrastructure) and the **superstructure.** The base consists of the **forces of production** and the **relations of production,** which, combined, allow people to produce the goods and amenities society needs. Marx and **Engels** argue that the base is mainly responsible for determining a society's superstructure,—that is, its ideas, culture, **religion,** and politics. The **capitalist mode of production,** for example, results in superstructural elements that enforce the power of the **bourgeoisie** and the exploitation of the **proletariat** (such as political systems where the bourgeoisie maintain control or religious

systems that justify the inequalities inherent in the system).

Marx's ideas are in direct opposition to those of **Hegel** (and many of the **Young Hegelians**), who argued the reverse: that it is the ideology of a society that determines its structure. Marx, however, did not posit a simple one-way directional causal relationship where the base determines all aspects of the superstructure and cautions against this type of determinism. Instead, he notes that the relationship between the two is reciprocal and that neither the base nor the superstructure is a static phenomenon. Because both are products of social behavior, the base can impact the superstructure in many possible ways. Likewise, changes in the superstructure can affect the base. For example, the **growth** of **revolutionary class consciousness** by the proletariat—an ideological shift in the superstructure—can ultimately result in changes to the base in the form of revolutionary-driven change in the mode of production and the relations of production.

BAUER, BRUNO (1809–1882). A **Young Hegelian,** an untenured lecturer at the **University of Berlin,** and a leader of the **Doctors' Club** when Karl attended the university in 1836–1839. Dr. Bruno Bauer became a mentor and friend to the young Marx, inviting him to his family home and advising him to pursue an academic career. Bauer's biblical criticism, which centered on attacking establishment **religion,** caused a sympathetic member of the Prussian government to arrange a transfer to the **University of Bonn** to improve his prospects of gaining a professorship. As a lecturer there, Bauer maintained his relationship with Karl, advising him on his dissertation and urging him to apply for an academic career at the university after Marx obtained his doctorate. On receiving his doctorate, Marx moved to Bonn; however, **Hegelian** philosophy fell out of favor with the conservative Prussian state, terminating Bruno's academic career in March 1842 before Marx could gain the position. "Before they parted company, Bauer and Karl 'rented a pair of asses' to ride through the city. Bonn society was astonished. We shouted with joy, the asses brayed'" (Stedman-Jones 2016, 104). Marx then moved to **Cologne** and turned to **journalism** for a living.

After losing any chance for academic positions, Bauer became increasingly forthright in his writings on religion, **atheism**, rationalism, and the origins of Christianity. In 1842, the philosophical views of Marx and Bauer diverged, as Marx was increasingly concerned with applying philosophy to political and social issues while Bruno remained focused on religion and spirituality. Bruno, Marx, and other Young Hegelians were writing for the *Rhineland News*. Karl eventually became an informal editor and came to believe that the focus of the newspaper should be on political conditions rather than religious criticism. Karl wrote to **Arnold Ruge**, "For religion is without content; it owes its being not to heaven, but to earth; and with the abolition of distorted reality, of which it is the theory, it will collapse of itself" (Stedman-Jones 2016, 120). As Karl became more a critic of the **political economy** of **capitalism** and an advocate of **socialism** and **social revolution**, his estrangement from Bauer increased.

Along with many Young Hegelians, Bauer's radicalism centered on critiques of religion, a rejection of social conventions, and a celebration of atheism. In 1844, Karl, along with **Engels**, wrote *The Holy Family or Critique of Critical Criticism: Against Bruno Bauer and Company*, which, true to its title, critiqued the lifestyle radicalism of Bruno Bauer and the Young Hegelians who followed.

BEBEL, AUGUST (1840–1913). Ferdinand August Bebel was a German socialist politician who helped form regional German workers' associations. The pamphlets of **Ferdinand Lassalle** initially attracted Bebel to socialism when August was a young woodworker. When Lassalle died in 1864, Bebel became an **Eisenacher** and, along with his mentor and colleague **Wilhelm Liebknecht**, struck a cautious middle path between the kind of revolutionary advocacy demanded by Marx and **Engels** and Lassalle's aspiration of leading the German **proletariat** into a coalition of German workers

and the King and Junker class against the **bourgeoisie**.

After the **Austro-Prussian War**, **Bismarck** unified northern German states under Prussian leadership and established a Reichstag (parliament) elected by universal manhood suffrage. Both Bebel and Liebknecht were elected to the North German Reichstag in 1867 on the ticket of the People's Party. In 1869, the two formed the **Social Democratic Workers' Party of Germany (SDAP)** and affiliated with the **International Workingmen's Association**. In 1871, Bebel expressed solidarity with the **Paris Commune** in the Reichstag, stating, "Before many decades have gone by the battle-cry of the Parisian proletariat—'War on palaces, peace to cottages, death to poverty and idleness!'—will be the battle-cry of the entire European proletariat" (Stedman-Jones 2016, 555). In 1875, the SDAP met with the Lassalleans of the **General German Workers' Association** in a unity conference held in the city of Gotha. In preparation for the meeting, representatives met to draw up a joint program, the **Gotha Program**, which led to bitter denunciations from Marx. In 1890, the group merged with other socialist parties into the **Social Democratic Party of Germany (SPD)**. Bebel became the leader of the SPD of Germany until his death in 1913, less than a year before the outbreak of World War I.

Bebel was unique among socialist leaders, coming from humble origins and having little formal education. As such, his skills lay primarily in organizing and inspiring German workers. He served several terms as a member of the German Reichstag. His opposition to additional war bonds (along with Liebknecht) and to continue the war against **France** in 1870 led to accusations that he was a French sympathizer or agent. He served several years in prison, both for caballing against the German state and for insulting the Kaiser, which further burnished his reputation among German workers.

His contemporaries did not consider Bebel to be a particularly sophisticated thinker, and as a revolutionary, many viewed him as too committed to parliamentarism. Bebel's skill instead lay in organizing and oratory, and he was a consistent voice favoring the cause of German workers. In various speeches before the Reichstag, Bebel inveighed against Germany's imperialist aspirations and the mistreatment of German soldiers by officers as well as the oppression of indigenous peoples in southwestern Africa. His most notable contribution to socialist literature was his *Women under Socialism* (1904), which argued for gender equality and the abolition of monogamous marriage.

BECKER, HERMANN "RED" (1820–1885). A **Cologne** democrat whose red hair and radical politics earned him the nickname "Red." He started the *West German News* in 1848; Prussian authorities suppressed the paper in July 1850, and shortly after, Becker became active in the **Communist League**. In 1851, he worked with Marx to print a multivolume collection of Marx's essays, but after the initial volume, the Prussian government suppressed the work. In May 1851, the Prussian government arrested Becker along with 10 other Cologne communists. The prisoners spent more than 18 months in solitary confinement in dark, narrow cells and were forbidden most visitors, including attorneys. They went to trial in October 1852 on charges to conspiracy to overthrow the Prussian government. The **Cologne Communist Trial** drew the attention of all of central Europe; crowds gathered at the courthouse to cheer on the defendants and curse the authorities. On 12 November, the court sentenced Becker to six years in prison. After serving his sentence, he remained active in democratic politics in opposition to the Prussian government. The people of Cologne elected him mayor in 1878.

BELGIUM. Under pressure from the Prussian government, **France** expelled Marx from Paris in January 1845, giving him one week to leave the country. Marx and his family settled in **Brussels** for the next three years. While there, Karl mixed with radicals and liberals from across Europe, particularly German émigrés and socialist intellectuals. While in Brussels, he worked on his **political economy** manuscripts as well as *The German Ideology*

(1845). It was in Belgium in early 1846 that Marx and **Engels** began to set up a network of communists across the continent by starting the **Communist Committee of Correspondence**, sending out propaganda and reports on the activities of fellow socialists. On 23 February 1848, the **Paris Uprising** occurred. When word reached Belgium, the government feared similar revolutionary activity. Because of his involvement in democratic activities as well as the **Communist League**, authorities believed Marx to be conspiring to overthrow the Belgium government. The government expelled Marx and his family on 4 March; Karl briefly relocated back to **Paris** before returning to **Cologne** to edit the *New Rhineland News*.

BERLIN. Karl Marx moved to Berlin when he enrolled at the **University of Berlin** in the autumn of 1836 at the behest of his father, **Heinrich**, who was not happy with Karl's extracurricular activities at the **University of Bonn**. Berlin was the Prussian capital at the time, a kingdom that was a major power in Europe but one without an independent judiciary, a free press, or a parliament. Berlin had a **population** of about 300,000 in 1836 and was Karl's first real experience with big-city life; he continued to live there for four and a half years. While not a center of commerce or industry, Berlin was rich in cultural life: —theater, opera, and the arts. It was while studying law and philosophy in Berlin that Karl began writing romantic poetry for **Jenny** as well as making other literary attempts to write a play, theater criticism, and even a novel. Not happy with the results, Karl destroyed most of these works. It was also in Berlin that he first encountered the work of the philosopher **Georg W. F. Hegel**, a significant intellectual influence. The **Young Hegelians** reinforced this influence, a group that also gave Marx the personal connections that would serve him well in beginning his **journalistic career**.

BERNSTEIN, EDUARD (1850–1932). Bernstein was a "second-generation Marxist" who eventually rejected key elements of Marx's interpretation of socialism in favor of a more **evolutionary**, Kantian interpretation of **socialism**. A dedicated member of the Marx faction in the

1870s, Bernstein spent 1878–1901 in exile following Germany's **Anti-Socialist Laws**. Bernstein split his time between Switzerland and **England**, where he befriended both Marx and **Friedrich Engels** and came to know **Karl Kautsky**. In the period between Marx's death in 1883 and Engels's death in 1895, fellow **Marxists** viewed Bernstein as a reliable member of the "**Eisenachers**." During his various travels to England, Bernstein encountered members of the **Fabian Society**, British socialists who advocated a gradualist and evolutionary approach to socialism. Although Bernstein rejected such accusations, his fellow Marxists suspected that Fabian influence led to his ultimate break with Marx on crucial aspects of his interpretation of socialism.

Bernstein was one of the architects of the **Erfurt Program** in 1891, which became the platform of the **German Social Democratic Party**. He returned to Germany in 1901 and became a member of the Reichstag (the lower house of the German Parliament) from 1902 to 1918. Although he continued to describe himself as a Marxist, Bernstein also engaged in a sustained revision of several essential elements of Marxist socialism and eventually rejected the inevitability of **violent revolution**. Bernstein also rejected **Hegelianism** and in his writings attempted to create a version of socialism that drew on the work of **Immanuel Kant**, fearing that violent means may hopelessly corrupt the end of any revolutionary project.

Bernstein also criticized Marx's economic determinism, contending that many of Marx's predictions regarding the "**immiseration**" of the **proletariat** had not presently occurred; while Marx had predicted the inexorable concentration of wealth in the hands of the **bourgeoisie**, Bernstein meticulously demonstrated that **trade unions** and **political parties** espousing socialist ideas were improving the lot of the working class. These developments persuaded Bernstein that the **LaSallean** view that the state could be a force for good was at least plausible. Remaining orthodox Marxists treated Bernstein's critique as a betrayal. Consequently, Bernstein became a figure of considerable controversy. Karl Kautsky, in particular, criticized Bernstein on the same grounds that Marx criticized the LaSalleans: that a working class dependent on the state for its well-being would remain a subservient class. **Rosa Luxemburg (1871–1919)**, a founding member of the **Communist Party of Germany**, criticized Bernstein in similarly harsh terms. Nevertheless, in the pre–World War I years, the German Social Democratic Party would move in the direction of **evolutionary socialism**, a pathway that Marx expressly opposed.

BISMARCK, OTTO VON (1815–1898). A reactionary, royalist member of the German nobility (e.g., Junkers), Bismarck stood foremost among the towering political figures of European politics from the mid- to the late 19th century. Bismarck effectively employed a mix of diplomacy and military force to secure a unified German state in 1871. He deftly managed the newly unified Germany's domestic and foreign policies, creating the first welfare state to mollify a potentially radicalized labor movement while stitching together a network of alliances that secured a tenuous peace in Europe for the remainder of the 19th century.

After roughly a decade serving as an ambassador, Bismarck became Prussian chancellor in 1862 at a time when German unification had been a dominant issue for more than a decade. Bismarck led Prussia through a series of military and diplomatic victories over Denmark, **Austria**, and **France**, culminating in Wilhelm I's ascension as first German emperor and subsequently Kaiser, or head of state of a unified German state. Bismarck deftly avoided calls for the creation of a unification of all German-speaking peoples, settling the long conflict between Prussia and Austria for hegemony over the hodgepodge of principalities and city-states of the **German Confederation**.

Over 17 years as German chancellor, Bismarck sought to manage German international and domestic affairs to avoid threats to Germany's security, with mixed success. He avoided joining in the race for colonies in Africa and Asia to prevent drawing Germany into conflict with **England** but ultimately reversed course and acquired overseas possessions in Africa and the South Pacific. Bismarck engaged in a long and ultimately fruitless *Kulturkampf* with the Catholic Church over control of church offices in Catholic-dominated areas of the newly unified state (1872–1878). Likewise, he counseled against victory parades and punitive concessions following Prussian defeat of Austria, but German seizure of Alsace-Lorraine following the **Franco-Prussian War** stoked long-standing anti-German sentiments in France. He established tariffs during the "Long Depression" of 1873–1879 to protect nascent and vulnerable German industries. Bismarck also engaged in the "Germanization" of newly annexed southern (French), northern (Danish), and eastern (Polish) territories. He appeared animated by anti-Polish animus, viewing Polish and German nationalism as a zero-sum conflict; with the Poles, he preferred expulsion to assimilation. His attempts to isolate France and provide indirect aid to the British in their disputes with Russia in central Asia helped set the stage for the interlocking alliances that would trigger World War I.

Domestically, Bismarck engaged in a series of policies calculated to centralize and strengthen the German state. His principal domestic fear was an emerging industrial workforce, organized by diverse and divergent groups of socialists. His justification for proposing the construction of the first welfare state in Europe was to establish ties of loyalty between German workers and the nation. He was not above attempts to encourage divisions among socialists. He appears to have engaged in a brief dialogue with **Ferdinand Lassalle** in the early 1860s in hopes of widening the divisions between the **Social Democratic Party** and the **General German Workers' Association**, the two leading German socialist labor organizations. Bismarck also exploited two assassination attempts on Kaiser Wilhelm I to institute the **Anti-Socialist Laws**, which banned socialist attempts at organizing workers and fielding candidates in elections. Police were also empowered to search and arrest anyone suspected of socialist tendencies. Bismarck hoped that the legislation would hamper the activities of the Social Democratic Party, which continued to field successful candidates running independently.

The death of Kaiser Wilhelm I in 1888 and the brief and ineffectual reign of Friedrich III that same year set the stage for Bismarck's exit. He lacked an understanding of Kaiser Wilhelm II, and his attempts at manipulating the young monarch backfired. Wilhelm II forced Bismarck into retirement over conflicting views on the renewal of the Anti-Socialist Laws.

No record exists of Bismarck's view of Karl Marx or **Marxism** in general, but he had a well-documented hostility toward socialism. His efforts alternatively to co-opt, divide, and ultimately suppress German socialist movements provided testament to his enmity. In contrast, Marx's opinion of Bismarck betrayed begrudging respect. Marx supported the war with Denmark as a necessary evil, believing that German unification was an essential condition for social and economic progress. Marx's view of Bismarck was likely akin to his historical perspective of capitalism: once a progressive force, destined for overthrow by historical forces beyond his control.

BLANC, LOUIS (1811–1882). Louis Blanc was a French politician, historian, and socialist reformer. Roughly a contemporary of Karl Marx, Blanc's *The Organization of Work* (1839) was widely influential and advanced the socialist principle, "From each according to his ability, to each according to his needs," which Marx viewed as the appropriate principle of distribution during the **dictatorship of the proletariat.** He was also among the first socialists to argue for a universal "right to work." He was a gradualist and a reformer, and as such, Marx viewed Blanc's work with suspicion, even as Marx adapted critical elements of Blanc's socialism.

Blanc was a leading member of the Provisional Government during the French **Revolution of 1848,** but his plans for the creation of workshop communes to guarantee French workers employment proved politically controversial. He fell out of favor with the Provisional Government and subsequently fled **France** for **England** when **Louis Bonaparte** established the Second Empire in 1852. He did not return to France until the fall of the Second Empire in the aftermath of the abdication of **Napoleon III** in 1870. On his return from exile, Blanc served in the National Assembly for eight years. While not participating in the **Paris Commune** of 1871, among his last official acts was to propose amnesty for the "**Communards**," its leaders and members still living.

Marx was at once influenced by and critical of important aspects of Blanc's interpretation of socialism. On the one hand, Marx drew from Blanc his conclusions regarding the centrality of industrial workers as well as his acceptance of Blanc's distributive principles as a waystation along the path to **communism**. On the other hand, according to Isaiah Berlin (2013), Marx viewed socialists like Blanc with a jaundiced eye. He saw them as "sentimental **petite-bourgeoisie** in disguise, sheep in wolves clothing." They might have the right ideals, but their "gradualist" tactics make them "enemies of the revolution" (93). As much as French socialists contributed to Marx's systematic account of **revolutionary socialism**, he ultimately rejected the evolutionary, moralistic, and individualistic strands of French socialism as promulgated by figures like **Pierre Proudhon** and Blanc.

BLANQUI, LOUIS-AUGUSTE (1805–1881).

A French socialist and rival of Marx whose principal *raison d'être* appeared to be plotting to overthrow a succession of French governments. Blanqui did most of his writing in prison, and he spent roughly half of his adult life behind bars. Blanqui's leadership and charisma generated a following, and "**Blanquism**" became a frequent target of Marx's critical attacks on rivals for control of the European socialist movement. Blanquism presented revolution as a sort of "silver bullet," an end in itself, where, with the rapid overthrow of the **state** and the destruction of the **bourgeoisie**, socialism would naturally take its place.

Marx's view on Blanqui varied over time. He appeared to express "Blanqui-like" solidarity during the **Revolutions of 1848** and appeared to have believed in 1871 that Blanqui—then in jail—would have been the ideal person to lead the **Paris Commune**. The more moderate elements of the **International** sometimes accused Marx and Engels of "Blanquist-Jacobinism."

At the same time, Marx's major writings express considerable impatience with Blanquism's recklessness and lack of fidelity to the cause of the working class. Marx coined the phrase "**alchemists of revolution**" in his 1850 debates with the **Willich-Schapper group** over the proper lessons to draw from the failures of the 1848 uprisings (Avineri 1995, 201).

Blanqui's socialism differed in significant respects from **Marxism**. The Blanquists were indifferent to **class politics**, believing that a small cadre of dedicated revolutionaries was all that was necessary to overthrow a state. Blanqui also did not appear to trouble himself too much with the shape of government after the revolution but unlike Marx did not appear committed to a required revolutionary sequence, including a "**dictatorship of the proletariat**." "Blanquism" among adherents of Marxism quickly became a kind of insult for short-term, emotive, and ultimately counterproductive **violence**. *See also* LENIN, VLADIMIR, VANGUARD PARTY.

BLANQUISM. Blanquism is a concept advocated by **Louis-Auguste Blanqui** that a relatively small group of professionals should forcibly carry out a **socialist revolution**. These professionals should be highly trained and organized revolutionaries who would overthrow the capitalist political-economic system. They would then set up a temporary dictatorship that would have the goal of ushering in the new socialist order. After the establishment of this new socialist system, the dictatorship would dissolve and hand power over to the proletariat. Marx was highly critical of Blanquism. He argued that the proletariat that had developed a **revolutionary class consciousness** must drive the **revolution**. That Blanquism focused on the revolution itself, with little thought or plan for how to implement a genuinely **classless society** after the revolution. *See also* LENIN, VLADIMIR, VANGUARD PARTY.

BOARD OF DIRECTORS. Marx (1885/1978) terms these governing boards of **joint-stock companies** (corporations) a new deception perpetrated by the **capitalist class**. He writes that they arise "over and above the actual

29

managing director, a number of governing and supervisory boards arise, for which management and supervision are in fact a mere pretext for the robbery of shareholders and their own enrichment" (514). He asserts that the wages for such supervisory personnel are "in inverse proportion, as a rule, to the actual supervision exercised by these nominal directors" (514). *See also* CAPITALIST CLASS, MANAGERIAL SKILLED LABOR.

BOLSHEVIK REVOLUTION. The **Bolsheviks** were a **revolutionary socialist** party initially formed in 1898 to unite the different leftist parties and organizations present in the Russian Empire at that time. By the time of the **Russian Revolution of 1905**, the Bolsheviks were an influential yet fragmented organization made up of factory workers and agriculturalists, led by **Vladimir Lenin**. The two main factions of the party split permanently in 1912, with Lenin supporters forming the **Russian Social Democratic Labor Party**, unofficially known as the Bolshevik Party.

After the collapse of the czarist autocracy of the Russian Empire in March 1917 that marks the beginning of the **Russian Revolution of 1917**, the **Soviets**, local councils made up primarily of industrial workers and soldiers, ruled alongside the Russian Provisional Government, which was made up mostly of capitalists and the remnants of the czarist noble aristocracy. There were frequent conflicts, protests, and strikes during this time, most notably by Lenin's Bolsheviks, who advocated for an immediate end to Russia's involvement in World War I, land for agricultural peasants, and bread for the workers ("Peace, Land, and Bread"—the slogan of the Bolshevik leaders in 1917). When the Provisional Government continued Russia's involvement in the war, the Bolsheviks were able to leverage resistance to the conflict to gain control over workers' militias and soldiers. They allied with the Soviets (collectively known as the **Red Guards** and, later, the **Red Army**), and in November 1917, the Bolshevik Revolution overthrew the Provisional Government, and the Bolsheviks became the main governing party of Russia. Once in charge of the government, Lenin and

the Bolsheviks set about reorganizing Russia into the world's first socialist republic, though conflict soon erupted between the Bolsheviks and other counterrevolutionary parties and non-Bolshevik socialists. Ultimately, the Bolsheviks were able to suppress these movements and reconstituted themselves as the **Communist Party of the Soviet Union**, paving the way for the creation of the **Union of Soviet Socialist Republics** in 1922. *See also* VANGUARD PARTY.

BOLSHEVIKS. *See* BOLSHEVIK REVOLUTION.

BOLSHEVISM. *See* BOLSHEVIK REVOLUTION.

BONAPARTE, CHARLES-LOUIS NAPOLEON. *See* NAPOLEON III.

BONAPARTE, NAPOLEON (1769–1821). Born into a Corsican minor noble family, Napoleon Bonaparte's rapid rise through the French republican army during the wars sparked by the **French Revolution** brought him from second lieutenant in 1785 to leading troops in the field by 1795. His unprecedented successes in campaigns on the Italian peninsula encouraged the launching of a military adventure in Egypt to break British control of the eastern Mediterranean. When Horatio Nelson's decisive defeat of the French navy in the Battle of the Nile rendered French supply lines tenuous, he returned to **France** and received national acclaim, quickly overbearing the politically bankrupt Council of 500 through a series of rigged "plebiscites" to assume an increasingly dictatorial position over the French state, even as he commanded armies in the field.

Following a brief respite afforded by the Peace of Amiens (1802), Napoleon succeeded through a plebiscite in being named "First Consul for Life." His plans for expanding French control in North America and reassertion over French Caribbean possessions ultimately proved fruitless, and he abruptly sold the Louisiana Territory to the United States in 1803. In 1804, at age 35, Napoleon declared himself "emperor" and launched a series of military campaigns that smashed a series of alliances of hostile European rivals. By

1808, Napoleon had imposed the "continental system" on much of Europe, a blockade calculated to cripple the economy of the one remaining undefeated European power: **England**.

Three factors led to Napoleon's downfall. First, England's Royal Navy won a series of devastating victories at sea that prevented Napoleon from invading the British Isles. Second, a festering insurgency in Spain—strongly supported by a small British army under the command of Arthur Wellesley, the Duke of Wellington—frustrated the French occupation of the peninsula. Third, Napoleon ignored his military advisers and launched an invasion of Russia, whose military adopted a Fabian strategy of avoiding pitched battle with the *Grande Armèe*. Napoleon succeeded in capturing Moscow, which the Russians burned rather than suing for peace. Napoleon bivouacked in Moscow for five critical weeks and then began a long retreat, with Russian cavalry harrying retreating French units in freezing weather. Fewer than 30,000 French soldiers survived the retreat. Napoleon raised more troops but remained heavily outnumbered by soldiers from the Sixth Coalition (e.g., Austria, Great Britain, Portugal, Prussia, and Sweden). Following the devastating French defeat at Leipzig, Napoleon abdicated and went into exile on the island of Elba. His brief, triumphant return to France and displacement of the newly installed Louis XVII led to the "Hundred Days" War, culminating in the Battle of Waterloo, where the combined British and Prussian armies—led by Wellington and Prince Blücher—defeated Napoleon and forced him into exile at St. Helena, a tiny island in the Atlantic, 150 miles off the African coast. He died there at age 51 amid rampant speculation that he was poisoned.

Marx adopted a distinctively Hegelian view of Napoleon as a heroic world-changing figure. For Marx, Napoleon's military exploits began the process of destroying the last vestiges of feudalism, a necessary accomplishment that would presage the consolidation of the bourgeoisie and proletariat. As Isaiah Berlin (2013) described it, "The demands of his historical environment inevitably made him an instrument of social change" (141). In *The Eighteenth Brumaire of Louis Bonaparte*, written in 1852, Marx famously compared **Napoleon III** unfavorably to his uncle, noting that Hegel had remarked that "all great, world-historical facts and personages occur, as it were, twice. He has forgotten to add: the first time as tragedy, the second as farce" (Tucker 1978, 594). Marx and, later, Lenin would deploy the term **Bonapartism** to denote counterrevolutionary bourgeois movements calculated to seize momentum from socialist revolutionaries to preserve the **ruling class**.

BONAPARTISM. In a general sense, Bonapartism refers to the takeover of civilian-led government by military leadership, usually in the form of a charismatic authoritarian state, a definition based primarily on the political ideology of **Napoleon Bonaparte**. Marx used the term specifically to refer to counterrevolutionary military forces that sought to seize control of the state from civilian and specifically **proletariat** revolutionary groups after a **socialist revolution**. He was critical of such approaches (most notably in his 1852 manuscript *The Eighteenth Brumaire of Louis Bonaparte*), arguing that they ultimately led to the consolidation of power among a small **ruling class** and thus defeated the purpose of a socialist revolution. Modern **Marxist** analysts sometimes use the term to refer to revolutionary methods used by leaders such as **Joseph Stalin** and **Mao Zedong**, who utilized the military to form authoritarian control of extensive bureaucratic socialist regimes.

BOURGEOIS DEMOCRACY. Marx (and, later, **Marxist** thinkers) argued that **capitalism** distorts democratic processes. This subversion is because **class** rights are proportional to the degree to which the class can influence political decision making through political donations, bribery, control of mass media, and propaganda. The ability of wealthy classes to influence the democratic process producing outcomes that favor policies that support their **capital accumulation** overrides the will of the people. In other words, capitalist democracies are just plutocracies, where small numbers of very wealthy individuals control policy. Marx viewed capitalist democracy and the electoral process in such systems as no more than a cynical attempt by the bourgeois owners of the **means of production** to deceive the populace. They provide an illusion of democracy by allowing people to choose from the bourgeoisie's predetermined choices, who, when elected, enact the policies that support bourgeois interests over the interests of the proletariat. *See also* DICTATORSHIP OF THE BOURGEOISIE, DICTATORSHIP OF THE PROLETARIAT.

BOURGEOISIE. A general term for the middle classes in the Middle Ages through the 19th century usually associated with towns and cities. In the Middle Ages, this class consisted of small manufacturers, financiers, and merchants. With the intensification of economic activity, this group began gaining wealth and political power through what Marx called **primitive accumulation**, thus appropriating the necessary **capital** to start the process of the endless accumulation that is **capitalism**. "Accumulate, accumulate! That is Moses and the prophets!" (Marx 1867/1976, 742). By the time of the **Industrial Revolution**, the bourgeoisie—consisting of industrial capitalists, merchants, and bankers—became the class that had controlling interest in the **means of production**, distribution, and finance for **England** and soon the world. "It has been the first to show what man's activity can bring about. It has accomplished wonders far surpassing Egyptian pyramids, Roman aqueducts, and Gothic cathedrals; it has conducted expeditions that put in the shade all former Exoduses of nations and crusades. The bourgeoisie cannot exist without constantly **revolutionising** the instruments of production, and thereby the **relations of production**, and with them the whole relations of society" (Marx and Engels 1848/1969, 16). Marx uses the label "bourgeoisie" interchangeably with the term "capitalist," using the latter term much more frequently in later writings. *See also* PREFACE, THE.

BRAVERMAN, HARRY (1920–1976). Harry Braverman was born in Brooklyn, New York. His parents, Morris and Sarah, were Jewish Polish immigrants, his father a shoe worker.

Attending Brooklyn College for one year, he withdrew for economic reasons to find employment. He became exposed to Marx and **socialism** during his year of college. Shortly after, he joined the Young People's **Socialist League.** In 1936, at the age of 16, he found work at the Brooklyn Naval Yards as a coppersmith apprentice, where he worked until 1941. As the trade of coppersmith was in decline, Braverman found jobs in similar trades around the county, such as pipefitting, and sheet-metal work. It was in these trades that Braverman got a sense of the impact of science-based **technology** on jobs. "I had the opportunity of seeing at first hand, during those years, not only the transformation of industrial processes but the manner in which these processes are reorganized; how the worker, systematically robbed of a craft heritage, is given little or nothing to take its place" (Braverman 1974, 5). Drafted into the army in 1944 or 1945, he spent the following years as a sergeant teaching and supervising pipefitting. After his service, he moved to Youngstown, Ohio, with his wife Miriam, finding work as a steelworker. Fired from one company "at the instigation of the FBI," he managed to find work at others (Foster 1998, x).

From his early year in college on, Braverman continued his commitment to socialist ideology and organizations devoted to the establishment of these ideals. He became a member of the Socialist Workers' Party (SWP) and attended a six-month course of Marxist study at their **Trotsky** School in the early 1950s. But there were deep divisions in the SWP in the early 1950s. In 1953, Braverman left (or was expelled from) the SWP and became a coleader of a splinter group, the Socialist Union. It was at this point that he began coediting and writing for its paper, the *American Socialist*, under his party name, Harry Frankel. While working and writing for this paper, he worked out many of the ideas expressed in *Labor and Monopoly Capitalism*.

When the *American Socialist* folded after some seven years, Braverman moved into book publishing, becoming an editor for Grove Press in 1960. "While at Grove he edited and published *The Autobiography of Malcolm*

X when that book was dropped by Random House, the publisher who had initially commissioned the project" (Livingston 2000). He then became a vice president and general manager at Grove Press until leaving in 1967, "when the president of the company refused to publish a book by Bertrand Russell on American war crimes in Vietnam" (Livingston 2000). Braverman then became the director of Monthly Review Press and worked there until his death from cancer on 2 August 1976 at the age of 55.

It was while working in publishing that Braverman experienced the typical office processes of the time as well as the changes taking place in the office as a result of automation. "As an executive in publishing," he says,

> I was able to see, and in fact design, some of the administrative processes involved in modern marketing, distributing, accounting, and book production routines; and this experience twice included the transition from conventional to computerized office systems. I would not pretend that this background is as extensive as that of many others who have worked for longer periods of time in larger organizations, but at least it does enable me to understand, in some detail and concreteness, the principles by which labor processes are organized in modern offices. (Braverman 1974, 5)

Braverman began writing *Labor and Monopoly Capital* in his "spare time" at night and on weekends starting in 1970. Initially published in 1974, it was well received, sold very well, and is still in print. This is a remarkable feat for a Marxist critique of American capital and society. While most will not agree with *Labor and Monopoly Capital* on every count, the book will give many an appreciation for the devastating effects of the **detailed division of labor** on human life and the role of capitalism in spreading this division. *See also* FOSTER, JOHN BELLAMY, WALLERSTEIN, IMMANUEL, WESTERN MARXISM.

BRITISH FACTORY ACTS. Early capitalists maximized the **surplus value** created by

workers through long working days. Industrialists argued that a working day of 12 hours was necessary for the worker to both reproduce his value and create at least a little surplus value for the capitalist. However, beginning in 1833 and throughout the 19th century, the British government gradually limited the **length of the working day** through a succession of Factory Acts. These measures passed in a **bourgeois democracy** to co-opt working-class movements and to prevent the depletion of the supply of workers through death or dismemberment. Overwork, unhealthy living conditions, and periodic epidemics threatened the economic and military success of the nation. Drawing on "the official statistics" regarding conditions in British factories by British inspectors, Marx describes the prevailing 60-hour average workweek (Marx 1867/1976, 348–49). Many capitalists saw even the limit of 60 hours as too restrictive, and he reports on widespread cheating on the part of capitalists, attempting to lengthen the workday whenever possible. However, capitalists eventually realized that they could increase surplus value created by workers through employing industrial **machinery**, at least in the short run. Because of this, he argues, the Factory Acts themselves contribute to the **centralization and enlargement** of industry by destroying "small-scale and domestic industries," thus eliminating an outlet for employment in small **workshops** for much of the **surplus population** (635).

BRITISH MUSEUM. The Library of the British Museum is one of the premier libraries in the world. In Marx's day, it contained books, periodicals, pamphlets, government documents, and parliamentary debates and hosted public discussions on all the scientific discoveries and political developments of the day. Beginning in 1850, when he obtained his ticket for the library, Marx spent a great deal of time in the reading room of the museum, often 10- or 12-hour days, conducting his research in **political economy** as well as gathering information for his **journalism**.

BRUSSELS. In January 1845, Marx and his family came to Brussels after the Prussian government pressured the **French** govern- ment to expel Marx from **Paris**. The family spent three years in the capital of **Belgium**. While there, Karl continued to write and asso- ciate with other European radicals. To avoid further trouble with the Prussian government, he renounced his Prussian citizenship and as- sured Belgian authorities that he would not engage in political activities—a promise he would not keep. His second daughter, **Laura**, was born in Brussels in October 1845, and his son **Edgar** in February 1847. While in Brus- sels, Marx and Engels started the **Communist Committee of Correspondence** as a clearing- house for socialist theory, propaganda, and news of the activities of various radical groups around the European continent. Shortly after the **League of the Just** reorganized itself as the **Communist League**, Marx became the head of the Brussels Congregation. At their second Congress in November 1847, the Commu- nist League adopted Marx's political program whole and commissioned Marx and **Engels** to write *The Communist Manifesto*. Finally, in 1847, Marx joined and became a very active member of the **Brussels Democratic Associa- tion**. The people overthrew the French mon- archy in February 1848, and the Republic was declared. The Belgian government took the opportunity on 3 March to give Marx 24 hours to leave the country. The **Revolutions of 1848** had begun, and after a brief stop in Paris to lay his plans, Marx returned to **Munich**.

BRUSSELS DEMOCRATIC ASSOCIATION. Marx and Engels played a role in the founding of the Brussels Democratic Association in the fall of 1847. The Association was composed mainly of political refugees with Marx as its vice chair. The Association's goal was to mo- bilize for struggle against monarchist regimes in Europe and to promote democratic reforms, free trade, and liberal positions on interna- tional affairs. Marx was interested in promoting democratic reforms as the first step in the evolution of **communism**. In a speech to the Association in January 1848, he denounced protectionism as a tactic of the old regime and praised free trade as destructive of the old so- cial order. He called for establishing the rule

of **capital**, thereby hastening the **evolutionary** process and ultimately bringing on the **revolu- tion**: "It [free trade] dissolves the old nationali- ties and pushes to the extreme the antagonism between the bourgeoisie and the proletariat. In a word, the system of commercial liberty hastens the social revolution. It is solely in that revolutionary sense, gentlemen, that I vote in favor of free trade" (quoted in Sperber 2013, 201). Karl's position of supporting democratic reforms against monarchies was at the heart of his editorials in the *New Rhineland News* and remained a consistent theme of his politics throughout his life. With the February 1848 revolution in **France**, the Belgian authorities cracked down on the more radical members of the Association and expelled Marx from **Brus- sels** on 4 March 1848. The Association ceased to exist by 1849.

BUKHARIN, NIKOLAI (1888–1938). Nikolai Bukharin was a **Russian revolutionary** whose extensive writings contributed to Russian **Marxist** revolutionary theory. An "Old **Bol- shevik**," Bukharin used his position as editor of *Pravda*, the Bolshevik Party newspaper, as well as his office as general secretary of the Executive Committee of the **Communist Inter- national** to wield considerable influence within the Bolshevik Party before the **October Revo- lution** and well into the 1920s. His brief alli- ance with **Stalin** led to the removal of Stalin's most significant rivals in the Fifteenth Com- munist Party Congress (1927), paving the way for Stalin's rise to absolute power. Bukharin would himself be sacrificed on the altar of Sta- lin's paranoia, denounced in "show trials" in 1938. Bukharin's questioning and subsequent show trial and execution influenced Arthur Koestler's writing of *Darkness at Noon* (1940).

Bukharin's pathway to radicalism was a fa- miliar one for Russian revolutionaries: student activism leading to arrest by the czarist secret police, internal exile, and eventual escape, leading to flight from Russia. He lived for a time both in Germany and in the United States in New York City, where he edited a Russian-lan- guage social democratic magazine. Bukharin's evident talent as a writer and budding theorist brought him to the attention of older Russian radicals like **Lenin**, who recognized Bukharin's popularity among younger Bolsheviks and who viewed Bukharin as supremely talented but lacking in fidelity to Marxist principles. The multitude of Russian exiles who returned at word of the February Revolution rapidly tilted the balance of power among the revolutionary factions from the **Mensheviks** to the Bolsheviks, whose October Revolution pushed Russia in a significantly more radical direction.

Within the Bolshevik Party, Bukharin's talent led him to the editorship of *Pravda* (Russian translation: "Truth"), the Communist Party's official newspaper in the aftermath of the October Revolution. He also rose to a position of leadership in the Communist International (**Comintern**), or **Third International**, a relatively small group of communist organizations dedicated to the support of **class struggle** from 1926 to 1929. Bukharin had supported Lenin's "New Economic Policy," which reintroduced market mechanisms in the hopes of stimulating the economy to combat seven years of severe economic depression. From 1924 to 1929, he served as a full member of the Politburo and in the aftermath of Lenin's death supported Stalin in his power struggle with **Leon Trotsky** and his allies. During the power struggle between Stalin and Trotsky, Bukharin, who had initially promulgated the idea of **"socialism in one country,"** supported Stalin and participated in the maneuvers that led to the removal of Trotsky and his allies from positions of authority and influence.

By 1929, Stalin purged Bukharin from the Politburo and his other leadership positions. His continued support for the New Economic Policy ran counter to Stalin's decision to engage in "forced collectivization" in 1928 to consolidate further party control over the economy. His attempts to appeal to former rivals exposed him to betrayal. He was briefly rehabilitated and given the editorship of *Izvestia* (Russian translation: "News"), the official newspaper of the Soviet government. However, by 1936, Stalin initiated the "Great Terror," a massive purge of the leadership of the Communist Party, the **Red Army**, wealthy landholders, and anyone else who might plausibly oppose Stalin's increasingly totalitarian rule. Bukharin was interrogated, forced into confessing to "betraying the revolution" (which he subsequently recanted), and shot.

Bukharin was a significant 20th-century theorist of revolutionary **Marxism** both in his influence with major historical figures and in the sheer volume of his writing. For example, Lenin drew on and borrowed liberally from Bukharin's writings on imperialism, and it was Bukharin who first established the notion of "socialism in one country," not Stalin. To no small extent, Bukharin's reputation as a theorist was somewhat tarnished by his associations with both Lenin and Stalin. Many scholars dismiss Bukharin as a "mere propagandist," a popularizer of the arguments of more powerful or more sophisticated colleagues. The seeming unawareness of his peril and his meekness in accepting his fate as a victim of Stalin's need for internal enemies to suppress contributed to his subordination as a lesser figure in the pantheon of 20th-century Marxist revolutionary theorists.

BURNS, LYDIA "LIZZIE" (1827–1878). Younger sister to **Mary Burns**, Lizzie served as a live-in housekeeper in the apartment that **Engels** and Mary shared until Mary's death, after which she and Engels became domestic partners. Both Lizzie and Mary were illiterate but intelligent, had strong working-class ties, and were passionate and informed supporters of Irish causes (Green 2009). After Mary's death, Engels left **Erman and Engels** and lived openly with Lizzie, moving to London in 1870 and socializing freely. Although he believed that marriage was a **bourgeois** institution (see *ORIGIN OF THE FAMILY, PRIVATE PROPERTY, AND THE STATE, THE*), he "married Lizzie only on her deathbed in respect for her religious sentiments" (Green 2009, para. 6). He wrote about her, "My wife was a real child of the Irish proletariat and her passionate devotion to the class in which she was born was worth much more to me—and helped me more in times of stress—than all the elegance of an educated, artistic middle-class bluestocking" (Henderson 1976, 567).

BURNS, MARY (1821–1863). Mary was a radical Irish mill worker who met **Engels** on his first visit to Manchester in 1842 or 1843. She guided Engels as he made his observations of working-class life and conditions for his book *The Condition of the Working Class in England.* At some point, she formed a more intimate relationship with Engels, sharing a cottage—apart from his formal residence—with him in Manchester until her death in January 1863. He referred to their place as "a refuge in his double life as a revolutionary and as a capitalist" (Green 2009, para. 5).

Mary was the object of some tension between Marx and Engels, probably due to **Jenny Marx**'s open dislike of her (Sperber 2013, 177; Stedman-Jones 2016, 225). While Engels's letters were often solicitous regarding Marx's family, Karl was rarely attentive toward Mary. When Mary Burns died suddenly, Marx responded to Engels's letter announcing her death by asking for money. "Engels was appalled at his friend's lack of empathy, so different from Engels's own attitude on the death of **Marx's children** and the life-threatening illness of his wife. Even Engels's 'Philistine acquaintances' had shown 'more sympathy and friendship' than did Marx over Mary's death" (Sperber 2013, 481). It took some time to repair the breach between the two. When Engels became romantically involved with Mary's younger sister, **Lizzie Burns,** Karl became more solicitous in his letters. "When Engels and Lizzie moved to London in 1870, the Marxes socialized with both of them. Some mutual concessions in his family enabled Karl to reconcile the two central personal relationships in his life and his obligations as friend and patriarch" (Sperber 2013, 482). *See also* HESS, MOSES, PESCHE, SYBILLE.

C

CABRAL, AMILCAR (1925–1973). A West African agricultural engineer, poet, political dissident, revolutionary, and statesman, Cabral led the African Party for the Independence of Guinea and Cape Verde (PAIGC) against Portuguese colonial rule. Influenced by Marx, as an anticolonial theorist, he ranks with Franz Fanon and **Che Guevara**. As a student in the late 1940s in Lisbon, Portugal, studying to become an agronomist, Cabral helped organize student protests against Portuguese colonial rule. He returned to Africa in the early 1950s and helped to found PAIGC and acted as an intelligence asset for Czechoslovakian intelligence.

In the late 1950s, Cabral began organizing training camps in neighboring Ghana and elsewhere in West Africa. His training in agronomy facilitated his implementation of training methods designed to enable PAIGC troops to live off the land rather than raid farmers and shop owners. Throughout the 10-year insurgency, Cabral became the de facto governor of significant portions of Guinea-Bissau. Portuguese intelligence successfully fomented divisions within PAIGC, resulting in Cabral's assassination on 20 January 1973, but his half brother Luis Cabral unified the PAIGC, purged it of infiltrators and discordant elements, and successfully led the PAIGC into independence, becoming its president in 1974 until his ouster in a military coup in 1980.

Immersed as he was in the anticolonialist movement, **Lenin** rather than Marx likely figured more prominently in Cabral's ideology. Nevertheless, he displayed an absolute fidelity to critical **Marxist** tenets: the belief in **class struggle**, a commitment to **historical materialism**, the conviction that only **revolutionary** means could overturn the existing political order, and the need for a high degree of **revolutionary consciousness** among the **proletariat**. Cabral had faith that "eternity is not of this world, but man will outlive **classes** and will continue to produce and make history, since he can never free himself from the burden of his needs, both of mind and of body, which are the basis of the development of the **forces of production**" (McLellan 1989, 386).

CAPITAL. Capital is not a thing but a process; it is always in circulation, always in motion. It is **money** and resources used to make more money or more **exchange value**—money purchases resources and labor to produce **commodities** sold in the **marketplace**. The goal of production is more money than was initially invested in the production process. Production is for the sake of increasing one's capital—for **surplus value**, not **use value**. The constant **growth** of surplus, goaded by **competition**, is the goal of each capitalist.

According to Marx, capital consists of **constant capital** and **variable capital**. Constant capital is the part of wealth used to acquire and maintain the material **means of production**—that is, the **tools** and **machinery**, factories, and **workshops**. While it is a necessary condition for producing surplus value, it does not produce surplus value itself. Only variable capital—that is, the **labor power** of workers—produces surplus value. The profit motive, as well as the competition for a greater share of the market, gives the capitalist great incentive to take steps to increase surplus value and thus **profits** for the enterprise. These steps take the form of constant capital investments in tools, machinery, factories, and **distribution systems**, all to improve the **productivity** of labor power. Further subdivision of the **detailed division of labor** can also increase productivity. By improving productivity, the capitalist shortens the time it takes for the worker to produce a single unit of a commodity, that is, an exchange value that equals the wage paid (**paid labor**) and that lengthens the time the worker is producing surplus value for the capitalist (**unpaid labor**). *See also* CIRCUIT OF CAPITAL, CONTRADICTIONS OF CAPITALISM, CREDIT SYSTEMS.

CAPITAL: A CRITIQUE IN POLITICAL ECONOMY (1867).

According to Ernest Mandel (1976), Marx had become a communist shortly after attaining his doctorate in philosophy (1841) through his experience with social problems in **Prussia** as well as strikes in **England** and **France**. **Moses Hess** also played a significant role in introducing Marx to socialism. In the course of the 1840s, Karl increasingly turned to economic studies, producing in rapid succession such works as *Economic and Philosophic Manuscripts of 1844*, *The Poverty of Philosophy* (1847), and *The Communist Manifesto* (1848). Marx's political activities, his work in journalism, constant financial troubles, personal illness, and the illness and death of three of his children constantly interrupted his writings on **political economy**. Throughout the 1850s, however, Marx filled dozens of notebooks.

The first volume of *Capital* is by Marx alone and based on these notebooks. He published it in the German language in 1867. The original English translation (1887) is based on the third German edition, published in 1883, and was translated by **Samuel Moore** and **Edward Aveling** and closely supervised and edited by **Frederick Engels**, Marx's longtime friend and collaborator. In volume 1, Marx aimed to lay bare the laws of motion that explain the origin, maintenance, decline, and disappearance of

the **capitalist mode of production**. It focuses on capital's continuous search of **surplus value** produced by workers in the process of producing **commodities**. This drive for surplus value is the engine of economic **growth** and technological development. Such development leads to the increasing **alienation** of all human beings—capitalist and **laborer**—and growing fears that "the **forces of production** will be transformed into forces of destruction" (Mandel 1976, 78).

Engels edited the last two volumes of *Capital* after Marx's death. These latter volumes are incomplete drafts based on Marx's notebooks compiled throughout the 1850s, with additional work by Marx before his death in 1883. Scholarship on the raw notebooks has led some to posit that Engels's edits were substantial and may have gone well beyond Marx's

An early cover for *Das Kapital*.

notes (Harvey 2013). Because of this, it is the first volume of *Capital* that scholars consider Marx's definitive work on political economy. It is also the volume that is most widely read.

While the focus of the first volume of *Capital* is on the rise and mechanisms of accumulation of the industrial **bourgeoisie**, volumes 2 and 3 integrate the financial and merchant capitalists into the analysis. Volume 2 (1885), which Engels published in German, deals with speeding up the circulation of commodities in the marketplace as the **capitalist class** intensifies commercial **banking, transportation, and communication** aimed at marketing and distributing commodities around the globe. This intensification has the effect of concentrating money in the hands of an ever-smaller percentage of the capitalist class (Mandel 1978).

Marx intended volume 3 (1894) to combine the analysis of surplus value creation in commodity production and distribution and thereby explain the capitalist mode of production in its totality, that is, its structure, dynamics, and how its various **contradictions** would lead to crises, working-class revolt, and the transition to socialism. Unfortunately, Marx's notes on these issues were somewhat incomplete (Mandel 1981).

When Marx wrote *Capital*, private industry was still in its infancy in England and western European countries; Marx was writing in a society still very much in transition from a **feudal mode of production** to a capitalist mode of production. Despite this, Marx's analysis of the capitalist mode of production remains invaluable in understanding the impact of capitalism on social life. *See also* PREFACE, THE, *THEORIES OF SURPLUS-VALUE* (1905).

CAPITAL CENTRALIZATION. *See* CENTRALIZATION AND ENLARGEMENT OF CAPITAL.

CAPITAL GROWTH. *See* CENTRALIZATION AND ENLARGEMENT OF CAPITAL.

CAPITALISM. *See* CAPITALIST MODE OF PRODUCTION.

CAPITALIST AGRICULTURE. It is not that capitalism transforms only the **factory system**. Capital's employment of science and **technology** also affects agriculture, causing it to transform into an **exploitative** relationship in which the crops, animals, and people become **commodities**. Marx argues that the "**large-scale industry**" has an even more "**revolutionary**" effect on agriculture. It substitutes the **wage laborer** for the foundation of feudal society, the **peasant** (Marx 1867/1976, 637). Marx goes on to detail the conscious application of technology to farming, which drastically reduces the rural **population** and concentrates them into cities to become the growing class of wage earners. This concentration has two effects: (1) with their rising population, urban areas gain increasing power in society, and (2) it has **environmental** consequences for the land and consequently for the physical health of the workers. Mechanical technology and chemistry replace care for the land; agribusiness transforms agriculture, exploiting not only the worker but also the earth itself. Capitalist agriculture concentrates the population into urban settings, having an impact on the environments of both city and rural life. "It disturbs the circulation of matter between man and the soil" (554). Marx's concern here is that such urban concentrations prevent the recycling of waste to the soil, thus ultimately destroying soil fertility. "The more a country proceeds from large-scale industry as the background of its development, as in the case of the United States, the more rapid is this process of destruction. Capitalist production, therefore, only develops the techniques and the degree of combination of the social process of production by simultaneously undermining the original sources of all wealth—the soil and the worker" (638). *See also* ECOLOGY, ENVIRONMENTAL CRISIS, METABOLIC INTERACTION.

CAPITALIST CLASS. Marx divides the capitalist class into four groups based on their source of revenue. Industrial capitalists, whose wealth comes from profits made from exploiting **surplus labor**; commercial capitalists, whose source of income is in exchange of commodities; bankers, who get revenue from both commercial and interest transactions;

and capitalist landowners, whose income comes from land rent. However, Marx considers the industrial capitalist as central to his analysis of the capitalist system, for it is wage labor that "creates the total mass of surplus-value" (Mandel 1978, 49). The other forms of capitalism preceded the rise of the industrial capitalist and, rather than create capital from surplus labor, accumulated it through buying cheap and selling dear, enclosure, plunder and piracy, fraud, usury, and other methods of exploiting others. These older forms of capitalism evolved with the development of industrial capitalism and are now essential for the redistribution of the surplus created by industrialism, but they are not *directly* involved in growing that surplus. However, they do speed up the **circuit of capital**, thus contributing indirectly to its increase (59–60). *See also* MANAGERIAL SKILLED LABOR, PRIMITIVE ACCUMULATION, PRODUCTIVE LABOR, UNPRODUCTIVE LABOR.

CAPITALIST CYCLES. Economic cycles are part of capitalist societies. In boom times, "feverish production" causes capitalists to induct members of the **industrial reserve army** into the workplace, causing wages to rise, profit margins to be squeezed, markets to be saturated, and contraction to occur, causing depression, throwing a part of the labor force out of work. As labor becomes cheap again, industry begins to recover, and the cycle begins anew. The lack of centralized planning, Marx asserts, is part of the structure of capitalism, causing these economic cycles of boom and bust (Marx 1867/1976, 580). The "uncertainty and irregularity of employment," the periodic return of mass unemployment, the long duration of recessions and depressions, play a significant role in the hardships of the mass of people who make up the **surplus population** (866). This surplus population is essential for periods of expansion and must, Marx asserts, be higher than the **growth** of **population**. "This increase is effected by the simple process that constantly 'sets free' a part of the working class; by methods which lessen the number of workers employed in proportion to the increased production. Modern industry's

whole form of motion, therefore, depends on the constant transformation of a part of the working population into **unemployed** or semi-employed 'hands'" (786).

The rise and fall of those in poverty or living on the edge reflect the changes as well as the growth of the capitalist industrial cycle (808). As capitalism matures, Marx asserts, the accumulation and the **productivity** of labor grows due to the expansion of wealth, credit, and the technical conditions of production (such as **machinery** and the **means of transportation and communication**), making possible a transformation into additional **means of production**—both in expanding old markets and in developing new ones. "In all such cases, there must be the possibility of suddenly throwing great masses of men into the decisive areas without doing any damage to the scale of production in other spheres. The surplus population supplies these masses. The path characteristically described by modern industry, which takes the form of a decennial cycle (interrupted by smaller oscillations) of periods of average activity, production at high pressure, crisis, and **stagnation**, depends on the constant formation, the greater or less absorption, and the re-formation of the industrial reserve army or surplus population" (785). Thus, the swings of boom and bust get progressively wider. As capitalism develops, the system must necessarily create enormous differences in wealth and power. The social problems it creates in its wake of boom and bust—issues of unemployment and underemployment, of poverty amidst affluence—continue to mount. *See also* CLASS CONFLICT, CRISES OF CAPITALISM, ECONOMIC EXPANSION AND CONTRACTION, PROLETARIAT, WORKERS AS CONSUMERS.

CAPITALIST MODE OF PRODUCTION. The early **manufacture mode of production** employed by capitalists was different from **handicraft production** only quantitatively, that is, in the number of workers employed. Once under the direction of the capitalist, however, handicraft production transforms into the manufacturing mode of production with its **detailed division of labor**. This period begins in the middle of the 16th century and lasts until the end of the 18th century. With the advent of the steam engine and other mechanical **innovations**, the capitalist mode of production fully comes into its own. The era of **large-scale industry** begins in which capitalists further centralize workers into **factories**, **deskilled** and **exploited** for their **labor**. Through the process of striving to maximize **profits** in growing **world markets**, capital becomes enlarged and **centralized** and **science** and **technology** consciously employed to improve **productivity**. *See also* PREFACE, THE.

CAPITALIST REVOLUTION. The capitalist revolution referred to by Marx in his historical analyses was not a single event but rather a combination of historical changes that led from the European system characterized by the **feudal mode of production** to the industrialized **capitalist mode of production** system characteristic of western Europe during Marx's lifetime. The changes leading to the dominance of **capitalism** in the late 19th century were, according to Marx, a result of two primary factors. The first, following Marx's **historical materialism** approach to history, was the development of new **technology** and new **productive forces**, such as mills and heavy plows, that increased agricultural **productivity**, generating **surplus** goods. These technological developments were vital in the change toward capitalist systems. A second factor leading to the genesis of capitalism had to do with changes in **class** structure and changes in the **relations of production**. The eventually successful struggle of **serfs** and the **peasantry** against feudal lordship, outlined by Marx in the **Eighteenth Brumaire of Louis Bonaparte**, led to the creation of a new class of rural **populations** who owned and managed agricultural land and who, important to the development of capitalism, had sole control over their **labor**. Ultimately, these changes, combined with technological advancements, led to a class of **wage laborers** denied access to the **means of production** and therefore required to sell their **labor power** to survive. The **growth** of wage labor was particularly crucial in the development of capitalism in urban centers of trade

and manufacturing. By the time of the **Industrial Revolution**, these combined technological and social class changes had established capitalism as the primary **mode of production**. *See also* FACTORY SYSTEM, MACHINES, TOOLS, WAGE SLAVERY.

CAPITALIST STATE. From early on, Marx and **Engels** viewed the state as an arm of the class that controls the **mode of production**. Society requires organizations that will maintain conditions of its continued production as well as keep the exploited classes in conditions of servitude. While the state always represents itself as the whole of society, in actuality, it represents only the exploiter. In **ancient society**, this meant that the state represented the interests of slaveholders and kept the exploited in **slavery**; in **feudal** society, the state served the lords and kept the exploited in serfdom; in a capitalist society, the state represents the **bourgeoisie** and keeps the exploited in **wage slavery**.

However, in revolutionary times, the state becomes the focus of conflict between the classes. Marx makes clear in *Capital* that the power of the state was critical in the transition from **feudalism** to **capitalism**. The state creates the conditions for capital accumulation through taxation, the establishment of national **banks**, enforcement of contracts, patents, and government purchases of goods and services. It is the state's brute force in fashioning the colonial system that provides the initial capital to fund the transition as well as protecting domestic markets and uprooting industry in dependent countries. "Force is the midwife of every old society which is pregnant with a new one. It is itself an economic power" (Marx 1867/1976, 916).

Nevertheless, it is not just the initial stages of capitalism where the state is critical. In *The Communist Manifesto*, Marx writes, "The executive of the modern state is but a committee for managing the common affairs of the whole bourgeoisie" (Marx and Engels 1848, 76). Marx regarded the state and political power as secondary to **class conflict**; political power is how the dominant class—the exploiting class—maintains its domination.

Engels echoes this view in *Anti-Dühring* as well as in the more popular *Socialism: Utopian and Scientific*, asserting that the state is an organization that supports the external conditions of the **capitalist mode of production**, protecting the system from the workers as well as the plundering of individual capitalists. "The modern state, no matter what its form, is essentially a capitalist machine, the state of the capitalists, the ideal personification of the total national capital" (Engels 1908, 123). The **Factory Acts**, for example, are laws to curb capital's tendency to exploit **labor power** to the maximum, depleting this vital and necessary resource to the detriment of all. The capitalist state limited the **length of the working day** to prevent this abuse by the unbridled pursuit of profit as well as the threat of working-class movements. "Periodical epidemics speak as clearly on this point as the diminishing military standard of height in **France** and Germany" (Marx 1867/1976, 348).

It would be a mistake to view the capitalist state as entirely dominated by the bourgeoisie; it is the arena of **class struggle**, and, occasionally, the state does not serve capital interests. The state can address some of the most egregious abuses of the working class or the environment. However, the state cannot grant fundamental reform that challenges the existence of capitalism through the normal political process. *See also* BOURGEOIS STATE, DICTATORSHIP OF THE BOURGEOIS, WITHERING AWAY OF THE STATE.

CENTRALIZATION AND ENLARGEMENT OF CAPITAL.

Over time, Marx writes, capital takes control over **handicraft production** processes and, later, **manufacturing**, where the workers are in control of the work process, centralizing the workers into **workshops** and **factories**. Through the process of competing for markets, some firms win and others lose, and capital becomes enlarged and centralized. With this concentration and centralization, there is an increasing and conscious application of science and **technology** to improve efficiency and **productivity**. This **innovation** naturally favors large enterprises, increasing mechanization, and a large workforce.

Marx writes of the inevitability of the centralization of capital through the **laws of capitalist production**. Through these laws, many capitalists fail or become absorbed by larger, more **technologically** advanced competitors. Along with this centralization, there occurs a more conscious and systematic application of science to the production process; this includes the **industrialization of agriculture** and its exploitation of the land (and, more recently, animals). Also, Marx argues, efficiency demands that the labor process transform into one in which large combinations of workers cooperate in the production process. A final characteristic of the centralization of capital, Marx asserts, is "the entanglement of all peoples in the net of the **world market**, and, with this, the **growth** of the international character of the capitalist regime" (Marx 1867/1976, 928).

Capitalists monopolize all advantages as the system enlarges and centralizes and the mass of misery and **exploitation** grows. However, Marx continues in the first volume of *Capital*, along with these developments, other, more positive developments take place that include the growing revolutionary consciousness of the working classes and their eventual revolt, a class, he adds, that is growing in number and who are "trained, united and organized" through the **capitalist mode of production**. "The **monopoly** of capital becomes a **fetter upon the mode of production** which has flourished alongside and under it. The centralization of the **means of production** and the **socialization of labour** reach a point at which they become incompatible with their capitalist integument [hardened shell]. This integument [hard shell] is burst asunder. The knell of capitalist **private property** sounds. The expropriators are expropriated" (Marx 1867/1976, 929).

Capitalism is a system of **contradiction**, Marx writes, that creates periodic crises. With each succeeding **crisis of capitalism**, the centralization and enlargement of capital become greater, and thus the next crisis becomes more severe. As the process continues, the system of capitalism—a system that has unleashed the most awesome productive powers the world has ever known—will become a restraint on the further increase of these powers; when the constraints become significant enough, the **proletariat**, in the name of all people, will revolt. *See also* CLASS CONFLICT, COMPETITION, CREDIT SYSTEMS, OVERPRODUCTION, WORKERS AS CONSUMERS, ZUSAMMENBRUCHSTHEORIE.

CHARTISM. The first mass movement of the working classes in Britain grew out of the failure of the 1832 Reform Act and the 1833 **Factory Act** to address working-class issues. The movement agitated against conditions in the factory and the cities. In 1838, William Lovett drafted a bill in response to the economic depression of 1837–1838. The bill focused on parliamentary reform and contained six demands: (1) universal manhood suffrage, (2) equal electoral districts, (3) vote by secret ballot, (4) Parliaments elected annually rather than every five years, (5) payment of members of Parliament, and (6) abolition of property qualifications for membership in Parliament. In February 1839, a Chartist convention prepared a petition to Parliament and gathered more than 1.25 million signatures. If Parliament ignored the petition, leaders threatened, there would be "ulterior measures." In June, Parliament rejected the petition out of hand. Riots ensued, and the leaders of the movement were arrested and sentenced to prison or banished to Australia. After this, the Chartists moderated their tactics, presenting a second petition to Parliament in 1842 with more than 3 million signatures. Again, Parliament refused, causing further unrest and arrests. The final petition of the Chartists was in 1848 as revolution was in the air in Europe. Parliament again ignored it. Marx, who was supportive of working-class parties for a time, writes about the demise of the Chartist movement as a "fiasco" in which the leadership was jailed and the organization disbanded. "Everywhere the working class was outlawed, anathematized, placed under the 'loi des suspects' [repressive laws passed in various countries after 1848]. The manufacturers no longer needed to restrain themselves. They broke out in open revolt, not only against the Ten Hours' Act, but against all the legislation since 1833 that had aimed at restricting to some extent

the 'free' exploitation of **labour-power**" (Marx 1867/1976, 397–98).

For a time in the 1850s, Marx was somewhat optimistic about a Chartist revival becoming a lasting working-class political party, but by the end of the 1850s, he had lost faith in such movements (Sperber 2013). He came to believe that political reform in the context of a capitalist society was futile and that revolution was necessary. *See also* EVOLUTIONARY SOCIALISM.

CHILD LABOR. Marx writes about the evils of child labor under 19th-century capitalism. Citing the work of inspectors for the **British Factory Acts** and other official reports, he documents the abuse of child labor. This abuse was both legal, as the successive acts permitted gross abuses of children, and illegal, as capitalists frequently violated even these regulations. Citing these reports, Marx writes of young children working 12- and 15-hour days in a variety of industries. In the manufacture of matches, for example, Marx details that conditions are so adverse that only the starving children of "half-starved widows" work there. Reporting on the British inspectors, Marx writes that in 1863, the children were working from 12 to 15 hours per working day, many working at night, getting meals haphazardly, and at their workstations. "Dante would have found the worst horrors in his Inferno surpassed in this industry" (Marx 1867/1976, 356).

The reason for such abuse, Marx asserted, lies in the nature of capitalism itself: the value of labor power is determined by the **labor time** necessary to earn enough to maintain a family. "Machinery also revolutionizes, and quite fundamentally, the agency through which the capital-relation is formally mediated, i.e., the contract between the worker and the capitalist." Industrial **machinery** reduces the need for workers to have adult strength and dexterity. The cost of purchasing the **labor power** of a child is significantly less than the value of an adult male. By requiring every member of a family of four to work in the **labor market** to maintain themselves, the value of the adult male's labor power depreciates and spreads over the whole family. While it might cost a little more to employ the entire family, Marx writes, the capitalist gets four days of labor instead of one. "Previously the worker sold his own labour-power, which he disposed of as a free agent, formally speaking. Now he sells wife and child." For the family to survive, four people must now labor for the capitalist, thus giving him their **surplus labor**. Therefore, machinery, which could save human labor, furthers the **exploitation** of workers (Marx 1867/1976, 518–19).

Capitalists much preferred children, as they are in the Global South today because their labor power costs far less than an adult's labor does. Children tend to be docile and take orders well, and ever more sophisticated **machines** take much of the heavy lifting out of work and are "so self-regulating that a child can superintend it" (Marx 1867/1976, 559). As evidenced in much of his writings, Karl was very much against child labor and advocated for its abolition. *See also COMMUNIST MANIFESTO, THE.*

CIRCUIT OF CAPITAL. In the second volume of *Capital*, Marx (1885/1978) focuses on the process of the circulation of capital. The "circuit of capital" is the phrase Marx uses to refer to the entirety of the transformation of **capital** as it moves through production and circulation in a continuous process. Marx analyzes the process by breaking it into three phases that capital passes through in the circuit: money capital, productive capital, and **commodity** capital.

The first stage begins with the capitalist exchanging **money** (M) on the commodity and **labor markets** for the acquisition of **capital** and **labor power**; his money transformed into commodities, denoted by Marx as M – C. The second stage, or productive capital, is the part

Photograph of child laborers at the turn of the 20th century.

of the circuit in which the capitalist processes the purchased commodities into a higher value of capital through the process of production, resulting in commodities of greater value than the input components. In the third stage, the capitalist returns "to the market as a seller; his commodities are turned into money, or they pass through the circulation act C – M" (Marx 1885/1978, 109). The complete formula for the circuit, then, is

$$M - C \dots P \dots C" - M"$$

where the dots indicate the interruption of the circuit during and after production (P) and the C" and M" indicate the increase of **surplus value** of C (commodities) and M (money) as a result of production.

Much of the second volume of *Capital* is devoted to the analysis of different aspects of this circuit, and Marx uses the different forms of the circuit for different analytical approaches, ultimately making the argument that the failure to recognize and distinguish between the various types of capital along the circuit results in severely compromised arguments by many **political economists**. *See also* CAPITALIST CLASS.

CIVIL WAR IN FRANCE, THE (1872).

A 36-page pamphlet written by Karl Marx in the aftermath of the **Franco-Prussian War** and the collapse of the **Paris Commune** in 1871, *The Civil War in France* was the last of Marx's major political pamphlets and marked a significant evolution in his thought regarding the necessary preconditions for a genuinely **proletarian** revolution. Drawing on contemporary journalistic accounts of events, Marx concluded that the Paris Commune was "in no way socialist, nor could it be" (Avineri 1968, 240). Marx believed that the Paris Commune uprising would fail in that it was premature and the proletariat had not yet achieved **revolutionary class consciousness**. He contended that such spontaneous uprisings like the Paris Commune lacked a directed critical mass that would enable the proletariat to seize the state and abruptly overawe counterrevolutionary forces.

Analysis of *The Civil War in France* has often focused on Marx's motivations in writing the pamphlet. For example, Isaiah Berlin (2013) characterized the pamphlet as a "tactical move. . . . He regarded [the Paris Commune], indeed, as a political blunder: his adversaries the **Blanquists** and **Proudhonists** predominated in it to the end; and yet its significance in his eyes was immense" (241). For Berlin, Marx was attempting to conjure up a heroic socialist legend. Avineri (1968) argued that Marx "does not discuss the commune as it actually was, but as it could be, not *in actu* but *in potentia*. He elevates the Commune's *possible* enactments and its *potential* arrangements to a paradigm of future society" (240). For Avineri, this dual language enabled Marx to speak sympathetically to different constituencies within the socialist movement and in that sense represented a political rather than a philosophical statement.

In 1891, Engels issued a 20th-anniversary reprint in which he highlighted the significance of the Paris Commune and Marx's analysis of the necessary conditions for a successful proletarian revolution. Regardless of his motivations, Marx was consistent in sympathizing with the spirit of the Paris Commune, even as he opposed it as a premature outburst, a revolt rather than a revolution.

CLASS. The lottery of birth determines the relation of the individual to the **means of production** and dictates one's class position. Once a person is born a master or a slave, a feudal lord or a serf, a worker or a capitalist, their behavior, attitudes, values, and beliefs are prescribed for them. For Marx, the class role broadly defines the person. He deals with capitalists and proletarians as the "personifications of economic categories, embodiments of particular class relations and class-interests" (Marx 1867/1976, 92). Individuals are subject to their relation to the production process whether or not they try to rise above these social forces. He views the formation of the economy as an evolutionary process, much like natural history. Marx does not deny the operation of other factors in affecting human beliefs and behaviors, but he contends that an individual's objective class position—as determined by his relationship to the means of production—exerts a predominant influence.

CLASS ANTAGONISM. Class antagonism intimately relates to the ideas of **alienation**, **class struggle**, and the **mode of production**. Marx contended that throughout history, the economic **mode of production** produced class divisions based on exploitation. Exploitation, in turn, generates alienation among members of the exploited class. Alienation would subsequently produce class antagonism. In the capitalist historical phase, class antagonism is antecedent to class struggle, a period in which a sense of resentment spreads among the **proletariat** toward the **bourgeoisie** and which the bourgeoisie repays in disdain and further exploitation.

Mid-19th-century Europe provided an eloquent illustration of class antagonisms. The upheavals of the **Napoleonic era** had broken up the **feudal** order, and economic **industrialization** was rapidly transforming the politics of western Europe. The **Congress of Vienna (1815)** had attempted to reimpose conservative, monarchical regimes, but economic circumstances were rapidly imposing wholesale changes on broad swaths of Europe. Industrialization, **urbanization**, and widespread education had produced a concentrated and at least semiliterate workforce. By 1848, a series of **revolutions** throughout Europe signaled the unsustainability of the existing political order. Small wonder that Marx's **historical materialism** would find a receptive audience among aggrieved **workers**. *See also* PREFACE, THE.

CLASS CONFLICT. The **contradiction** between capital and labor is the conflict that Marx focused on intently in the first volume of ***Capital***. The contradictions begin on the factory floor, where management has an interest in **expropriating** the maximum amount of **surplus value** from labor and the worker an interest in conserving energy and maximizing rewards. Nevertheless, it is broader than the factory floor. Over time, Marx writes, in the process of **competing** for **markets**, some firms win and others lose, capital becomes **centralized and enlarged**, and unsuccessful capitalists fall into the proletarian class. "One capitalist always strikes down many others" (Marx 1867/1976, 929). The quest for profit leads corporations to adopt sophisticated **technology**, to reorganize labor into ever more **detailed divisions** for the sake of efficiency, and to squeeze wages to the lowest amount possible as determined by prevailing social standards. The maximization of capital increasingly exploits workers, stripping them of their skills. Capitalists directly harness **science** through the research and development of technologies that will ever more efficiently automate production and distribution processes (Marx 1867/1976, 590).

As capitalism **evolves**, the system must necessarily create enormous differences in wealth and power. The social problems it creates in its wake will continue to mount. The vast majority of people will fall into the **proletarian** class; the wealthy will become richer but ever fewer in number. Capitalists will apply mass-production techniques, **machine technology**, and **economies of scale** to economic activities—**unemployment** and misery result for many. The lack of centralized planning under capitalism results in cycles of **economic expansion and contraction**, thus causing crises such as inflation and depression. Capitalism becomes international in scale; the people of all nations become part of the capitalist **world system** with the industrial center exploiting much of the world for raw materials and cheap labor.

Over time, capitalism brings into being a working class (the proletariat) consisting of those who have a fundamental antagonism to the owners of capital. The control of the state by the wealthy (**dictatorship of the bourgeoisie**) makes it ineffective in fundamental reform of the system and leads to the passage of laws favoring their interests and incurring the wrath of a growing number of workers. Now highly **urbanized** and concentrated in **factories** and workplaces by the forces of capital, the workers increasingly recognize their exploitation. Eventually, achieving **class consciousness**, they begin to realize that the **monopoly** of **capital** is preventing the production of goods and services for the many.

The capitalists who control the forces of production will not produce goods and services unless there is the possibility of profit. Many will be increasingly impoverished amid exorbitant wealth for the few—and the unfulfilled potential to supply the many. In such a crisis, the proletariat will become more progressive. However, the organization, money, and power of capitalists within the state will block real structural reform.

The capitalists harness all of these economic and political transformations and developments to their commercial interests. Nevertheless, with this growing monopoly of economic, political, and social power, the misery of the oppressed grows. With capitalism's continued development, the **contradictions** become worse, and periodic **crises** of **overproduction** occur in which economic **contraction** throws many out of work as well as destroying the fortunes of many of the smaller capitalists. Concentration and enlargement of surviving enterprises grow with the recovery, making the next crisis potentially worse.

The further development of production becomes impossible within a capitalist framework. In time, the proletariat will recognize that the capitalist system is not serving social needs and will develop revolutionary consciousness; the framework of capitalism becomes the target of revolt, the **contradictions of capitalism** producing a **revolutionary** crisis. "The monopoly of capital becomes a fetter upon the mode of production which has flourished alongside and under it. The centralization of the **means of production** and the **socialization of labor** reach a point at which they become incompatible with their capitalist integument [hardened shell]. This integument is burst asunder. The knell of capitalist **private property** sounds. The expropriators are expropriated" (Marx 1867/1976, 929). With the revolution, production processes that previously served the needs of capital accumulation will serve broad human needs.

Marx further asserts that the coming revolution will not be as protracted and violent as the **capitalist revolution** itself, in which individual means of production of the masses was expropriated by the few into concentrated means of production owned by a few, in a violent and barbarous manner. With the **socialist revolution**, it will be the expropriation of the few capitalists by the "mass of people" (Marx

1867/1976, 930). Public ownership of factories will carry on production in the same manner, though surplus value and thus exploitation will no longer be the goal. The **dictatorship of the proletariat** will rule in the interests of that class.

Marx does not assert that capitalism will collapse due to its contradictions, only that these contradictions will produce periodic crises, growing in intensity. The end of the system depends on the revolutionary consciousness, actions, and success of the proletarian class. When the revolution occurs during one of these crises, the contradiction will be apparent to all, and the **ruling class** will be at its most vulnerable. Further, he posits the establishment of a socialist state after a successful proletarian revolution. Capital's **centralization and enlargement** of the mode of production, as well as its socialization of labor, set the conditions for socialism to evolve. "No social order is ever destroyed before all the **productive forces** for which it is sufficient have been developed, and new superior **relations of production** never replace older ones before the material conditions for their existence have matured within the framework of the old society" (Marx 1859, para. 7).

Nevertheless, the establishment of socialism is not automatic in Marx's theory; much depends on the outcome of **class struggle**. While Marx posited that late developments of capitalism set the foundations for socialism as a possible solution to the inherent contradictions of capitalism, barbarism is also a genuine possibility. Such regression could occur if a new ruling class defeated or co-opted progressive revolutionary forces. *See also* PREFACE, THE, ZUSAMMENBRUCHSTHEORIE.

CLASS CONSCIOUSNESS. A term frequently employed by Marx and **Engels** to denote a particular state of awareness combined with a determination to act collectively and cohesively on those interests. Plamenetz (1992) characterizes the importance of the concept by discussing the class consciousness of the **bourgeoisie:**

> they do not merely know what they want
> as individuals; they do not merely have

personal ambitions. They have demands which they make in common; they know what they want done on their behalf as a class, or, if all of them do not know, they have leaders who do know, and whose leadership they accept. They are organized to make collective demands, and could not even decide what demands to make unless they were organized. To act as a group—to be able to formulate collective aims and to pursue them—a class must be organized. Any class, to be actively engaged in a conflict with other classes, must be class-conscious in this sense. (191–92)

From a **Marxist** perspective, the bourgeoisie's class consciousness includes control of the **forces of production** but also of the "**superstructure**," the religious, moral, ethical, and cultural narratives that justify **capitalism** and the bourgeoisie's exploitation of the **proletariat**. The bourgeois commitment to maintaining the capitalist system is essentially a reactionary class consciousness in Marxist terms and demands that a **revolutionary class consciousness** take shape committed to the overthrow of capitalism.

For Marx, proletarian class consciousness begins to form when members of the working classes become aware of their treatment collectively as a category of people and that, as a class, workers are subject to **exploitation**. The process of the **immiseration** of many brings workers to the realization of their exploited status. As workers become more **alienated** from their **labor** and from the products of their work and their fellow workers, class consciousness begins to form. Marx and Engels were under no illusions that the class consciousness would amalgamate simultaneously throughout the capitalist world. Marx recognized that some states had a greater coercive capacity over the proletariat; on those grounds, he deemed Russia and the United States to be particularly poor candidates for proletarian consciousness raising. Marx and Engels also suspected that the bourgeoisie would attempt to play "divide and conquer" games within the proletariat. They also viewed the capitalists as capable

of easily manipulating the **lumpenproletariat** into acting as reactionary shock troops.

Elster (1985) defined class consciousness as "the ability to overcome the free-rider problem in realizing class interests" (347). This ability suggests that class consciousness includes new conditions for bargaining and coalition building, reducing factionalism, and reducing incentives for proletarian factions to defect. Alienation plays a significant role in intensifying **class antagonism** and reducing **competition** among workers. Importantly, class consciousness is distinct from revolutionary class consciousness. The working class may be motivated by class consciousness and aware of their status as members of a class with distinct interests and pursue goals and achievements short of revolution. However, for Marx and Engels, even the achievement of short-term goals would likely contribute to further consciousness raising among the proletariat, a further coalescence of a more coherent class consciousness. Even modest successes on such fronts would lead to the creation of organizational structures and, eventually, the overthrow of capitalism. *See also* CLASS CONFLICT, CLASS STRUGGLE, DICTATORSHIP OF THE PROLETARIAT, INTERNATIONAL WORKINGMEN'S ASSOCIATION (IWA), SECOND INTERNATIONAL, THE.

CLASS STRUGGLE. It is in the opening pages of *The Communist Manifesto* (1848) that Marx and Engels make their declaration that the history of all societies is the history of class struggle between oppressors and oppressed. In **ancient** societies, this consisted of freemen and slaves; in **feudal** society, lords and **serfs**; and in the burgeoning capitalist society, capitalists (**bourgeoisie**) and workers (**proletariat**). The struggle is not always open, but ultimately ending in a revolutionary reconstitution of the larger society or the common ruin of all (1). All societies, except those of prehistory and the communist utopia to come, are fundamentally divided between classes who clash in pursuit of their interests. The **forces of production** shape the relations between people.

The class that owns or controls the **mode of production** (the combined forces and relations of production) is, by definition, the **ruling class**. "What else does the history of ideas prove, than that intellectual production changes its character in proportion as material production is changed? The ruling ideas of each age have ever been the ideas of its ruling class" (Marx and Engels 1848/1969, 19). These ruling ideas tend to emphasize maintaining the status quo or promoting ideas that enhance the position of the already powerful. Because the ruling class controls the forces of production, the class can dominate noneconomic institutions as well. Through influence or control over critical institutions such as media, government, foundations, and higher education, the viewpoints of the ruling class become the widely accepted view of society.

The oppressed class, those who do not own or control the forces of production, usually internalize these elite ideologies. However, under certain conditions, counterideologies opposed to elite domination become widespread among the oppressed. It is under these conditions that the struggle between classes becomes **revolutionary**, with the potential of transforming the entire society. *See also* CLASS CONFLICT, CLASS CONSCIOUSNESS, PREFACE, THE, REVOLUTIONARY CLASS CONSCIOUSNESS.

CLASS STRUGGLES IN FRANCE 1848–1850 **(1895).** The *New Rhineland News* originally published this work as a series of three (of a planned four) articles under the title "1848–1849." The work sums up the results of the **1848 Revolution** in **France** and came out in book form in 1895, with the formal title and an introduction by **Engels**. Marx researched the work through French newspaper reports, witness accounts of French and German radicals, as well as reports from the *New Rhineland News* Paris correspondent. In introducing the work in 1895, Engels wrote that it was Marx's first attempt to explain contemporary events through the materialist conception of history worked out in *The Communist Manifesto*, tracing political events to economic causes.

Marx identifies the roots of the February Revolution as crop failures in the mid-1840s,

followed by a general economic crisis of factory closures and bankruptcies throughout Europe. "In common with the bourgeoisie the workers had made the February Revolution, and alongside the bourgeoisie they sought to secure the advancement of their interests, just as they had installed a worker in the Provisional Government itself alongside the bourgeois majority. Organize labor!" (19). However, the bourgeoisie co-opted the revolution when writing the new constitution, Marx writes. "The bourgeoisie has no king; the true form of its rule is the republic" (34). The work of the Constituent National Assembly consisted of replacing the old royalist labels with republican ones. While the proletariat insisted that the constitution enumerate the "right to work" (in the literal sense, not the American), the bourgeoisie transformed this into the "right to public relief," and Marx adds "and what modern state does not feed its paupers in some form or other?" (35).

Nevertheless, it was not just the proletariat that was co-opted, for the petit bourgeois republicans gave power to the large capitalists. With the coup of **Louis Bonaparte** in December 1851, the period of **revolution** was over for the time being. The **Revolutions of 1848** were premature; the proletariat of Europe were but a minority, lacking in revolutionary consciousness. However, Marx writes, conditions were now ripe for industry to grow, thus setting the stage for a real proletarian revolution. *See also* BLANC, LOUIS.

CLASSLESS SOCIETY. The ultimate and, according to Marx, the inevitable outcome of **social evolution** was **communism**, characterized most saliently by the absence of any form of social or economic **class**. In such a society, the role of the **state** (a force Marx argued exists primarily to repress lower classes) is no longer needed and would "**wither away**." Marx also argued that "primitive" hunter-gatherer societies were classless, operating under a system of **primitive communism**. *See also CRITIQUE OF THE GOTHA PROGRAMME.*

COLLAPSE OF CAPITALISM. *See* ZUSAMMENBRUCHSTHEORIE.

COLLECTED WORKS OF MARX AND EN-GELS (MECW). The Collected Works of Marx and Engels is a 50-volume English-language collection of all works published by the two in their lifetimes as well as many unpublished manuscripts and letters. Originally published in the Soviet Union in 1931 under the sponsorship of the **Marx-Engels Institute**, they issued the English edition from 1975 to 2004. In addition to the well-known works of the two, the collection includes Marx's poetry to **Jenny**, letters to his father, extensive correspondence between **Engels** and Marx, and newspaper articles written by the two. The entire collection is available at https://archive.org/details/MarxEngelsCollectedWorksVolume10MKarlMarx. *See also* MARX'S JOURNALISTIC CAREER, *NEW RHINELAND NEWS, NEW YORK TRIBUNE, RHINELAND NEWS.*

COLLECTIVE ANARCHISM. *See* SOCIAL ANARCHISM.

COLOGNE. Sperber (2013, 107) labels the years 1842–1852 as "Marx's Cologne decade." Marx begins the decade as an editorial writer at the *Rhineland News*, which lasted about six months, before emigrating to **Paris** and then to **Brussels**, all this time keeping contact with his supporters in Cologne. He returned along with several of his followers during the **Revolutions of 1848**, establishing the radical *New Rhineland News*, becoming a crusading editor mainly against Prussian rule. In May 1849, the Prussian Ministry of the Interior accused Marx of being involved in a planned insurrection and expelled him from the country. However, he continued his ties with the city's active **Communist League** Congregation. *See also* BECKER, HERMANN "RED," COLOGNE COMMUNIST TRIAL, HESS, MOSES, JUNG, GEORG, RUTENBERG, ADOLF.

COLOGNE COMMUNIST TRIAL. In May 1851, the Prussian government arrested a **Communist League** member who was carrying documents of the League. Over the next few weeks, authorities rounded up many members of the League. The authorities held the accused in prison for 16 months, often in solitary confinement. The trial lasted from 4 October through 12 November 1852. The Prussian government charged 11 members of the League with treason. The prosecution focused on the communists' calls for revolution against the government, their antireligious ideology, and their desire to confiscate the property of capitalists. Prosecutors tied the radicalism of the League directly to the events of the **Revolutions of 1848**. The prosecution worried that the case was flimsy, consisting of forged documents to incriminate the League further. From **England**, Karl worked to expose the forgeries, writing articles for newspapers in defense of the accused and raising money for their defense. Both Marx and **Engels** wrote pamphlets about the trial, charging that the prosecution's case consisted of false testimony given by police informants as well as forged documents. They claimed that the Prussian police state provoked the arrests against the international working-class movement. The court found seven of the accused guilty and sentenced them to prison for terms ranging from three to six years. The trial put a damper on **revolutionary** activity in Germany and brought about the dissolution of the Communist League in 1852. *See also* BECKER, HERMANN "RED."

COLONIALISM. Marx held a complex view of colonialism, a policy of a **state** that seeks to extend or retain authority over other people and territories. Early on (in the 1840s and 1850s), it was assumed by Marx that the coming **proletarian revolution** in western Europe would necessarily end the colonization of the undeveloped world, and in his work, he often vehemently condemned the violence and misery thrust on colonized **populations**. In the case of India (outlined most completely in Marx's [1853] *New York Tribune* article "The British Rule in India"), Marx noted that colonization destroyed the old world of India "with no gain of a new one." He concluded, "Whatever may have been the crimes of **England** she was the unconscious tool of history in bringing about that revolution" (para. 12). In other words, colonization, though fraught with problems for the colonized, nonetheless is necessary to industrialize a nation like India. Industrialization and the establishment of capitalism, then, is an essential step toward the eventual proletarian revolution. However, Marx argued that once industrialized, India must first gain independence from Britain before the revolution could take hold (Chandra 1998). In the case of British rule in Ireland, Marx and **Engels** argued that the most productive route forward for Ireland would involve first overthrowing British rule and implementing an agrarian revolution, thereby hastening the overthrow of the British **bourgeois**, who depended on importation of Irish agricultural goods to maintain economic power.

COLONIZATION. *See* COLONIALISM.

COMINTERN. Known alternatively as the "Third International" and the "Communist International," the Comintern was an organization dedicated to the cause of global **communism**. The Comintern formed out of the schism between doctrinaire **Marxists** and **anarchists** that stalemated the **Second International**. Led by Russian Leninists, the Comintern held numerous meetings between 1919 and 1943. The **Russian Revolution** provided a powerful impetus in forming the Third International. Russia's Communist Party provided much of the leadership, along with the communist parties of the constituent members of the Soviet Union and communist parties of eastern Europe. The Soviet Union's control by a communist government enabled the **Bolshevik Party** to influence the Comintern's platform and activities. The Comintern met through a series of congresses and plenums intended to establish a broad platform for coordinating the activities of like-minded **revolutionary socialist** organizations.

In the formative years, the Comintern fomented revolutionary action in eastern European countries like Hungary and Poland and the successful prosecution of the Russian Civil War (1917–1922). Although organizationally small and modestly funded, the Comintern proved adept at manipulating the activities of communist parties in other regions. **Vladimir Lenin** insisted on "Twenty-One Conditions" necessary for communist parties to join the Comintern. Among those conditions was the requirement for a periodic "purge" of communist parties, establishing the ideological nature of leadership struggles among communists. Throughout the 1920s, **Grigory Zinoviev** was able to use the leadership of the Comintern as a base of popular support in the immediate post-Lenin scrum for the leadership of the Bolshevik Party.

The ineffectiveness of Soviet efforts to overthrow governments in eastern Europe compelled a more realistic appraisal of its goals. Post-1925, the Comintern focused its efforts on fostering a more favorable "revolutionary environment" in select countries. Internal power struggles in the Soviet Union resulted in **Joseph Stalin**'s rise to power. His tactical decision to advocate "**socialism in one country**" influenced the Comintern's cautious approach giving higher priority to the preservation of the Soviet Union. Opposition to fascism provided a basis for popular appeals in western European countries and elsewhere. The Comintern facilitated the formation of "popular front" organizations, acting ostensibly as leftist political organizations while functionally responsive to Comintern direction. This strategy gave rise to the term "fellow traveler" in the United States and elsewhere, a pejorative reference to individuals who were intellectually sympathetic to the political goals of communism but who chose not to join the communist party formally.

Between 1928 and 1935, the Comintern began advancing a more explicitly revolutionary doctrine, arguing that capitalism was entering its death throes. The Comintern directed communist front organizations to adopt confrontational policies advocating more immediate and violent actions. Stalin's purge of the Communist Party affected the Comintern in the 1930s through his "show trials" in a purge of rival "Old" Bolsheviks. He installed NKVD secret police throughout the Comintern and executed roughly one-quarter of its staff members during the subsequent **Great Purge**. Numerous German communists who had relocated to the Soviet Union in the aftermath of the Nazi takeover of the Weimar Republic met a similar fate.

The Comintern advocated ""nonintervention" at the outset of World War II. The Nazi invasion of the Soviet Union and the subsequent entrance of the United States into the war created powerful incentives for Stalin to seek military support. To forestall Western opposition to supporting the Soviet war effort against Germany, Stalin dissolved the Comintern in 1943. After World War II, in the formative years of the Cold War, Stalin formed a successor organization, the Cominform, to coordinate among communist parties.

COMMODITY. Marx defined a commodity as an object or service that is produced for exchange with others and that satisfies a human need. The need can be a **primary need**, such as the need for food and water, sleep, or breathing, or a **secondary need**, such as fashionable clothing or the latest cell phone, created by the individual's imagination, by contact with others, or through advertising. If an external object satisfies a human need and its creation is for exchange or trade with others, it is a commodity (Marx 1867/1976, 125). If a man satisfies his needs through his labor, he is not creating a commodity, for it becomes a commodity only through the medium of exchange with others (131).

Marx looks at commodities from two standpoints: "**use value**" and "**exchange value.**" The physical properties of the commodity—its quality and quantity—determine its use value. "This property of a commodity is independent of the amount of labour required to appropriate its useful qualities" (Marx 1867/1976, 126). Exchange value, on the other hand, represents a quantitative relationship between the use values of one commodity for the use values of another and is determined by the quantity of **abstract human labor** expended to produce it. By "abstract human labor," Marx means the labor time necessary given the average **productivity** of a society's workforce. This measure naturally varies with the productivity of a nation's workforce, the degree of automation, the workers' average degree of skill, the **detailed division of labor**, and other factors. According to Marx, the exchange value of any object is the labor time socially necessary to produce it. Commodities are of equal value if they contain equal quantities of socially necessary labor time. "As exchange-values, all commodities are merely definite quantities of congealed labour-time" (129–30).

In general, then, Marx writes, the higher the productivity of labor, the less labor goes into a commodity and the less its value. The reverse is also true: the less productive the labor, the higher the labor invested into the commodity and the higher its exchange value (Marx 1867/1976, 131). *See also* LAW OF VALUE.

COMMUNARDS. The Communards were members and supporters of the **Paris Commune**. Coming mainly from the working classes, the Communards included republicans, socialists, **Blanquists**, **anarchists**, and members of the **First International**. They briefly formed a rebel government in the French capital from 18 March to 28 May 1871. The National Guard, stationed in defense of Paris, refused to disarm, and the workers of Paris—primarily idle industrial workers **unemployed** because of the war—seized power in Paris and declared the Paris Commune in rejection of the efforts by the interim government to manage the collapse of the Second Republic. The Communards wanted independence from the national government, demanding and electing a municipal council to rule the city.

In September 1870, toward the end of the **Franco-Prussian War**, the Prussians began a four-month siege of Paris, starving the city, and in January of the following year started shelling the town. In February 1871, the central government of **France** signed an armistice with Prussia; the peace treaty ceded the French provinces of Alsace-Lorraine and levied massive reparations on France. Radicalized by the opulence and growing class divisions in the Second Empire and provoked by the humiliating French defeat at the Battle of Sedan and the subsequent German siege of Paris, the call by the hastily formed national government to disarm the military in preparation for surrender provided the proximate cause for the insurrection. Parisians were furious. The national government sent troops to seize cannons from surrounding French forts.

The people resisted and executed generals, and full-scale revolt broke out. The Commune lasted for roughly two months from mid-March until 28 May 1871. French conservatives viewed the National Guard's backing of the Commune as intolerable. The national army entered Paris and fought a weeklong street-to-street series of battles with the Communards, known as the "the "Bloody Week." Twenty years later, Engels estimated some 30,000 killed. Contemporary estimates of those killed vary from 7,000 to 18,000, with significant portions of Paris destroyed in the fighting. The newly installed **Adolphe Thiers** administration arrested an estimated 25,000, eventually releasing some on humanitarian grounds, sentencing others to prison or forced labor. However, the French government's preferred solution to the Communards' insurrection was deportation, transporting thousands to colonial island possessions in the South Pacific. *See also CIVIL WAR IN FRANCE, THE.*

COMMUNISM. Marx and Engels often used the terms "communism" and "socialism" interchangeably, never consistently or systematically differentiating the two words. Many Marxist scholars, however, suggest that Marx intended the term "communism" to refer to the end product of **revolutionary socialism**. That is, a socialist system is where the private ownership of the **means of production** is abolished and all members equally share its fruits. Notably, a communist society in Marx's view is a **classless society**. The abolition of **classes** would not be immediate, and Marx recognized that socialist organized economies could exist while class structures were still in place. Communism, then, for Marx is the final evolutionary stage of socialism (following the progression from **primitive communism** to **slave societies** to **feudalism** to **capitalism**) that exists only after the total elimination of class structure in a society.

After Marx's death and the rise of the **Union of Soviet Socialist Republics (USSR)**, the term "communism" came to take on additional meaning. In the USSR, the communist system was one in which a strong centralized government exerted complete control of economic

and social elements within society. This sort of near-autocratic form of centralized control was characteristic of most modern communist states like the USSR, East Germany, and China. Socialist countries in the modern era, in contrast, are generally those that blend some elements of capitalism and socialism under a democratic political system and typically characterize themselves as **social democracies**. However, Marx did not make this type of distinction between the two terms. *See also COMMUNIST MANIFESTO, THE,* COMMUNIST PARTY OF THE SOVIET UNION (CPSU), DICTATORSHIP OF THE PROLETARIAT, GERMAN COMMUNIST PARTY, PROLETARIAT.

COMMUNIST COMMITTEE OF CORRESPONDENCE. A network of communists across the European continent founded by Marx and **Engels** in 1846 in **Belgium**. The Committee intended to act as a communications hub, sending out propaganda on socialism and **political economy** to radicals across Europe, keeping members abreast of political activities, and keeping socialists in contact with one another. Stedman-Jones (2016) asserts that there was another mission of the Committee: "Equally important from the start, however, whether avowed or not, was the ambition to eliminate rival visions of socialism" (212). The network consisted mainly of German communists, but **English** socialists were involved through Marx's contacts in the **League of the Just**. Marx's activities with the Committee led to his breaking contacts with former allies. "Favorable observers have described these breaks as necessary steps toward theoretical clarity and unity of action; more hostile ones attribute them to Marx's dictatorial tendencies and his desire to turn allies into subordinates. There were certainly elements of both motives, but they primarily reflected Marx's attempt to carve out a position for himself among émigré German radicals who were on their own in foreign countries, generally in difficult personal and financial circumstances, all the while facing the constant pressure of hostile Prussian and Austrian governments" (Sperber 2013, 176–77). The Correspondence Committee was never very successful; by 1848, the **Brussels** branch had become a part of the **Communist League**. *See also* MARX'S CHARACTER.

COMMUNIST CONFESSION OF FAITH. *See* PRINCIPLES OF COMMUNISM.

COMMUNIST INTERNATIONAL, THE. *See* COMINTERN.

COMMUNIST LEAGUE (BUND DER KOMMU-NISTEN). The Communist League was an international political organization established in London on 1 June 1847. The League was the result of the merger of the **League of the Just**, led by **Karl Schapper**, and the **Communist Committee of Correspondence** of Brussels, led primarily by Marx and **Friedrich Engels**. On its creation, the Communist League adopted a new charter that explicitly cited the work of Marx and Engels, calling for a **revolution** to overthrow the **bourgeoisie** and establish a **classless society** governed by the rule of the **proletariat** and adopting Marx's phrase "Working Men of All Countries, Unite!" as its motto. The second congress of the Communist League in December 1847 tasked Marx and Engels with writing ***The Communist Manifesto*** to outline the goals of the organization.

By 1848, the League had begun publishing the ***Neue Rheinische Zeitung*** under Marx's editorship, though the Prussian government terminated publication by May 1849. The League developed disputes with Marx and Engels, who wished to focus on building an international movement for workers and Schapper's wish to focus on promoting and participating in **revolutions**. Subsequent crackdowns by European governments saw the capture and imprisonment of several of the League members, and following the **Cologne Communist Trial** in 1852, the League disbanded. *See also* WILLICH-SCHAPPER GROUP, WILLICH, AUGUST.

COMMUNIST MANIFESTO, THE **(1848).** First published in February 1848 as the *Manifest der Kommunistischen Partei*, the *Manifesto* is widely considered the most influential political manuscript ever written. Commissioned by the

Bust of Karl Marx.

Communist League, Marx revised the 23-page pamphlet a few months later, correcting misprints and punctuation that upped the pages to 30 and served as the basis for future translations and editions. Marx designed the work to state the theory, nature, and goals of the Communist League. He also created it for wide distribution and to instigate revolutionary action. The *Manifesto* was soon translated to Danish, Polish, and Swedish toward the end of 1848. The first English translation appeared in 1850; to date, it has been translated into more than 200 languages.

Friedrich Engels wrote ***Principles of Communism*** as a catechism, a sort of confession of faith in **communism**. Becoming dissatisfied with the format, he sent the manuscript to Marx, asking him to rewrite in the form of a manifesto. Although it bears the name of Engels as a coauthor, Marx is responsible for almost all of the writing (Laski 1948). It consists of a preamble and four sections. The preamble, with the heading "Manifesto of the Communist Party," outlines the belief that communism is widely recognized by European powers to be a legitimate opposition to existing structures and that communists "should openly, in the face of the whole world, publish their views, their aims, their tendencies"" (Marx and Engels 1848). Section 1, titled "**Bourgeois** and **Proletarians**," begins with the well-known statement that "the history of all hitherto existing society is the history of **class struggles**" and seeks to outline and explain the **materialist** conception of history that underlies Marx's understanding of the appearance and nature of capitalist systems. Here, Marx outlines the development and ascendancy of the bourgeoisie through "constant revolutionizing of production." The rise of the bourgeoisie is due to their exploitation of the proletariat. Marx predicts that the proletariat will eventually serve as the "gravediggers" of the bourgeoisie. That is, as the proletariat ultimately becomes conscious of their **exploitation** and potential to overthrow the bourgeoisie through **revolution**, they will inevitably do so.

Section 2, "Proletarians and Communists," outlines Marx's vision for the relationship between the Communist party and other working-class parties, noting that the communists will never oppose existing or future working-class parties but will defend the interests of the proletariat, independent of political party, labor union, or nationality. Marx also addressed common criticisms and objections to communism in this section. Most notably, Marx defends communism against the claim that it would disincentivize people from working and reaffirms the communist goal of abolishing **private property**. The section concludes by outlining the immediate goals of communism in pursuit of establishing a **classless society**. These include the abolition of private ownership of the **means of production** as well as private property, the abolition of the inheritance of wealth, the establishment of progressive income taxes, the abolition of **child labor**, the establishment of free education for all, the nationalization of the **means of transport and communication**, and the establishment of a national **bank**.

Section 3, "Socialist and Communist Literature," explains the difference between communism and other prominent socialist doctrines that existed at the time of the *Manifesto*'s publication. Marx groups these other social doctrines as "Reactionary Socialism, Conservative or Bourgeois Socialism, and Critical-**Utopian Socialism**." In all cases, Marx criticizes and dismisses these approaches because they all fail to recognize the critically important role of the working-class proletariat as revolutionary actors in bringing about change.

The final section, "Position of the Communists in Relation to the Various Opposition Parties," concludes by briefly noting the Communist Party's alliance with the Social-Democratic Party against the bourgeoisie. This section also notes the party's positions concerning ongoing struggles and revolutionary actions in several European countries, finally declaring that "the Communists turn their attention chiefly to Germany, because that country is on the eve of a bourgeois revolution" that Marx suspects to be "the prelude to an immediately following proletarian revolution" (Marx and Engels 1848/1969, 34). The final paragraph of the *Manifesto* is a call to action: "The Communists disdain to conceal their views and aims. They openly declare that their ends can be attained only by the forcible overthrow of all existing social conditions. Let the **ruling classes** tremble at a Communistic revolution. The proletarians have nothing to lose but their chains. They have a world to win. Working Men of All Countries, Unite!" *See also SOCIALISM: UTOPIAN AND SCIENTIFIC.*

An early cover of *The Communist Manifesto.*

COMMUNIST PARTY OF GERMANY (KPD) (KOMMUNISTISCHE PARTEI DEUTSCH-LANDS).

In 1918, the **Social Democratic Party of Germany (SDAP)** split over disagreements about Germany's involvement in World War I. The more left-leaning members of the SDAP opposed the war, and the party split into the centrist **Independent Social Democratic Party of Germany** (which remerged with the SDAP four years later) and the more radical **Spartacus League**. The League, led by **Karl Liebknecht** and **Rosa Luxemburg**, held a founding congress in **Berlin** in December 1918. The merger of the Spartacus League with other radical left-wing groups officially became the Communist Party of Germany (Kommunistische Partei Deutschlands [KPD]). The KPD advocated **socialist revolution** and attempted several times to seize control of the German government.

The Nazi Party became a bitter enemy of the KPD. In 1933, when Adolf Hitler became chancellor of Germany, he publicly blamed the Reichstag fire on communist agitators and the KPD specifically. The new regime systematically arrested members of the KPD and forced senior leaders into exile in the **Soviet Union.** The party briefly revived after World War II. However, the Soviet occupation of East Germany undermined its support. By decree of the Soviet Union, it ultimately merged with the SDAP. In 1956, the West German government formally banned the KPD. *See also* FREI-KORPS, SPARTACIST UPRISING, SPARTACUS LEAGUE.

COMMUNIST PARTY OF THE SOVIET UNION (CPSU).

Initially, the party began as the majority faction of the **Russian Social Democratic Labor Party**. In 1912, the **Bolsheviks**, under the leadership of **Vladimir Lenin**, founded the Communist Party of the Soviet Union. The party seized control after the **Russian Revolution (1917)**, combining forces with the **Soviets** to form the Russian Socialist Federative Soviet Republic (SFSR), the world's first constitutional socialist state. After a period of civil war and instability, in 1922, the SFSR united with former Russian Empire territories to form the **Union of Soviet Socialist Republics (USSR)**, electing Lenin to the leadership position.

After the death of Lenin in 1924, a struggle for control between **Joseph Stalin** and **Leon Trotsky** ensued, with Stalin ultimately gaining power. Stalin guided the party under an ideological position combining classical Marxist ideas and Leninist philosophies. Stalin promoted industrialization in the USSR, which proved to be problematic in several ways, leading to years of economic uncertainty. In 1933, when Hitler came to power in Germany and began violent and systematic suppression of communist organizations, Stalin began the "Great Purge," a severe crackdown on both real and perceived enemies within the USSR. Hundreds of thousands of people were arrested, sent to prison camps, or executed (many were later recognized to be innocent). In 1941, Germany invaded the USSR; after a long and bitter struggle, Russia played a major role in the defeat of Germany.

After World War II, the party committed to establishing socialist governments in eastern Europe and began efforts to install USSR allied socialist regimes in other countries as well. These efforts were often through proxy wars and espionage acts that led eventually to the Cold War. By the 1980s, continued economic problems (many fueled by the arms race and other Cold War issues) led to waning power for the CPSU, ultimately leading to the dissolution of the USSR in the early 1990s. The party dissolved and underwent a variety of reformations, with the **Communist Party of the Russian Federation** representing the present-day form of the CPSU, with a focus on the classic Marxist-Leninist ideology.

COMPETITION.

Competition is a critical feature of the capitalist system; it keeps corporations focused on **innovation** and the expansion of capital. However, competition implies winners and losers, and over time, firms become more substantial as their competitors go out of business or become absorbed by the winners. "That which is now to be **expropriated** is no longer the **laborer**. This expropriation is accomplished by the actions of the immanent **laws of capitalist production** itself, by the **centralization** of capitals. One capitalist always strikes down many others" (Marx 1867/1976, 928). As capital becomes enlarged and centralized competition becomes a charade, **monopolies** and oligopolies form and begin to dictate to the market acceptable quality and price, innovation slows, labor costs are allowed to rise, and the system goes into a crisis of **stagnation**, or low economic **growth** and rising **unemployment**. "'The answer to this crisis [beginning in 1980 in the United States] was the neoliberal counterrevolution that not only smashed the power of **labor** but also effectively liberated and unleashed the coercive laws of competition as '"executor"' of the laws of capitalist development by all manner of stratagems (more open foreign trade, deregulation, privatizations and the like)" (Harvey 2010a, 314). *See also* CLASS CONFLICT, CONTRADICTIONS OF CAPITALISM, UNDERCONSUMPTION, WORKERS AS CONSUMERS.

CONDITION OF THE WORKING CLASS IN ENGLAND, THE (1845). In 1842, **Friedrich Engels Sr.** sent his son **Friedrich** to **England** to learn the family business of textile manufacturing at a cotton mill in which the elder held a partnership. Friedrich, in his early twenties at the time, worked in the business office of the **Ermen and Engels** cotton-spinning mill near the city of Manchester for the next two years. Already somewhat radicalized by his experiences in Germany, Engels formed an early liaison with **Mary Burns**, a radical Irish mill worker, and developed connections with **Chartists** and **Owenites** around Manchester. While in England, he researched conditions of the English working class for his first book, published in German in 1845 and English in 1887. He addresses his 1845 introduction to the "Working Classes of Great Britain." He writes of his method, "I have studied the various official and non-official documents as far as I was able to get hold of them—I have not been satisfied with this, I wanted more than a mere abstract knowledge of my subject, I wanted to see you in your own homes, to observe you in your every-day life, to chat with you on your condition and grievances, to witness your

struggles against the social and political power of your oppressors."

Engels first delves into the state of the working classes before the **Industrial Revolution** and then moves on to the impact of **machine** work over handwork and the emergence of an industrial **proletariat**. He then goes on to discuss the living conditions of the great industrial towns, the lot of the poor in the slums, the interior of workers' dwellings, the homelessness, the overcrowdedness, the cellar dwelling, their clothing, tainted food, and the appalling conditions of night refuges. These living conditions affect the health of the workers, and Engels details how disease and mortality are much higher among workers and their families, as are rates of crime and mental illness. The living and working conditions of the working classes, Engels asserts, lead to drunkenness, sexual irregularities, child neglect, and "social war." Marx cites this work in volume 1 of *Capital*, also citing statistics about the excessive infant mortality in working-class districts of England, pointing to official reports of child neglect, insufficient nourishment, unsuitable food, dosing with opiates, and even infanticide (Marx 1867/1976, 520–21).

What is most remarkable about the work is not only his keen eye for the misery and social disintegration around him but also his analysis of the causes of working-class degradation. He writes of the sheer numbers of workers competing for jobs that keep their wages at a minimum, how the **surplus population** forms a **reserve army** of workers that keeps wages down even in **boom** times of full employment. It is during boom times that wages rise, he writes, and thus profits fall and crisis strikes.

From this, it is clear that English manufacture must have, at all times save the brief periods of highest prosperity, an **unemployed** reserve army of workers to be able to produce the masses of goods required by the market in the liveliest months. "This reserve army is larger or smaller, according as the state of the market occasions the employment of a larger or smaller proportion of its members. . . . This reserve army, which embraces an immense multitude during the crisis and a large number during the period which may be regarded as the average between the highest prosperity and the crisis, is the "'surplus population'" of England, which keeps body and soul together by begging, stealing, street-sweeping, collecting manure, pushing handcarts, driving donkeys, peddling, or performing occasional small jobs. In every great town a multitude of such people may be found" (66–67).

Engels likens the lot of the working class to the lot of slaves. The worker thinks himself free because he is not sold to another, but economic circumstance forces him to sell himself piecemeal for a day, a week, or a year. He is not a slave to a single person but a slave to the whole "property-holding class" (64). The capitalist is thus far better off under this arrangement, Engels asserts, because he can dismiss his employees whenever it is profitable to do so. Under capitalism, he writes, production is for profit, not for the sake of supplying needs for people (65).

In addition, Engels writes about the impact of immigration on the **competition** among workers; unique problems experienced by the proletariat working in the mines, factories, and agriculture; and the influence of labor movements. Engels capped off his analysis with a chapter on the attitude of the **bourgeoisie** toward the proletariat, pointing out the hypocrisy of class as a whole. Despite the oppression and degradation of the workers, Engels believed that the **growth** in the numbers of the industrial proletariat, as well as their emerging labor movement, would soon usher in a social revolution in England, a prediction that Engels looked back on in 1892 and wrote about in a new preface to the English translation: "I have taken care not to strike out of the text the many prophecies, amongst others that of an imminent social revolution in England, which my youthful ardour induced me to venture upon" (7). *See also* INDUSTRIAL RESERVE ARMY, SURPLUS LABOR, WAGE SLAVERY.

CONGRESS OF VIENNA (1815). In the aftermath of **Napoleon Bonaparte**'s surrender and (brief) exile in May 1814, the victorious powers sought to reestablish a balance of power and a lasting basis for peace in the aftermath of decades of warfare. Delegates for the victorious powers began negotiating in late September 1814 and met formally from November of that year until June 1815. The Congress continued work through Napoleon's escape from Elba and his Hundred Days War, culminating in his defeat at Waterloo on 18 June 1815. Scholarship on the Congress of Vienna produced various interpretations, with many historians judging the Congress as a reactionary failure to acknowledge the **nationalist** ambitions of ethnic groups subordinated under the **Austrian Empire**. Later revisionist interpretations focused on the diplomatic skills of several of the delegates, particularly Austria's Clemons von Metternich.

Five principal "powers" were represented at Vienna, while numerous lesser principalities were present as well. Austria, **Great Britain**, **Prussia**, and **Russia** largely controlled the negotiations, while Charles-Maurice de Tallyrand-Pèrigourd, who had served under Napoleon until 1807 but had subsequently betrayed Napoleon and was at the time serving Louis XVIII, worked skillfully and duplicitously to constrain the urge of the victorious powers for punitive measures. Numerous "lesser" states, such as Spain, Portugal, Denmark, and Sweden, among others, hoped to steer the Congress in directions favorable to their interests. Despite the deeply reactionary nature of the leading figures that met in Vienna, the disruptive nature of Napoleon's sweeping military victories and subsequent political dominance compelled a new form of diplomacy where principals sent representatives to Vienna instead of diplomatic representatives ferrying back and forth between capitals.

Two important contemporaneous events complicated the negotiations. The first concerned conflict over the status of Poland and Saxony. Alexander II of Russia wanted Poland, while Prussia wanted Saxony. The Austrian and British delegations balked at such an enlargement for either power and secretly signed a pact with **France** to go to war in the eventuality that the Prussia-Russia faction decided to attempt a fait accompli. Ultimately, the revelation of the military agreement induced

Russia and Prussia to accept more modest territorial gains and preserve lesser surrounding kingdoms.

Into this squabbling entered a second and far more disruptive occurrence: Napoleon's escape from his first exile in Elba and his triumphant return to France. The threat that Napoleon posed to the delicate negotiations compelled the Duke of Wellington to leave Vienna to oppose Napoleon's return to power. Taking joint command of forces with Prussian Field Marshal Gebhardt Leberecht von Blücher, they defeated Napoleon at Waterloo. Their subsequent threatened invasion of France ended the threat of renewed general warfare and undermined Talleyrand's diplomacy, provoking the great powers to impose far harsher terms on France.

In practical terms, Russia gained territories in Poland, and Prussia obtained nearly two-thirds of Saxony. The Congress reduced the patchwork of German principalities and city-states from more than 339 states, jointly controlled by Prussia and Austria. Additionally, the Congress formally codified Switzerland's neutrality, and the Kingdom of the Netherlands joined the Dutch Republic with Spanish and Austrian Low Country territories. Over the longer term, the peace created by the Congress of Vienna proved short lived. The attempt to patch together ersatz monarchies over territories whose citizens felt no sense of filial loyalty likely fed Europe's mounting political ferment in the mid-19th century, rising to a crescendo in the **Revolutions of 1848.**

CONSPECTUS OF BAKUNIN'S STATISM AND ANARCHY (1874–1875). The Russian anarchist **Mikhail Bakunin** became one of Marx's chief adversaries within the **First International.** In 1873, he published *Statism and Anarchy,* in which he expressed concern that Marx believed in a need for a **dictatorship of the proletariat** to transition society from **capitalism** to **communism.** This dictatorship, Bakunin claimed, would essentially mean trading one **ruling class** for another. In late 1874 and early 1875, Marx took notes on Bakunin's book by copying passages and writing critical comments on Bakunin's thoughts—a standard

practice for Marx in his studies. In his critique, Marx makes several assertions about this transitional society after the **revolution,** providing a window on his thoughts regarding a postrevolutionary future.

After the revolution, Marx asserts, the **proletariat** will rule as a class "so long as the other classes, especially the **capitalist class,** still exists" (para. 2). Through their government, the proletariat "must employ forcible means" until the economic conditions of the **class struggle** are removed. Marx is aware that the **peasantry** in his day constitutes a considerable majority in most states in western Europe. He believed that over time, **capitalist agriculture** would replace the peasants with agricultural day laborers, as it had in **England.** If that transition has occurred, then the capitalist tenant farmer is as much a proletarian as the urban **wage laborer** and thus has the same interests.

However, should the peasants still be in the majority of society after the revolution, Marx writes, the proletarian government must act with caution. This caution is necessary because the peasantry made a wreck of the workers' revolution in **France.** Therefore, the government should take steps that will "facilitate the transition from the private ownership of the land to collective ownership, so that the peasant arrives at this economically of his own accord; but it is important not to antagonize the peasant, e.g., by proclaiming the abolition of the right of inheritance or the abolition of his property" (para. 4).

The revolution, Marx insists, can take place only where capitalist production is fully developed and where "the industrial proletariat accounts for at least a significant portion of the mass of the people." Real social revolution is based on economic conditions, on the full development of capitalist production, that such a revolution cannot "be carried out on the level of the Russian or Slav agricultural and pastoral peoples" (para. 6).

Marx asserts that the transitional government (the dictatorship of the proletariat) is analogous to an executive committee of a labor **union.** Bakunin objects that such elected leaders would no longer be workers: "They will no longer represent the people, but themselves and their pretensions to people's government. Anyone who can doubt this knows nothing of the nature of men" (para. 27). Marx responds that a manager in a **workers' cooperative factory** does not dominate in Bakunin's political sense, the implication being that the economic interests of the managers and the workers are the same.

Once in power, the proletariat will no longer have to focus on its struggle against the economically privileged class but can employ general economic means in its effort to achieve a communist society. This class rule can exist only as long as the economic basis of classes remains. "With its complete victory its own rule thus also ends, as its class character has disappeared" (para. 8). *See also CIVIL WAR IN FRANCE, THE, CLASS STRUGGLES IN FRANCE 1848–1850* (1895), *CRITIQUE OF THE GOTHA PROGRAMME, EIGHTEENTH BRUMAIRE OF LOUIS BONAPARTE* (1852), PARIS COMMUNE (1871).

CONSTANT CAPITAL. Constant capital refers to the material **means of production**. The **capitalist class** holds a **monopoly** over this capital, thus preventing the working class from access to the means of producing their livelihood and forcing them to sell their **labor power**. Marx defines constant capital as the **raw materials**, **tools**, and **machinery** used in the process of the production of a **commodity**. Constant capital is the product of past **labor**, the value of which is already set in the commodities used in the production process. The value of constant capital depends on the **productivity** of the industries that produce the tools, machinery, or raw materials used in a given production process. Marx calls this constant capital because it "does not undergo any quantitative alteration of value in the process of production" (Marx 1867/1976, 317). Constant capital does not add value to the commodity; it merely transfers its value to the new commodity. The amount of value constant capital transfers per unit of production depends on the life of the machine, the tool, or the amount of the raw material incorporated into the commodity. Only **variable capital**, or the capital used to buy the **labor time** of the worker, adds value in the production process.

This labor time consists of the production of enough value to reproduce the worker at a given standard of living and the **surplus value** that they produce in the labor process. *See also* ABSTRACT SOCIAL LABOR, DEAD LABOR, DIVISION OF LABOR, LABOR THEORY OF VALUE, LIVING LABOR, MONEY, SOCIALLY NECESSARY LABOR TIME, VALORIZATION PROCESS, WAGE GOODS.

CONTRADICTIONS OF CAPITALISM. The **crises** that will ultimately transform **capitalism**, according to Marx, are rooted in its contradictions, that is, structural features that, with development over time, will undermine the foundations of the system itself. The internal contradictions are features of capitalism that arise to block the flow of continued **growth** and expansion of **capital**. The capitalist system can often temporarily overcome these blockages, for the system is both dynamic and elastic. However, the actions taken to address one blockage often contribute to another obstruction, and as capitalism evolves, the contradictions become more acute. Two significant contradictions will cause a periodic crisis that, in time, Marx writes, will lead to a **socialist revolution**.

The focus of *Capital: Volume I* is the contradiction caused by the exploitative relationship between capital and labor itself, which leads to **class conflict**, and Marx predicted eventual **revolution**. With the **centralization and enlargement of capitalist** enterprises, their power and wealth increase, and they use this power to dominate the sociocultural system, monopolizing all advantages as the mass of the people suffer. With this development, the **proletariat** will become more progressive, Marx argues, though the dominance of the capitalists and their organization, money, and power will block governments from providing real structural change. Eventually, Marx writes, this contradiction, combined with **overproduction**, will produce a **revolutionary** crisis.

The second contradiction of capitalism, a focus of *Capital: Volume II*, is the disjunction between production and exchange. The goal of capitalist production is endless growth; this inevitably comes into conflict with the limited consumption capabilities of the proletariat.

Overproduction, as used by economists, refers to a condition where the supply of any given **commodity** exceeds the market demand for that product. The result is a devaluation of price and labor and a likely increase in **unemployment**. Marx argued in the first volume of *Capital* that there is an inevitable trend toward **crisis** in capitalist systems because of the inherent tendency for overproduction. For Marx, this intrinsic tendency is driven by continual **technological** improvements in **manufacturing** (and resultant increases in **productivity**), which increases the amount of **use value** in an economy, leading to a drop in **surplus value** and thus a **declining rate of profit**. This paradoxical condition, with increasing use value co-occurring with declining profits, is a paradox at the heart of what Marx refers to when discussing contradictions of capitalism and periodic crises in capitalist systems. *See also* ALIENATION, ECONOMIC EXPANSION AND CONTRACTION, EXPROPRIATION OF THE CAPITALIST CLASS, MACHINES, MONOPOLY, PREFACE, THE, TECHNOLOGY, UNDERCONSUMPTION, UNDEREMPLOYED, WORKERS AS CONSUMERS.

CONTRIBUTION TO THE CRITIQUE OF HEGEL'S PHILOSOPHY OF RIGHT, A

(1844/1883). Except for the introduction, this manuscript remained unpublished during Marx's lifetime. In it, Marx analyzes **Hegel**'s 1820 book *Elements of the Philosophy of Right*. In the book, Marx formulates his theory of **alienation**, based on the work of **Ludwig Feuerbach**. In the introduction, Marx analyzes the functions of **religion**:

> The foundation of irreligious criticism is: *Man makes religion*, religion does not make man. Religion is, indeed, the self-consciousness and self-esteem of man who has either not yet won through to himself, or has already lost himself again. But *man* is no abstract being squatting outside the world. Man is *the world of man*—state, society. This state and this society produce religion, which is an *inverted consciousness of the world*, because they are an

inverted world. Religion is the general theory of this world, its encyclopaedic compendium, its logic in popular form, its spiritual *point d'honneur*, its enthusiasm, its moral sanction, its solemn complement, and its universal basis of consolation and justification. It is the *fantastic realization* of the human essence since the *human essence* has not acquired any true reality. The struggle against religion is, therefore, indirectly the struggle *against that world* whose spiritual *aroma* is religion.

> *Religious* suffering is, at one and the same time, the *expression* of real suffering and a *protest* against real suffering. Religion is the sigh of the oppressed creature, the heart of a heartless world, and the soul of soulless conditions. It is the *opium* of the people (paras. 3 and 4)

See also ATHEISM.

CONTRIBUTION TO THE CRITIQUE OF POLITICAL ECONOMY, A (1859).

This book by Marx provides an analysis of capitalism by analyzing the work of the classical economists **Adam Smith** and **David Ricardo**. Marx refined many of the ideas in this book and incorporated them into **Capital**, published in 1867. Consequently, *Contribution* is not widely read today. However, **The Preface** to the work, in which Marx summarizes his **economic theory of history**, the "leading thread" of his studies, is an exception.

COOPERATIVE FACTORIES.

Cooperative factories have separated the work of supervision from the ownership of capital, the capitalist thus becoming superfluous to production. In a cooperative factory (either a **workers' cooperative** or a **joint-stock company**), the wages of management are part of the cost of labor, or **variable capital**, separate from the **profit** of the enterprise. Marx adds that in these cooperative enterprises, the profit for the money capitalist tends to be higher than average since there is a greater economy in the use of **constant capital** (or a greater **scale of production**). *See also* BANKS, CREDIT SYSTEMS, MANAGERIAL SKILLED LABOR.

COOPERATIVE LABOR. One of the positive aspects of **capitalism**, according to Marx, is that compared to previous systems, it employs a large number of **workers** who work cooperatively in producing **commodities**. "When numerous workers work together side by side in accordance with a plan, whether in the same process, or in different but connected processes, this form of labour is called co-operation" (Marx 1867/1976, 443). This cooperation can produce effects that are unattainable to an isolated individual worker or an individual with a significant expenditure of time. Cooperative labor increases the productive power of the individual and creates new productive power. Marx asserts that this is apart from the fusion of many individual forces into a single force—as when men combine to raise a heavy weight—but because man is a social animal, the social contact of working together to achieve a task heightens rivalry and stimulates the energy, the "animal spirits," of each worker. Marx calls this "simple cooperation" (443). In and of itself, it is a powerful cooperative force harnessed by any power than can concentrate large numbers of workers. Marx points to the megaliths erected by ancient societies as a result of simple cooperation as an example of its power.

This cooperative force can intensify, Marx asserts, if the labor process is complicated and the number of workers permits the **detailed division of labor**. This form of cooperative labor was dominant in early capitalism in what Marx calls the **manufacture period**. It can significantly speed up the production process, shortening the time necessary to complete the task (Marx 1867/1976, 445). **Adam Smith** first described the detailed division of labor in *The Wealth of Nations* (1776/2000) in the manufacture of pins:

> The greatest improvement in the productive powers of labor, and the greater part of the skill, dexterity, and judgment with which it is anywhere directed, or applied, seem to have been the effects of the **division of labor**. . . . To take an example, therefore, the trade of the pin-maker; a workman not educated to this business,

nor acquainted with the use of the machinery employed in it, could scarce, perhaps, with his utmost industry, make one pin in a day, and certainly could not make twenty. But in the way in which this business is now carried on, not only the whole work is a peculiar trade, but it is divided into a number of branches, of which the greater part are likewise peculiar trades. One man draws out the wire, another straightens it, a third cuts it, a fourth points it, a fifth grinds it at the top for receiving, the head; to make the head requires two or three distinct operations; to put it on is a peculiar business, to whiten the pins is another; it is even a trade by itself to put them into the paper; and the important business of making a pin is, in this manner, divided into about eighteen distinct operations, which, in some factories, are all performed by distinct hands, though in others the same man will sometimes perform two or three of them. (1)

Smith goes on to point out that he had observed small factories of some 10 men who, engaged in the detailed division of labor, could produce some 48,000 pins a day. This would amount to some 4,800 pins for each man. However, Smith estimates, if they had worked at fashioning the pins independently, each man performing all of the steps himself, each would be hard pressed to produce 20 in a day. By dividing the work, Marx argues, the commodity becomes the "social product of a union of craftsmen, each of whom performs one, and only one, of the constituent partial operations" (457). Twelve workers in one day engaged in cooperative labor, whether simple or complex, create a higher quantity of **use values** than a single isolated laborer working 12 days.

Capitalism taps the full potential of cooperative work. The scale of cooperation depends on enormous amounts of capital to employ hundreds of workers simultaneously in a single enterprise. As with **variable capital**, so too with **constant capital**. "Hence, concentration of large masses of the **means of production** in the hands of individual capitalists is a **material** condition for the co-operation of **wage-labourers**, and the extent of co-operation, or the scale of production, depends on the extent of this concentration" (Marx 1867/1976, 448).

Once numerous wage laborers are working for the capitalist, the capitalist must coordinate and direct **social labor**. Of course, the individual capitalist does not do it alone; like an army, there are officers (managers) and non-commissioned officers (foremen) who oversee the production process in the name of capital. With **large-scale industry**, the technical necessity of the instruments of labor (i.e., **machines**) determines the organization, speed, and actions of cooperative labor. The machine, Marx writes, necessitates the replacement of "human force" by "natural forces" and the replacement of human judgment by the "conscious application of natural science." The organization of social labor in the manufacture period was haphazard and subjective. "Large-scale industry, on the other hand, possesses in the machine system an entirely objective organization of production, which confronts the worker as a pre-existing material condition of production" (Marx 1867/1976, 508). The overriding purpose of capitalist management is to maximize the **valorization** of capital to optimize surplus value through the **exploitation** of **labor power**. Potentially labor-saving machinery instead exploits workers.

Thus ensues the antagonistic character of the management–labor relationship. According to Marx, it is the **centralization and enlargement** of the means of production and the socialization of the workforce to cooperate in labor that sets the economic preconditions for **socialism**. The proletariat will revolt because of the ever more severe crises caused by the **contradictions of capitalism**. These crises will eventually cause the **proletariat** to revolt, overthrowing the system and collectivizing the means of production. The proletariat will employ the means of production for the good of all rather than for the valorization of capital. *See also* EXPROPRIATION OF LABOR.

CREDIT SYSTEMS. Credit systems are the primary way of expanding the function of **money**, for credit facilitates large-scale commercial transactions. The credit system, according to Marx, is essential for the **centralization and enlargement of capital**. Capitalists compete in the market by lowering the cost of the production of a given **commodity** and thus reducing its **market price**. This cheapening of commodities depends on the **productivity** of labor, which in turn relies on the introduction of more efficient **technologies** and the **scale of production**, both of which require large amounts of **capital**. Therefore, larger capitalists tend to drive smaller capitalists out of business. As capitalism develops, it takes more and more capital to enter many industries, and smaller capitals tend to gravitate to industries where large-scale production has not yet dominated. However, over time, **competition** will ruin many small capitalists as their capital flows to the winners or vanishes completely (Marx 1867/1976, 777–78).

The centralization of capital accelerates the accumulation process. **Joint-stock companies** and credit systems provided by **banks** increase accumulation, both speeding it up (capital, you will recall, is a process) and intensifying production processes through the scale of production, **machinery**, and **transportation** systems. All of this makes "possible a very rapid transformation of masses of surplus product into additional **means of production**. The mass of social wealth, overflowing with the advance of accumulation and capable of being transformed into additional capital, thrusts itself frantically into old branches of production, whose market suddenly expands, or into newly formed branches, such as railways, etc., which now become necessary as a result of the further development of the old branches" (Marx 1867/1976, 784–85).

The credit system accelerates the development of **productive forces** and the world market through the **growth** of joint-stock companies, thus fulfilling capitalism's historical task of bringing the mode of production to full development and forming the material basis for a new form of production. It intensifies the contradictions between the **forces** and **relations of production** and amplifies economic **crises**. "The credit system has a dual character immanent in it: on the one hand it develops the motive of capitalist production, enrichment by the exploitation of others' labour, into the purest and most colossal system of gambling and swindling, and restricts ever more the already small number of the exploiters of social wealth; on the other hand however it constitutes the form of transition towards a new mode of production" (Marx 1894/1981, 574). *See also* CAPITALIST CLASS, CAPITALIST CYCLES, CIRCUIT OF CAPITAL, ECONOMIC EXPANSION AND CONTRACTION, INDUSTRIAL REVOLUTION, LARGE-SCALE INDUSTRY, PRODUCTIVE FORCES, WORKERS AS CONSUMERS.

CRISES OF CAPITALISM. The crises that will ultimately help to transform **capitalism** are rooted in its **contradictions**, that is, structural features that, with development over time, will undermine the foundations of the system itself. Writing in the early 1860s, Marx details these contradictions in *Capital: Volume I* (1867/1976). Capitalism begins by first taking over **handicraft production** and then develops the **manufacturing period** by exploiting an ever more **detailed division of labor**. This period, occurring in the middle of the 16th century and lasting to the last third of the 18th century, had the effect of **deskilling** much of the labor force, allowing manufacturing firms to hold wages down despite gains in **productivity**.

In the initial stages of **large-scale industry**, the deskilling process led to the widespread employment of women and children of all ages (Marx 1867/1976, 504); once governments stepped in with such reforms as the **British Labor Laws** to stop the most egregious abuses, capitalists increasingly employed **machinery** in the production processes. With the advent of the steam engine and other mechanical **innovations**, workers are further crowded into factories and **exploited** for their **labor power**. Through the process of striving to maximize **surplus value** in growing **world markets**, capital becomes **centralized and enlarged** and consciously employs **science** and **technology** to improve productivity. "With the development of the **factory system** and the revolution in agriculture that accompanies it, production in all the other branches of industry

not only expands, but also alters its character. The principle of machine production, namely the division of the production process into its constituent phases, and the solution of the problems arising from this by the application of mechanics, chemistry and the whole range of the natural sciences, now plays the determining role everywhere" (590).

Competition forces firms to innovate their production technologies to produce goods at a lower cost. If the company cannot provide such products, its competitors will, and the company will either innovate or go out of business. The drive for ever-increasing profit leads **monopoly capitalism** to adopt technology that is ever more sophisticated and to further the **division of labor** to increase productivity. Inevitably, over time, some firms win, and others lose and are thrown out of business or absorbed by their former competitors. Capital becomes less dependent on **skilled labor**, replacing it with **constant capital** and low-skilled **variable capital**. Productivity increases through ever more sophisticated technology, but the buying power of labor becomes more limited. Increasingly, capital strips workers of their skills, and they become mere **commodities** exploited, underemployed, or **unemployed**. The **surplus population** grows. Mass unemployment causes periodic crises of **overproduction** (**Engels** estimates once every eight years or so), each more severe than the last because each crisis leads to further **centralization and enlargement of capital** and thus the power of capital to control the state. Eventually, the crises become so severe that the proletariat comes to recognize their self-interest, successfully revolt, and establish socialism. *See also* CLASS CONSCIOUSNESS, REVOLUTIONARY CLASS CONSCIOUSNESS, WORKERS AS CONSUMERS.

CRITIQUE OF THE GERMAN IDEOLOGY, A. See *GERMAN IDEOLOGY, THE.*

CRITIQUE OF THE GOTHA PROGRAMME (1875). Published after Marx's death, the *Critique* is a letter that Marx wrote to the **Social Democratic Workers' Party of Germany (SDAP)**. The **Gotha Program** was a proposed manifesto for a planned party congress between the SDAP and the **Ferdinand Lassalle**–influenced **General German Workers' Association**. The congress was to take place in the town of Gotha, which advocated a moderate and evolutionary path to **socialism**. Before the congress convened, a faction of the party sent the proposed draft to Marx for comment. Marx critiqued its Lassalle-influenced elements, which gave the draft too much of a German nationalist cast and an **evolutionary** strategy. "But the whole program, for all its democratic clang, is tainted through and through by the Lassallean sect's servile belief in the state, or, what is no better, by a democratic belief in miracles; or rather it is a compromise between these two kinds of belief in miracles, both equally remote from socialism" (Marx 1875, Part IV, para. 22).

Marx thoroughly objected to the program, considering it "vulgar socialism" focused on distribution rather than the mode of production. Distribution, he asserts, is a function of the mode of production. In this regard, he writes,

The **capitalist mode of production**, for example, rests on the fact that the **material** conditions of production are in the hands of non-workers in the form of property in capital and land, while the masses are only owners of the personal condition of production, of **labor power**. If the elements of production are so distributed, then the present-day distribution of the means of consumption results automatically. If the material conditions of production are the co-operative property of the workers themselves, then there likewise results a distribution of the means of consumption different from the present one. Vulgar so-

cialism (and from it in turn a section of the democrats) has taken over from the bourgeois economists the consideration and treatment of distribution as independent of the mode of production and hence the presentation of socialism as turning principally on distribution. After the real relation has long been made clear, why retrogress again? (Part I, #3, para. 26)

In addition to this, Marx criticized the program for its focus on reform through the action of the state rather than the **revolutionary** action of the proletariat. The proletariat cannot reform the state because it is, first and foremost, a **capitalist state**. Despite this criticism (and more), the original program was later adopted by the congress with only minor changes, and the combined parties later became the **Social Democratic Party of Germany**.

What is most notable today about Marx's critique is his discussion about the role of the **state** after the **proletarian** revolution. **Communist** society will not develop on its own foundations, he argues; rather, it must emerge from a capitalist society. The foundations of the old society—economic, moral, and intellectual—will leave its mark even after the **revolution**. There must be a transition period. "Between capitalist and communist society there lies the period of the revolutionary transformation of the one into the other. Corresponding to this is also a political transition period in which the state can be nothing but the revolutionary **dictatorship of the proletariat**" (Part IV, para. 11). *See also CONSPECTUS OF BAKUNIN'S STATISM AND ANARCHY, DISTRIBUTION IN A COMMUNIST SOCIETY, EISENACHERS, ERFURT PROGRAM, EVOLUTIONARY SOCIALISM, GOTHA PROGRAM.*

D

DARWIN, CHARLES (1809–1882). Darwin was an English naturalist and biologist best known for his contributions to the science of biological **evolution**, in particular his 1859 book *On the Origin of Species*. This groundbreaking book presented his detailed and thoroughly researched theory of the formation of new species by the process of natural selection. It is widely considered one of the most important scientific works of the 19th century. **Friedrich Engels** obtained a first-edition copy (of which there were only 1,250) and after reading it sent a letter to Marx saying that it was "absolutely splendid." The next year, Marx replied, "Although it is developed in the crude English style, this is the book which contains the basis on natural history for our view" (Foster 2000, 197). Subsequently, Marx cites Darwin's ideas in the second edition of *Capital*. Referring to the book as an "epoch-making work," he relates Darwin's notion of natural selection and evolution to his own ideas about changes in the **forces of production** and **technology**. Marx essentially makes the argument that the same process of change and transformation observable in the natural world also occurs in the social world. *See also* ENGELS'S EULOGY FOR MARX, HISTORICAL MATERIALISM, PREFACE, THE.

DEAD LABOR. As **living labor** is another name for **variable capital**, dead labor is another name for **constant capital**. Marx likens dead labor to a vampire that lives only by sucking living labor "and lives the more, the more labour it sucks" (Marx 1867/1976, 342). Dead labor refers to **raw materials**, **tools**, and **machinery** used in the process of the production of a **commodity**. Such constant capital is the product of past **labor** (thus dead), the value of which is already set in the commodities used in the production process. If not for living labor, such capital equipment lies idle. "In **handicrafts** and **manufacture**, the worker makes use of a tool; in the factory, the machine makes use of him." Workers are in control in earlier modes of production, and now they are subject to the control of machines. Workers become the "living appendages" of a "lifeless mechanism" (dead labor) (Marx 1867/1976, 548). It is the rule of dead labor over the living, workers spending their lives in service to machines, creating **surplus value** for capital rather than for the living. "Hence the rule of the capitalist over the worker is the rule of things over man, of dead labour over the living, of the product over the producer. For the commodities that become the instruments of rule over the workers (merely as the instruments of the rule of capital itself) are mere consequences of the process of production; they are its products" (990).

As **machine** production increases the **productivity** of **large-scale industry** and **industrial agriculture**, it is the **growth of unproductive labor** in service and clerical work that has absorbed additional labor. However, much of this labor, as well as traditional **productive labor** in large-scale industry, is susceptible to further **innovations** in **technology**. *See also* ALIENATION, CAPITALIST CLASS, MANAGERIAL

SKILLED LABOR, PROLETARIAT, VALORIZA-
TION PROCESS.

DEATH OF KARL MARX (1883). Karl survived the death of his wife, **Jenny**, by a little
over a year. During that time, his health was
in decline. He developed a chronic cough that
became more severe toward the end, leading
to coughing up blood as well as difficulty in
speaking. The symptoms were consistent with
tuberculosis, the disease that killed his father
and several siblings. "Marx also complained of
a weakness in one side, an inability to write
with correct grammar and spelling, and loss
of memory: he could have suffered a small
stroke, a result of his high blood pressure. The
physicians' treatments, as with Marx's other
maladies, only made things worse. There was
the inevitable arsenic and the use of inflammatory chemicals to raise blisters on the skin
and eliminate moisture—just useless torment"
(Sperber 2013, 542).

He traveled some in the last year of his
life, visiting Ventnor, the Isle of Wight, Algiers,
Monte Carlo (where he visited a casino), Switzerland, and **France** to spend some time with
his daughter Jenny and his grandchildren.
On 11 January 1883, on returning to the Isle
of Wight, he received news that his daughter
Jenny had died of cancer. He returned to
London and was looked after by **Helene Demuth (Lenchen)**, but his health was in rapid
decline. On 14 March, a tearful Lenchen
greeted Engels when he came to visit. She told
him that Marx had lost consciousness after his
midday meal. Engels found him dead. *See also*
ILL HEALTH OF KARL MARX.

DECLINING RATE OF PROFIT. A theory, first
postulated among classical economists such
as **Adam Smith** and **David Ricardo**, that the
rate of profit will decline over time. In simple
terms, the idea is that the repetitive selling
the same amount of a product—say, wheat,
iron, or cotton—would result in a steady di-
minishment of the financial gains to the seller.
Smith explained the declining rate of profit by
citing increasing **competition**. Due to the law
of supply and demand, he argued, as more
sellers enter the marketplace, the selling price

of that good would decline. Ricardo took issue
with Smith's explanation, contending that
competition might have a leveling effect but
would not affect the rate of profit. For Ricardo,
the only factor that could erode profit was a
rise in **wage labor** needed to produce the good.

Karl Marx, in *The Grundrisse* and at various points in *Capital*, emphasized the significance of this phenomenon and viewed the
declining rate of profit as dispositive evidence
of the unsustainability of **capitalism**. He criticized the classical economists for failing to
discern that the declining rate of profit might
signal a systemic issue with capitalism as a
mode of production. According to Marx, **constant capital** does not create value but only
transfers its value to the **commodity**. Moreover, as it is the **exploitation** of labor that
produces **surplus value** and thus profit, in
the long run, the employment of **technology**
to the production process must lead to a declining rate of profit. While **technological innovation** might introduce greater efficiencies in
production, only additional labor would generate higher value. **Machinery** might produce
greater physical output, increasing the crude
amount of **capital**, but this higher output sans
labor could be only temporary. Prices would
have to decline to sell the increased amount
of goods, and competitive forces would push
rivals to adopt similar technological innovations, thus increasing supplies of the commodity and lowering the price. Although Marx
identified some countervailing tendencies,
such as patents, **monopoly** rents, and the like,
these forces pushing technological innovation
would tend to produce lower rates of profit over
time. For Marx, the declining rate of profit was
symptomatic of the **contradictions** inherent in
capitalism; because profit derived from the **exploitation** of labor, the declining rate of profit
required that the **bourgeoisie** increase the exploitation to maintain the rate of profit.

The declining rate of profit, a centerpiece of
Marxian economic analysis, has been subject
to intensive research and sustained criticism
across the ideological spectrum. Questions
regarding the sustainability of profits persist,
evidenced in the work of Thomas Piketty
that capital returns in industrially developed

countries are higher than the rate of economic **growth**. This imbalance would lead over time to higher levels of economic inequality, suggesting that Marx's intuitions regarding the rate of profit had some merit.

DEMOCRATIC FEDERATION. *See* SOCIAL DEMOCRATIC FEDERATION.

DEMUTH, HELENE (LENCHEN) (1820–1890). Family servant of the Marx family, she came to the household in April 1845 from **Jenny Marx**'s mother and stayed with the family for the rest of Jenny's and Karl's lives. Her son, **Frederick Demuth**, was the son of Karl Marx. The birth caused considerable strain in Jenny and Karl's marriage, but it survived. Lenchen continued as their maid. She died in 1890, and in accordance with the wishes of Jenny, she was buried in the Marx family grave. Her body was later moved to the tomb of Karl Marx at Highgate Cemetery.

DEMUTH, HENRY FREDERICK (FREDDY) (1851–1929). Illegitimate son of Karl Marx born on 23 June 1851 to **Helene Demuth**. **Friedrich Engels** claimed paternity, although the dark complexion of the child made it discernable that Karl was the father. Engels admitted as such on his deathbed, saying he did it to save Marx's marriage—a real issue in that both **Jenny** and Karl hinted at the severe marital strain in their correspondence at this time. "The births of Freddy and [Jenny Marx's] **Franziska** were within three months of each other. The atmosphere in the tiny two-room flat occupied by two heavily pregnant women—both with children sired by him—can only be imagined" (Stedman-Jones 2016, 324). Sperber (2013) characterizes it as "one of those open family secrets, which everyone knows but no one will acknowledge, even to themselves" (263). Jenny's acquiescence to the fiction probably saved the marriage. Working-class parents in East London fostered Freddy, but he returned on occasion to visit his mother, **Lenchen**. A laborer throughout his life, he became a close friend and confidant to **Eleanor Marx**. Freddy died without known descendants in 1929. Because of Engels's confession, the **German Social Democratic Party** knew about Freddy's paternity but covered it up. The **Soviets** also hid the fact; it became widely known only after the fall of **communism** in the **Soviet Union**. *See also* MARXIAN MYTHOLOGY.

DESKILLING. The drive for ever-increasing profit leads **capitalism** to adopt increasingly sophisticated **technology** and to further the **division of labor** to increase **productivity**. Such division has the effect of deskilling much of the **labor force**, allowing corporations to hold wages down despite these gains in productivity. In the initial stages of **large-scale industry**, the deskilling process led to the widespread employment of women and children of all ages (Marx 1867/1976, 517). Once governments stepped in to regulate the most egregious abuses of **child labor** and 16-hour workdays, capitalists increasingly employed **machinery** in production processes, consequently allowing capitalists to employ unskilled, low-**wage labor** and thus increasing the **surplus value** extracted from the workers. Machine production and the application of chemistry and other science-based technologies squeeze themselves "into manufacture for one specialized process after another" (590).

The machine becomes a competitor of the worker as capital expands by utilizing technology; it destroys the livelihood of the worker. Specialized **labor power** morphs from the specialized skill in handling a tool to the unskilled labor of tending a machine. With evolution, "the **use-value**, the **exchange-value** too, of the workman's labour-power vanishes; the workman becomes unsaleable, like paper money thrown out of currency by legal enactment" (Marx 1867/1976, 470). Workers stripped of their skills become cheap commodities **exploited** by capital and thus rendered superfluous, and the **unemployed** flood the **labor market** and further sink the **price of labor**.

DETAILED DIVISION OF LABOR. The detailed division of labor (or **manufacturing division of labor**) is the breaking down of production tasks into simple discrete steps and becomes prominent in the early **manufacturing mode of**

production practiced by early capitalists as described by Marx. It has several advantages that are due to its particular form. First, a worker who performs the same simple operation for his working life becomes a human machine. He takes less time to do his task than the true craftsman who conducts a series of activities in succession. The specialized worker perfects his method, continuing repetition of the same simple task that teaches him by experience to perform with the minimum of exertion. A craftsman, who performs all of the operations in the production of a commodity, must change his **tools** with each task, interrupting the flow of his labor; a specialized laborer has no such interruptions, both increasing his **productivity** by the intensity of his labor and decreasing the time spent in **unproductive labor**. This collection of specialized workers is the living mechanism of manufacture, producing more in far less time—the goal of capitalist organization. As against these advantages, however, Marx notes that constant repetition of a single, simple task "disturbs the intensity and flow of a man's vital forces, which find recreation and delight in the change of activity itself" (Marx 1867/1976, 460).

A second characteristic of the detailed division of labor, often overlooked in the literature, is the specialized nature of the tools employed in production. In **handicraft production**, Marx writes, all stages of the production process use general tools, such as knives, hammers, drills, and the like. However, with the detailed division of labor, the different operations narrow, and the specialized worker acquires a tool specifically designed for the task. Tools that once served multiple tasks become altered and specialized. Marx reports that Birmingham produces some 500 types of hammers, each one designed for such a specialized task. By specializing and simplifying these tools, the manufacturing period is creating "the material conditions for the existence of machinery, which consists of a combination of simple instruments" (Marx 1867/1976, 460–61). The detailed division of labor as well as the specialized tools of the trades are the essential elements of the **manufacture period**.

Marx describes two types of manufacture. The first is to manufacture many products only by assembling parts made independently in separate **workshops** by independent craftsmen, for example, in the production of watches, some making the mainspring, another shop the dials, and yet another the screws and the like. Under such an organization, only a few parts of the watch pass through several hands, coming together only when assembled into the finished product. The second type of manufacture, Marx writes, produces articles that go through continuously connected phases of development. As an example, he writes of the wire used in the manufacture of needles, which pass "through the hands of seventy-two, and sometimes even ninety-two, different specialized workers" (Marx 1867/1976, 463).

This mode of production is far more potent than traditional handicraft production due to the cooperative nature of the division of labor. However, Marx avers, it requires the transportation of the unfinished product from one hand to another, which both is costly and presents problems of coordination, as the work product of one stage of production becomes the raw material of the next. Each worker is, therefore, dependent on the work of others. Different operations, Marx points out, require unequal time to complete and thus produce unequal quantities of parts. Experience determines the number of workers needed for each operation. The detailed division of labor acquired its form first by experience, and when it attains a degree of consistency, it becomes the conscious method of capitalist production. This interdependence of specialized workers compels each to complete their task in the time allotted efficiently. "This creates a continuity, a uniformity, a regularity, an order, and even an intensity of labour, quite different from that found in an independent handicraft or even in simple cooperation" (Marx 1867/1976, 464–65). It substantively changes its form, Marx asserts, only when there is a **revolution** in the instruments of labor.

Within the workshop, the various tasks performed by the workers can run the gamut between unskilled and highly skilled. The manufacturing period develops a hierarchy of labor as well as a scale of wages to match. "If it develops a one-sided specialty to perfection, at the expense of the whole of a man's working capacity, it also begins to make a specialty of the absence of all development" (Marx 1867/1976, 469). The value of the labor power of the latter is minimal, but even among the skilled, their functions grossly simplified, and compared to the artisans of old, the wages they can command for their labor falls.

The detailed division of labor, Marx writes, reacts on the **social division of labor**, multiplying, and differentiating its subdivisions. The social division of labor is the foundation for specialization that affects every aspect of life. The colonial system in Marx's day extended the world market, which promoted the manufacturing period as well as the division of labor within and between societies. Nevertheless, while there are many linkages and analogies between the division of labor in society and the detailed division of labor, they "differ not only in degree, but in kind" (Marx 1867/1976, 474). The detailed division of labor is the specific creation of capital (479). Manufacture revolutionizes labor, converting the worker into "a crippled monstrosity by furthering his particular skill as in a forcing-house, through the suppression of a whole world of productive drives and inclinations, just as in the states of La Plata they butcher a whole beast for the sake of his hide or his tallow" (481). The worker becomes utterly dependent on employment by capital, unfit to exist independently, his productivity realized only through employment in the workshop. He becomes, in effect, the property of capital.

The independent peasant and the handicraftsman exercise their knowledge, judgment, and will, their total faculties, while from above, the capitalist rules the specialized worker. The detailed division of labor "mutilates the worker, turning him into a fragment of himself" (Marx 1867/1976, 482). In manufacture, the exploitation of workers enriches the profits of capital. Some crippling of the mind and body is due to the social division of labor itself, but the detailed division of labor carries this to extremes: "it is the first system to provide the materials

and impetus for industrial pathology" (484). *See also* ALIENATION.

DIALECTICAL MATERIALISM. Although never explicitly defined by Marx, the philosophical approach known as "dialectical materialism" formed the theoretical basis for Marx's method of reasoning. The concept emerges in his writing most clearly in the second edition of *Capital*, where he states his intention of using a modified form of **Hegelian dialectics** in his analyses. Subsequent **Marxist** thinkers and writers popularized the term, most notably including **Joseph Stalin** (Moore 1971). Marx was a student of **Georg W. F. Hegel**, and it is from his work that Marx derives his conception of dialectics. Dialectics is the philosophical belief that all things (ideas mostly for Hegel, material and social conditions for Marx) are connected and contain contradictory sides or aspects. Further, it is the tension or conflict between these contradictions that drive changes in systems.

Marxian dialectical materialism differs from Hegelian dialectics in that it recognizes the primacy of material conditions—a view that held that the material, concrete world (which includes the **forces of production** essential to human life) shapes the **relations of production** (socioeconomic interactions) and that this **base**, in turn, determines the nature of social and political reality (the **superstructure**). Combining this **materialist** view with the dialectical view of the importance of conflict and contradiction in producing social change is at the heart of Marx's **historical materialism**. Between the forces and relations of production, therefore, exist the contradictions to bring about change in social form. Within the **capitalist mode of production**, this took the form of conflict between the **bourgeoisie** and **proletariat** that he predicted would lead to significant **crises**, eventual **revolution**, and the destruction of **capitalism** and the establishment of a **classless** form of social organization. *See also* PREFACE, THE.

DIALECTICS. In classical philosophy, dialectics refers to a discourse between two or more individuals who hold differing points of view about a given subject with a stated goal of arriving at the truth through reason-based argumentation. Notably, in this sense, dialectics implies a process of exposing contradictory states or ideas, which often can exist simultaneously. Traditional dialectics (and the dialectical methods of **Georg W. F. Hegel**) focus on the validity and truth of ideas and the role that they play in producing change. Marx based his concept of **dialectical materialism** on the basic premises of dialectics, but the focus was on material aspects of the historical development of social and economic forms of human organization rather than Hegel's ideational formulation. In the Postface to the second edition of *Capital: Volume I*, Marx writes about the influence of **Hegelian dialectics** on his theory: "My dialectical method is, in its foundations, not only different from the Hegelian but exactly opposite to it. For Hegel, the process of thinking, which he even transforms into an independent subject, under the name of 'the Idea', is the creator of the real world, and the real world is only the external appearance of the idea. With me the reverse is true: the ideal is nothing but the material world reflected in the mind of man, and translated into forms of thought" (Marx 1867/1976, 102). *See also* HISTORICAL MATERIALISM.

DICTATORSHIP OF THE BOURGEOISIE.
The phrase refers to representative democracies of the West. The label is consistent with Marx's and **Engels**'s view of the modern **state** as a committee for managing the affairs of the **capitalist class**. Marx (1850) used the phrase in referring to the republican government of **France** (27, 23, 58). **V. I. Lenin** (1919) wrote,

Marxists have always maintained that the more developed, the "purer" democracy is, the more naked, acute and merciless the **class struggle** becomes, and the "purer" the capitalist oppression and bourgeois dictatorship. The Dreyfus case in republican France, the massacre of strikers by hired bands armed by the capitalists in the free and democratic American republic—these and thousands of similar facts illustrate the truth which the **bourgeoisie**

are vainly seeking to conceal, namely, that actually terror and bourgeois dictatorship prevail in the most democratic of republics and are openly displayed every time the exploiters think the power of capital is being shaken.

Lenin is also using the term to legitimate the term "**dictatorship of the proletariat**" and to equate his party's rule in the **Soviet Union** with the **bourgeois democracies** of the West. In the same document, he goes on to write, "In these circumstances, proletarian dictatorship is not only an absolutely legitimate means of overthrowing the **exploiters** and suppressing their resistance but also absolutely necessary to the entire mass of working people, being their only defence against the bourgeois dictatorship which led to the war and is preparing new wars." *See also CONSPECTUS OF BAKUNIN'S STATISM AND ANARCHY, CRITIQUE OF THE GOTHA PROGRAMME.*

DICTATORSHIP OF THE PROLETARIAT.
As a sequence in Marx's vision of the **revolutionary** cycle, the "dictatorship of the proletariat" described a period of indeterminate length in which the **proletariat** overthrows the **bourgeoisie state** and would then use the power of the modern state to destroy class distinctions. Marx maintained that such a dictatorship would be a necessary phase in *The Communist Manifesto*, *Critique of the Gotha Programme*, and *The Civil War in France*. Marx also consistently cautioned against premature revolutions and suggested that a kind of "revolutionary tipping point" would begin in one (undetermined) country and move to other countries when a large enough proportion of the **proletariat** had reached **revolutionary class consciousness** to overcome whatever obstacles **reactionary forces** might throw in their way.

Marx believed that **revolutionary class consciousness** would unite and motivate the proletariat. This consciousness is required to counter to the **bourgeoisie**'s already existent consciousness of their privileged position in society and their determination to maintain their place. Unlike the transition from **feudalism** to

capitalism, Marx and **Engels** hypothesized that the transition from capitalism to a socialist dictatorship of the proletariat would be relatively swift and need not entail excessive violence or bloodshed, although they anticipated that there might be some of both. Marx is using the term "dictatorship" well before **Stalin**, Hitler, and other 20th-century dictators and their attempts to exert total control of their societies. In addition, Marx's "dictator" is that of a whole class governing in the interests of the proletariat rather than an individual. Still, the term is fraught with problems that go beyond 20th-century interpretations. **Bakunin**, fearing anything related to state control, criticized the concept of a dictatorship of the proletariat, saying, "If you took the most ardent revolutionary, vested him in absolute power, within a year he would be worse than the Tsar himself" (Guerin 1970, 25–26).

Marx, aware of the objections of Bakunin and other anarchists, still insisted that a proletarian "dictatorship" would be required to uproot capitalist control over the **forces of production**. Because the urge to profit taking is so ingrained in the capitalist mind-set, the proletariat must harness the power of the **state** to suppress human greed. Policies to ensure the **socialization** of the forces of production would drain off those impulses toward greed by following the distributional principle, "From each according to his ability, to each according to his contribution." Marx reasoned that, over time, the need for dictatorship would recede as people habituated themselves naturally to socialist sensibilities. Relief from the need to exploit one another would unleash humanity's creative capacities, producing such superabundance that a new principle—"From each according to his ability, to each according to his need"—would take precedence. In such a superabundant environment, the need for a dictatorship—indeed, for the state itself—to use Marx's famous terminology, would "**wither away**." *See also* BOURGEOIS DEMOCRACY, *CONSPECTUS OF BAKUNIN'S* STATISM AND ANARCHY, DICTATORSHIP OF THE BOURGEOISIE.

DISTRIBUTION IN A COMMUNIST SOCIETY. In Marx's *Critique of the Gotha Programme*, he writes of the distribution of the proceeds of labor in a communist society. It is not a matter of merely distributing all the proceeds of labor to the **worker**. He is aware that funds must be set aside for such economic necessities as capital investment for replacement and expansion as well as administration.

Besides, he writes, it is necessary to provide for a reserve or insurance fund to provide against accidents and the like. Further, there is a need to deduct for social needs:

> Before this is divided among the individuals, there has to be deducted again, from it: *First*, the general costs of administration not belonging to production. This part will, from the outset, be very considerably restricted in comparison with present-day society, and it diminishes in proportion as the new society develops. *Second*, that which is intended for the common satisfaction of needs, such as schools, health services, etc. From the outset, this part grows considerably in comparison with present-day society, and it grows in proportion as the new society develops. *Third*, funds for those unable to work, etc., in short, for what is included under so-called official poor relief today. (Marx 1875, Part I, #3, para. 14)

Marx advocated the distribution of the remaining social product be according to the labor that each worker contributes. This distribution, he admits, is a holdover from **bourgeois** society, a defect that is inevitable when a communist society first emerges from **capitalism**. It is only after **communism** has a chance to develop, when work no longer enslaves the individual, that the establishment of a just society is possible. "After the **productive forces** have also increased with the all-around development of the individual, and all the springs of co-operative wealth flow more abundantly—only then can the narrow horizon of bourgeois right be crossed in its entirety and society inscribe on its banners: From each according to his ability, to each according to his needs!" (Part I, #3, para. 25). *See also* DICTATORSHIP OF THE PROLETARIAT.

DIVISION OF LABOR. *See* SOCIAL DIVISION OF LABOR.

DOCTOR'S CLUB. The Doctor's Club was a loose association of **Young Hegelians** in **Berlin** when Marx was there in 1836–1837. Meeting in coffee houses and pubs, the club included faculty, journalists, and students. Dr. **Bruno Bauer**, a lecturer at the **University of Berlin** at the time, was a leading member. The network of Young Hegelians was critical in Marx's developing theoretical orientation as well as his securing employment at the ***Rhineland News***. *See also* HEGEL, GEORG WILHELM FRIEDRICH.

E

EBERT, FRIEDRICH (1871–1925). Friedrich Ebert stands among the most prominent and controversial figures of the second generation of German socialists. Born into a family of saddlers, Ebert trained and apprenticed traditionally, traveling extensively to fill the needs of the equestrian gentry. Early in his apprenticeship, he encountered representatives of the German **Social Democratic Party of Germany (SPD)** and joined the party when he was 18. In the late 1890s, membership in the SPD drew the attention of the Kaiser's secret police, and Ebert frequently moved to avoid arrest. Less of an ideologue than a practical organizer, Ebert ran for Reichstag seats for various districts before winning a post in 1912. With the death of **August Bebel** in 1913, Ebert was elected party chair of the SPD. Ebert did not have a philosophical turn of mind and was far more pragmatic and an active organizer. He rapidly rose through the ranks as a reliable representative of moderates in the SPD, which at the start of World War I was the largest political party in the Reichstag.

Ebert played a significant role as leader of the SPD during the **German Revolution 1918–1919**. By November 1918, Germany's prospects in the war had deteriorated significantly. Its ally, Austria-Hungary, had capitulated, U.S. entrance into the war had blunted Germany's brief manpower advantage garnered from **Russia**'s withdrawal, and its territorial losses left the Imperial Army in an increasingly dangerous state. In late October, rebellious sailors seized the naval ports in protest of orders to leave port to take on the British fleets. By late September 1918, the German Supreme Army Command had briefed Kaiser Wilhelm II that the military situation was untenable. In response to U.S. President Woodrow Wilson's call for Germany to replace its monarchy with a more democratic government, the German Supreme Command recommended the Kaiser's abdication, and through a series of complicated machinations, Ebert became the first socialist chancellor of the Weimar Republic.

Ebert came into office at a turbulent time, confronted with establishing an entirely new regime, negotiate an end to World War I, and resist attempts from both left and right to overthrow the fledgling Weimar Republic. Ebert's first action was to call for calm, subsequently allying the SPD with moderate and conservative factions in suppressing the **Spartacist Uprising** in January 1919. Elected president in August 1919, he signed the **Treaty of Versailles**, which was universally unpopular in Germany, contributing to an already mounting narrative of the "Stab in the Back" rumors that leftists had betrayed Germany's war effort. The unsuccessful right-wing Kapp Putsch of March 1920, which aspired to reverse the 1918 Revolution and replace the Weimar regime with an autocratic government, compelled Ebert to flee **Berlin**. The coup fell apart following six days of paralysis. Over the balance of his time in office, Ebert repeatedly employed emergency powers as Weimar lurched from crisis to crisis. Vicious political attacks from both left and right may have contributed to Ebert's rapidly declining health and his sudden death on 27 February 1925.

Ebert made no significant contributions to **Marxism** as a body of thought, but his status as the first leftist politician to ascend to high office in Germany carries significance. At the same time, his frequent use of violence in defense of the Weimar Republic—often against attacks from the far left—render him a polarizing figure among socialists. In particular, his willingness to deploy the **Freikorps**—former German World War I veterans serving in right-wing–funded militias—in suppressing the Spartacist Uprising drew intense criticism. From a **Marxist** perspective, Ebert's modest origins and pragmatic record of governance highlight the importance of a proletariat properly imbued with **revolutionary class consciousness**. See also LIEBKNECHT, KARL, LUXEMBURG, ROSA.

ECOLOGY. Marx's contribution to ecological thought was largely ignored by those that followed, but **John Bellamy Foster** (2000) has brought it to light in a recent study titled *Marx's Ecology: Materialism and Nature*. According to Foster, Marx and **Engels** rooted their ecology in **materialism** in the observation that the natural world is the foundation for all life. The natural environments that make life and society possible, as well as the **mode of production** that men and women use to obtain and exchange goods and services, are the foundation of Marx's social theory. Foster cites Marx in the *Economic and Philosophical Manuscripts of 1844*: "The universality of man manifests itself in practice in the universality which takes the whole of nature as his inorganic body, (1) as a direct means of life and (2) as the matter, the object and tool of his activity. Nature is man's inorganic body, that is to say, nature in so far as it is not the human body. Man lives from nature, i.e., nature is his body, and he must maintain a continuing dialogue with it if he is not to die. To say that man's physical and mental life is linked to nature simply means that nature is linked to itself, for man is a part of nature" (72). According to this view, corporal human beings are very much part of and rooted in nature; nature forms the "inorganic body" that provides air, water, food, sun, and shelter—the necessities of life itself—as well as the **tools** and materials needed to access these needs.

All **modes of production** mediate between the natural environment and society; labor is necessary for appropriating materials from nature and fashioning these materials for human use. The fact that the mode of production is essential for life itself is why Marx designates it as the **base** of the social systems.

Foster argues that Marx's theory is central to the concerns of human ecology. The amount and type of resources needed from nature depend on a society's mode of production (**forces and relations of production**) as well as the **population**'s overall size, **growth**, age and sex ratios, class position, and other demographic factors. These population characteristics, according to Marx, are highly dependent on the mode of production; the two factors combined are the primary factors that affect human ecology (i.e., the type of resources exploited) and the amount of depletion and pollution caused by this **exploitation**:

> Just as the savage must wrestle with nature to satisfy his needs, to maintain and reproduce his life, so must civilized man, and he must do so in all forms of society and under all possible modes of production. This realm of natural necessity expands with his development, because his needs do too; but the **productive forces** to satisfy these expand at the same time. Freedom, in this sphere, can consist only in this, that socialized man, the associated producers, govern the human **metabolism** with nature in a rational way, bringing it under their collective control instead of being dominated by it as a blind power; accomplishing it with the least expenditure of energy and in conditions most worthy and appropriate for their **human nature**. (Marx 1894/1991, 959)

It is through the mode of production that humans relate to the environment, the material conditions that make life possible. The **capitalist mode of production**, according to Marx, is particularly exploitative of both human beings and of the environment.

For Marx and Engels, the most thorough exploitation and abuse of both nature and workers occurs. Marx writes of the pollution of the cities of his day, of the raw sewage, the dirt, and the hovels of the workers where even the light of the sun is blocked (Marx 1867/1976, 814–19). It is the search for new markets, investment opportunities, products, workers, resources, techniques, and technologies to expand capital—all to the exclusion of other values and considerations—that first drove peasants off the land and has led capitalism to so thoroughly exploit and abuse both **workers** and the environment (638). Nevertheless, this exploitation will pass, Marx writes in *Capital: Volume III*, for it is unsustainable and morally wrong. "From the standpoint of a higher socio-economic formation [future socialist society], the **private property** of particular individuals in the earth will appear just as absurd as the private property of one man in other men. Even an entire society, a nation, or all simultaneously existing societies taken together, are not the owners of the earth. They are simply its possessor, its beneficiaries, and have to bequeath it in an improved state to succeeding generations as *boni patres familias*" [good heads of household] (Marx 1884/1991, 911). This passage alone should establish Marx's bona fides as a theorist well ahead of his time, one who has integrated ecology into his perspective.

While **historical materialism** takes the relationship between society and the environment as the foundation of societies, Marx himself does not fully explore the limiting factors that geography, resources, climate, or pollution might have on capitalist production and growth. Nor does Marx explicitly posit that ecology will eventually become a constraining factor on **capital growth** much less one of the crises that have the potential to precipitate **revolution** and collapse. These factors are more fully explored by contemporary Marxists, such as Foster and **Immanuel Wallerstein**. *See also* CAPITALIST AGRICULTURE, OVERPRODUCTION, URBANIZATION.

ECONOMIC AND PHILOSOPHIC MANUSCRIPTS OF 1844.

The *Economic and Philosophic Manuscripts of 1844* (sometimes called the *Paris Manuscripts*) are a series of three manuscripts written by Karl Marx between

April and August 1844. Marx never had them published during his lifetime, receiving their first publication in 1932 in the **Soviet Union** and later translated and published in English in 1959.

The manuscripts offer a view of a young Marx's analysis of economic issues and philosophical issues, with the first manuscript (divided into four sections: "Wages of Labor," "Profit of Capital," "Rent of Land," and "Estranged Labor") focused primarily on a critique of the ideas of **Adam Smith**. It deals mainly with issues of **wage labor** and **capital** and is one of Marx's first detailed explanations and analyses of how capitalist systems can result in **alienation** and **fetishism of the commodity**:

We proceed from an actual economic fact. The worker becomes all the poorer the more wealth he produces, the more his production increases in power and size. The worker becomes an ever cheaper commodity the more commodities he creates. The devaluation of the world of men is in direct proportion to the increasing value of the world of things. Labor produces not only commodities; it produces itself and the worker as a commodity—and this at the same rate at which it produces commodities in general. This fact expresses merely that the object which labor produces—labor's product—confronts it as something alien, as a power independent of the producer. The product of labor is labor which has been embodied in an object, which has become material: it is the **objectification** of labor. Labor's realization is its objectification. Under these economic conditions this realization of labor appears as loss of realization for the workers; objectification as loss of the object and bondage to it; appropriation as estrangement, as alienation. (Marx 1844, 28–29)

The second manuscript is a short entry titled "Antithesis of Capital and Labor, Landed Property and Capital," which discusses the issue of **private property** and **landlords**, topics more thoroughly addressed in the third manuscript. That manuscript consists of five sections: "Private Property and Labor," "Private Property and **Communism**," "Human Needs & Division of Labor under the Rule of Private Property," "The Power of Money," and "Critique of the Hegelian Dialectic Philosophy as a Whole."

ECONOMIC EXPANSION AND CONTRACTION. According to Marx, the system of capitalism is subject to boom and bust, and this has a devastating impact on working families. The system is dependent on the **markets** of the world; increasing demand sets off feverish **production**, followed by overfilling the markets and then contraction of these markets and the crippling of production. "The life of modern industry becomes a series of periods of moderate activity, prosperity, **overproduction**, **crisis**, and **stagnation**" (Marx 1867/1976, 495). The instability in employment wreaks havoc on the lives of the proletariat. As capitalism **evolves**, Marx asserts that economic booms and busts must swing wider, causing a constant churning of employment. This expansion and contraction are not possible "without disposable human material, without an increase in the number of **labourers** independently of the absolute **growth** of the **population**" (785). This increase is ensured by consistently "setting free" a part of the workforce through layoffs, plant closings, mergers, downsizing, automation, and other methods that lessen the number of workers needed to maintain production. Therefore, Marx states, modern capitalism depends on the transformation of a large part of the **proletariat** to be periodically **unemployed** or **semiemployed** as well as to become a semipermanent underclass, or **lumpenproletariat**. *See also* CAPITALIST CYCLES, INDUSTRIAL RESERVE ARMY, OVERPRODUCTION, UNDERCONSUMPTION, WORKERS AS CONSUMERS.

ECONOMIC STAGNATION. *See* CAPITALIST CYCLES.

ECONOMIC SURPLUS. In precapitalist societies after the agrarian revolution, independent producers—**serfs**, slaves, peasants, or artisans—produced economic surpluses. In most

of these societies, elites expropriated the bulk of the surplus directly through force, tradition, law, theft, or piracy or indirectly through taxes, forced labor, fraud, usury, or other means. Regardless of the methods used to separate the producers from their surplus products, these means were transparent, open, and evident to both exploited **populations** and the exploiters. The system of **capitalism**, Marx argues, is very different in that both surplus creation and expropriation are opaque, obscured by the **commodification** of **wage labor**.

The essence of capitalism is the creation of surplus—now called **surplus value**. Suppose, for example, that a person in business for herself making pottery vases pays $10 for the material to make each vase and sells each for $20. Suppose further that she can comfortably make one vase in one hour. She needs $40 per day for the necessities (**commodities**) to live on (food, clothing, and shelter), so she needs to work only four hours per day to make a living. This is simple commodities production. You have goods for which you have no need (a surplus), and you exchange them with someone who wants them for products you need. This exchange can be through barter or the exchange of **money**. Either way, it is an exchange of goods based on equal value; there is no surplus value created in the transaction, no profit.

Now suppose this same individual decides to become a capitalist and is therefore intent on increasing her wealth or capital. Some workers have no access to the **means of production** and therefore have nothing to sell on the market except their **labor power**. She hires a man from this pool at $5 per hour. This man can also make one vase per hour. The material for each vase still costs $10; she still sells each vase for $20. Minus the material and labor costs, her profit is now $5 per vase. This profit is possible only because there is a difference between the cost of the labor ($5 per hour) and the amount of value added (**valorization**) by that labor to the raw materials ($10). In this case, the worker adds $10 to the value of the materials in the course of his hour's work but is paid only $5 for his efforts. The owner of the means of production takes this surplus value of $5 per hour created by the worker and calls it **profit**. In effect, in an eight-hour day, the worker is laboring four hours for himself and four hours for the capitalist. According to Marx, only human labor in commodity production can create surplus value in **exchange value**.

Continuing the example, for the capitalist to live, she still needs at least $40 per day. To get this in profit, she will have to work her employee at least eight hours per day. For the employee to live, he also needs $40, and therefore he has to work the capitalist's required eight hours per day. Where she had to work only four hours per day to live through simple commodities production, he works eight hours per day under capitalist production to do the same. The increase in work hours under capitalism is because his labor is now supporting both himself and the capitalist.

The creation of surplus value is the essence of capitalism, not the satisfaction of social needs. Commodities are merely the vehicle for surplus production, that is, the labor power invested in the item. It is in exchange that the capitalist realizes surplus value. It is the disconnection between production and realization that is the primary **contradiction** within the capitalist system. *See also* ACCUMULATION OF CAPITAL, BOURGEOISIE, CLASS CONFLICT, COMMODITY, CRISES OF CAPITALISM, LABOR THEORY OF VALUE, PRIMITIVE ACCUMULATION, SOCIAL LABOR, SURPLUS LABOR.

ECONOMIC THEORY OF HISTORY. *See* HISTORICAL MATERIALISM.

ECONOMIES OF SCALE. It is the **laws of capitalist production** that **centralize and enlarge** capital (Marx 1867/1976, 929). Large enterprises consciously apply **science** in developing productive **technology**. It is only through economies of scale that most technical processes can be utilized. That is, large organizations and a massive, **socialized labor** force are necessary to employ such technologies successfully. This same applied science develops the **means of transportation and communication** systems that expand markets worldwide. In this capitalist system, all of the advantages of wealth and power are in the hands of a continually decreasing number of capitalist magnates (929). *See also* LARGE-SCALE INDUSTRY.

EIGHTEENTH BRUMAIRE OF LOUIS BONAPARTE (1852). An essay written by Marx between December 1851 and March 1852 discussing the French coup of 1851 in which **Louis Napoleon Bonaparte** assumed dictatorial powers. The title is a historical reference to Napoleon Bonaparte's "Coup of 18 Brumaire," which occurred on 9 November 1799 and ended the **French Revolution**. In the French Republican calendar, the date of that coup was 18 Brumaire. Marx drives home the meaning of the title in the opening line of the essay: "Hegel remarks somewhere that all great world-historic facts and personages appear, so to speak, twice. He forgot to add: the first time as tragedy, the second time as farce." In the Preface to the work, Marx compares his analysis of the rise of the dictator with two of his contemporaries:

Of the writings dealing with the same subject at approximately the same time as mine, only two deserve notice: Victor Hugo's Napoleon le Petit and **Proudhon's** Coup d'Etat. Victor Hugo confines himself to bitter and witty invective against the responsible producer of the coup d'etat. The event itself appears in his work like a bolt from the blue. He sees in it only the violent act of a single individual. He does not notice that he makes this individual great instead of little by ascribing to him a personal power of initiative unparalleled in world history. Proudhon, for his part, seeks to represent the coup d'etat as the result of an antecedent historical development. Inadvertently, however, his historical construction of the coup d'etat becomes a historical apologia for its hero. Thus he falls into the error of our so-called objective historians. I, on the contrary, demonstrate how the **class struggle** in **France** created circumstances and relationships that made it possible for a grotesque mediocrity to play a hero's part. (Marx 1852, 1)

Regarding the role of the individual in history, "Man makes his own history, but he does not make it out of the whole cloth; he does not make it out of conditions chosen by himself, but out of such as he finds close at hand. The tradition of all past generations weighs like an alp upon the brain of the living" (5). Like his *Class Struggles in France, 1848–1850*, Marx analyzes the coup in terms of class struggle and **historical materialism**, like the original 8 Brumaire, the coup of Louis Napoleon ended the **1848 Revolution**, and the Republic. It was a "Parody of restoration of empire" (58). *See also* PEASANTRY.

EISENACHERS. The **Social Democratic Workers' Party of Germany** began in Eisenach, Germany, in 1869. **August Bebel** and **Wilhelm Liebknecht** led the "Eisenachers" (a moniker that stuck). The party affiliated with the **International Workingmen's Association**, and although influenced by Marx's and **Engels's** **political-economic** analyses, they were somewhat more moderate than their mentors were. *See also* ERFURT PROGRAM, GENERAL GERMAN WORKERS' ASSOCIATION (ADAV), GOTHA PROGRAM, LASSALLE, FERDINAND, SOCIAL DEMOCRACY, SOCIAL DEMOCRATIC PARTY OF GERMANY (SPD).

ENGELS, FRIEDRICH (1820–1895). Born into a family of German industrialists in the Rhineland, Friedrich Engels eventually collaborated with Karl Marx to become one of the most influential German socialists of the 19th century. Giving up a formal university education to enter the family business, Engels developed a romantic, rebellious side, writing poetry and social criticism. Biographers frequently note the resulting dualism between loyal service to his families' textile business and his convictions regarding the necessity for social reform and close association with Marx.

In his youth, constitutionalism and liberal republicanism informed his social criticism of the poverty afflicting working-class Germans. He accused pietistic German Protestants like his parents of hypocrisy in tolerating the poverty, poor housing conditions, and fragile health of German **workers** in the 1830s. His brief service in the peacetime Prussian military freed Engels from his family business and widened his intellectual circles. In his posting to **Berlin**, he became acquainted with the **Young Hegelians**, with whom Engels engaged primarily in the Christian dimensions of their discourse. Engels's first meeting with Karl Marx in 1842 left the latter unimpressed with what he likely perceived as a wealthy dilettante social critic. Engels's subsequent critique of English industrialization impressed Marx, and they began a long writing collaboration, starting with *The Holy Family*. This collaboration was somewhat of a rant aimed at the Young Hegelians, also offering an initial glimpse into Marx's theory of history (Berlin 2013, 113).

While Engels consistently deferred to Marx as the senior collaborator and authority on **historical materialism**, several of Engels's solo writings constitute an essential contribution to the corpus of revolutionary Marxist writings. Isaiah Berlin (2013) offers valuable insight into the complex dynamic of mutual needs and drives that formed the Marx–Engels collaboration. Engels, he writes, began studying **socialism** under **Moses Hess** and independently arrived at positions similar to Marx. He often simplified Marx's ideas for a mass audience, sometimes to the point of oversimplification. "Most important of all, he possessed a quality essential for permanent intercourse with a man of Marx's temperament, a total uncompetitiveness in relation to him, absence of all desire to resist the impact of that powerful personality, to preserve and retain a protected position of his own; on the contrary, he was only too eager to receive his whole intellectual sustenance from Marx, unquestioningly, like a devoted pupil, and he repaid him his sanity, his enthusiasm, his vitality, his gaiety, and finally, in the most literal sense, by supplying him with means of livelihood at moments of desperate poverty" (95). In an important sense, each man possessed qualities that the other lacked, and both men respected those qualities lacking in themselves that they saw in the other. Engels appreciated Marx's prophetic vision and deep intellect. In Engels, Marx saw a man with a capacity to quickly absorb and synthesize prodigious amounts of information and a gift for articulating Marx's vision of **revolutionary socialism** in compelling and easily understood terms.

Engels wrote his first published book, *The Condition of the Working Class in England* (1845), during his stay in Manchester. It was comprised of personal observations and contemporaneous reports and argued that the **Industrial Revolution** had left English workers far worse off. After both men joined the **League of the Just** in 1847, Engels contributed an early draft that Marx would later rewrite as *The Communist Manifesto* (1848). The work offered the most succinct distillation of Marx's and Engels's version of revolutionary socialism, its publication coming perspicaciously amid the **Revolutions of 1848**. In 1849, both Engels and Marx had drawn the attention of increasingly reactionary Prussian authorities, and both relocated to **England**.

While Marx feverishly devoted himself to Volume I of his masterwork *Capital*, Engels subsidized Marx and his family as best he could. However, Engels's dependence on his family and their disapproval of his revolutionary activities limited the extent of his financial patronage. Nevertheless, on settling his father's estate in 1864, the family made Engels a partner in **Erman and Engels**. Selling his interest in the firm in 1869, he was able to better support Marx and his family as well as devoting himself to the labor movement.

In writing anonymous reviews for *Capital*, Engels developed a shorthand version of **Marxism** that would offer a distinctive perspective on **revolutionary Marxism**. He rendered "Marxism" into more ideologically rigorous terms at the cost of accentuating the more teleological and deterministic aspects. In the midst of Marx's feverish writing of Volume II of *Capital*, German socialist Eugene Dühring began producing works critical of revolutionary Marxism with the intent of supplanting Marxism as the dominant German interpretation of socialism. Engels replied with *Anti-Dühring* (1878), which exerted tremendous influence over the younger generation of Marxists, including **Eduard Bernstein**, **Karl Kautsky**, and **Georgi Plekhanov**. In that work, Engels elaborated on his conception of "**scientific socialism**," founded on two of Marx's unique philosophical advances. First, the **materialist conception of history** focused attention on the ways that societies meet their material needs rather than on moral sentiments. Second, Engels espoused Marx's insight regarding the importance of **surplus value** in sustaining **capitalism**, thus emphasizing the inherently **exploitative** nature of capitalism. In *Socialism: Utopian and Scientific*, a pamphlet based on several chapters of *Anti-Dühring*, Engels argued that scientific socialism represented positivistic and law-like reflections of the laws operating in the universe. The two works also contained the famous Marxist declaration that eventually the **dictatorship of the proletariat** will cause the state to "**wither away**" (Stedman-Jones 2016, 560).

Engels's role in the partnership steadily became more prominent throughout the 1870s. Marx's obsessive work habits and unsanitary living conditions contributed to his **ill health**. From 1873 on, Marx suffered from attacks of headaches and insomnia, and his **productivity** declined precipitously. Marx deferred increasingly to Engels in matters related to the promotion and defense of Marx's revolutionary socialism.

Following Marx's death in 1883, Engels exerted considerable influence as principal editor and publisher of Volumes II and III of *Capital* and for the last 12 years of his life as the authoritative defender and advocate of Marx's philosophy and legacy. In this period, Engels also produced *The Origin of the Family, Private Property, and the State* (1884), published a year and a half following Marx's death. In this work, Engels relied heavily on the notes Marx had written on American anthropologist **Lewis H. Morgan**'s *Ancient Society* (1877). Engels advanced his positivistic interpretation of historical materialism. He asserted that Marx had intended a book-length treatment of Morgan's work. He wrote that Marx believed that Morgan's evidence—derived from the study of North American Indians—provided evidence of **primitive communism**. In such societies, social relationships were more matrilineal and egalitarian, lacking the capacity for capital accumulation. Engels further contended that the development of **private property** began the process of subordinating women and overthrowing matrilineal kinship bonds, this subordination being the first act on the path to successive stages of economic development, creating the conditions for capitalism.

The divergence between Marx's and Engels's thought is a frequent topic of speculation among scholars and biographers. Part of the differences in how Marx and Engels understood "Marxism" is explained by temperament and life experience. Marx, as a trained philosopher and committed **Hegelian**, was disciplined and, at times, intolerant. Engels, in contrast, lacking a formal education, was far more capable of "outside-the-box thinking" but was also far more susceptible to intellectual trends. Engels synthesized **Charles Darwin**'s view of natural history into Marxism. While Marx accepted the importance of Darwin's accomplishments, he never engaged in intensive study of *On the Origin of Species* (1859). Marx took extensive notes when he encountered anything that he could synthesize into his materialist conception of history. The lack of such notes on Darwin's work is an important indication of Marx's wariness toward Darwin. It appears that Marx was suspicious of Darwinism, particularly of Darwin's belief in evolution's "accidental" nature. Marx's

Hegelianism brought with it a teleological conviction that nothing was accidental. Marxism would move in a decidedly Darwinian direction following Marx's death, driven by Engels's enthusiasm and by influential German and Russian Marxists like Karl Kautsky and **Georgi Plekhanov**. *See also* BURNS, LYDIA (LIZZIE), BURNS, MARY, ENGELS'S EULOGY FOR MARX, *PEASANT WAR IN GERMANY, THE.*

ENGELS, FRIEDRICH, SR. (1796–1860). Friedrich Engels Sr., the father of Friedrich, was a textile manufacturer and a conservative Christian. He sent young Friedrich to Bremen as a commercial apprentice, where, on reading some literature of the **Young Hegelians**, he had a crisis of faith regarding Christianity. When young Engels joined the army and stationed in **Berlin**, he became a member of the **Free Men** and began writing for the *Rhineland News*. In 1842, the senior Engels sent his son to Manchester, **England**, to work at **Erman and Engels**, a textile mill in which he had a partnership. He insisted that young Friedrich work there both to further his commercial training and to separate him from his radical friends. "The paternal plan backfired badly: the stay in Manchester only reinforced the young Engels's radical and communist sympathies. Manchester was, as contemporaries said, 'Cottonopolis,' the global symbol and global center of

Statues of Friedrich Engels and Karl Marx.

the **industrial revolution**" (Sperber 2013, 138). Returning to the continent, Friedrich wrote *The Condition of the Working Class in England* (1845), continued writing for the radical press, and began his lifelong partnership with Marx. Estranged from his father for the next several years, in 1850, he relocated to England after the **Revolutions of 1848**, and living in genteel poverty, he asked his father for a position at the Manchester firm, becoming a middle-level manager in the business. When his father died, Friedrich eventually received a partnership in the firm as part of his inheritance.

ENGELS'S EULOGY FOR MARX. Karl Marx died in **England** in 1883 and was buried in Highgate Cemetery in London. His friend, **Friedrich Engels**, delivered the eulogy. In the excerpt below, Engels points to what he considers to be the two most essential contributions Marx made to our understanding of human societies: (1) **historical materialism** and (2) the "laws of motion" or **evolution** of capitalist society:

> Just as **Darwin** discovered the law of development of organic nature, so Marx discovered the law of development of human history: the simple fact, hitherto concealed by an overgrowth of **ideology**, that mankind must first of all eat, drink, have shelter and clothing, before it can pursue politics, science, art, **religion**, etc.; that therefore the production of the immediate **material** means, and consequently the degree of economic development attained by a given people or during a given epoch, form the foundation upon which the state institutions, the legal conceptions, art, and even the ideas on religion, of the people concerned have been evolved, and in the light of which they must, therefore, be explained, instead of vice versa, as had hitherto been the case.
>
> But that is not all. Marx also discovered the special law of motion governing the present-day **capitalist mode of production**, and the bourgeois society that this mode of production has created. The discovery of **surplus-value** suddenly threw

light on the problem, in trying to solve which all previous investigations, of both bourgeois economists and socialist critics, had been groping in the dark. (Marx and Engels 1975a, 467)

Marx's analysis of the structure and the internal forces of change within the capitalist system led him to make several predictions of the immediate evolutionary path of the capitalist mode of production. Through the development of such theories as the **law of value**, Marx predicted a future of ever-intensifying **technological** progress, accelerated **productivity**, the **centralization and enlargement of capital**, a **declining rate of profit** (although he also identified countervailing trends in this decline), periodic **economic cycles** of boom and recession, as well as **class struggle** between the **bourgeoisie** and **proletariat**. While he may have been wrong about the inevitability of a **socialist revolution** (at the very least, he was wrong about the timing) and his lofty visions of a communist future, his analysis of the system of capitalism as well as its centrality in understanding modern society is first-rate. *See also* CRISES OF CAPITALISM, DEATH OF KARL MARX, PREFACE, THE.

ENGELS'S RELATIONSHIP WITH MARX. Various biographies of the two revolutionaries have thoroughly discussed and analyzed one of history's most celebrated intellectual partnerships: the relationship between Karl Marx and **Friedrich Engels**. They first met in the office of the *Neue Rheinische Zeitung* while Marx was working as the editor. Engels had been anonymously contributing articles to the increasingly left-wing paper and only briefly met Marx this time while on his way to **England** for work (where, notably, Engels met **Mary Burns** the following year and began formulating what would become *The Condition of the Working Class in England* [1845]). In 1844, after Marx had moved to Paris, Engels met him for the second time, and the two recognized their similar worldviews and, more important, began what would become a lifelong friendship. They immediately agreed to begin collaborations on what would become *The Holy Family*, with

Engels writing his sections in the 10 days following their second meeting and, repeating a pattern that would later become evident in their working relationship, Marx taking much longer to finish his sections of the work.

While the two bonded over their revolutionary visions, they also bonded over their mutual love of alcohol, meeting in the pubs of Paris and **Brussels** to discuss socialism and revolution in the mid-1840s. Engels was Marx's "man on the ground" over the next several decades, feeding Marx direct observations of how the wage system worked, how stock markets functioned, and how the working class felt about their position in the capitalist system. Despite his **bourgeois** upbringing and status and his family-supplied employment in the textile industry, Engels used his gradually increasing income promoting **class consciousness** and **revolutionary socialism**.

More directly, he used his income to support Marx, who was by all accounts a poor manager of money, often having to pawn belongings to meet his debts. On many occasions, Engels would step in and provide Marx with monetary gifts so that he could continue his writing. Engels's visible position in industry led him ultimately to realize that he would need to cede the intellectual spotlight to his friend Marx. Although the two collaborated on many projects, including works attributed solely to Marx in some cases, Engels came to see his role in the relationship as somewhat of a "general"—providing the money necessary to get works like *Capital* published and to propagandize Marx's revolutionary ideas.

Eventually, Engels was able to leave behind his work in **Erman and Engels**, noting to Marx in an 1845 letter that "it is impossible to carry on communist propaganda on a large scale and at the same time engage in huckstering and industry." As Marx's health declined, Engels was able to take over many of the "revolutionary" duties Marx was obligated for, especially as a member of the General Council of the **International Workingmen's Association**. Engels was much more organized and energetic than Marx, and he again saw it as his role to take on these duties to

allow Marx to pursue his more intellectually oriented goals further.

Engels appreciated his friendship with Marx and saw him as "the greatest living thinker" of their time (as he noted in his **eulogy** for Marx), and Marx appreciated his friendship with Engels. There is scant evidence of the two fundamentally disagreeing or arguing—though some awkwardness existed between the two as a result of Marx's indifference toward Engels's relationship with Mary Burns—or, perhaps more accurately, **Jenny Marx**'s dim view of Engels's relationship with Mary. Nonetheless, the Engels and Marx families were close up to Marx's death.

One of the most controversial aspects of the relationship between Marx and Engels is the role that Engels took on concerning Marx's legacy. After his death, Engels saw it as his duty to continue promoting and propagandizing Marx and his ideas. He brought significant portions of Marx's unpublished work to publication, most notably Volumes II and III of *Capital*. Also, he wrote several books and pamphlets based on ideas developed by Marx (such as *The Origin of Family, Private Property and the State*). This role—as executor of Marx's intellectual contributions—resulted in Engels putting an indelible personal stamp on the material that would serve as the basis for the developing ideology of **Marxism**. Much analyses by subsequent scholars have focused on unraveling what Marx might have meant and what Engels may have added through his interpretations of Marx's true meanings and purposes. *See also* PESCH, SYBILLE.

ENGLAND. Marx arrived in London in August 1849, his family following a few weeks later. He was to reside there for the rest of his life. He came because the English government there had a more liberal policy toward political refugees than did other Western countries. The family had to exist on Marx's meager income from writing for many years, living in the slums of SoHo and often turning to pawn shops, loans, and help from **Engels**. This poverty probably contributed to the death of several of his children. It was in England that Marx spent hours at the Library of the **British Museum**, researching his newspaper and **journal** articles as well as his writings on **political economy**. In addition to his writings, Karl was very active in the life of the émigré community as well as socialist and union politics. *See also* CAPITAL, INTERNATIONAL WORKINGMEN'S ASSOCIATION (IWA).

ENLIGHTENMENT. The Enlightenment was a complex intellectual and philosophical movement during the late 17th and 18th centuries, taking place primarily in Europe and North America. It marked attention to reason as the primary force guiding human endeavors. Many credit the rationalist philosophy of René Descartes as foundational to the movement, and Enlightenment thinking came about in concert with the scientific revolution. Many argued that reason, human liberty, and the empiricism of the scientific method should be how human lives (and, by extension, the societies and institutions in which humans lived) could be improved. Enlightenment thought formed the basis of new ideas about government and, in many ways, led directly to the French and American revolutions. Likewise, Enlightenment ideas were critically important in the development of economics and contributed in many ways to the development of the capitalist systems on which Marx focused. The Enlightenment profoundly influenced Marx. His work was concerned with such ideals as freedom, equality, independence, rationality, and a scientific understanding of history and society. *See also* MARX, HEINRICH, WYTTENBACH, JOHANN HEINRICH.

ENVIRONMENTAL CRISIS. There is a **contradiction** between **capitalism**'s need for continual **growth** and the limits of the natural environment. The issue, much commented on by modern-day ecologists, is somewhat surprising to many that Marx wrote of it in the 19th century. Marx calls it our "metabolic relation to nature." In modern terms, he is referring to **ecology**. Both the forces and the **relations of production** are essential in determining the relationship of humans to the natural world. However, the focus of Marx's analysis quickly moves to the relations of production. The **class**

interests that the **forces of production** serve—the purpose as well as the extent of their use—are central in human ecology. The **exploitation** of the environment and the worker is endemic to the capitalist system because those who control the **mode of production** profit from this exploitation.

Moreover, capitalists value profit above all else. The profit motive is at the heart of the environmental crisis. Capitalism needs **perpetual growth**, but Marx recognized limits to this growth. Once capitalists fully revolutionized **large-scale industry** in its exploitation and transportation of raw materials, he writes, the mode of production is capable of "sudden extension by leaps and bounds, which comes up against no barriers but those presented by the availability of raw materials and the extent of sales outlets" (Marx 1867/1976, 578–79). *See also* CAPITALIST AGRICULTURE, CLASS CONFLICT, CONTRADICTIONS OF CAPITALISM, FOSTER, JOHN BELLAMY, METABOLIC INTERACTION.

ERFURT PROGRAM (1891). Many came to see the platform of the **Social Democratic Party of Germany (SPD)** established by the **Gotha Program** in 1875 as a capitulation to the German state in the heady days immediately after German unification. In the intervening years, the German state had consolidated political control and embarked on military expansion and industrial production, but German workers had seen little benefit. Workers' status and economic well-being had deteriorated in the years since the SPD had entered competitive elections and participated in the government as an opposition party. Additionally, the mood of German workers had soured on the intense nationalism that had swept Germany in the aftermath of the stunning military victories over first **Austria** and then **France** that had forged the German state. In 1878, German Chancellor **Otto von Bismarck** supported the passage of **Anti-Socialist Laws** in the aftermath of two assassination attempts on Kaiser Wilhelm. Drafted scarcely a year after lifting this 12-year prohibition, the Erfurt Program reflected these darker realities.

Initial drafts, written, respectively, by **August Bebel** and **Wilhelm Liebknecht**, removed the salutary language regarding the state. However, the platform avoided any directly inflammatory challenges to the legitimacy of the Hohenzollern monarchy. As befitting Liebknecht's history of political agitation, the platform called on the SPD to work for the elimination of the adverse conditions caused by **capitalism**. In July 1891, **Karl Kautsky** wrote an extensive critique of the Liebknecht drafts of the SPD platform, calling for reforms of the platform to include references to **communism** "as a necessity resulting directly from the historical trend of capitalist production methods" (Dominick 1982, 361). While Liebknecht's draft of the platform called on German workers to continue the struggle against capitalism, Kautsky's more esoteric alternative proposal posited the inevitability of the **socialist revolution** without necessarily conceiving of a definitive set of actions required of German workers. In a last-minute bit of maneuvering, August Bebel threw his support behind Kautsky's revised platform and persuaded Liebknecht to support Kautsky's version, which received unanimous ratification.

The Erfurt Program was at once much more explicitly a "Marxist" platform in its language and analysis, even as it pragmatically avoided pursuing Marx's revolutionary prescriptions. Adopting Marx's critical analysis of capitalism in whole cloth, the platform conceived the role of the SPD to protect and preserve the rights of German workers and not to pave the way to the revolutionary replacement of the **capitalist state** with a socialist democratic regime, however conceived. The drafting of the Erfurt Program marked the rise of Kautsky as a leader within the SPD and the eclipse of Wilhelm Liebknecht as the principal SPD theorist. The resulting "Marxification" of the SPD's public program suggested a sense in which the German left had succumbed to new, defanged "orthodox" interpretation of **Marxism**, one that meekly accepted the power of the German state even as it disparaged the capitalist state's legitimacy. This line of thought would represent a dominant line of **Marxist** theory into the 20th century and illustrate an approach that **Lenin** would dismissively characterize as "**trade union consciousness.**" *See also* ZUSAMMENBRUCHSTHEORIE.

ERMEN AND ENGELS. The Manchester cotton-spinning mill partly owned by **Friedrich Engels**'s father, **Friedrich Engels Sr.** The elder sent the younger Friedrich there in 1842 to learn the business. Spending much of his life there as a manager, Engels spent his initial years researching his book *The Condition of the Working Class of England.* On his return in 1850, Engels was a manager in the firm and used some part of his wages to supplement the income of Marx. Engels's father died in 1861. Rather than allow Friedrich any share of the textile business in Germany, the family decided to use their Manchester resources to secure Friedrich a partnership in Ermen and Engels. He became a full partner in 1864, and in 1869, he sold his interest in the firm to the Ermen brothers and invested in the stock market. From this, he was able to retire and eventually move to London, devoting himself to the labor movement. In addition, he was able to settle Marx's debts and provide the family with a £350 annual income (Green 2009).

ETHNOLOGICAL NOTEBOOKS OF KARL MARX, THE. Based on notes written between 1880 and 1882, they were published posthumously in 1974 (Marx 1880–1882/1974). Among the very last works written before his death, the collected notes offer Marx's views and ideas regarding the work of several prominent anthropologists and ethnologists of the time: **Lewis Henry Morgan**, John Budd Phear, Henry Sumner Maine, and John Lubbock. Marx's interest in ancient societies was long-standing and informed many of his theories of the origin of the state and the development of **capitalism** outlined throughout much of his work. Much of the attention paid to Phear, Maine, and Lubbock are polemical and critical. However, most of the notes are on Morgan's ideas—particularly those outlined in Morgan's *Ancient Society* (Morgan 1877). Notably, **Engels** drew heavily from *Ancient Society* (and partially from Marx's notes) for his

1884 manuscript *Origin of the Family, Private Property and the State*, and Marx's notes confirm that Engels and Marx fundamentally agreed on most of the ideas presented in *Origin of the Family*.

Marx read Morgan's *Ancient Society* in 1880, and in it, he saw support for his **historical materialism**–based understanding of the **evolution** of human social systems. Morgan's work focused on empirical and material understandings of the nature of changes in such social realms as the family, the state, and the origins of **private property**. His basic premise that changes in the sources of subsistence result in changes to other parts of society (in a more or less progressive linear manner) is similar in many ways to Marx's analysis of the relationship between the **mode of production** and **superstructure**. *See also* PREFACE, THE.

EVOLUTION. The idea of historical progress, which contends that human societies pass through stages of development, grew out of the **Enlightenment** philosophical traditions. Many thinkers in Marx's day commonly held an evolutionary view. Further, the idea that social forms inevitably change is one that was central to **Hegelian dialectics**, which served as the basis for Marx's theoretical approach to understanding the world. As such, evolution—change in ideas, social forms, economic organization, and political organization—was a central concept for Marx's ideas about history and the role of **revolution** in the progress of historical development. This approach to history, known as **historical materialism**, holds that there are predictable forms through which societies pass. These stages are determined primarily by the dominant material **forces of production** and associated **relations of production** and where revolutionary changes in form (from **primitive communism** to **feudalism** to **capitalism** and ultimately to **communism**) occur due to inherent conflicts in the system.

Charles Darwin published *On the Origin of Species* in 1859, outlining the theory of evolution by natural selection: a formalized, materialist framework for biological change in species. Although Marx had already begun formulating his ideas about changes in social

forms by the time Darwin published *Origin*, the book was well received by Marx, who called it an "epoch-making work" (Marx 1867/1976, 460) and "the book which contains the basis in natural history for our view" (Marx and Engels 1975b, 232). That Darwin explained nature using the same historical and materialist principles underlying his explanation of human societies was, for Marx, confirmation of the correctness of his approach. The link between Darwin's ideas of natural selection and evolution and Marx's ideas about the evolution of human societies was perhaps best summarized at Marx's funeral in 1883 by **Engels**'s **Eulogy for Marx**: "just as Darwin discovered the law of development of organic nature, so Marx discovered the law of development of human history" (467). *See also* DIALECTICAL MATERIALISM, HISTORICAL MATERIALISM, SOCIAL EVOLUTION.

EVOLUTIONARY SOCIALISM. In contrast to **revolutionary socialism**, evolutionary socialism proposes that a socialist, class-free society can come about through nonviolent incremental changes won through democratic processes rather than through **violent revolution**. During Marx's life and in the decade after his death, **Eduard Bernstein** argued this view most forcefully, with a full treatment in his 1899 book *Evolutionary Socialism: A Criticism and Affirmation*. Bernstein argued that, given the rapid economic **growth** in Germany in the late 19th and early 20th centuries, **capitalism** would successfully adjust to a growing middle class and would not, contrary to Marx's supposed predictions, collapse. Further, he warned against violent proletarian revolution as ultimately undermining workers' rights through the establishment of reactionary, autocratic, or otherwise undemocratic political systems. Evolutionary socialism is a central guiding tenet of the **Social Democratic Party of Germany**. *See also* SOCIALISM: UTOPIAN AND SCIENTIFIC, ZUSAMMENBRUCHSTHEORIE.

EXCHANGE VALUE. Marx argues in *Capital: Volume I* that **commodities** have two very different values: **use value** and exchange value. The use value is a measure of how useful a commodity is to society. Exchange value is a measure of the quantity of money (or other commodities) exchanged for a given product in trade. Notably, Marx points out that use value and exchange value need not be the same for any given commodity and offers a detailed critique of the interchangeable usage of different forms of value, arguing that philosophers and economists have frequently misinterpreted and confounded the different types of value.

All commodities have value, defined by Marx as the product of labor needed to produce the product. However, exchange value can differ from use value, according to Marx, due to a variety of factors, including the supply of a commodity, the existence of a societal need for a given commodity (or the demand for a product), and the degree of **fetishism of the commodity** that may act to distort the exchange value of a commodity. Further, exchange value represents the price required to purchase not just the product but also the labor needed to produce said commodity. While Marx was interested in detailing and understanding the underlying structure of market behavior and exchange, modern economics views exchange value largely as merely the **market price** (in monetary form) required to purchase any given commodity at a given time. *See also* LABOR THEORY OF VALUE, THE.

EXPROPRIATION OF LABOR. Private property exists when the **means of production** belong to private individuals. It has a very different character in terms of whether private individuals are **workers** or nonworkers. Individual workers who own their means of production are the foundation of **small-scale industry**. Marx avers that small-scale industry also exists under **slavery** and **feudalism**, but he asserts that it truly "unleashes the whole of its energy" only where the worker is free to set the conditions of his **labor**—owns the land and **tools** and controls the execution of the tasks. This **mode of production**, where the worker sets the terms of work, necessitates both small size and the dispersal of the means of production. It excludes centralization and enlargement, the **detailed division of labor**,

cooperative labor, and the social control of the forces of nature. "It is compatible only with a system of production and a society moving within narrow limits which are of natural origin" (Marx 1867/1976, 927–28).

This fragmented mode of production is, of course, **dialectical** and contains the seeds of its destruction. Small-scale worker–ownership relations that characterize this mode of production fetter new **material** forces and accompanying passions. A few then expropriate the individual fragments of production, removing the masses from the soil, their instruments of labor, and their livelihood. Marx details this expropriation in some detail in his writing on **primitive accumulation**. He characterizes the process as barbarous, using a variety of forcible methods that mercilessly transform the individual property of the many into the socially concentrated means of production owned by the few.

With the **rise of capitalism**, the old society decomposes, and new technological developments, organizational forms, norms, and values come to dominate. Rural **peasants** become urban **proletarians**, and their labor becomes **variable capital** harnessed to **constant capital** to increase the amount of **surplus value** expropriated by the capitalist. As **capitalism** evolves, the means of production becomes more **centralized and enlarged**, furthering the **socialization of labor**.

With this concentration, other developments take place at an ever-increasing rate: (1) conscious application of **science and technology**; (2) **industrialization of agriculture**; (3) cooperative, **socialized labor** suitable for **large-scale industry**; (4) the growing entanglement of all people into the **world market**; and (5) the ever-increasing international character of the capitalist regime. The capitalists, of course, monopolize the advantages of this system, and the exploitation of the masses grows. However, concurrent with these developments, the working class also increases in number. This class, concentrated in **factories** and **urban** environments by the **capitalist mode of production** itself, exploited for its labor, is primed for revolt. *See also* CLASS CONFLICT, CLASS STRUGGLE, MANAGERIAL SKILLED LABOR, WAGE GOODS.

EXPROPRIATION OF THE CAPITALIST CLASS. The **laws of capitalist production** lead to the expropriation of many capitalists by a few. As **competition** for markets continues, many capitalists fail, and others thrive and grow. "After every **crisis** one can see many ex-manufacturers in the English factory districts who are now supervising their own former factories as managers for the new owners, often their creditors, in return for a modest wage" (Marx 1894/1991, 511–12). Over time, capital concentrates into the hands of a few.

Consistent with Marx's theory of **historical materialism**, **monopoly capitalism** becomes a fetter on the further development of the mode of production. Millions are homeless, yet capital cannot produce housing without profit. Millions are hungry, yet capital restricts production or destroys food to prop up prices. Millions are **unemployed**, yet capital cannot integrate them unless there is a market for the commodities that they can produce. When the **crises** become severe and the proletariat becomes sufficiently conscious of their exploitation, they will revolt, expropriating capitalist **private property** and establishing a socialist society. Marx asserts that the coming **revolution** will not be as protracted or as violent as the **capitalist revolution** itself. That transition involved the taking of property and livelihood away from the mass of people by a few usurpers, but because of the prior expropriation of capital, the transition to **socialism** will involve the expropriation of a few usurpers by the mass of people (Marx 1867/1976, 930). *See also* OVERPRODUCTION, PREFACE, THE, ZUSAMMENBRUCHSTHEORIE.

F

FABIANISM. Its culture strongly influenced socialism in **England**. While inequality and attending economic injustice was present in the United Kingdom, a deep-seated cultural revulsion of revolution exerted a powerful influence on English socialism. This repulsion was particularly true for those members of the Fabian Society, a prominent variant of English socialism. The sobriquet "Fabian" drew on the Roman Quintus Fabius Maximus Verrucosus, who became known as "Fabius the Delayer" for his strategy in avoiding pitched battle with the Carthaginian army led by Hannibal during the Second Punic War. Members of the Fabian Society—who included such prominent members of the British gentry as Sydney and Beatrice Webb and George Bernard Shaw—advocated an evolutionary path to a more just society. A highly heterodox and elitist group, the Fabians rejected violence and confrontation as political tactics, believed strongly in the improvement of society through rational planning, and were instinctively repelled by most continental socialists' beliefs in **violent revolution**.

Part of the diversity of Fabianism lay in its intellectual wellsprings. Decidedly non-Hegelian thinkers, such as Auguste Comte, Samuel Coleridge, and the American Ralph Waldo Emerson, exerted varying amounts of influence and inspiration on Fabians, as did an earlier generation of English liberals, socialists, and utilitarian thinkers, such as John Stuart Mill and T. H. Green. The nonliberal nature of some Fabian thought is also present. Sydney Webb, for example, expresses the conviction that the "perfect and fitting development of each individual is not necessarily the utmost and highest cultivation of his own personality but the filling, in the best possible way, of his humble function in the great social machine" (Lewis 1952, 445). While Fabians rejected atomistic individualism and many Fabians found Marx's economic analysis in *Capital* illuminating, most rejected Marx's deterministic view of history and his inverted **Hegelianism** as a kind of metaphysics.

The Fabians were implacably committed to a gradualist approach to political reform. They rejected violence and rapid political change as likely to unleash uncontrollable forces and wreak unnecessary havoc. They believed that steady, remorseless pressure in the form of reasoned argument would eventually break down the barriers to reform and that initial reforms, once accepted, would create an impetus to more comprehensive reforms. Fabians generally favored the extension of voting rights, believing that the working class would support many Fabian initiatives. However, they doubted that an uneducated working class could correctly apprehend their collective interests and so advocated for the widespread extension of public education. Lewis (1952) wrote that the "intense practicality of Fabianism was based instinctively upon Burke's remark that the essence of statesmanship is in knowing how much of an evil to tolerate" (446). This doctrinal heterodoxy immunized Fabianism to some extent from Marx's tendency to excoriate allies who failed to hew to his exacting (if opaque) doctrine. In this sense, the Fabians resisted the lures of **religion** or religious fanaticism because of the group's relentless egalitarianism. No one positioned himself or herself as a prophet; indeed, it appears not to have occurred to any of them to do so.

Fabianism demonstrates the truism that, while all Marxists are socialists, not all socialists are Marxists. The Fabians represented an alternative interpretation of socialism, one that embraced a clear recognition of the connection between means and ends and one that expressed a commitment to participatory democracy. The Fabians exerted a significant influence on British politics, particularly in the formation and early platforms of the Labor Party. Many of its members were public figures and public servants. One of its founding members, Beatrice Webb, founded the London School of Economics.

Many second-generation Marxists, particularly future leaders of the **Social Democratic Party of Germany** like **Eduard Bernstein** and **Karl Kautsky**, who spent time in England due to **Bismarck's Anti-Socialist Laws**, were aware of and in some instances interacted with members of the Fabian Society. Some have claimed that the Fabians influenced Bernstein's evolutionary approach to **Marxism**, a charge Bernstein himself denied. In any event, the Fabians stood as a genuine force for reform in England, offering a more profound commitment to improving the living and working conditions of the English working class than the transactional palliatives of Tory Democracy. *See also* EVOLUTIONARY SOCIALISM, SOCIAL DEMOCRATIC FEDERATION, SOCIALIST LEAGUE.

FACTORY SYSTEM. Large-scale industry builds on the **detailed division of labor**, no longer dependent on skilled artisans. The worker becomes an **unskilled** minder of **machines** rather than a hierarchy of specialized workers in the **manufacturing** era. Besides, the simplified nature of the work—though incredibly boring and low paying—causes a rapid turnover of workers. The capitalist separates creative and manual labor in the production process. Both become the province of capital's rule over labor. Large-scale industry, with its reliance on machine production, has compounded this rule. The machine deprives the work of all content and meaning. "The special skill of each individual machine-operator, who has now been deprived of all significance, vanishes as an infinitesimal quantity in the face of the **science**, the gigantic natural forces, and the mass of **social labour** embodied in the system of machinery, which, together with those three forces, constitutes the power of the 'master'" (Marx, 1867/1976, 548–49). The capitalist misuses machinery, Marx writes; rather than serving man, it causes man to serve the machine. It makes the worker into a cog, a small part of a specialized machine. It makes the worker dependent on both the factory and the capitalist (547).

Discipline on the factory floor is much like the discipline in military barracks, with manual laborers and foremen becoming much like "the private soldiers and N.C.O.s of an industrial army" (Marx, 549), training men, women, and children to serve the machines, to become useful factory hands. Rather than the slave driver's lash, punishments are in the form of fines deducted from wages; often, Marx writes, such penalties are a form of profit for the capitalist.

Finally, Marx details the material conditions of the factories of his day. "Every sense organ is injured by the artificially high temperatures, by the dust-laden atmosphere, by the deafening noise, not to mention the danger to life and limb among machines which are so closely crowded together, a danger which, with the regularity of the seasons, produces its list of those killed and wounded in the industrial battle" (Marx 1867/1976, 552). Through the factory, capital robs the worker of the necessities of life—space, light, air, and protection from dangerous machinery, chemicals, and other contaminants. The factories, Marx opines, are little better than jails. *See also* BANKS, BRITISH FACTORY ACTS, *CONDITION OF THE WORKING CLASS IN ENGLAND*, CREDIT SYSTEMS, DESKILLING, EXPROPRIATION OF LABOR, JOINT-STOCK COMPANIES, RELATIVE SURPLUS VALUE, WORKING DAY, LENGTH OF THE.

FALLING RATE OF PROFIT. *See* DECLINING RATE OF PROFIT.

FALSE CONSCIOUSNESS. A term employed by Marxists referring to the role of **ideology** and **religion** in rationalizing an unfair set of economic relationships. Marx drew heavily on **Ludwig Feuerbach**'s analysis of religion as a kind of fantasy. Nevertheless, Karl did not employ the term itself. **Friedrich Engels** used the word pejoratively to describe a body of ideas conceived and configured to imbue existing class inequities with a legitimacy they could not otherwise assume. This view is illustrated in Marx's statement in *The German Ideology* that the "ideas of the **ruling class** are the ruling ideas, i.e., the class which is the ruling material force of society, is at the same time the ruling intellectual force" (Tucker 1978, 136). Marx consistently referenced ideology as a kind of gaslighting, as an illusion designed to deceive. After Marx's death, Engels's understanding of ideology evolved somewhat, continuing to refer to all nonproletarian "ideology" in a negative sense but elevating "**proletarian**" doctrines to a privileged, "scientific" status.

Aside from ideology, Marx and Engels also contended that morality and religion were significant sources of ideology or false consciousness. Society's moral rules and norms reflect **class divisions**; as such, ethical directives inevitably support the ruling class. People acting on some normative impulse are likely deluded. Plamenatz (1992) describes Marx's view of religion like this:

> Religion is the fantasy of man afflicted by the sense of his own inadequacy and will disappear when he is no longer afflicted. But why is he so afflicted? He is so because he lives in a social environment which does not allow him to realize his potentialities. He is the victim of circumstances which, though they are effects of human activities, he cannot control. He is the victim of forces which he has himself produced, though he does not know how he had done so. He engages in production to satisfy his wants, but the system of production is such that he is impelled into

courses which do not satisfy him. Only when man ceases to be the victim of the product system and the money economy brought into being by his efforts to satisfy his needs will he be able to live a full satisfying life. Only then will he cease to be a frustrated, a deprived creature, and have no need to resort to fantasy. (221)

This collapse of moral, ethical, and religious thinking under the heading of "ideology" helps to explain Marx's curt dismissal of religion as the "opiate of the masses" in Marx's *Critique of Hegel's Philosophy of Right*. While Marx's broader passage is not as comprehensively dismissive of religion as the decontextualized statements would suggest, Marx is contending that religion is a mere palliative, incapable of providing a cure for the **alienation** that is the source of distress.

Within the framework of **dialectical materialism**, false consciousness is part of the constellation of obstacles to overcome for the ignition of the **revolutionary** sequence. The **proletariat**'s progressive alienation and achievement of **revolutionary class consciousness** on the part of a critical mass of the working class are essential elements of the proletariat's emergence from the collective state of false consciousness.

FETISHISM OF THE COMMODITY. According to Robert Tucker (1986), Marx's assertion that **commodities** appear to be nearly self-evident is "really full of metaphysical subtleties and theological whimsies" (205). Tucker observes that Marx's use of "fetishism" dates back to the *Economic and Philosophic Manuscripts of 1844*. Marx describes the relationship between producer and product as a social relation but one confounded in some mystical way to obscure the labor that created the commodity. For Ollman (1980), "metamorphosis of value is a tale about man, his productive activity and products, and what happens to them all in capitalist society. Misreading this story as one about the activities of inanimate objects, attributing to them qualities which only human beings could possess, positing living relations for what is dead, is what Marx calls the 'fetishism of commodities'" (195). For Marx, the dominant social relationships within a capitalist society are relationships among objects, and their value derives from comparisons with other commodities rather than with the labor that produced it.

This worship or obsession with inanimate objects provides a powerful source of the broader **alienation** of the **proletariat**. An essential aspect of the fetishism of the commodity is the related fetishism of **money**, which is an advanced form of fetishism. As a vehicle of "stored value," money is the ultimate expression of **objectification**: people come to worship money as an end in itself. In his *Economic and Philosophic Manuscripts of 1844*, Marx wrote, "If I have the vocation for study but not money for it, I have no vocation for study—that is, no effective, no true vocation. On the other hand, if I have really no vocation for study but have the will and the money for it, I have an effective vocation for it" (quoted in Tucker 1978, 105). In capitalist societies, money—and the possession or lack of it and, in particular, the worship of it as the ultimate basis for social transformations—deranges social relationships with the external world and one another. Worship of money creates the foundation for **profit**, and the obsessive need for ever-increasing profit is the engine that drives the **immiseration** of the proletariat. Marx believed that one of the most critical actions of the "**dictatorship of the proletariat**" would be the abolition of money on the belief that in a **classless society**, money would be unnecessary and the incentives for such fetishes eliminated. *See also* DICTATORSHIP OF THE BOURGEOISIE.

FEUDAL MODE OF PRODUCTION. In Marx's theory of the successive **evolution** of socioeconomic forms driven by changes in the **mode of production**, Marx places the feudal mode of production as the formation directly preceding **capitalism**. He developed the concept most completely in the section "Pre-capitalist Economic Formation" in *Grundrisse* as well as chapter 47 of *Capital: Volume I*. According to Marx, the feudal system arose after the fall of the Western Roman Empire when western

Europe returned to small-scale subsistence agriculture. A new social form appeared to replace the clan as the primary organizational feature, and the relationship between **peasants** and **serfs** and landowning lords now formed the basis of legal citizenship. This **ruling class** is usually a nobility or aristocracy legitimated by some form of theocratic right. The aristocratic **landlord** leverages one's political and legal power to extract **economic surplus** from the peasantry. The landlord is, in turn, a **vassal**—subordinate to a higher-level noble who recognizes the landlord's authority in exchange for military services. All feudal systems have these essential characteristics, though the geographic span of this mode of production resulted in significant local variability in many social and economic aspects of the system.

In systems characterized by the feudal mode of production, Marx recognized the seeds for the subsequent **capitalist mode of production**. Notably, the development of new **productive forces**, such as mills, heavy plows, and other **technology** that increased agricultural **productivity**, was essential in generating surplus and enabling the **growth** of a healthy merchant class. Another critical development in this period was the increasing difference in **urban** and rural areas; for the first time, the **relations of production** were different in urban centers than rural agricultural areas, and Marx saw this development of trade and manufacturing in towns as an essential element in the transition from feudalism to capitalism. *See also* PREFACE, THE.

FEUERBACH, LUDWIG (1804–1872). Ludwig Feuerbach was a German philosopher. Feuerbach came from a prominent family and began his studies in theology but quickly changed to philosophy. He studied under **G. W. F. Hegel** at the **University of Berlin**. Scholars often link him to the **Young Hegelians**, a younger generation of German philosophers. Among this group, some— known as "Left Hegelians"— recognized the radical implications of Hegel's use of the **dialectical method**.

Feuerbach's most significant work was *The Essence of Christianity* (1841), which exerted considerable influence over several mid- and late 19th-century thinkers, including Karl Marx. Feuerbach suggested that **religion** was "a fantasy":

> Into his notion of God, man projects his idea of what he aspires to and cannot yet attain; he creates God in his own image, or rather in the image of himself as he unconsciously desires to be. His life to come, in the company and love of God, is the dream in which he seeks the satisfactions still denied him in the world. The idea of God expresses man's sense of his own worth, of the worth of his fully realized self. As his understanding and his opportunities increase, as he comes nearer to being able to live the sort of life which seems to him worthy of his kind, he will give up seeking in fantasy the satisfactions which he will at least be able to get in the real world. (Plamenatz 1992, 220)

While Feuerbach worked within Hegel's system of thought, he jettisoned the idea of "Spirit," arguing that Hegel was engaging in the externalization of human needs and aspirations.

Feuerbach deserves some credit for providing Marx with an avenue of escaping the influence of Hegel's **idealism**. While Marx retained Hegel's dialectical approach to philosophy, he jettisoned idealism in favor of **historical materialism**, viewing history in terms of **class struggle**. Marx's inversion of Hegel's ontology in preference for economic determinism provided a more congenial foundation for an emancipatory view of history and of moving beyond mere contemplation to "**praxis**," or the process of acting toward the realization of ideas. As Marx would declare, "The philosophers have only interpreted the world, in various ways; the point is to change it!" (Tucker 1978, 145).

Feuerbach's analysis of religion likely contributed to Marx's and Engels's characterization of religion as a part of **capitalism**'s "**ideological superstructure**," a component that serves to sustain and reinforce the legitimacy of capitalism, to imbue an otherwise oppressive system with the patina of legitimacy.

Others contributed to the role that religion would play within **Marxism**, but Feuerbach certainly added to Marx's and Engels's conviction that religion was the "opiate of the masses" and a powerful obstacle to the proletariat's development of **revolutionary class consciousness**. *See also THESES ON FEUERBACH* (1845).

FIRST INTERNATIONAL. *See* INTERNATIONAL WORKINGMEN'S ASSOCIATION (IWA).

FIXED CAPITAL. *See* CONSTANT CAPITAL.

FORCES OF PRODUCTION. Marx uses the term "**means of production**" about a range of factors included in the production process. The list consists of the **tools**, machinery, factories and **workshops**, roads and canals, and raw materials used to create something of value. In addition to these **material** aspects, the forces of production include **labor power**, or the knowledge and skills of those directly involved in the production process as well as the organization of collective labor. Previous labor power (also called **dead labor**) goes into fashioning the means of production—the tools, machinery, factories, and workshops—and thus is part of the forces of production. "Nature builds no **machines**, no locomotives, railways, electric telegraphs, self-acting mules [a machine to spin cotton], etc. These are the products of human industry; natural material transformed into organs of the human will over nature, or of human participation in nature. They are organs of the human brain, created by the human hand; the power of knowledge, objectified" (Marx 1857–1861, 706). However, it is labor power that is part of the forces of production, not the labor process itself. Marx considers the ongoing labor process—that is, the organization of work, **division of labor**, and ownership relations—as part of the **relations of production** and dependent on the forces of production. Again, work relations are part of the relations of production. It is the forces of production, or the way that a society wrests the material conditions necessary for survival from the environment, that determine the relations of production; together, the two form the economic **base** of a society

According to Marx and Engels, the forces of production form the base of sociocultural systems; this base is the determining element in history. However, while material conditions are "ultimately determinant" in historical change, superstructural elements (political, legal, philosophy, ideologies, and religious beliefs) react on this material base, often determining the direction, speed, and character of social change. It is not that Marx explains everything by reference to economic production. While the **superstructure** rests on the economic base, it is not that it is merely a passive effect. Engels (1894) clarifies: "Political, juridical, philosophical, religious, literary, artistic, etc., development is based on economic development. But all these react upon one another and also upon the economic base. It is not that the economic position is the *cause and alone active,* while everything else only has a passive effect. There is, rather, interaction on the basis of the economic necessity, which *ultimately* always asserts itself" (1).

Marx posits that, over time, the material forces of production come into conflict with the existing relations of production, that is, the property and work relations within which these forces have developed. The connections between the forces and relations of production are critical in Marx's theory. When the relations of production no longer promote the **growth** of the forces of production, when they become a fetter on their further development, **crisis** and the potential for **revolution** become possible. **Capitalism**, for example, fostered the phenomenal growth of **productive forces**—factories, tools, **technology**, labor power, and the exploitation of raw materials—but Marx posits that capitalist relations of production will inevitably constrain further development. As capitalism continues to expand, periodic crises of **overproduction** will ensue—markets will crash, factories will shutter, and unemployment will rise. These crises will become more severe as capitalism expands, capital enterprises become enlarged and concentrated, and the working classes become ever more significant in number and conscious of their exploitation.

At some point, Marx predicts the situation will lead to a **socialist revolution**. *See also* MODE OF PRODUCTION, PREFACE, THE, *WAGE LABOUR AND CAPITAL*, WORKERS AS CONSUMERS.

FORDISM. Fordism refers to the modern industrialized system of mass production and mass consumption of commodities and is named for Henry Ford, who was largely responsible for introducing the "assembly-line" style of **commodity** production (automobiles in his case). In this type of production, unskilled and semiskilled **laborers** produce vast volumes of standardized, low-cost commodities. The mass scale of industrial output allows a reduction in the price of such goods to the point that laborer wages are enough to purchase such mass-produced products. The term was first introduced and popularized in the 1930s by **Antonio Gramsci** and has been used among **Marxist** scholars since. Aldous Huxley also used the word in his novel *Brave New World. See also* ECONOMIES OF SCALE, LARGE-SCALE INDUSTRY, WAGE GOODS.

FOREIGN MARKETS. *See* WORLD MARKETS.

FORTY-EIGHTERS. The Forty-Eighters were European political refugees from the failed **Revolutions of 1848**, settling in countries in the Americas and Australia. Historians estimate that the German group who came to the United States to be about 4,000 to 10,000 (Dictionary of American History 2003). They contributed significantly to German American cultural life in the United States, especially in cities like Cincinnati, St. Louis, and Milwaukee, where German numbers were high. While hard liquor was the drink of choice in America at that time, German Americans brought their love of beer to the country. Politically, they tended to be abolitionists, equating southern **slavery** with the repressive aristocratic regimes in Germany. As a voting bloc in the Republican Party, German Americans, often led by these political refugees, were a progressive force advocating Lincoln's election and serving in the Union army and later took active roles in Reconstruction. "Throughout the second half of the nineteenth-century Forty-Eighters in the United States supported improved labor laws and working conditions. They also advanced the country's cultural and intellectual development in such fields as education, the arts, journalism, medicine, and business—notably insurance" (Lich 2010, para. 2). *See also* SCHURZ, CARL, WILLICH, AUGUST.

FOSTER, JOHN BELLAMY (b. 1953). Foster is a social theorist strongly influenced by Karl Marx's critique of **capitalism**. He is also the editor of the *Monthly Review*, an independent socialist magazine, the oldest continuous socialist journal in America (established in May 1949). Foster has written extensively on **ecology** (see particularly *Marx's Ecology*) as well as such topics as the **political economy** of capitalism, **imperialism**, **monopoly**, the increasing dominance of the financial sector in a capitalist economy, and American militarism. *See also* BANKS, CAPITALIST AGRICULTURE, METABOLIC INTERACTION, MONOPOLY CAPITALISM, WALLERSTEIN, IMMANUEL, WESTERN MARXISM, WORLD MARKETS.

FOURIER, CHARLES (1772–1837). Charles Fourier was a French socialist thinker and writer considered to be one of the primary founders of **utopian socialism**, a belief that an equal, ordered, and just society is possible. In his work, he maintained that mutual concern and cooperation among individuals could significantly increase not just the **productivity** of society but also the overall well-being of all individuals. He proposed the organization of communities into what he termed "phalanxes," where individuals would literally inhabit hierarchical levels within community buildings, with wealthier individuals on higher floors. The type of job would determine wealth, though he proposed a minimum wage for all individuals to eliminate poverty. Fourier was also an early supporter of women's rights, arguing that all jobs should be open to both men and women and that skill and aptitude should be the only characteristics considered in job placement.

Both Marx and **Engels** were highly critical of Fourier and the concept of utopian socialism. In one of his most famous pamphlets,

Socialism: Utopian and Scientific, Engels critiqued idealistic approaches to socialism, arguing that **scientific socialism**, such as the kind proposed by Marx and himself, was a much more practical, realistic, and workable approach to building socialist societies. *See also* OWEN, ROBERT, SAINT-SIMON, HENRI DE.

FRANCE. The French intellectual scene during Marx's lifetime was vibrant, and Marx developed both friendships and intellectual rivalries with several French thinkers—most notably **Pierre-Joseph Proudhon**. Marx first met Proudhon after moving to **Paris** in 1843 (beginning a relationship that was both friendly and antagonistic). At the time, Paris was home to several expatriates who fled their countries due to their revolutionary ideas and activities. Many critical events in Marx's life occurred while living in France, including his first introductions to Proudhon, **Mikhail Bakunin**, **Arnold Ruge**, and, critically, **Friedrich Engels**. While in Paris, Marx's first daughter, **Jenny Marx**, was born. During this period of 1843–1844, Marx also began working on what would become *Economic and Philosophic Manuscripts of 1844* (also known as the *Paris Manuscripts*, eventually published in 1932). At the behest of the Prussian government, France expelled Marx from Paris in 1845. He and his family then moved to **Brussels**, where they remained until 1848, when the **Belgium** government expelled them. Marx then briefly returned to Paris and subsequently to **Cologne** to participate in the **Revolutions of 1848**.

Like many intellectuals of his day, Marx was fascinated with the **French Revolution**, and though he never published a major work specifically focused on it, references to the revolution occur throughout his writings. Marx subsequently wrote several pieces covering contemporary events in France, notably the **1848 Revolution**, the **Paris Uprising**, and the **Paris Commune**. Marx wrote about these events in several works, including *The Class Struggles in France, 1848–1850*, *The Eighteenth Brumaire of Louis Bonaparte*, and *The Civil War in France*. Many scholars see these works as Marx's first attempts at analyzing contemporary events using his **historical ma-terialist** methodology. *See also* BLANC, LOUIS, BLANQUI, LOUIS-AUGUSTE, BONAPARTE, NAPOLEON, FOURIER, CHARLES, FRANCO-PRUSSIAN WAR, *GERMAN-FRENCH ANNALS*, LAFARGUE, PAUL, LONGUET, CHARLES, NAPOLEON III, SAINT-SIMON, HENRI DE, THIERS, ADOLPHE.

FRANCO-GERMAN YEARBOOKS. *See GERMAN-FRENCH ANNALS.*

FRANCO-PRUSSIAN WAR. Carried away by **nationalism** at the beginning of the Franco-Prussian War of 1870, many German Revolutionaries—including Marx and **En-gels**—supported the Prussian cause. Marx considered the French as the aggressors and the Prussian government fighting a defensive war. Marx wrote, "The French deserve a good hiding. If the Prussians win, then centralisa-tion of the STATE POWER will be beneficial for the centralisation of the German working class. German predominance would then shift the centre of gravity of the West Euro-pean workers' movement from **France** to Germany" (quoted in Stedman-Jones 2016, 488). With the French army defeated in a se-ries of battles culminating with the capture of the emperor, the people of Paris proclaimed a republic. The new government was more to the liking of Marx. When Prussia demanded the provinces of Alsace-Lorraine and the pay-ment of 5,000 million francs from France and began to arrest leaders of the **Prussian Social Democratic Labor Party,** Marx and Engels switched sides and declared their support for the French Republic. However, the new French government was ultimately defeated and agreed to an armistice. **Bismarck** refused to sign a permanent peace treaty with the French Republic and insisted on the election of a new French National Assembly, which would then end the war. "Duly held in Feb-ruary 1871, the elections resulted in a vic-tory for the conservative monarchists, who favored making peace, even a peace of de-feat. It was above all in Paris that pro-war rad-icals were victorious" (Sperber 2013, 378). It was the pro-war radicals who proclaimed

the **revolutionary** government in Paris on 18 March, or the **Paris Commune**. At the end of the war, the German states unified as the **German Empire** under Wilhelm I, and the Treaty of Frankfurt in 1871 ceded Alsace-Lorraine to Germany. *See also CIVIL WAR IN FRANCE, THE.*

FREE LABORER. The difference between a free laborer under capitalism and a slave is that the former has the "liberty" of changing his master and therefore thinks himself free. Citing Thomas R. Edmonds (1828, 56–57), Marx (1867/1976, 1027n) notes that the mo-tive that drives the free man is the threat of starvation and that what drives the slave is physical punishment. The master of the slave has some interest in keeping the slave in good health, but the master of a freeman has little care for the health of the worker in that the injury done does not fall on him alone but also on the entire class of capitalists. *See also* WAGE SLAVERY.

FREIKORPS. Freikorps (Free Corps) were volunteer military organizations that existed in Germany throughout the 18th, 19th, and early 20th centuries. In many cases, they were mostly mercenary or private forces that fought for either compensation or, in other in-stances, for patriotic or nationalistic reasons. During the Napoleonic era, the Freikorps often took on the role of a guerrilla force be-hind **French** lines, achieving praise and fame among German nationalists. After Germany's defeat in World War I, the Freikorps formed primarily from returning soldiers and were put to use by the ruling **Social Democratic Party of Germany** to suppress communist upris-ings, in particular the **Spartacus League**. The Freikorps were instrumental in the arrest of Spartacus League members and the assassi-nation of Spartacus leaders **Karl Liebknecht** and **Rosa Luxemburg**. The Freikorps also fought against communist revolutionaries in the Baltics, Poland, and Prussia in the period following World War I. The formation of the Nazi Party in the 1920s saw many former Frei-korps leaders take up positions of leadership in the party, though Hitler came to see many of the Freikorps units as potential threats and eventually targeted some of the Freikorps leaders for arrest or assassination.

FRENCH REVOLUTION (1789). Beginning in 1789, the French Revolution resulted in the overthrow of the monarchy and the feudal system and the establishment of a **French Republic**. The revolution had far-reaching implications throughout the world, leading to the establishment of many other republics and liberal democracies. The majority of the revolutionary events that occurred during Marx's time looked back on the French Revolution both as a predecessor and as a framework for a successful **revolution**. While Marx never covered the French Revolution as the primary subject of a significant work, he scattered references to it throughout his writings, especially those that focus on the historical trajectories leading to a **capitalist mode of production**. In *The German Ideology*, for example, he asserted that the French Revolution was "the most colossal revolution that history has ever known" (Marx 1845, 208). Subsequent analyses of Marx's voluminous notes suggest that he had planned to write a work focused on the revolution itself eventually. Of particular interest to Marx was the historical importance of the revolution in that it represented the end stages of the **feudal mode of production** and the establishment of **bourgeois** rule in **France**, all conditions Marx saw as an essential and necessary step toward an eventual **socialist revolution**. *See also* BONAPARTE, NAPOLEON.

G

GANS, EDWARD (1797–1839). A professor of legal history at the University of Berlin when Marx attended. Despite conservative Prussian dominance of the university, Gans advocated constitutional government, parliament, and guaranteed civil liberties. Concerned with the plight of workers, he rejected the socialism of Saint-Simon and advocated workers' productive cooperatives. Marx attended Gans's lectures. "The ideas expressed there clearly made an impression on the young Marx, and several passages in *The Communist Manifesto* would be taken, almost verbatim, from Gans's writing. Gans was a mentor and adviser in the making; had he not died of a stroke in 1839 at the age of 42, Marx's life might have taken a quite different path" (Sperber 2013, 60).

GENERAL GERMAN WORKERS' ASSOCIATION (ALLGEMEINER DEUTSCHER ARBEITER-VEREIN). Ferdinand Lassalle founded the General German Workers' Association (ADAV) in 1863. The goal of the party was to support and advance workers' rights and establishing a socialist government through lawful electoral processes. Marx and Engels initially endorsed the party and promised to write editorials for the ADAV's publication, *The Social Democrat.* However, they subsequently refused to provide support due to their disagreements with Lassalle. Wilhelm Liebknecht was also an early member of the ADAV, though he soon quit the organization due to its friendly stance with Otto von Bismarck's government. In 1875 in the city of Gotha, the ADAV combined with the Social Democratic Workers' Party of Germany to form the Socialist Workers' Party of Germany (SDAP). The SDAP was later renamed the Social Democratic Party of Germany, which still exists today as the oldest Marxist-influenced party in the world.

GENERAL LAW OF CAPITALIST ACCUMULATION *See* LAWS OF CAPITALIST PRODUCTION.

GERMAN COMMUNIST PARTY. *See* COMMUNIST PARTY OF GERMANY (KPD).

GERMAN CONFEDERATION. A league of states created by the Congress of Vienna in 1815 after the defeat of Napoleon. In 1866, after the Austro-Prussian War, Bismarck abolished the Confederation and expanded Prussia by annexing German states that fought on the side of Austria. In addition, he incorporated smaller states into a new North German Confederation under Prussian domination. This Confederation dissolved at the end of the Franco-Prussian War when the German states unified as the German Empire.

GERMAN EMPIRE. In 1871, concurrent with the Franco-Prussian War, Prussian leadership formed the German Empire (also called Imperial Germany). The southern German states, except for Austria, joined the North German Confederation in prosecuting the war and after the war in forming the new nation-state. Otto von Bismarck became chancellor of the new nation; Berlin became its capital, and a new constitution was approved; and the Prussian king Wilhelm I became emperor. Imperial Germany lasted until the end of World War I in 1918 with the founding of the Weimar Republic. *See also* ANTI-SOCIALIST LAWS OF GERMANY, COMMUNIST PARTY OF GERMANY, FREIKORPS, LIEBKNECHT, KARL, LUXEMBURG, ROSA, SOCIAL DEMOCRATIC PARTY OF GERMANY.

GERMAN-FRANCO YEARBOOKS. *See GERMAN-FRENCH ANNALS.*

GERMAN-FRENCH ANNALS (*DEUTSCH–FRANZÖSISCHE JAHRBÜCHER*). When Marx's editorship at the *Rhineland News* ended, he and **Arnold Ruge** decided in the spring of 1843 to coedit a journal called the *German-French Annals* with the goal of publishing essays by French and German radicals. The journal headquartered in **Paris** and anticipated both French and German authors and audiences. When Ruge fell ill, Marx took over editing the *Annals* but failed to get any French writers interested. While language was a barrier, "There were also political and intellectual differences that made cooperation difficult. Most of the French socialists the German editors met rejected political action as a means to bring about their new society, counting instead on the voluntary formation of communes, without the need for subversive activities or revolutionary struggles" (Sperber 2013, 120). Stedman-Jones (2016, 147) adds that the **atheism** of the Germans was also a factor in their reluctance to get involved. Marx did recruit enough German writers to put out a double edition in February 1844, including two articles by Marx and one by Engels. However, Prussian authorities confiscated the journal, and the venture failed. Shortly after its publication, the Prussian government pressured **France** to expel Marx. *See also ON THE JEWISH QUESTION.*

GERMAN IDEALISM. *See* IDEALISM.

GERMAN IDEOLOGY, THE (1845–1846). Written by Karl Marx and **Friedrich Engels** in 1845–1846 but never published while either

lived. In 1932, the **Marx-Engels Institute** first published the manuscripts in Moscow. Many scholars consider the essays included in the book to be the most direct and comprehensively detailed explanation of **historical materialism**, and in many ways, they mark the transition of Marx away from philosophical works toward works focusing on revolutionary materialism.

Much of the volume consists of criticisms of the **Young Hegelians: Bruno Bauer, Max Stirner,** and **Ludwig Feuerbach.** Part I appears to be a work from which the *Theses on Feuerbach* (first published in English in the 1932 version of *The German Ideology*) served as the initial outline. The major criticism was that the Young Hegelian belief that historical change is due to changing ideas (and therefore that ideas alone change the world) is wrong. Rather, to understand history, social change, and the nature of the current state of social and economic affairs (and, indeed, to understand the future of those things), we must look to the **material** world. For Marx and Engels, that involved analyzing how the **mode of production** influences and shapes social forms. Through criticism of idealist approaches, they outline the materialist understanding of such subjects as **labor, production, alienation, class conflict, revolution,** and the establishment of **communism.**

It was in *The German Ideology* that Marx and Engels first outlined their much-quoted vision of a communist society:

> And finally, the **division of labour** offers us the first example of how, as long as man remains in natural society, that is, as long as a cleavage exists between the particular and the common interest, as long, therefore, as activity is not voluntarily, but naturally, divided, man's own deed becomes an alien power opposed to him, which enslaves him instead of being controlled by him. For as soon as the distribution of labour comes into being, each man has a particular, exclusive sphere of activity, which is forced upon him and from which he cannot escape. He is a hunter, a fisherman, a shepherd, or a critical critic, and must remain so if he does not want

to lose his means of livelihood; while in communist society, where nobody has one exclusive sphere of activity but each can become accomplished in any branch he wishes, society regulates the general production and thus makes it possible for me to do one thing today and another tomorrow, to hunt in the morning, fish in the afternoon, rear cattle in the evening, criticise after dinner, just as I have a mind, without ever becoming hunter, fisherman, shepherd or critic. This fixation of social activity, this consolidation of what we ourselves produce into an objective power above us, growing out of our control, thwarting our expectations, bringing to naught our calculations, is one of the chief factors in historical development up till now. (9)

How this vision accords with Marx's later economic analysis on the necessity of capital's development of **productive forces** as a foundation for socialism is problematic. The image is more suitable to agrarian than to industrial **forces of production**.

GERMAN WORKERS' EDUCATIONAL ASSOCIATION (*DEUTSCHER ARBEITER-BILDUNGS-VEREIN*).

The German Workers Educational Association (GWEA) was an organization founded by **Karl Schapper** in London in 1840. Its purpose was to act as a public front and educational resource of the underground revolutionary **League of the Just**. After the reorganization of the League of the Just into the **Communist League**, the GWEA remained allied with the group. Ultimately, the Communist League split due to differences in opinion between Marx and Schapper, and the GWEA remained affiliated with the Schapper group, leading Marx to quit the organization. After the **First International** in 1865, the GWEA affiliated with the **International Workingmen's Association** and continued to operate until the crackdown on German political immigrants in **London** during World War I.

GERMAN WORKERS' SOCIETY. *See* GERMAN WORKERS' EDUCATIONAL ASSOCIATION (*DEUTSCHER ARBEITER-BILDUNGS-VEREIN*).

GODWIN, WILLIAM (1756–1836). William Godwin was a prominent **English** literary figure and one of the first modern proponents of **anarchism**. In his book *Enquiry concerning Political Justice, and Its Influence on General Virtue and Happiness*, published first in 1793, Godwin argued that while society was a source of good, government was always a source of evil. Ultimately, human perfectibility and progress would render it an unnecessary evil and abolish it. He also published many popular novels dealing with similar political and philosophical issues. Marx and **Engels** cited Godwin's work as having contributed to their theories regarding exploitation and noted that his popular work was effective in bringing issues of exploitation to the mind of the proletariat.

GOLDMAN, EMMA (1869–1940). Emma Goldman was a prominent American political activist who was instrumental in the development of **anarchism** in the United States and Europe in the early 20th century. A Russian immigrant to the United States, she was initially supportive of the **Bolsheviks**. Consequently, the U.S. government deported her to Russia in 1920. While in Russia, she met with **Vladimir Lenin** but became disillusioned with government-sponsored **Marxism** and, in particular, the Soviet state and its suppression of free speech documented in two of her books: *My Disillusionment in Russia* (1923) and *My Further Disillusionment in Russia* (1924). Leaving the Soviet Union in 1923, she continued her writing while living in **France**, **England**, and Canada.

GOTHA CONGRESS (1875). *See* GOTHA PROGRAM.

GOTHA PROGRAM. Following the internecine conflicts within the **International Workingmen's Association** and its subsequent collapse, Marx suspended his attempts to unify the various strands of European **socialism**. The LaSalle wing of German socialism favored working within the government for reform. The **Eisenach** faction, secretly supported by Marx, favored revolutionary action. Marx, in extended exile in **London**, had begun to lose influence even among his closest followers, such as **Wilhelm Liebknecht, Eduard Bernstein,** and **August Bebel,** who read the mood in the newly unified Germany as hostile to a **revolutionary socialist** movement. Liebknecht, in particular, had his feet planted in both the **Eisenach** and the **LaSalle** wings of German socialism. In general, by the mid-1870s, Marx's supporters in the **Social Democratic Workers' Party** were inclined to unify with the LaSalle-influenced **General German Workers' Association** and seek a voice in the new German government.

The two socialist parties held their Congress in Saxe-Coburg-Gotha in the **German Empire**; the two parties were to unite to form the **Social Democratic Party of Germany**. The compromise platform retained Marx's critique of capitalism but mostly embraced LaSalle's vision of a socialist-inflected nationalism. The platform called for many of the central political aspirations that united 19th-century socialists of all stripes: universal suffrage, freedom of association, workplace safety provisions, and limits to the **length of the working day** (16-hour workdays were typical). However, implicit in these progressive nostrums was an abandonment of any commitment to the overthrow of the capitalist system. This capitulation to LaSallean persuasions emblemized the mood of German socialism at the cusp of the formation of a unified German state, flush with nationalistic sentiments and yearning for its place in the sun.

Marx's reaction was to pen a vitriolic response, *Critique of the Gotha Programme*, in the marginal notes of the draft of the platform sent to him. As Isaiah Berlin (2013) noted, for Marx, the "program itself seemed to him to be permeated by the spirit of compromise—especially in accepting the permanent compatibility of socialism with their worst enemy, the state—and to rest on a belief in the possibility of attaining social justice by peacefully agitating for such trivial ends as a 'just' remuneration for labour, and the abolition of the law of inheritance—**Proudhonist** and **Saint-Simonian** remedies for this or that abuse, calculated to prop up the state and the capitalist system rather than hasten collapse" (249). Marx's

repudiation of the Gotha Program would be his last sustained articulation of a vision of **revolutionary socialism**, paving the way to a more just and, by necessity, stateless society. Nevertheless, the Congress approved of the original draft of the program with few changes. *See also* EISENACHERS.

GOTTSCHALK, ANDREAS (1815–1849). Andreas Gottschalk was a German physician practicing in **Cologne** starting in 1842, where he began treating indigent patients often free of charge and was publicly supportive of increasing access to health care to the poor and underserved. Subsequently, he became a prominent member of the Cologne **Communist League** and played a leading role in the foundation and leadership of the Cologne Workers' Association until his arrest in June 1848. After his release in December 1848, he remained in Cologne, where he worked as a doctor for the poor until his death from cholera in 1849.

GRAMSCI, ANTONIO (1891–1937). Antonio Gramsci was a founding member and leader of the Italian Communist Party. His *Prison Notebooks*, consisting of more than 3,000 pages of historical analysis, influenced the development of **Western Marxism** as an alternative to the more dominant **Stalinist** interpretations of **socialism** and **Marxism** of the mid-20th century. Gramsci's elaboration of cultural **hegemony** as an explanation for the persistence of capitalism and his criticism of Marx's **dialectical materialism** and the more deterministic elements of orthodox Marxism marked original contributions to socialist theory and established Gramsci's importance as a 20th-century political theorist.

Gramsci was born into an affluent family in Sardinia. Due to a childhood accident or as the result of Pott disease (a form of tuberculosis that deforms the spine), Gramsci grew up severely stunted and suffered poor health throughout his life. A gifted student, Gramsci won a scholarship to the University of Turin, where he studied linguistics and literature. He joined the Socialist Party in 1913; forced by ill health to suspend his studies, he began writing for socialist newspapers and developed a reputation as a perceptive and elegant writer. He worked as a socialist organizer as well, advocating for the formation of workers' councils as an organizing vehicle that he hoped would replace unions as the primary unit of working-class political participation.

Gramsci helped found the Italian Communist Party (PCI) in 1921. Gramsci traveled to the Soviet Union in 1922 and was a member of the **Communist International (Comintern)** and subsequently returned to Italy to assume leadership of the PCI. The Mussolini regime swept up members of the PCI and arrested Gramsci and following a pro forma trial sentenced him to 20 years' imprisonment. He would spend the next 11 years in prison, where—denied adequate medical care—his health declined rapidly until his death at age 46. Despite his ill health and the denial of access to any socialist writings, Gramsci wrote more than 30 notebooks, often in code to deceive prison censors, on a vast array of topics. He drew on a wider variety of sources than an orthodox Marxist, frequently referencing Niccoló Machiavelli and Benedetto Croce, the latter one of the most influential Italian intellectuals of the early and mid-20th century.

Gramsci's interpretation of socialism was decidedly unorthodox. He rejected the more deterministic elements of Marx's analysis, expressing skepticism that a **proletarian revolution** was "inevitable" in the industrially developed countries. Gramsci significantly expanded the concept of hegemony, first advanced by **Lenin**, to provide a much more granular analysis of Marx's **social relations of production**. Drawing on Machiavelli's fondness for martial metaphors, Gramsci argued that capitalism was more deeply "entrenched" than assumed by Marx and other **revolutionary socialists**. The capacity of the bourgeoisie to successfully impose a cultural hegemony connected to folklore, **religion**, myth, and, importantly, popular culture, internalized among the proletariat the sense that bourgeois norms represent common sense rather than norms that buttress oppressive social and political arrangements and institutions. Gramsci rejected Marx's view that material conditions would produce an inevitable revolutionary sequence; instead, he argued that socialist intellectuals must create a "counterhegemony" and wage a "war of position," a slow, often imperceptible war over control of political discourse.

Gramsci's convictions regarding the power of cultural hegemony led him to reject the more deterministic and positivistic aspects of Marx's analysis. Believing in the power of free will, Gramsci believed that people must contest and overcome cultural domination to pave the way to more durable communist politics. Gramsci viewed Marx's positivistic belief that the social sciences were similar to the natural sciences as a mistake and that socialists must appeal to workers on emotional terms. Whether Gramsci was more of a **revolutionist**—and committed to the violent overthrow of **capitalism**—or an **evolutionist**—and more committed to **social democracy** and an evolutionary path is a point of ambiguity over which Gramsci scholars have long debated.

As Dante Germino (1986) observed, Gramsci "defied imprisonment in any intellectual system. Instead, he produced his own theory of politics. His aversion to established intellectual schemes helped him develop the qualities of political theory at its best, including openness to new development, disinterestedness, the ability to distinguish the essential from the accidental, a determination to speak truth to power, and the discernment of the differences between a paradigm and a utopia" (291). Gramsci's resistance to subsuming his critical voice to any particular system of thought opened him to a broad vista of essential narratives. For Germino, the "most prominent quality of Gramsci's mind and spirit was empathy for those at the 'margins' of social life" (292). His capacity to draw on but avoid captivation by system-building philosophers like Marx lent him a distinctive voice and contributed significantly to his influence among 20th-century socialist theorists.

GROWTH. *See* PERPETUAL GROWTH.

GRUNDRISSE **(1857–1858).** The *Grundrisse* (or *Fundamentals of Political Economy Criticism*) is an unfinished manuscript written by

Marx in 1857 and 1858. In 1939, the **Marx-Engels Institute** translated, edited, and published an edition in Russian. A German-language edition was published in 1953, and it was subsequently published in several other languages, with an English translation appearing in 1973. Marx did not intend the work for publication. It consists of a series of seven topically wide-ranging handwritten notebooks that Marx wrote primarily for self-clarification of his ideas, many of which would eventually find their way into *Capital: A Critique in Political Economy.*

Grundrisse is some 800 handwritten pages long, and its subject matter is broad, covering many significant elements of Marx's key ideas found in his other published work. Throughout the works, Marx's analytical methods exemplify those associated with **dialectical materialism** and classic **Hegelian dialectics.** The introductory material consists of extensive discussion of production and the relationship between production, distribution, exchange, and consumption, demonstrating the interrelatedness of each of these concepts in the economy. The manuscript includes sections on **money** and the nature of **capital** and its circulation, outline Marx's theories on **exchange value, commodities, marketplaces,** and the **circuit of capital** that form the main ideas found in *Capital: Volume I.* A section devoted to production delves into Marx's ideas about the **relations of production** as well as the issues of **surplus labor, labor power, surplus value, profit,** and other related concepts.

Other key ideas discussed in the *Grundrisse* notebooks include discussions of precapitalist **modes of production** (including extensive examinations of the **Asiatic mode of production** and the **feudal mode of production**), the sources of the original **accumulation of capital,** the rise of **technology** and **automation,** and the characteristics and preconditions necessary for successful **revolutionary socialism.**

While many of these ideas found a treatment that is more systematic in *Capital,* scholars note that *Grundrisse* contains a thorough discussion of Marx's theoretical method of analysis. Marx does not explicitly discuss dialectical materialism and its analytical methods in *Capital,* though these methods serve as the basis for the analysis presented in Marx's later works. Many later Marxist writers see *Grundrisse* as a link between Marx's earlier philosophical works (such as *The German Ideology* and *Economic and Philosophic Manuscripts*) and his later, more mature scientific writings, such as the three volumes of *Capital.* In *Grundrisse,* Marx makes it clear that to understand concepts like production, one must use a historical approach and that the key to understanding these concepts is through generating abstract definitions using historical particularities and examples. *See also* HISTORICAL MATERIALISM.

GRÜN, KARL (1817–1887). A democratic-socialist politician and journalist, Grün played a major role in the radical politics of the era and the **Revolution of 1848.** Grün was a classmate of Marx at the **University of Berlin** and a member of the **Young Hegelian** group. Fearing Prussian arrest for his radical activities, Grün left the German states in 1844 and moved to **Belgium.** In 1848, the government expelled him along with Marx, and he moved to **Paris.** There, he worked with **Pierre-Joseph Proudhon** and became an acquaintance of **Mikhail Bakunin.** When the **Revolution of 1848** spread to states in Germany, Grün returned. Settling in **Trier** and again taking up journalism and democratic politics, supporters elected him to the short-lived Prussian National Assembly. When the Prussian government dissolved the Assembly, Grün organized a protest rally that turned violent. Prussia charged him with "intellectual responsibility" for the violence and, after trial, sentenced him to prison. On his release, he returned to Belgium, where he lived from 1850 to 1861 and worked as a tutor and writing **political-economic** criticism. Grün returned to the German states in 1861 when Prussia granted amnesty. He remained active in politics, opposing Prussia in the **Austro-Prussian War,** and after **Austria**'s defeat, he moved to Vienna in 1868, where he continued to write and lecture on democracy, materialist philosophy, literature, and the politics of the era until his death in 1887.

GUESDE, JULES (1845–1922). A **French** socialist who led the "intransigent" faction of the French Workers' Party, which he helped to found in 1880. Guesde was a close collaborator with **Paul Lafargue** (1842–1911), who had married Karl Marx's second daughter, **Laura** (1845–1911). Guesde began his career as a journalist writing in republican newspapers and journals during the Second Empire. Like many socialists of the period, Guesde spent the years 1871–1876 in exile in Switzerland, where he became acquainted with the works of Karl Marx. Returning to **France** in 1876, the government briefly imprisoned him for his participation in a congress of socialist organizations.

During the factional in-fighting that emerged almost immediately within the French Workers' Party, Guesde led the "Intransigents," a faction advocating the formation of an international workers' movement organized along revolutionary principles, against the "Possibilists," a faction of more pragmatically oriented leftists. In 1902, the French Workers' Party and the **Blanquist** Central Revolutionary Committee merged to form the Socialist Party of France. Guesde served several terms in the Chamber of Deputies. During World War I, Guesde moderated his revolutionary position, supporting the war effort and, at times, even expressing nationalist sentiments.

Guesde's interactions with Marx occurred in 1880 when Guesde traveled to London to share his draft of the French Workers' Party's platform. Marx helped with the redrafting of the platform but fell into dispute with Guesde over the purpose of the platform's demands for improvement in the treatment of workers. Where Marx viewed them as a basis for agitation, Guesde took a more calculated approach, seeing these demands as an inducement to lure French workers away from the more radical anarchist socialist groups competing with the French Workers' Party for support. This conflict provoked Marx to observe to **Friedrich Engels** that if Guesde and Lafargue were **Marxists**, then he himself was no Marxist.

GUEVARA, ERNESTO "CHE" (1928–1967). Born in Argentina, Guevara trained as a medical doctor. Traveling widely throughout South and Central America in the early 1950s, Guevara became convinced that **revolutionary socialism** was the only way to improve the lives of Latin Americans. He became Fidel Castro's second in command during the Cuban Revolution. "Influencing Fidel to move toward a more **Marxist** perspective from his initial anti-imperialist **socialism**, Guevara turned his attention to pursuing world revolution" (Johnson, Walker, and Gray 2014, 180). Rejecting Marx's assertion of the necessity of capitalist development before the **revolution**, Guevara espoused a version of **vanguardism**, called "*foquismo*," or armed struggle. He called for well-trained paramilitary units relying on speed of movement to evade entrapment by a country's armed forces and providing a "focus" for the poor. By demonstrating the impotence of regime forces to stop such attacks, Guevara argued that *foquismo* tactics could rapidly topple brittle **colonialist** regimes in the developing world, particularly in Africa and Latin America. His *foquismo* was much less successful outside of Cuba; special forces captured and summarily executed him in Bolivia after he failed to attract the support of the **peasantry**.

GUILDS. The guilds were a **feudal** form of **handicraft production** in which a master craftsman could employ apprentices and journeymen within stringent limits in terms of their number and duties. These rules of the guild placed severe restrictions on the transformation to **capitalism**. "A merchant could buy every kind of **commodity**, but he could not buy labour as a commodity" (Marx 1867/1976, 479). In addition, the guilds prohibited further **division of labor** within the workshop; if additional division was needed, new guilds formed to supply the old ones. The system isolated and perfected handicrafts, but it excluded the "autonomy of the **means of production**," including the **detailed division of labor** necessary for **manufacture** (480). Marx adds that while the division of labor at large can exist in many types of societies, the detailed division of labor as it exists in the **manufacture period** is specific to the **capitalist mode of**

production. *See also* COMMODITY, HANDI-CRAFT PRODUCTION.

GUILLAUME, JAMES (1844–1916). Guillaume was **Mikhail Bakunin**'s friend and right-hand man and a leading member of the **anarchist** wing of the **First International**. Even before meeting Bakunin, he was one of the founding members of the **International** in Switzerland in 1866 and attended all its conferences and also wrote a four-volume history of the organization (**Marxist Internet Archives**, Bakunin Archive). Marx had him expelled from the International, along with Bakunin, at the 1872 **Hague Conference**. In addition to several socialist and anarchist works of his own, Guillaume edited the last five of the six volumes of Bakunin's collected works. He also wrote a brief biographical sketch of Bakunin as an introduction to these works.

H

HAASE, HUGO (1836–1919). Hugo Haase was a German socialist lawyer and politician who served in the **Reichstag**. He was a prominent member of the **Social Democratic Party of Germany (SPD)** in the years just before and during World War I. Haase is notable as the first socialist lawyer allowed to practice law in **Prussia**. As a lawyer, Haase generally represented workers, journalists, and socialists. As a member of the Reichstag, he opposed the vote for the appropriation of funds for the war effort but went along with the rest of the SPD in an optimistic political environment in Germany, where most were confident of a quick and decisive victory. As the war quickly degenerated into a seemingly unwinnable quagmire, Haase led a significant faction of the SPD in opposing the continuation of the war effort.

Following the death of **August Bebel**, the SPD selected Haase and **Friedrich Ebert** as cochairmen. However, Haase and several other influential SPD members split from the party in 1917, forming the **Independent Social Democratic Party of Germany (USPD)**, which earned him a great deal of hostility among rank-and-file SPD members. He rejected the appeals of those former SPD members who called for a violent **proletarian** overthrow of the German state but was appalled by the brutal and violent suppression of the **Spartacist Uprising** by the Provisional Government following the **German Empire**'s defeat in World War I. In early 1919, Haase unsuccessfully called for the reunification of the SPD and the USPD.

Haase, like many socialists in the immediate post–World War I era, was assassinated in late 1919. Like many SPD parliamentarians, Haase was not a doctrinaire **Marxist**; instead, he adhered to a less revolution-minded culture within the organization. These pragmatic socialists resisted Marx's and **Engels**'s aspirations for using the SPD as a platform for **revolution**.

HAGUE CONGRESS, THE (1872). The fifth congress held by the **International Workingmen's Association (IWA)**. In preparations for the September conference, Marx outmaneuvered **Mikhail Bakunin**, ensuring majority support for his positions in control of the **International**. Marx pushed for the organization's support for the establishment of **proletarian** political parties. "His slate for the officers of the Congress handily beat out that of the Bakuninists. Votes on crucial issues—the reaffirmation of the right of the General Council to suspend the membership of affiliated societies, the condemnation of Bakunin's International Alliance of Social Democracy, and the expulsion from the IWA of Bakunin and his right-hand man, the Swiss anarchist **James Guillaume**—went Marx's way, and by substantial majorities" (Sperber 2013, 513). Marx was planning to leave his leadership position in the IWA to concentrate on his economic writings, so he sought to neuter the organization rather than let it fall into the hands of **anarchists**. Toward the end of The Hague conference, **Engels** made a motion to move the location of the General Council of the IWA to New York City. With the passage of the proposal, the IWA gradually lost its relevance and by the late 1870s ceased to exist.

HANDICRAFT PRODUCTION. The production of goods by individuals or in **workshops** under the direction of master craftsmen of the **guilds**. Handicraft production tends to be small scale, with a simple **division of labor**, skilled workmanship, and the use of simple **tools**. It encompasses a wide variety of crafts involving textiles, woodworking, metalworking, and fashioning other materials for human consumption. Handicrafts were fundamental in the production of goods used in preindustrial societies and were the **mode of production** first adapted by early capitalists. *See also* CAPITALIST MODE OF PRODUCTION, DETAILED DIVISION OF LABOR, MANUFACTURE MODE OF PRODUCTION.

HEGEL, GEORG WILHELM FRIEDRICH (1770–1831). At the time of his death in 1831, Hegel was the most prominent philosopher in Germany. He is one of the most important figures of the philosophical school referred to as **German idealism**. As a student, Hegel studied classical Greek and Roman philosophy as well as the work of more recent

Bust of Georg Wilhelm Friedrich Hegel.

philosophers. Students of his writings, including Karl Marx, **Ludwig Feuerbach, Bruno Bauer**, and **Friedrich Engels** (a group generally referred to as **Young Hegelians**, whose collective work greatly influenced the work of Marx and later **Marxist** thinkers and revolutionaries), all went on to become prominent philosophers, thinkers, and **revolutionaries**.

Hegel's philosophical aim was to develop a system of thought to describe any aspect of reality (what he referred to as the Absolute). This process involves conceptualizing all thought as **dialectical**. That is, all thought consists of a thesis and antithesis, or competing and conflicting opposites; the goal of **Hegelian dialectics** is to synthesize the thesis and antithesis or reconcile the conflicting opposites to form a synthesis. For Hegel, the focus was on ideas. For example, the thesis may be any given idea and the antithesis a competing or conflicting idea. The synthesis reconciles the conflict into a more complete "truth." This truth, in turn, becomes the new thesis, eventually opposed by a conflicting antithesis. The dialectical process is continual, and Hegel envisioned it as ultimately leading to a genuine understanding of the Absolute.

Although Marx was critical of the idealist base of Hegel's philosophy, the concept of **dialectics** was central to Marx's theory of **historical materialism**. Rather than the resolution of dialectical contradictions in ideas, however, Marx saw progress and change resulting from the resolution of contradictions present within material life. *See also* DIALECTICAL MATERIALISM, HEGELIAN DIALECTICS.

HEGELIAN DIALECTICS. Hegelian dialectics is a method of thought developed by German philosopher **G. W. F. Hegel** in which he utilizes the concept of **dialectics**—that all ideas have inherent in them opposing (or dialectical) sides, thought of by Hegel as a "thesis" and "antithesis." The goal of Hegelian dialectical thought is to reconcile these opposing or contradicting ideas into a "synthesis" that, through reconciliation, produces a new idea that is closer to the truth and ultimately can lead to a full understanding of reality as a whole—what Hegel refers to as "the Absolute." All aspects of reality (ideas, history, politics, economy, society, and the like) are subject to Hegelian dialectics, and progress toward understanding them can proceed only through reconciliation of competing or contradictory ideas. Although Marx was critical of the ideological focus of Hegel's version of dialectics, his theory of historical development and change (**historical materialism**) is a dialectical understanding of the world. For Marx, the inherent conflicts in any given social or economic system can, through reconciliation (or, in Marx's term, **revolution**), lead to change in the system toward an ultimate end. For Hegel, that end was an ideological notion of the Absolute; for Marx, the ultimate purpose was the establishment of a **classless society** characterized by **communism**.

HERR VOGT: A SPY IN THE WORKERS' MOVEMENT **(1860).** Karl Vogt (1817–1895) was a German scientist and politician. Active in left-wing political circles, he was a visible supporter of German democracy and unification. However, while exiled in Switzerland, he privately became a supporter of **Napoleon Bonaparte III**, and in 1859, Vogt published a pamphlet highly critical of Marx. Amid writing *Capital*, Marx replied in 1860 with *Herr Vogt*. In it, Marx offers a biting criticism of the contemporary politics of Napoleon and his czarist allies in Europe. Although it was not public knowledge, Marx was also able to deduce that Vogt was a paid agent for Napoleon and accused Vogt of such. Marx's work was meticulous, and his critique ruined Vogt's political career. After the fall of Napoleon, government documents revealed that Marx was correct. Napoleon's government had secretly paid Vogt 40,000 francs to support Napoleon and to attack Marx and other German revolutionaries.

HERZEN, ALEKSANDR (1812–1870). A 19th-century **Russian** writer and philosopher, Herzen was a child of an "irregular liaison" between a wealthy Russian landholder with familial ties to the Romanovs and a German Protestant daughter of a minor Württemberg official (then part of the **German Federation**) whom he never married. His father

nevertheless doted on Herzen, who was provided a lavish private education with a French tutor. He eventually did his formal studies at the University of Moscow, where Herzen discovered forbidden republican writings. Realization of his status as a privileged bastard child, was according to Isaiah Berlin (1998), "probably one of the determining factors of his life" (503). Herzen was, on several occasions, banished by authorities for possession of forbidden writing. However, his father's intervention frequently mitigated his exiles. His experience as an internal exile provided him with standing for membership in the dissident Russian intelligentsia.

In 1847, at his father's death and the inheritance of much of his father's considerable wealth, Herzen emigrated to Italy. He spent the rest of his life abroad, taking Swiss citizenship and traveling to **Paris**, Italy, and **London**. He launched a literary career, publishing the Russian periodical *Kolokoi* ("Bell"), widely read among the Russian émigré **populations** of Europe. His call for the emancipation of Russian **serfs** contributed to Czar Alexander II's abolishment of that institution in 1861. He also used his wealth to support itinerant socialists like **Pierre Proudhon**. Herzen's love of the Russian **peasantry** and his convictions regarding the ineluctable dignity of individual life oriented him more toward **anarchists** like his fellow Russian **Mikhail Bakunin** than **Marxists**. However, he ultimately became equally unacceptable to both anarchists and Marxists alike, as he was too republican for the anarchists and too libertarian for the Marxists. He was also too committed to individual dignity to accept the sacrifice of individuals on the altar of what he characterized as abstractions. He nevertheless exerted tremendous influence over Russian elite thought. The **Narodniks**, in particular, drew heavily on Herzen's writings, particularly their convictions regarding the innate virtue of the Russian peasantry.

HESS, MOSES (MOISHE) (1812–1875). Hess, an early socialist writer, led a weekly discussion and reading circle in **Cologne** on social issues and **communism**. Marx joined the reading circle in October 1842, when he became a journalist at the paper shortly after receiving his doctorate. It is in Cologne that Hess introduced Marx to socialism, though it was some time before Marx fully adopted (and adapted) the perspective. Hess was among the group of liberal Cologne industrialists, lawyers, and writers who founded the *Rhineland News* (*Rheinische Zeitung*). **Engels** also wrote several articles for the newspaper and on visiting Cologne met Hess, "who convinced him of the virtues of communism" (Sperber 2013, 138). Hess's ideas on the centrality of **cooperative labor** for human existence were to become central in Marx's **historical materialism**. Hess moved to **Brussels** in the fall of 1845 and lived next door to the Marx family, making plans with both Marx and Engels to publish a journal under their control, though the plans fell through. Hess also worked with Marx and Engels on the manuscripts of *The German Ideology*, though they published little of that work in their lifetimes. While in Brussels, tension developed between the three, some of it based on personal relationships among their partners, some based on differences in socialist theory. For the remainder of Hess's life, his relationship with Engels and Marx was somewhat strained—sometimes cooperating, sometimes in private slights and criticisms, and sometimes in open hostility between them. Hess later came to advocate a Jewish homeland in Palestine, thus becoming one of the first Zionists. *See also* BURNS, MARY, MARX, JENNY (NÉE WESTPHALEN), PESCH, SYBILLE.

HISTORICAL MATERIALISM. In The Preface to *A Contribution to the Critique of Political Economy* (1859), Marx summarized his **economic theory of history**. The summary begins with a discussion of the **forces of production**, which consists of the **tools, machinery, transportation systems, raw materials**, and **labor power** that go into the production process. The material forces of production cause men to enter into social relations with one another, independent of their will but indispensable to their survival. These **"relations of production"** are the economic structure of society. Together, the forces and relations of production

form the **mode of production**, which serves as the **base** for the **superstructure** of the social order, or the general character of the social, political, legal, and spiritual life as well as humankind's very social consciousness. "It is not the consciousness of men that determines their existence, but, on the contrary, their social existence determines their consciousness" (Marx 1859, para. 6).

At a particular stage of development, Marx continues, the material forces of production come into conflict with the existing relations of production, that is, with the property relations within which the relationships have developed. It is at this point that these property relations turn into constraints on the further development of the forces of production. As an illustration, consider the capitalist relations of production regarding agriculture—that is, the private ownership of the forces of agricultural production—oil companies, chemical and seed companies, farm implement manufacturers, farms, concentrated animal feeding organizations, food-processing plants, distribution systems, and supermarkets. In a time of capitalist crisis, amidst economic depression and widespread poverty and hunger, agricultural production operating under capitalist constraints cannot intensify production and profitably sell additional **commodities**. While **capitalism** has been a great intensifier of the forces of production, there will come a time of crisis, Marx hypothesizes, when further development of these forces—despite ever-growing need—will no longer be possible. "From forms of development of the forces of production these relations turn into fetters" (Marx 1859, para. 6). In such a severe crisis, social revolution throws off these constraints. If successful, the revolution will change the economic foundation of society and necessarily transform the entire superstructure.

In studying such transformations, Marx writes, one should make a distinction between the changes in the material economic conditions of production, for these are measurable and can be determined with scientific precision, and the ideological forms—legal, political, religious, or philosophic—in which men become conscious of conflict and fight it out. Such periods of transformation cannot be understood by these ideological struggles, for it is the contradictions of material life, the conflict between the forces and relations of production, that explain men's consciousness.

Karl's view of social change is more **evolutionary** than **revolutionary**. "No social order ever disappears before all the **productive forces**, for which there is room in it, have been developed; and new higher relations of production never appear before the material conditions of their existence have matured in the womb of the old society" (Marx 1859, para. 7). He then posits a broad outline of evolutionary stages: **Asiatic, ancient, feudal,** and the modern **bourgeois** (or capitalist), each epoch based on different methods of production, each a distinctive period in the economic history of society. Finally, he forecasts a new social order developing in the womb of bourgeois society. "The bourgeois relations of production are the last antagonistic form of the social process of production—antagonistic not in the sense of individual antagonism, but of one arising from conditions surrounding the life of individuals in society; at the same time the productive forces developing in the womb of bourgeois society create the material conditions for the solution of that antagonism. This social formation constitutes, therefore, the closing chapter of the prehistoric stage of human society" (para. 8).

HODGSKIN, THOMAS (1787–1869).

An **English** socialist and advocate of anticapitalist individualist **anarchism**, Hodgskin was considered to belong to the school of **Ricardian** socialists, a group of English and Irish political economists who saw in **David Ricardo** (and other classical political economists like **Adam Smith**) radically egalitarian implications. Hodgskin was born into a naval family in the Chatham Naval Dockyard and joined the Royal Navy at 12 and at age 18 served in the Battle of Trafalgar (1805). His criticisms of the brutal authoritarianism of the British Navy led to his eventual court-martial and dismissal. His first written work was a jeremiad on naval discipline. Hodgskin studied at the University of Edinburgh and subsequently traveled to **London**, where he became acquainted with the utilitarian thinkers Jeremy Bentham and James Mill, who sponsored Hodgskin's further travels and more in-depth studies.

Although influenced by the utilitarians, Hodgskin parted ways with influential utilitarians on major economic issues. For example, while utilitarians and classical economists supported "combination laws" that prohibited union formation, Hodgskin argued in favor of allowing labor organization, invoking Ricardo's **labor theory of value** to criticize income inequality. However, Hodgskin was likely never so much a socialist as he was an individualist anarchist. Hodgskin committed most of his later years to journalism, writing for the liberal magazine *The Economist* for 15 years. Hodgskin's career illustrates the relentlessly antirevolutionary character of British socialism. Hodgskin himself, although a consistent and trenchant critic of **capitalism**, hewed to more anodyne individualist anarchism than to the revolutionary visions of leftist anarchism prevalent in **France**, Germany, and **Russia**.

HOLY FAMILY, THE (1845).

During a short stay in Paris in 1844, **Friedrich Engels** met Marx face-to-face for just the second time, and in their conversations, it became evident that the two shared deep theoretical agreements. Marx suggested that the two of them write a critique of the currently academically popular idealistic philosophy and theory of the **Young Hegelians**. This meeting led to the first joint work between the two comrades. They divided the chapters between them. Engels finished his sections before leaving Paris (on his way to **England** for employment), and Marx, who had a larger share of the writing, finished his parts by the end of 1844, with the work published in early 1845. Marx drew a significant portion of his contributions to the work from his *Economic and Philosophic Manuscripts of 1844*.

The book is fully titled *The Holy Family or Critique of Critical Criticism: Against Bruno Bauer and Company* and was primarily a criticism of the **idealism** at the core of Young Hegelian thought—with particular emphasis placed on a critique of their view of **religion**. The title of the book, as well as many of the headings within the text, were bitingly satirical (e.g., the heading of Section 1, Chapter VIII: "Critical Transformation of a Butcher into a Dog"), and throughout, Marx refers to the leaders of the Young Hegelians (**Bruno Bauer** and **Max Stirner**) as "Saint Bruno" and "Saint Max." The apparent purpose of the book was to criticize idealist approaches and present their alternative materialist approach to understanding human beings and their societies. In doing so, Marx and Engels also outline their **dialectical materialist** logic, laying the framework for **revolutionary socialism**. They argue for an eventual **proletariat** uprising, making a materialist, dialectical argument that the proletariat and **private property** are opposites and, therefore, part of a single whole and that, ultimately, as the antithesis of private property, the proletariat will annihilate it. **Vladimir Lenin** later wrote extensively about *The Holy Family* (published as part of Lenin's Collected Works in the 1930s), drawing attention to it as one of the first clear arguments for revolutionary socialism.

HOLY ROMAN EMPIRE. A decentralized collection of kingdoms, duchies, free cities, and principalities governed by an emperor with limited powers over the various lords who had independence within their territories. **Napoleon** dissolved the Holy Roman Empire in 1806. **Trier**, the home of **Heinrich Marx** and later birthplace of Karl, was part of the empire until 1797, when it became part of the **French Republic** and then, after Napoleon's defeat, a province of **Prussia** (1815). The changes in the governance of the city had a profound effect on the life and career of Heinrich and, subsequently, his son. *See also* JEWISH LIFE IN TRIER, MARX, SAMUEL.

HUMAN NATURE. What essential characteristics make up a "person"? What do human beings need to create and sustain a political community? These sorts of questions form a vital springboard for philosophical inquiry. When Aristotle declared that human beings are "social animals," he was identifying human social needs as an essential and universal human trait, one that structured the kind of community that humans require to live meaningful lives.

Likewise, in arguing that human life within the "state of nature" (e.g., without government) was "poor, solitary, nasty, brutish and short," Thomas Hobbes was arguing that human beings are essentially egoistic and in the absence of overwhelming political authority will use force in the service of self-aggrandizement. Many regard such assumptions regarding humans as a starting point of political philosophy and political theory.

Karl Marx makes no explicit reference to human nature in any of his writings; however, his *Economic and Philosophic Manuscripts of 1844* establishes human beings as imbued with needs and drives, some "primordial" (e.g., food, sleep, sex, and the like) and some ineluctably creative, setting humanity apart. Rather than attempting to model some essential "human nature," Marx refers to humanity as a **"species-being,"** bound up within broader historical forces. Human needs were species needs, with people fulfilling these needs within the more comprehensive framework of Marx's vision. That vision included the **materialist conception of history,** or the interplay between the **forces of production** and the **social relations of production.** For Marx, the fulfillment of basic human needs was malleable: as the forces of production evolved, so too human nature evolves in response to changing **material** conditions. Marx appears to be less interested in delineating the essence of human nature than in contending that material circumstances shape human beings for better or worse.

Essential to Marx's treatment of human nature is his analysis of **capitalism.** He founded his entire project on the premise that human beings required emancipation from an economic system, a system that deranged human nature and **alienated** human beings from their creative capacities. In this broadly historical sense, Marx's thoughts related human nature to a historical **dialectical** transition. In Marx's mind, historical circumstances could not long contain humanity. Eventually, when the time was ripe, humanity would find a way to transcend the constraints of history and material conditions and more fully employ humanity's creative capacities. Marx was convinced that human beings were more fully human when unshackled by the oppression of an economic system obsessed with **economic growth** and **profit**. Once freed from concerns of basic material needs and the **division of labor**, liberated human beings would become fully "social beings." Marx famously discusses the emancipatory potential of a communist society in *The German Ideology* (1845):

> For as soon as the distribution of labour comes into being, each man has a particular, exclusive sphere of activity, which if forced upon him and from which he cannot escape. He is a hunter, a fisherman, a shepherd, or a critical critic, and must remain so if he does not want to lose his means of livelihood; while in communist society, where nobody has one exclusive sphere of activity but each can become accomplished in any branch he wishes, society regulates the general production and thus make it possible for me to do one thing today and another tomorrow, to hunt in the morning, fish in the afternoon, rear cattle in the evening, criticise after dinner, just as I have a mind, without ever becoming hunter, fisherman, shepherd, or critic. ("Private Property," para. 2)

For Marx, the achievement of a communist society would mark the blossoming of human nature and the full realization of human potentiality.

HYNDMAN, HENRY (1842–1921). Hyndman converted to socialism after reading Marx and formed Britain's first socialist political party, the **Democratic Federation**, in 1881. The party later changed its name to the **Social Democratic Federation** in 1884. Hyndman was an extremely unpopular leader, perceived as dictatorial and nationalistic and an anti-Semite. *See also* SOCIALIST LEAGUE.

I

IDEALISM. Idealism is a philosophical approach to questions related to epistemology or matters related to the nature of reality or knowledge (e.g., How do we know what we know?). There is potentially an ontological dimension to idealism as well. As an epistemological issue, idealism focuses on "Subject and Object," or how self-aware minds struggle to make sense of the world. What unites idealism of all variants is the significance of language as a mediating phenomenon between the mind and "external" reality, and this theory of knowledge was an essential feature of idealists' respective political philosophies. There are several variants of idealism, but for understanding Marx, discussion of the **German idealism** of Kant, Fichte, and **Hegel** deserves special attention.

Immanuel Kant (1724–1804) advanced a transcendental refutation of idealism that begins with the premise that the active, rational, and autonomous human mind categorizes phenomena in the world. These aspects of the human mind are "transcendental" in the sense that the mind's process of categorizing experience is universal. Kant conceded that while a "noumena" (or "thing-in-itself") may exist independently of human senses, there is no knowledge outside of human experience. Therefore, all that human beings know is "phenomenological" in nature; that is, knowledge is a product of human experience. In *The Critique of Pure Reason* (1781), Kant concluded that the physical world is "real" and transcendentally "ideal" and that the mind categorizes phenomena, creating a rational picture of reality.

Johan Gotlieb Fichte (1762–1814) built on Kant's transcendental idealism to establish an interpretation of idealism known as *Wissenschafslehre*, or "science of knowledge." He contended that the use of reason presupposes self-consciousness ("the I simply supposes itself"). Additionally, the self also imagines an objective world as well as a world of free and rational beings. The act of categorization involves a process and a transition from sensation to intuition to concept. Fichte stressed the "intersubjective" nature of knowledge: self-awareness is a compound cognizance of consciousness among other conscious selves. He contended that it is necessary to constrain individual freedom to facilitate a community of free beings and that a just community was an essential condition for self-consciousness.

George Wilhelm Friedrich Hegel (1770–1831) articulated a version of idealism described as absolute idealism and borrowed from his predecessors to erect a systematic philosophy that incorporated the entire corpus of cognition and action. Hegel criticized Kant for making a false distinction between appearance and "reality." Resolving the challenges that such false dichotomies produce requires the realization that "knowing or thinking and the object of knowledge or thought are but two sides of a single experience, separable in our minds but not in fact, and we must realize as well that knowledge is active and not passive" (Plamenatz 1992, 6). Hegel's idealism is also absolute in the sense that it claims to be comprehensive in explaining all human experience as well as assuming the rationality of human history as an unfolding of human consciousness. Hegel believed that a transcendental "Spirit" (e.g., Geist) imbues each historical epoch. Spirit is evolving, and self-creating, a manifestation of reality realized (somewhat mystically) through a dialectical synthesis of that particular historical epoch's "Spirit."

Idealist approaches to politics insist on the importance of language and experience, and that history unfolds according to some larger, **teleological** purpose, which Hegel described as the "cunning of reason." Idealists presuppose that existing political and economic relations fit the particular Spirit of a given age. They view political institutions from an idealistic perspective, as adapted to the needs of the evolving subjective consciousness of that historical period. Thus, Hegel could conclude that the modern state suited the needs of human beings in 19th-century Europe.

Karl Marx would begin his philosophical career as a Hegelian idealist but developed an alternative approach—**dialectical materialism**—criticizing the conservatism embedded in Hegel's idealism and, in particular, Hegel's view of the state as a potentially appropriate embodiment of "Spirit." According to Avineri (1968), Marx "accepts both Hegel's concepts and his system as a whole, and then subjects both to [Ludwig] **Feuerbach**'s transformative criticism" (13). Marx contended that Hegel hypothesized the German monarchy as idealized Spirit: "Marx saw, hidden behind Hegel's formula and the elevation of the monarch's will into general consciousness, the given historical situation which he felt should be viewed as it really was, not as an incidence of a general pattern" (15). Ultimately, Marx found Hegel's idealism too confining for his emancipatory project and discarded those aspects of Hegelianism that he did not need in favor of approaches that justified a more transformative politics.

ILL HEALTH OF KARL MARX. Karl Marx was often in ill health as an adult. His father, **Heinrich Marx**, suffered from pulmonary weakness, and the majority of his children were susceptible to consumption, with five of the nine dying before the age of 25 (Stedman-Jones 2016, 33). The military exempted Karl from service because of a tendency to respiratory illness. "From 1849 onwards he was afflicted by complaints of liver and gall. As **Jenny** told **Lassalle** in April 1858, Karl was incapable of writing to him at that time, because 'the liver complaint from which he was already suffering at the time—unfortunately it recurs every spring—had got so much worse that he has had to dose himself constantly'" (321). In addition to his genetic predispositions, the fact that he lived in poverty most of his adult life probably contributed to his suffering. After the death of his wife Jenny in 1881, Marx became ill with bronchitis and pleurisy, which, some 15 months after Jenny, led to his death in 1883.

Karl also complained of "boils" or "carbuncles" erupting on his skin, so severe were some outbreaks that they would often incapacitate him for weeks. Examining Marx's descriptions of this affliction in letters to **Engels** and others, Sam Shuster (2007), a professor of dermatology, established that Marx suffered from "hidradenitis suppurativa (HS)," a skin disease in which the apocrine sweat glands become blocked and inflamed. According to Shuster, the painful skin condition causes boil-like lumps, particularly in the armpits and groin, linked to more widespread infections; lesions on the body, scalp, and face; scarring; swelling, joint pain; and a painful eye condition. The condition can be very debilitating and may explain the difficulty Marx had throughout his adult life in keeping a steady work schedule. Shuster writes that

this new diagnosis has the importance of and beyond historical correctitude: the skin is an organ of communication and its disorders produce much psychological distress; it produces loathing and disgust, depression of self-image, mood and well-being. These aversive effects are particularly severe in patients with hidradenitis suppurativa, and there is much evidence of this in Marx's letters; in particular, Marx's hidradenitis contributed to his poverty and greatly reduced his "self-esteem," as he told FE [Engels] (24 Jan 1863). His loathing of the lesions ("curs," "swine," "Frankenstein" as he variously called them), and the **alienation** they produced is apparent from the violent joy of his attack on them: KM [Marx] to FE [Engels] 20 Feb 1866: "I took a sharp razor . . . and lanced the cur myself. The sang brule [burnt blood] . . . leapt right up into the air."

Shuster links the psychological effects of the disease to some of Marx's writings, particularly his theories of alienation. However, his radical political views, as well as his status as a political refugee for most of his adult life, could have had a similar effect on his psychological outlook. *See also* DEATH OF KARL MARX.

IMMISERATION HYPOTHESIS. Many commentators claim that Marx forecast that as **capitalism** evolved, it would impoverish the **proletariat.** Based on Marx's early writings, the **"pauperization"** hypothesis was "formulated before he had brought his theoretical understanding of the **capitalist mode of production** to its final, mature conclusion. It is only in the years 1857–8 that we have the birth of Marx's economic theory in its rounded, consistent form. After he had written *A Contribution to the Critique of Political Economy* and the *Grundrisse*, there was no longer a trace of any such historical trend towards absolute impoverishment [of the working class] in his economic analysis" (Mandel 1976, 70). In *Capital: Volume I*, he did assert that the **surplus population,** so necessary for the success of capitalism, would increase in numbers, **pauperism,** and misery, but the context of this assertion refers to the **unemployed** and semiemployed poor. Regarding the working class itself, he asserted that they would get a smaller share of the **surplus value** they produced and that even as their wages rise in advanced industrial societies, the system would continue to deny their human needs of education, health, leisure, housing, and culture. The needs of the worker "to develop a full personality, to become a rich and creative human being, etc.; these needs are brutally crushed by the tyranny of meaningless, mechanical, parceled work, **alienation** of productive capacities and alienation of real human wealth" (72).

In *Critique of the Gotha Programme*, Marx (1875) writes, "It was made clear that the wage worker has permission to work for his own subsistence—that is, to live, only insofar as he works for a certain time *gratis* for the capitalist (and hence also for the latter's co-consumers of surplus-value); that the whole capitalist system of production turns on the increase of this gratis labor by extending the working day, or by developing the **productivity**—that is, increasing the intensity or labor power, etc.; that, consequently, the system of **wage labor** is a system of **slavery,** and indeed of a slavery which becomes more severe in proportion as the social **productive forces** of labor develop, whether the worker receives better or worse payment" (Part II, para. 5). By the last line, Marx makes clear that he is not asserting that the wages of the proletariat must fall or that they will become pauperized as capitalism continues to evolve. *See also* INDUSTRIAL RESERVE ARMY, LUMPENPROLETARIAT, WORKERS AS CONSUMERS.

IMPERIAL GERMANY. *See* GERMAN EMPIRE.

INDEPENDENT SOCIAL DEMOCRATIC PARTY OF GERMANY (UNABHANGIGE SOZIALDEMOKRATISCHE PARTEI DEUTSCHLANDS) (USPD). Established in 1917 by **Karl Kautsky** and **Hugo Haase,** the Independent Social Democratic Party of Germany (USPD) was the result of a split in the **Social Democratic Party of Germany (SPD).** The USPD under the leadership of Haase called for an end to Germany's involvement in World War I and charted a centrist position oriented toward electoral revision and a milder, less revolutionary-minded version of **Bolshevism** (as opposed to the more revolutionary **Spartacus League,** which also formed out of this split of the SPD). By the time of the parliamentary elections in June 1920, the USPD had grown to more than 750,000 members, making it the second-largest faction in the Reichstag (after the SPD). The USPD split in 1920 over a debate on whether to join the Third **Communist International,** with the left-wing, pro-**Comintern** group merging into the **Communist Party of Germany** and the other half remaining as the USPD. Over time, differences in positions between the USPD and the SPD became less critical, and in September 1922, the two groups remerged as the United Social Democratic Party of Germany, then two years later readopted the original name as the SPD.

INDUSTRIALIZATION OF AGRICULTURE. *See* CAPITALIST AGRICULTURE.

INDUSTRIAL RESERVE ARMY. Engels first uses the term in *The Condition of the Working Class in England* (1845/1969) to refer to the **surplus population** of workers—the **unemployed** and underemployed. It is a critical means of capitalist accumulation. Engels writes, "From this, it is clear that English manufacture must have, at all times, save the brief periods of highest prosperity, an unemployed reserve army of workers, in order to be able to produce the masses of goods required by the market in the liveliest months. This reserve army is larger or smaller, according as the state of the market occasions the employment of a larger or smaller proportion of its members" (66). This army serves to keep wages down for the workers during normal times and puts a curb on their demands in times of prosperity (Marx 1867/1976, 784). Marx calls it a disposable workforce created by capital, always ready for exploitation when it is in the interests of capital to tap it. Under the law of supply and demand as it applies to labor, it ensures that the action of this law is limited to the needs of capital to "exploit and dominate workers" (792).

The growth of this surplus population parallels the **perpetual growth** of capital and the **proletariat**. Higher concentrations of wealth contribute directly to the "absolute mass of the proletariat and the **productivity** of its labour" and to the larger size of the industrial reserve army (798). Marx goes on to write that the more this army grows in proportion to **active labor**, the more extensive the **pauperization** of the industrial reserve army. This growth, he says, is the "absolute **law of capitalist accumulation**." Automation and recession swell the ranks of the industrial reserve army. In times of prosperity, the existence of the unemployed curbs wage demands and moderates the law

of supply and demand in favor of the capitalists, thereby allowing the capitalist to more efficiently exploit and dominate the workers (792). As **capitalism** accumulates capital, "it thrusts itself frantically" into old areas of production or entirely new regions, suddenly expanding markets. It is often necessary to expand the workforce suddenly without disrupting other industries. The surplus population supplies the fodder for the oscillations of boom and bust of modern capitalist industry (785). So essential is this surplus population for the existence of capitalism, Marx writes, that it is as if capitalism "had bred it at its own cost" (784).

INDUSTRIAL REVOLUTION. The Industrial Revolution began around 1750 in Great Britain and spread throughout western Europe and the United States over the following century (Horn, Rosenband, and Smith 2010). It was characterized by a transition from hand production methods and small-scale agriculture to new, technologically driven manufacturing and agricultural techniques, including the use of steam power and other **mechanized** machine **tools** and the **growth** of the modern **factory systems** of production. The massive increases in **productivity** made possible by these new technologies led to significant changes in society. Included among these changes was a gradual increase in life expectancy (and concomitant rapid increase in **population**) due mainly to improved sanitation and public health, nutrition, and the large-scale movement of people into urban settings (the location of most factories).

For Marx, the Industrial Revolution was the "climax of the long transition from feudalism to **capitalism**" (Heller 2011, 176). Industrialization introduced **capital** into the productive process, making possible the establishment of the **bourgeoisie** and **proletariat classes** that so concerned much of Marx's work. Further, increases in productivity due to technological improvements made the **exploitation** of the proletariat in the pursuit of extracting **relative surplus value** possible. Marx recognized the nature of economic and social changes leading up to the Industrial Revolution as well as the effects of this revolution on the rest of the sociocultural system. However, Marx argued that it was not the Industrial Revolution itself but rather the establishment of a **capitalist mode of production** that was truly transformative. The transition to capital began more than a century before the Industrial Revolution. The capitalist system adapted and intensified industrial production and employed industrial technologies to extract the surplus from the proletariat class rather than engage it for the betterment of all. *See also* LARGE-SCALE INDUSTRY, MACHINES, MANUFACTURE PERIOD.

INDUSTRIAL WORKERS OF THE WORLD (IWW). Formed by a loose confederation of **Marxists**, **anarchists**, socialists, and other radicals and proponents of strong **trade unions** from throughout the United States, the Industrial Workers of the World (IWW) formed in Chicago in 1905. Sharply critical of the American Federation of Labor's pro-capitalist positions and refusal to allow unskilled workers into craft unions, the IWW promotes a more Marxist view of the solidarity of all workers as well as revolutionary struggle to overthrow the employing class. When founded, it was the only American union to welcome all workers regardless of gender, nationality, or race and was open to membership from all countries throughout the world. For reasons unknown, members of the organization acquired the nickname of "Wobblies." The organization was involved in many labor disputes in the United States and abroad throughout the 20th century and faced many instances of government suppression. The IWW is still active throughout the world. The preamble to the current constitution begins, "The working class and the employing class have nothing in common. There can be no peace so long as hunger and want are found among millions of the working people and the few, who make up the employing class, have all the good things of life. Between these two classes, a struggle must go on until the workers of the world organize as a class, take possession of the **means of production**, abolish the wage system, and live in harmony with the Earth."

INNOVATION. As it relates to economics, innovation refers to the use of creativity and imagination to identify and apply **technology** to improve **productivity** or efficiency in distributing goods and services. Within Marxist theory, innovation in the form of technical change is the engine for **surplus value**, contributing to **the bourgeoisie's profits** and the **alienation** of the **proletariat** (Elster 1985, 143–54). **Competition** for market shares, as well as the **declining rate of profit**, creates powerful incentives for capitalists to pursue innovations. The resulting **mechanization** imposes downward pressure on the working class, threatening workers with both displacement and a downward spiral of wages.

For Marx, innovation tends to contribute to higher levels of **immiseration**, eventually fostering the gradual emergence of **revolutionary class consciousness** among the proletariat. In *Capital* and elsewhere, Marx predicts a **revolutionary sequence** culminating in the proletarian seizure of the state and the resulting period of proletarian rule that Marx described as the "**dictatorship of the proletariat**," a phrase expressly deployed by Marx only in his *Critique of the Gotha Programme*. After the **socialist revolution**, innovation would contribute to the replacement of **capitalism** with socialism, and further technological change would eliminate the compulsory need for work; relieved of the obligation to coerce people to work, labor itself would transform into a voluntary, pleasurable activity.

INSTRUMENTS OF LABOR. Marx defines instruments of labor as objects that are between the laborer and the product. The laborer makes use of these objects to work on other substances, using the physical or chemical properties of these objects to fashion **use values** consistent with his purpose (Marx 1867/1976, 284). Within this definition, Marx is including natural objects used as **tools** in gathering and producing food and shelter. The land itself is an instrument, though agriculture requires the development of many other instruments as well. These instruments of labor, Marx asserts, are as crucial to the study of prehistoric societies as are fossils for the study of extinct animals.

"It is not what is made but how, and by what instruments of labour, that distinguishes different economic epochs" (286).

Among the essential instruments of labor are tools and **machines** that enter directly into the production process. In addition, the instruments of labor include things that do not directly come into the production process but that serve as "objective conditions for carrying on the labour process," without which production would not be possible or greatly hampered (286). These would include the earth itself as well as instruments created by prior labor, such as **workshops**, **factories**, and **transportation systems**. *See also* ABSTRACT LABOR, CONSTANT CAPITAL, DEAD LABOR, LIVING LABOR, SOCIALLY NECESSARY LABOR TIME.

INTERNATIONAL DIVISION OF LABOR.

Marx argues that from its very beginnings, **capitalism** has had a **division of labor** that encompassed several nation-states. Under the spur of accumulation, capital expanded over the centuries to cover the entire globe. The capitalist world economy established long-distance trade in goods and linked production processes worldwide, all of which allowed the significant **accumulation of capital** in Europe. Political interests played a vital role in the creation of these economic relationships. Europeans created the modern nation-state along with capitalism to serve and protect the interests of capitalists. What was in the interests of early European capitalists was the establishment of a world economy based on an unequal division of labor between European states and the rest of the system. Also, their interests were in the establishment of strong European nations that had the political and military power to enforce this inequality. In addition to national markets, Marx (1867/1976) described an emerging **world market** based on a twofold division of labor. Different classes have differential access to resources within nation-states, and the different nation-states have differential access to goods and services on the world market. Political power very much distorts both types of markets—those within and those between nation-states:

On the other hand, the cheapness of the articles produced by **machinery** and the **revolution** in the means of **transport** and **communication** provide the weapons for the conquest of **foreign markets**. By ruining **handicraft production** of finished articles in other countries, machinery forcibly converts them into fields for the production of its raw material. Thus India was compelled to produce cotton, wool, hemp, jute and indigo for Great Britain. By constantly turning workers into "supernumeraries," **large-scale industry**, in all countries where it has taken root, spurs on rapid increases in emigration and the **colonization** of foreign lands, which are thereby converted into settlements for growing the **raw material** of the mother country, just as Australia, for example, was converted into a colony for growing wool. A new and international division of labour springs up, one suited to the requirements of the main industrial countries, and it converts one part of the globe into a chiefly agricultural field of production for supplying the other part, which remains a pre-eminently industrial field. (579–80)

For Marx, the capitalist world economy is a mechanism of surplus appropriation that is both subtle and efficient. Following his concept of **surplus value**, the world economy relies on the creation of **surplus** through constantly expanding the **productivity** of the labor force of constituent nation-states. It extracts this surplus for the benefit of the elite through the creation of **profit**. As with the extraction of profit through the creation of **surplus labor** within capitalist enterprises, it has the advantage of disguising the **exploitative** relationship. In such arrangements, it becomes difficult for the victim to identify the exploiter or even for the exploiter to recognize that they are **expropriating** surplus. All of it is left to—and defined by—market forces. In such situations, it is challenging to organize and coalesce against an enemy and difficult to revolt.

As with capitalism within nation-states, many contest the global power of capitalism. It is the subject of struggle, and there are internal contradictions that, over time, cause political and economic instability and social unrest. Eventually, according to Marx, a worldwide crisis will result, the exploited will revolt, and the system will necessarily collapse, opening the way for revolutionary change. *See also* FOSTER, JOHN BELLAMY, WALLERSTEIN, IMMANUEL.

INTERNATIONAL WORKINGMEN'S ASSOCIATION (IWA). The International Workingmen's Association (IWA), also known as the **First International**, is an organization formed in London in 1864 to unite international socialist, communist, **social anarchists**, and other left-wing groups and **trade unions**. At the first meeting, the organization decided to draft a program and constitution and formed a subcommittee to do the writing. The group elected Marx to the general council and as a primary member of the writing subcommittee, with several subsequent meetings in the weeks following the initial meeting occurring at his house. Ultimately, the subcommittee decided to defer writing to Marx as the sole author for the organization's founding documents. Among these documents was his inaugural address titled "Address and Provisional Rules of the International Working Men's Association," where he stressed the potential for positive achievements through cooperative actions and cited concrete examples of working-class organizational successes. The **International** grew in prestige and numbers, reaching a maximum of about 800,000 members in 1869 (some reports put the numbers as high as 8 million, though the "hard-core" membership likely never exceeded about 20,000) and had several successful interventions in labor struggles on behalf of its member European trade unions.

Antagonisms within the International, however, continued to grow. An **anarcho-socialist** wing, led by **Mikhail Bakunin**, advocated for a **Blanquist** approach to revolution, with Bakunin particularly against Marx's leadership in the International and highly critical of his belief in a **dictatorship of the proletariat**, opting instead for direct and immediate revolutionary action against European governments. After

Marx's support of the **Paris Commune**, Bakunin began organizing factions of the International under his control to overthrow Marx's leadership, which he deemed as authoritarian. This growing factionalism led to the expulsion of the Bakunists from the IWA at **The Hague International** of 1872 and the development of one of the most notable schisms in European socialism between anarchists and Marxists. This schism ultimately led to the dissolution of the IWA four years later in 1876.

INTERNATIONAL, THE. *See* INTERNATIONAL WORKINGMEN'S ASSOCIATION (IWA).

IRON LAW OF WAGES. An economic concept frequently attributed to German socialist **Ferdinand Lassalle** (1825–1864), who posited that the **price of labor** correlates with the minimum subsistence of workers; increases in the workforce would tend to lower subsistence wages, while decreases would raise them. Lassalle first invoked the phrase around 1863 but drew on earlier classical political economists like **David Ricardo**, whose more nuanced perspective on labor was that the "natural" cost of workers depended on the cost needed to maintain labor. However, Ricardo also observed that market forces could generate higher labor costs. Lassalle invoked this concept to reject the idea of proletarian "self-help." Instead, Lassalle called for an alliance between the state and labor, with subsidies from the state calculated to improve the lives of workers, implicitly dismissing the notion of both **class struggle** and a **classless society** as an attainable end point.

Socialists like Marx vehemently rejected Lassalle's economic views, rejecting the state as an unreliable partner. Marx accused Lassalle of fundamentally misreading Ricardo. In *Critique of the Gotha Programme*, published posthumously, Marx engaged in a sustained attack on Lassalle's economic theories, initially noting that "nothing of the 'iron law of wages' is Lassalle's except the word 'iron' borrowed from Goethe's 'great eternal iron laws'" (quoted in Tucker 1978, 534). For Marx, the reliance of the Gotha Program on Lassallean concepts signaled the adoption of moderate, evolutionary socialism, and republican principles. Negotiations by the **Social Democratic Workers' Party** for unification with the Lassallean **General German Workers' Association** amounted to capitulation and a turn away from the **proletariat**'s commitment to the **revolutionary** overthrow of **capitalism**. Marx derided Lassalle's republicanism like this: "It is as if, among slaves who have at last got behind the secret of **slavery** and broken out in rebellion, a slave still in thrall to obsolete notions were to inscribe on the program of rebellion: 'Slavery must be abolished because the feeding of slaves in the system of slavery cannot exceed a certain low maximum!'" (quoted in Tucker 1978, 535).

J

JANUARY UPRISING. *See* SPARTACIST UPRISING.

JEWISH LIFE IN TRIER. In the Middle Ages, the Rhineland was part of the **Holy Roman Empire**, and birth determined rights and privileges as well as obligations and restrictions. The "society of orders" regulated group rights. In Catholic-dominated **Trier**, for example, Protestants were forbidden to practice specific crafts, Catholic clergy had the privilege of collecting dues from peasants, and Jews had to pay special taxes and were restricted in what occupations they could pursue and where they could live. In 1794, French armies of the Revolutionary Republic conquered Trier and set about establishing their revolution there. In 1797, the French Republic formally annexed Trier. "Chartered privileges of the society of orders were replaced by a government in which all citizens were equal under the law, and in which the basis of sovereignty was no longer the hereditary property of a monarch but the will of the nation. **Guilds** were abolished, and occupational freedom instituted; seigneurial dues came to an end. The property of monasteries and the nobility was confiscated and sold at auction—in Trier and vicinity, about 9,000 hectares (the use of metric measures was another revolutionary step), or 14 percent of useful agricultural land, including most of the very best vineyards" (Sperber 2013, 7–8).

Napoleon Bonaparte ended the Republic when he declared himself emperor in 1804. In February 1807, Napoleon summoned some 71 rabbis and prominent Jewish laymen in his empire to the Great Sanhedrin in **Paris**. Among the group that attended was **Samuel Marx**, rabbi of Trier, the brother of Karl's father, Heinrich, and future uncle to Karl. Because of the Sanhedrin, rabbis became state employees like the Protestant ministers and Catholic priests within the empire. Also decreed were discriminatory laws on Jews, called the Infamous Decree, regarding the rights and duties of Jews. The Decree forbade them to exact usury from Christians or Jews. It levied mandatory licenses for Jewish dealers for them to engage in trade. It forbade Jews (though not Christians) to pay a substitute to serve in the military if conscripted. It required Jews to change their names to make them consistent with the needs of civil registration and encouraged them to engage in occupations such as agriculture, manual occupations, and the arts. In 1814, **Heinrich Marx** began studying to become a lawyer.

In 1815, the **Congress of Vienna** gave the Prussian state the Rhineland as a reward for participating in the defeat of Napoleon in the Napoleonic Wars. Prussia, a Protestant kingdom, had previously issued an Edict of Emancipation for the Jews in 1812; despite its title, Jews were now forbidden to serve the government as attorneys, even in private practice. For this reason, Heinrich Marx converted to Protestantism and was baptized into the Christian Evangelical church of Prussia sometime after 1816. Karl was born in 1818; his father had him baptized in 1824. *See also ON THE JEWISH QUESTION.*

JOINT-STOCK COMPANIES. Marx noted that the spread of joint-stock companies (corporations) represented a tremendous expansion of the scale of production, as enterprises that would be impossible for the individual capitalist would now be feasible. However, he notes, it also changes the nature of private capital, as its enterprises now *appear* as social in character ("corporations are people") though still acting "within the confines of the **capitalist mode of production**" (Marx 1894/1991, 567). The joint-stock company replaces the owner-manager of an enterprise by "a mere manager in charge of other people's capital" and pays a "wage for a certain kind of **skilled labor**." The capitalist becomes "a mere owner, a mere money capitalist"; the profit is a reward for capital ownership completely separated from control or even participation in the actual production process, merely appropriating "other people's surplus labour" (567). Marx continues,

> This is the abolition of the capitalist mode of production within the capitalist mode of production itself, and hence a self-abolishing contradiction, which presents itself prima facie as a mere point of transition to a new form of production. It presents itself as such a contradiction even in appearance. It gives rise to **monopoly** in certain spheres and hence provokes state intervention. It reproduces a new financial aristocracy, a new kind of parasite in the guise of company promoters, speculators and merely nominal directors; an entire system of swindling and cheating with respect to the promotion of companies, issue of shares and share dealings. It is private production unchecked by private ownership. (569–70)

The **credit system** is the basis for the transformation of private capitalist enterprises into joint-stock companies. It intensifies the development of **productive forces** and the **world market**, consequently causing contradictions between **production** and **consumption**, **crises**, and outbreaks of social violence. "If the credit system appears as the principal lever of overproduction and excessive speculation in commerce, this is simply because the reproduction process, which is elastic by nature, is now forced to its most extreme limit; and this is because a great part of the social capital is applied by those who are not its owners, and who therefore proceed quite unlike owners who, when they function themselves, anxiously weigh the limits of their private capital" (574). Marx argues that **capitalism** pushes to these extremes because nonowners are gambling with other people's money rather than owners, who are far more cautious regarding risks to their private capital. Moreover, these developments set the stage for the eventual dissolution of capitalism and the true socialization of these enterprises to serve the producers (the **proletariat**). *See also* COOPERATIVE FACTORIES.

JOURNALISTIC CAREER. *See* MARX'S JOURNALISTIC CAREER.

JUNG, GEORG ROBERT. A **Cologne** attorney and **Young Hegelian** who worked with **Moses Hess** to secure funding—through the sale of shares of stock—to fund an alternative newspaper in Cologne, the *Rhineland News*. Both Jung and Hess were much impressed with Marx's keen mind and invited him to submit articles when they established the paper in January 1842. They were also instrumental in hiring Marx on the editorial staff of the newspaper in October of that year and supported him against both stockholders and Prussian authorities when a government decree on 23 January demanded the paper cease publication on 1 April 1843. Jung remained a friend and admirer of Marx throughout his life. *See also* MARX'S JOURNALISTIC CAREER, *NEW RHINELAND NEWS, NEW YORK TRIBUNE.*

JURA FEDERATION. Around the middle of the 19th century, Switzerland had emerged from a period of intense religious sectional conflict. Inspired by the American experiment with republican government, the Swiss people achieved a consensus to merge the religious and economic interests of the Catholics and Protestants, along with the French-, German-, and Italian-speaking cultural segments of the

population. The resulting constitutional revisions abolished the Swiss nobility, legally banned (with minor exceptions) the deployment of Swiss troops abroad, and significantly liberalized its government. As a result, Switzerland's reformed government had significant incentives to loosen its immigration laws to stimulate economic **growth**, making Switzerland a particularly inviting country of refuge for European socialists and radicals who faced imprisonment in their home countries. In particular, the canton of Jura, comprised of Roman Catholic, French-speaking Swiss, developed strong antistate, egalitarian ideological sympathies among the watchmaking artisans in the Saint-Imier valley in this period, making the cities in the Jura region a particularly inviting sanctuary for those socialists with **anarchist** convictions.

The Jura Federation coalesced as a rival organization of anarchist-oriented socialists formed by **Mikhail Bakunin** in 1869 in Switzerland in a region where anarchist ideology had flourished. Bakunin recruited anarchist members of the **International Workingmen's Association (IWA)** as a potential base of support and as a way of opposing the "statist" thrust of Karl Marx's ideological aspirations. The IWA leadership accused Bakunin of forming a secret cabal within the IWA in 1871 and subsequently expelled him. The Jura Federation's meetings in 1872 demonstrated the strength of the "antistatist" faction of European socialism, as the defecting members of the IWA were vociferously opposed to Marx's conviction that the proletariat must seize and control the state and inaugurate a "**dictatorship of the proletariat**" to transition to a communist society.

Influential members of the Jura Federation included Mikhail Bakunin, **James Guillaume**, Carlo Cafiero, and Élisèe Reclus. Bakunin exerted exceptional influence in forming the Jura Federation, but ill health caused his retirement in 1873. In 1877, the recruitment of **Peter Kropotkin** as principal spokesman of **anarchism** caused a rift among Bakunin's original followers, causing Guillaume and others to defect from the organization. The subsequent source of conflict within the Jura Federation and among European socialists was the advisability and utility of the "propaganda of the deed," or the spontaneous use of violence and terrorism as a way of inspiring a more generalized revolution.

K

KAUTSKY, KARL (1854–1938). Karl Kautsky was a Czech German social theorist and one of the most prominent Marxists of the period following the death of **Friedrich Engels** to the onset of World War I. Born in the **Austro-Hungarian Empire**, Kautsky attended the University of Vienna, where he studied history, philosophy, and economics. He joined the Social Democratic Party of Austria in 1875. In 1880, he moved to Zürich, Switzerland, where he worked for a time for Karl Höchberg, a committed socialist who was engaged in smuggling socialist pamphlets and literature into Germany during the 12 years in which the **Anti-Socialist Laws** banned any socialist propaganda in Germany.

In 1883, Kautsky established the political magazine *Die Neue Zeit* (The New Times) in Stuttgart in southwestern Germany. He would retain the editor's position of that periodical until 1917, a position that provided both a steady income and a platform for advancing **Marxist** and **Darwinist** ideas. In 1885, he befriended Friedrich Engels and frequently traveled to **London** to help Engels's ongoing efforts in promoting Marx's theories within European socialism. Engels employed Kautsky in 1888 editing Marx's posthumous *Theories of Surplus-Value*, and in 1891, the **Social Democratic Party of Germany (SPD)** adopted Kautsky's rival draft of the **Erfurt Program** over **Wilhelm Liebknecht**'s initial draft, sealing Kautsky's reputation as a preeminent socialist theorist and authoritative voice of the post-Marx/Engels generation.

In response to **Eduard Bernstein**'s criticisms of Marxist analysis in *Evolutionary Socialism* (1899), Kautsky (among others) rose in defense of Marxist orthodoxy, accusing Bernstein of failing to understand the nature of **class conflict** and of embracing **Ferdinand Lassalle**'s brand of national socialism. Kautsky initially advised SPD deputies to abstain from voting for war credits in advance of World War I, believing that Germany would wage a principally defensive war against Russia. As the war progressed, however, Kautsky defected from the pro-war SPD, forming an alternative **Independent Social Democratic Party of Germany** comprised of those factions of German socialists who opposed the war.

After briefly serving in the interim German government following its defeat, Kautsky's prominence steadily declined. He rejoined the SPD in 1920 and during that period wrote a book about his travels in independent Soviet Georgia criticizing the **Bolshevik** regime's conspiratorial tendencies. In essence, Kautsky accused the Bolsheviks of replacing czarist absolutism with a different brand of authoritarianism. Kautsky joined Russian Marxist Georgi Plekhanov in believing Russia to be unready for a **socialist revolution**; lacking the necessary economic **productivity** to provide the required abundance, Kautsky and Plekhanov followed Marx in believing that Russia would need to develop through a capitalist phase before transitioning to socialism. Prominent Bolsheviks, in turn, characterized Kautsky and like-minded socialists as opportunists unwilling to recognize the historic nature of the Bolshevik's revolutionary undertaking.

Like his mentor Engels, Kautsky was a more deterministic, dogmatic thinker than was Marx himself. As much a Darwinist as a Marxist, his interpretation of Marx's **materialism** took on clear overtones of Darwinist **social evolution**. As a theorist, Kautsky offered evidence that the German **peasant** class was hostile to the political aspirations of the **proletariat**, and he provided a contemporaneous interpretation of **imperialism** to **Lenin**'s argument as the tertiary stage in the historical development of **capitalism**. With Engels, Kautsky shared a more naturalistic account of **Marxism**: where Marx's view of science was more contingent and malleable, Engels and Kautsky asserted a "scientific **dialectics**" as accessing eternal and unchangeable laws.

KINGDOM OF PRUSSIA. Prussia played a vital role in the defeat of **Napoleon Bonaparte** in the Battle of Waterloo, and it benefited greatly from the **Congress of Vienna**, regaining most of the territory that it had lost to the **French** in 1806 as well as some new territory in Saxony and the Rhineland. The kingdom then became part of the new **German Confederation**, a confederacy that included 39 sovereign states replacing the **Holy Roman Empire**. The German Confederation included Prussia's archrival, Austria. With the appointment of **Otto von Bismarck** as the prime minister, Prussia embarked on a program of unification of the German states under Prussian leadership. *See also* AUSTRO-PRUSSIAN WAR, FRANCO-PRUSSIAN WAR, NORTH GERMAN CONFEDERATION, WARS OF GERMAN UNIFICATION.

KROPOTKIN, PETER (1842–1921). A Russian aristocrat with a royal lineage, Kropotkin was a philosopher, geographer, scientist, and **anarcho-socialist** whose dissident activities led to his renunciation of lands and titles at a very young age. He served briefly in the Russian army and a greater length of time in Siberia working as a geographer; there, the experience of observing Russian peasants eking out a perilous existence on the steppes further radicalized him. He made significant contributions to the discipline's understanding of the topography of Asia. Kropotkin's writings have enjoyed an enduring influence among libertarian anarchists.

Kropotkin's travels in Europe as a geographer included a trip to Switzerland, where he joined the **International Workingmen's Association (IWA)** in 1872, although he developed a closer affinity with the more anarchist-oriented approach of **Mikhail Bakunin**'s **Jura Federation**. His return to Russia included his joining the Circle of Tchaikovsky, a diverse literary society of **Narodniks** that dabbled in revolutionary subversion. Arrested for his subversive activities, Kropotkin was able to use his aristocratic status to escape to Europe, where he traveled in socialist circles before settling in Geneva, Switzerland, and found work editing the anarchist newspaper of the Jura Federation. The assassination of Czar Alexander II caused his expulsion from Switzerland, and he traveled between **England** and **France**. The French government arrested him in Lyon for his membership in the IWA and imprisoned him for four years. He subsequently spent many years living in England, developing relationships with English socialists like **George Bernard Shaw**. In 1917, Kropotkin returned to Russia, where he quickly became disillusioned with the course of the **Bolshevik Revolution**. He died in 1921.

Kropotkin's principal contribution to socialist thought lay in offering an empirical basis for countering the movement of **evolutionary** theory toward social **Darwinism**. More than a generation younger than Karl Marx, the two never interacted, and Kropotkin was closer to Bakunin's convictions regarding the inherently authoritarian nature of the state, but he was also suspicious of the scheming and machinations of Bakunin. A libertarian anarchist, Kropotkin's central contention was that individuals have a natural right to well-being and that humanity's inherent tendencies toward cooperation and "mutual aid" provided a far superior basis for a coercion-free society than a centralized industrial economy backed by an innately violent state.

His first published work, *The Conquest of Bread* (1892), initially serialized in an anarchist journal, extolled the spontaneous communalism of Russian peasant villages coping with otherwise crushing poverty. His best-known work, *Mutual Aid* (1902), rejected the social Darwinists' claims that life involved a remorseless **competition** between eater and eaten. David Priestland (2015) observes of *Mutual Aid* that, "unlike Social Darwinists such as Herbert Spencer, who argued that all forms of life were driven by a competitive 'struggle for existence' between organisms, Kropotkin insisted that another type of struggle was more important—between organisms and the environment" (para. 8). Cooperation rather than competition was, for Kropotkin, the most significant contributor to the evolution of the human species.

L

LABOR. What distinguishes man from animals, Marx asserts, is that man first conceives what he builds in his mind. "But what distinguishes the worst architect from the best of bees is that the architect builds the cell in his mind before he constructs it in wax." Ideally, the worker first conceives the product of labor in her mind and fashions the material of nature to this purpose. This purpose determines her activity "with the rigidity of law" (Marx 1867/1976, 284). Marx goes on to say that this purpose is necessary to keep the laborer focused for the duration of the work. If the worker's purpose is absent—that is, if others determine the nature of the work, the **tools**, and the techniques they use—the more significant the resulting **alienation** of the laborer.

LABOR MARKET. The labor market refers to the supply and demand for **labor** in which employees provide the supply and capitalist employers supply the demand. The existence of an **industrial reserve army** supplements the **active labor army** in **capitalism**, which serves to moderate the supply side of the equation in favor of the capitalist. In times of expansion, **capital** calls the reserve army into the workforce and dampens the demands of existing workers on wages; in times of contraction, employers easily slough off the reserves. The flexibility of workforce size ensures that the rate of **surplus value** that the capitalist can extract from workers remains profitable. "If 'traditional' means of increasing or maintaining that 'reserve army' are drying up (where, for example, independent peasants, handicraftsmen

and shop-keepers have declined as a proportion of the total active **population**, or where substitution of **machines** for men in industry is slowing down), then new sources can always be tapped through sweeping transformation of housewives into wage-labourers; mass immigration of labour; extensive re-deployment of student youth onto the labour market, and so on" (Mandel 1978, 22).

LABOR POWER. Part of Marx's concept of the **forces of production** (or **productive forces**), the term refers to the skills, knowledge, and experience of the **labor** force. Marx defines labor power as the sum of mental and physical capabilities set "in motion whenever he produces a **use-value** of any kind" (Marx 1867/1976, 270). Labor power is the capacity for labor, not the labor itself. Along with the **means of production** (technological and resource factors such as raw materials, **tools**, and machinery), labor power is a critical part of the forces of production. The capitalist purchases labor power on the market, just as other components in the production process.

Marx writes that there are two necessary conditions for labor power to become a commodity for sale to the capitalist. First, the individual must be free to sell it as a **commodity** for a limited time rather than selling himself as a slave. Workers must treat their labor power as their "own property," a commodity that can be sold to a buyer and consumed for a specified period of time (Marx 1867/1976, 272). The second essential condition for labor power to become a commodity is that workers have no other commodity to sell and so are compelled to offer their labor power on the market to meet their material needs. *See also* MODE OF PRODUCTION, RELATIONS OF PRODUCTION, SOCIAL DIVISION OF LABOR.

LABOR THEORY OF VALUE. Marx's labor theory of value is a refinement of the classical economist's concept, particularly in the work of **David Ricardo**. According to Marx, the **law of value** governs exchange relationships between **commodities**; as **labor power** is a commodity under the **capitalist mode of production**, the law of value regulates the relationship between **capital** and labor as well. The **use value** of labor consists of specific commodities that it produces, such as a rug or a pizza. Departing from Ricardo, Marx makes a distinction between the concrete labor, which determines the use value of the commodity, and **abstract labor**, which determines their **exchange value**. By abstracting from its use value, it is no longer a table, a house, or a sweater. It is not the product of a carpenter, a mason, or a spinner. "With the disappearance of the useful character of the products of labour, the useful character of the kinds of labour embodied in them also disappears; this in turn entails the disappearance of the different concrete forms of labour. They can no longer be distinguished, but are all together reduced to the same kind of labour, human labour in the abstract" (Marx 1867/1976, 128).

The amount of **abstract human labor** necessary for its production determines the exchange value of a useful article. This abstract human labor is measured by the average labor time *socially necessary* for the production of a given commodity. Note that this is the *average* labor time, not the actual time to make the product. Capitalists strive to produce goods at or below this average labor time to maximize the **surplus value** extracted from their workforce and thus increase their **profit**. If it takes a given workforce to expend twice as much labor on a commodity than the society's average labor time for that commodity, the exchange value remains the same.

To summarize, commodities produced in the same abstract labor time have the same exchange value. The equating of different quantities of commodities in exchange depends on the socially necessary labor time for the production of these commodities. "As exchange-values, all commodities are merely definite quantities of congealed labour-time'" (Marx 1867/1976, 130). Under the capitalist mode of production, the production of commodities is specifically for exchange to reap surplus value. **Money**, according to Marx, is a universal commodity used as a medium of exchange as well as representing the exchange values of different products. Capital is the money and resources used to make more money or more exchange value. **Constant capital** acquires and maintains the material **means of production**, that is, the raw materials, **tools**, **machinery**, factories, and **workshops**. Constant capital cannot create surplus value. **Variable capital** is money invested in labor power; only labor power can create surplus value.

The law of value is very much the heart of Marx's economic analysis of **capitalism** and has all sorts of consequences for the system as a whole. For example, the competitive nature of capitalist society, as well as the drive for increased profit, pushes capitalists to intensify their production and increase the **productivity** of their workforce. The capitalist accomplishes productivity increases through the introduction of ever more powerful and efficient machinery as well as through a more refined **division of labor**. With this increase in productivity, the surplus value created by the workforce increases, but less labor time is needed to produce the commodity. Therefore, following supply and demand, the less the commodity's exchange value, the more products the capitalist must sell to maintain or increase profit levels. At the same time, because of increased machine production, there are fewer workers receiving wages to buy the commodities produced, thus draining demand. Consequently, capitalism goes through periods of **economic expansion and contraction** (Marx 1867/1976, 581–82). Moreover, this is but one of the **crises** that are produced by the **contradictions** between use value and exchange value within the capitalist system.

LAFARGUE, PAUL (1842–1911). A French revolutionary, political journalist, theoretician, and propagandist, Paul Lafargue was Marx's son-in-law, married to Karl's second daughter, **Laura**. He was born in Cuba to French and Creole parents, but he would spend most of his life in **France**, with periods of exile in **England** and **Spain**. In 1865, he participated in demonstrations as a medical student in France and was banned from all French universities and left for London, where he became a frequent visitor to Marx's house and met Laura.

Karl was not too happy with his manner of "paying court," taking a dim view of "all-too great intimacy" (Sperber 2013, 471). Once they announced their intentions to marry, Paul's economic prospects became an issue, Marx fearing that his daughter would live in poverty. "Before the final arrangements of your relationship to Laura, I must have serious information about your economic circumstances. . . . You know that I have sacrificed my entire fortune in revolutionary struggle. I do not regret it. Quite the opposite. Were I to start my career over again, I would do the same. Only I would not marry. As much as it is in my power, I wish to keep my daughter from the cliffs on which the life of her mother has been shattered" (471–72).

Nevertheless, Paul and Laura married in 1868 and moved to **Paris**. Although he studied medicine, he refused to practice it, instead trying his hand at a variety of occupations throughout his life. Rarely having a steady income, **Engels** often supported the family. While in Paris, Paul worked on behalf of the **International Workingmen's Association**. Following the fall of the **Paris Commune**, he fled to Spain, where he continued working for **the International**. Returning to London for 10 years and then France, he helped found the French **Marxist** party and was the first Marxist to sit in the French legislature. On 25 November 1911, Laura and Paul committed suicide together. Lafargue left a suicide note:

> Healthy in body and mind, I end my life before pitiless old age which has taken from me my pleasures and joys one after another; and which has been stripping me

of my physical and mental powers, can paralyse my energy and break my will, making me a burden to myself and to others. For some years I had promised myself not to live beyond 70; and I fixed the exact year for my departure from life. I prepared the method for the execution of our resolution, it was a hypodermic of cyanide acid. I die with the supreme joy of knowing that at some future time, the cause to which I have been devoted for forty-five years will triumph. Long live **Communism**! Long Live the **Second International**.

LANDLORD. The term "landlord" originated within **feudalism**, and Marx discusses the role of aristocratic landowners (i.e., landlords) in his description of the **feudal mode of production** (most notably in *Grundrisse* and in *Capital: Volume I*). Divine rights to political and legal power normally legitimized the feudal landlord. After the **capitalist revolution** and the establishment of the **capitalist mode of production**, political and legal systems align themselves to the new economic order. Nation-states allow for the ownership of **private property**, including land and other fixed features and resources (e.g., minerals, timber, and the like). Marx identifies four primary groups of the **capitalist class**, one of which are landowners who derive revenue from the rent of land. Marx's work was most concerned with landlords in the context of those who own agriculturally productive property and the political and legal systems that allow them to generate profits from the rent of that land to agricultural workers. In an essay titled "Rent of Land" (in the *Economic and Philosophic Manuscripts of 1844*), Marx criticizes the writings of **Adam Smith** on the nature of rent. Smith argues that the interests of the property owner are also the interests of society as a whole because they may increase the rent of land only through improvements to that land. The tenants who pay rent then derive revenue from these improvements through the sale of crops. However, Marx notes that given the domination of the capitalist class in legal and political systems, those landowners can exploit tenants, raising rents even when no improvements are made to the land by the landowners themselves. He notes, "It is absurd to conclude, as Smith does, that since the landlord exploits (through the collection of rent) every benefit which comes to society, the interest of the landlord is always identical with that of society."

Marx further argues that, unlike regular capitalist **competition** among the producers of consumer goods, the availability of land (and land-based products, such as minerals) is scarce and ultimately finite. As such, rent for agricultural land (or the price of minerals) is determined primarily by the highest production costs within an industry, resulting in higher surplus profits for those farms and mines that have relatively low production costs. Contemporary **Marxists** point to the confirmation of Marx's theory of land and mineral rent (often referred to as a general theory of rent) in recent economic patterns in energy production. The price of oil, for example, is determined by the oil fields, where the highest production costs occur, resulting in much higher profits for the cheaper oil fields. Although Marx did not explicitly write about landlords and the rental of domestic dwellings, its commonality in modern capitalist systems has led many Marxists to address habitation rental through the same general theory of rent. They assert that the contemporary system is one in which property owners hold virtually all of the legal and political power compared to tenants. Landlords, therefore, can exploit the tenant class through charging maximum amounts of rent without investing in actual improvement of the dwellings. This imbalance of power leads to significant problems with inadequate housing among poor segments of the **population**. *See also* MONOPOLY, MONOPOLY CAPITALISM.

LARGE-SCALE INDUSTRY. Large-scale industry is the second stage of the **capitalist** transformation of the **mode of production**. The first was the transformation of **handicrafts** to a **detailed division of labor** located in cottages and **workshops** under the control and organization of capitalists. In this stage, employers break up crafts into simple discrete steps and assign workers each simple task. This, Marx asserts, robs the worker of real skill and consigns him to repeat a simple task for his working life. The second stage completes the process in which large-scale industry further **deskills** and fragments the worker through yoking him to **machine** production. The employment of machines to increase the **productivity** of labor is the result of the application of **science** and **technology** in the service of **capital** (Marx 1867/1976, 482). By making the **worker** more productive, the capitalist can increase the production of **commodities**, thereby shortening "the part of the working day in which the worker works for himself, to lengthen the other part, the part he gives to the capitalist for nothing" (492). In other words, the industrial machine functions to increase **surplus value**.

The transformation of the mode of production in one industry often necessitated a change in others. For example, "machine spinning made machine weaving necessary, and both together made a mechanical and chemical revolution compulsory in bleaching, printing and dyeing" (505). The revolution in cotton spinning called forth the invention of the cotton gin, by which it was possible to produce cotton on an industrial scale. Finally, the revolution in large-scale industry necessitated a revolution in the **means of communication and transportation**. There was a need to transport massive amounts of raw materials as well as manufactured goods around the globe. There was a need to coordinate production and trade activities. Transportation and communications systems rapidly adapted themselves to the new mode of production of large-scale industry.

In the early stages of the machine revolution, **handicraft** and manufacture dominated their production, that is, through the use of the detailed division of labor and specialized **tools**. However, this material basis for producing machines proved inadequate over time. "Large-scale industry therefore had to take over the machine itself, its own characteristic instrument of production, and to produce machines by means of machines. It was not until it did this that it could create for itself an adequate technical foundation and stand on its own feet. At the same time, as machine production was becoming more general, in the first decades of the nineteenth century, it gradually took over the construction of the machines themselves" (506).

One of the earliest impacts of machinery on the worker was on the physical strength needed in the production process. Because the machine largely dispenses with the need for muscular power, the capitalist can employ women and children to tend many of their machines. Thus, one of the first results of the application of machinery was to increase the number of women and children working in the factory. This increase, of course, lowers the **labor market** value of men by spreading out the cost to the whole family. Now, in order to live, four people must give their **surplus labor** to the capitalist. Therefore, not only does the machine increase the productivity of the worker—and thus the short-term profits of the capitalist—but it also increases the number of workers that it exploits. A further problem with the widespread use of women and children in the labor process, according to Marx, is that such labor is no longer a "free" exchange of commodities, the capitalist possessing the **means of production** and the worker his **labor power**. Now the laborer exchanges not only his labor but also that of his wife and children. Marx writes extensively of the moral degradation of **capitalism**'s exploitation of women and children, citing **Engels**'s *Condition of the Working Class in England* as well as other writers.

A second initial impact of large-scale production on the worker is extending the **length of the working day**. There are several reasons for this relationship. First, according to Marx, is the greed of the capitalist. The capitalist must strive to get the maximum use out of a machine to maximize the surplus value extracted from his workers. Machine production, Marx writes, ties up a large portion of capital in a form that is capable of continuously returning value to the capitalist whenever it is in contact with workers and loses value whenever idle.

Consequently, he lengthens the working day to the maximum allowed by law and the physical limits of his workers. The capitalist feels justified in doing this because much of the work is less physically demanding. He can do this because the women and children he employs are more pliant and responsive to discipline than men. Access to this new class of workers, as well as access to workers laid off because of these technological **innovations**, produces a **surplus population** willing to submit to the long hours demanded by capitalists. Finally, the fact that the capitalists were successful early on in defeating, watering down, or ignoring the most meaningful industrial reforms proposed through government allowed them to lengthen the working day and freely exploit its workforce.

Along with the length of the workday, the intensity of factory labor also increases its pace with the unvarying uniformity of the machine. Nevertheless, there were limits to this. It is not possible to have both high intensity and long working days without worker revolt. However, once Parliament shortened the working day beginning with the **British Factory Acts** (1848), capitalists began intensifying work processes as well as the development of the machine system. Capitalists were speeding up the machines as well as giving workers more of them to supervise or operate and increasing the exploitation of labor power (Marx 1867/1976, 533–34). *See also* CREDIT SYSTEMS, EXPROPRIATION OF LABOR, FACTORY SYSTEM, JOINT-STOCK COMPANIES, RELATIVE SURPLUS VALUE.

LASSALLE, FERDINAND (1825–1864). Lassalle was a Prussian lawyer, socialist, and labor activist who offered an alternative vision of the role of workers in society. Jewish on his father's side, the government formally barred him from most avenues of political advancement, and by all accounts, he "threw himself with immense passion into the revolutionary movement, where his exceptional ability, his enthusiasm, but most of all his genius as an agitator and a popular orator, swiftly raised him to leadership" (Berlin 2013, 194). Lassalle was an intense, charismatic figure who exerted considerable influence among German workers long after his untimely death and decisively influenced the formation of the **Social Democratic Party of Germany (SPD)**.

Like many figures of the German left, the government jailed Lassalle for his activities in support of the **Revolutions of 1848**, but released him after only a six-month sentence. He was officially banned from living in **Berlin** for the years 1855–1859 but successfully appealed to the court of the Prussian king Frederick William IV. In 1863, Lassalle formed the **General German Workers' Association (ADAV)** and commanded a considerable loyal following among German workers. Within the framework of the then-fragmented German socialist movement, Lassalle had a complicated relationship with Karl Marx. Lassalle admired Marx's intellect and worked collaboratively with Marx where he felt he could. Marx, in turn, acknowledged Lassalle's genius as an organizer and agitator "but was repelled by him personally, and was deeply suspicious of him politically" (196). The origins of Marx's mistrust lay in Lassalle's republicanism: where Marx remained convinced of the necessity of a **violent revolution** to overthrow **capitalism**, Lassalle was a committed republican and advanced a kind of **trade unionism** joined to **nationalism**. Lassalle aspired to a type of "social monarchy" in which a unified German monarch would extend to German workers greater political rights and improved working conditions in exchange for support for a united German state. Such a platform, conjoined with Lassalle's vanity and ambition, could only disgust Marx.

Lassalle died an untimely death in 1864 at 39 years of age in a duel with a rival suitor. Lassalle's principal contribution to socialist theory is the **iron law of wages**, which declared that real wages would tend over time to align with the minimum salary required to sustain the life of the worker. His lasting legacy within socialism was the formation of the ADAV, which continued to organize and expand its hold within the German labor movement and persisted as the kind of nationalist republicanism that so vexed Marx and his followers. Marx would spend his remaining years struggling for the soul of the German **proletariat**. The merging of the ADAV and the **Social Democratic Workers' Party** into the SPD would bear Lassalle's imprint and provoke Marx's

stinging *Critique of the Gotha Programme*, in which Marx denounced the betrayal of the socialist principles enunciated in *The Communist Manifesto*.

LAW OF VALUE. According to Marx, the law of value governs exchange relationships between **commodities**. The law of value determines the relative amounts of **social labor** and **material** resources of a society that will be devoted to producing different products; it does this through governing the exchange values of commodities. Through these exchange relations, it distributes resources in response to effective demand. Mandel (1976) adds, "In the third place it rules economic **growth**, by determining the average rate of **profit** and directing investment towards those firms and sectors of production where profit is above average, and away from those firms and sectors where profit is below average" (41).

Value is a social construct. That is, value does not inhere in the commodity; social interaction determines value. It begins with a product, a good that satisfies a human need for others. Commodities have two types of value of concern: **use value** and **exchange value**. Use value is simply a quality that is useful to society. Every successful commodity produced under capitalism has a use value, or its production would not continue for any significant length of time. As use values, commodities differ in quality by their physical properties and have no existence apart from the product itself. Use values are realized in consumption; they are material wealth, but they are also the bearers of exchange value.

Exchange value, according to Marx, is a quantitative relationship between two different commodities. The relation between the two commodities changes over time and place. Nevertheless, an equation can express whatever the relationship may be at any one time or place. For example, a given amount of corn is equal to a given quantity of iron, or x pounds of coffee is equal to y ounces of wine. "It follows from this that, firstly, the valid exchange-values of a particular commodity express something equal, and secondly, exchange-value cannot be anything other than the mode of expression, the 'form of appearance,' of a content distinguishable from it" (Marx 1867/1976, 126–27).

This common element in such exchanges is in terms of quantity, Marx argues, as the physical properties of commodities constitute their use value. The exchange relation of commodities is an abstraction from their use values. One use value is worth just as much as another use value in an exchange of the appropriate quantities of the two. "As use-values, commodities differ above all in quality, while as exchange-values they can only differ in quantity, and therefore do not contain an atom of use-value" (Marx 1867/1976, 127). The use value of corn is qualitatively different from the use value of iron. However, the amount of iron exchanged for an amount of corn is a quantitative relationship that is socially determined. This exchange value differs in quantity over time and across societies. However, if in exchange the use value of the commodity is no longer a factor, what then is the common social substance of all commodities that is the basis of exchange value? Marx answers that it is **abstract human labor** (128). *See also* LABOR THEORY OF VALUE, MONEY.

LAWS OF CAPITALIST PRODUCTION. The laws of capitalist production are Marx's term for the constraints that the capitalist system puts on the individual capitalist and on **labor**. **Capital**, Marx writes, takes no account of the health or well-being of **workers** unless the government forces them to do so. In general, the welfare of the worker is not dependent on the character of the capitalist, whether that be good or bad. "Under free **competition**, the immanent laws of capitalist production confront the individual capitalist as a coercive force external to him" (Marx 1867/1976, 381).

It is the laws of capitalist production that motivate the capitalist to reinvest, to frantically search for new ways of **valorization**, to force workers to produce more for the sake of production itself, not for the enjoyment of **use values**, though the acquisition of **luxury goods** among capitalists grows over time. The main spur, however, is the external laws of capitalist production, which continually compels each

capitalist to increase his capital further without limit (739).

It is the laws of capitalist production and its inherent competition that forces capital to **mechanize** production, thus lessening the demand for labor while at the same time "setting free" workers into the **industrial reserve army**, which further depresses wages (793). Through this law, Marx relates the **growth** and success of capitalism to the expansion of **active labor army** as well as the industrial reserve army. The more extensive this reserve army, the larger the **surplus population** and the greater the **pauperism** of a significant section of the working class. "Like all other laws, it is modified in its working by many circumstances" (798). The modifications of the law might include the creation of new needs and industries to meet these needs, the development of a **world economy**, or the rise of welfare states that ameliorate some of the worst forms of poverty.

Finally, it is the law of capitalist production that distributes capital on the world market without thought to the social consequences of investment. To the capitalist, it is irrelevant whether the investment is in poison gas or automobiles, cigarettes, or food. The law is that capital invests in producing as much **surplus value** as possible (1051). The law "takes the form of a compulsion which the capitalists impose upon the workers and on each other—in reality, then, it is the law of capital as enforced against both" (1056). *See also* LABOR THEORY OF VALUE, LAW OF VALUE, PREFACE, THE.

LEAGUE OF THE JUST. A **secret society** of German exiles in **London** founded in 1836 and lasting to the mid-1840s. Its membership consisted of radical artisans and some intellectual leaders, including **Karl Schapper** and **Wilhelm Weitling**. The group initially focused on conspiracy and **revolution** and various forms of socialism. Their motto was "All men are brothers," and they sought to establish a social republic based on the ideals of civic virtue, equality, and justice. The League also sponsored **German Workers' Educational Associations**, open organizations with hundreds of members focused on adult education, social-ization, and mutual aid. **Engels** and Marx met many of the members of the group in 1845 when visiting London, and Marx continued to have contact with several members of the group while in **Belgium**. The two dominant personalities of the League were of different minds regarding revolution. Schapper favored a long-term campaign of education to prepare the people for an eventual revolution. Weitling advocated immediate revolt. This confusion of goals would continue throughout the League's existence. In June 1847 at a League congress that Engels attended, the group merged with the **Communist Correspondence Committee** and renamed itself the **Communist League** and shifted its focus from conspiracy and revolution to education and propaganda, even establishing a journal. Marx joined and became president of the **Brussels** branch (such branches were called congregations) of the Communist League and wrote *The Communist Manifesto*, which became the official political program of the new group.

LENIN, VLADIMIR (1870–1924). "Vladimir Lenin" was the *nom de guerre* of Vladimir Ilich Ulyanov, the most influential Russian Marxist theorist of the 20th century. Lenin was born into a middle-class and politically conservative family. The czarist regime executed his older brother Alexander Ulyanov (1866–1887) for his participation in a plot to assassinate Czar Alexander II when Lenin was 17. He was already dabbling in radical politics at Simbirsk Classical *Gimnazia* (a preparatory academy), but his brother's execution further radicalized Lenin. His commitment to revolutionary activities and organizing led to his arrest in 1893 and a three-year stint in internal exile. From 1900 until the onset of World War I, Lenin moved within socialist circles in western Europe and increasingly began associating with the **Bolshevik** faction of the **Russian Social Democratic Labor Party**, which advocated **violent revolution**. In the aftermath of the failed **Revolution of 1905**, Okhrana—the czarist secret police force—began cracking down on revolutionary organizations; Lenin fled Russia, establishing a base in Switzerland while moving

throughout eastern Europe organizing revolutionary cells.

Lenin famously returned to Russia in the midst of the Russian Revolution, conveyed through German territory on a closed railcar. He organized the Bolshevik faction to engage in militant action to overthrow the Provisional Government led by the more moderate **Mensheviks**. Rejecting calls for the formation of a coalition government of rival revolutionary factions, Lenin seized power and began issuing a series of directives reorganizing the government and establishing a one-party state. Throughout 1918, he also survived multiple assassination attempts, one of which left him severely injured. Lenin began the process of withdrawing Russia from World War I. From 1918 through 1922, Lenin directed a military campaign against "White" military forces intent on returning to a monarchical system. Blaming the wealthy Kulaks for chronic food shortages, one of Lenin's first acts was the formation of the Emergency Commission for Combatting Counter-Revolution and

Statue of Vladimir Lenin.

Sabotage, known as Cheka, which launched the "Red Terror," which targeted affluent Russians suspected of supporting a return of czarism. Confronting severe famine in 1921, Lenin enacted the "New Economic Policy," which introduced market mechanisms in an attempt to increase agricultural output. Denounced by hard-liners as a retreat from socialism, Lenin appealed to Marxist doctrine to contend that Russia's economy needed to mature into a capitalist economy before the country's economy would be sufficiently fallow ground for socialism.

Lenin's injuries from the assassination attempt severely compromised his health, which steadily declined throughout 1923. At various points, he contemplated suicide. He also became concerned regarding the fitness of key members of leadership. He recommended the removal of **Joseph Stalin**, then general secretary of the Communist Party, alarmed by his overt efforts to consolidate his power and influence within the party. He died on 21 January 1924, leading to Stalin's rapid assumption of absolute control over the Soviet party apparatus and with it the Soviet state.

Lenin stands among the foremost theorists of **Marxism** and made several notable contributions to Marxist theory. While Lenin agreed on the centrality of the **proletariat**, he contended that too many obstacles existed to prevent the formation of **revolutionary class consciousness**; as a result, he argued that a **vanguard party**—a small, highly organized, rigidly disciplined and ideologically orthodox group—was required to inspire and guide the proletariat in the desired direction. For Lenin, the small, underdeveloped nature of the Russian industrial class and the prevalence of a vast and uneducated **peasantry** made a vanguard necessary. In such a state, Lenin reasoned that the highest level of consciousness to which the proletariat could aspire was "trade union consciousness," a brand of **false consciousness** in which the proletariat allows itself to be "bought off" by the bourgeoisie. Another important contribution to the Marxist vocabulary was the idea of "democratic centralism," which encouraged the free exchange of ideas and open debate within the vanguard

party but which strictly prohibited dissent outside of internal party deliberations.

Perhaps Lenin's most significant contribution to Marxist theory was **imperialism**, which Lenin characterized as the "highest" and final stage of capitalism. Arguing that Marx had not anticipated that the advanced industrial capitalist nations would engage in conquest and oppression of non-European societies, Lenin argued that imperialism enabled capitalist countries to forestall the economic crises that Marx predicted would forge a revolutionary class consciousness among the proletariat. Taken together, Marxism-Leninism reinforced a commitment to revolutionary violence and a decisive rejection of the more nonviolent, **"evolutionary"** interpretations of early 20th-century socialists like **Eduard Bernstein**. Lenin also doubled-down on Marx's notion of a **"dictatorship of the proletariat,"** arguing for an extended tutelary role for a vanguard party as a necessary stage in the process of destroying the last vestiges of capitalism and the establishment of **communism**. Marxism-Leninism would prove to be an influential iteration of Marxism, providing considerable inspiration with the various waves of anticolonialism that swept through the 20th century.

LEVI, PAUL (1883–1930). A leader of the **Communist Party of Germany (KPD)**, Levi was born into an affluent family of Jewish merchants and earned his law degree, specializing in the legal defense of leftists. At age 23, Levi joined the **Social Democratic Party of Germany (SPD)**, joining a major left-wing faction with **Rosa Luxemburg** and **Karl Liebknecht** within the organization. With Luxemburg and Liebknecht, he formed the **Spartacus League**. Levi opposed the **Spartacist Uprising** of January 1919. With the deaths of Luxemburg, Liebknecht, and **Leo Jogiches (1867–1919)** in the wake of the uprising, Levi assumed leadership of the Communist Party of Germany.

Levi led the German delegations to the Second World Congress of the **Communist International (Comintern)** in 1920. As leader of the KPD, Levi argued that communists needed to appeal to the workers for public support, and criticized the advocacy of **violent revolution** among communists. The KPD expelled him from the party for that criticism. In his later years, he resumed his legal practice and worked in journalism. In 1922, he rejoined the SPD and was subsequently elected to the Reichstag. Throughout the 1920s, Levi was subject to several anti-Semitic attacks and in turn became a sharp public critic of emerging Nazi Party leaders like Adolf Hitler.

LIBERAL DEMOCRACY. *See* BOURGEOIS DEMOCRACY.

LIEBKNECHT, KARL (1871–1919). Karl Liebknecht was a German socialist, lawyer, revolutionary, and son of **Wilhelm Liebknecht**. Formerly a member of the **Social Democratic Party of Germany (SPD)**, Liebknecht cofounded with **Rosa Luxemburg**, **Leo Jogiches**, **Paul Levi**, and others both the **Spartacus League** and the **Communist Party of Germany (KPD)**. Trained as a lawyer, Liebknecht built a practice with his brother Theodor defending fellow leftists. Elected to the Reichstag in 1912 as a member of the Social Democratic Party, he began moving in a more radical direction as World War I approached.

Liebknecht excelled as an organizer of German working-class youths but generally left deeper theoretical considerations to his fellow leader, Rosa Luxemburg. To the extent that he did express himself on such matters, Liebknecht departed from orthodox **Marxism** on some important issues. Liebknecht was not, for example, an economic determinist. Additionally, he did not collapse history into a history of "**class struggle**," and he accepted the state as the arena of conflict between the forces of labor and the forces of reaction. In that sense, Liebknecht believed that the struggle between the **proletariat** and the **bourgeoisie** required organization and mobilization. Only a unified and fully committed labor movement would be in a position to contest the bourgeoisie for control of the state.

Liebknecht spent a considerable portion of the years 1904–1918 alternating between electoral office and prison. Like many labor leaders, he was initially ambivalent regarding Germany's entrance into World War I. At first, he abstained from votes on war bonds to support the German war effort (Luxemburg called for civil disobedience). However, his left-wing views and mounting opposition to German participation in the war provoked his arrest and conviction for treason. His sentence involved his forced conscription and assignment to the Eastern Front. Refusing to fight, forced into manual labor, and in ill health, Liebknecht returned to Germany in 1915. Arrested again in 1916 after returning to the Reichstag, the state tried Liebknecht for high treason for organizing antiwar protests. He was convicted and sentenced to a four-year term, which, following a grant of amnesty to all political prisoners, was reduced to two years. As German defeat in World War I became apparent, civil unrest began to spread, leading to the abdication of Kaiser Wilhelm II and the replacement of the German monarchy with a democratic republican government.

With Rosa Luxemburg and others, Liebknecht formed the **Spartacus League** in 1914, named after the leader of a famous slave revolt in the Roman Republic. The League was later renamed the KPD. He formed a close alliance with Luxemburg, considered by many the most gifted Marxist theorist of the early 20th century. On 5 January 1919, radicals called a general strike that launched the **Spartacist Uprising**, also known as the **January Uprising**. Inspired by the Bolshevik seizure of power in Russia, Liebknecht and Luxemburg found themselves supporting a revolution they believed to be ill advised. Right-wing **Freikorps** militia made up of returning veterans brutally suppressed the revolt. Liebknecht was among the leaders of the rebellion captured, tortured, and summarily executed.

Karl Liebknecht represented a more radical generation than his father's, a generation that rejected the accommodation to the German state, embittered by the alternating accommodation and oppression of German labor unionists. Liebknecht and Luxemburg called for the violent overthrow of the German state and the end of the German monarchy. This call produced a resurgence of radicalism inspired by the **Bolshevik Revolution** in Russia.

For Karl Liebknecht, Marx's analyses of **capitalism**'s ills were esoteric and irrelevant to the facts on the ground. Liebknecht's passion was for organization and protest. In death, he became a martyr for German communists of the mid-20th century. The Communist Party of Germany would become a significant party in Weimar Germany in the post–World War I period until the Nazi seizure of government. After World War II, the KPD became the ruling party in the German Democratic Republic (i.e., East Germany) from 1949 until German unification in 1990.

LIEBKNECHT, WILHELM (1826–1900). Wilhelm Martin Philipp Christian Liebknecht was a leading figure in the emerging German socialist workers' movement in the mid-19th century. Over a long career as a journalist, party leader, and professional revolutionary, Liebknecht was a unifying figure in the formation of the **Social Democratic Party of Germany (SPD)** and the father of **Karl Liebknecht** (1871–1919).

Born into a middle-class German family and orphaned at an early age, relatives raised Liebknecht. Educated during a rising tide of student radicalism in Germany, due to some difficulties with German authorities, he took an unpaid instructional position in Switzerland in 1847. There he reported on the civil war in that country for a German newspaper, thereby launching a five-decade-long journalistic career. Inspired by the **Revolutions of 1848**, he joined a troop of émigré Germans seeking to foment a revolution among the German states. He was arrested for treason when a resurgence of political unrest led to his release. He returned to Switzerland, where his efforts to unify the German-speaking Swiss workers' unions led authorities to declare him *persona non grata*. He subsequently relocated to **England**, where he lived for 12 years (1850–1862), developing a warm friendship with the similarly displaced Karl Marx.

Liebknecht returned to Germany in 1862, starting work as a journalist for the magazine *The Social Democrat* in 1864. He fell out with the editorial staff's friendly position regarding Prussian aspirations toward German unification. He served as a member of the national legislature as well as editing the Saxon People's Party newspaper, *The People's State*. In both positions, Liebknecht vigorously opposed the **wars of German unification** and was subsequently (and repeatedly if only briefly) jailed for his political agitation.

Returning to politics in 1874, Liebknecht played an instrumental role in unifying the **Social Democratic Workers' Party of Germany**—often described as the "**Eisenach** Party"—and the **Ferdinand Lassalle**–organized **Socialist Workers' Party of Germany** in Gotha, Germany, a year later. The platform of the unified SPD was expressly socialist in principle. Nevertheless, in *Critique of the Gotha Programme*, Marx vehemently criticized it as excessively moderate and displaying a tendency to believe that the state would negotiate in good faith with the **proletariat**.

Liebknecht resisted **anarchist** impulses from the left and the Lassalle wing's urges toward accommodation with **Bismarck** and the unified German state. Liebknecht consistently argued for a more Marxist orientation for the SPD's platform and helped secure the ratification of the **Erfurt Program** in 1891, superseding the **Gotha Program**. The Erfurt Program, while employing a more Marxist vocabulary, nevertheless eschewed organizing the proletariat for **revolution** and instead contended that the paramount task of the proletariat was to seek reforms that were favorable to workers and trust that the revolution will come at its appointed time. The commitment to Marxist vocabulary without the dedication to revolution provoked **Engels**'s denunciations. Engels viewed the Erfurt Program as a departure from **Marxist orthodoxy**. However, the SPD would widely distribute its brand of **Marxism** in the period before World War I.

LIVING LABOR. **Variable capital** is that part of **capital** with which the capitalists buy the **labor power** of the **workers**. Another name that Marx gives to variable capital is "living labor." **Constant capital** is the **machinery** and property used in the **means of production**. Another name that Marx gives to constant capital is "**dead labor**." Constant capital is a precondition for the production of **surplus value** but does not produce value by itself. Only variable capital or living labor can produce surplus value. "But capital has one sole driving force, the drive to **valorize** itself, to create surplus-value, to make its constant part, the means of production, absorb the greatest possible amount of **surplus labour**. Capital is dead labour which, vampire-like, lives only by sucking living labour, and lives the more, the more labour it sucks" (Marx 1867/1976, 342).

LONGUET, CHARLES (1839–1903). A journalist and activist in the working-class movements of **France**, including the French branch of the **International**, spending eight months in prison for such activities in 1866 and participating in the 1871 **Paris Commune**. After the defeat of the Commune, he moved to **England** as a refugee and met and married Karl's oldest daughter, **Jenny**, in 1872. While in England, he worked as a teacher of French. Returning to France with the amnesty in 1880, Longuet wrote for a newspaper owned by his friend, Georges Clemenceau, the future prime minister during World War I. Politically, Longuet was a follower of **Proudhon**, though he borrowed some ideas from Marx. Karl was not too fond of him, questioning his politics as well as the neglect of his children (Stedman-Jones 2016, 469). When Karl's wife **Jenny** died in 1881, his son-in-law wrote her obituary for the French newspaper *Justice*. "'We might guess that her marriage with Karl Marx, son of a **Trier** attorney, was not made without difficulty. There were many prejudices to vanquish, most of all that of race. We know that the illustrious socialist is of Israelite origins.' Sending the notice on to his daughter, Marx snorted, 'The entire story is simply made up; there were no prejudices to vanquish,' and added some cutting remarks about what a nitwit his son-in-law was" (Sperber 2013, 42). Marx also added, "Longuet would greatly oblige me in never mentioning my name in his writing" (Stedman-Jones 2016, 167). *See also* JEWISH LIFE IN TRIER.

LUKÀCS, GEORGES (1885–1971). Lukàcs was a Hungarian **Marxist** philosopher and social critic and led the emergence of **Western Marxism** as an alternative to the Marxist-Leninist-Stalinist orthodoxy of the **Soviet Union** of the mid-20th century. Born into a titled Hungarian family of the **Austro-Hungarian Empire**, Lukàcs earned multiple doctorates in economics, political science, and philosophy. In the period before World War I, Lukàcs led an eclectic life, moving at once within broad literary, artistic, and philosophical circles in Germany and Hungary. He became acquainted with noted intellectuals like Bertolt Brecht, Georges Simmel, Max Weber, and Karl Manheim. His elite status and social connections preserved his career—and life—on several occasions.

Influenced by the Russian Revolution, Lukàcs became a committed **Marxist** and joined the abbreviated Hungarian Soviet Republic in 1919. On the collapse of the Hungarian revolutionary government, Lukàcs fled to Austria. He spent considerable time in the Soviet Union, at times involuntarily, in the 1930s, returning to Hungary at the culmination of World War II. Lukàcs participated in the attempt by Hungarian communists to throw off Soviet domination in 1956; at the revolution's suppression, he narrowly avoided execution, spending a period of "exile" in Romania. He returned to Hungary in 1957 with a much more cautious approach to politics.

Lukàcs wrote widely on a variety of topics. His principal contribution to Marxist theory was *History and Class-Consciousness* (1921). In that work, which the Bolsheviks censured, Lukàcs criticized late 19th-century Marxists (especially **Kautsky** and Plekhanov) for attempting to replace its **Hegelian** foundations with scientific principles drawn from the physical sciences. The Fifth **Comintern** (1924) officially condemned Lukàcs's aspiration to "re-Hegelianize" **Marxism**; despite that official rebuke, Lukàcs remained a faithful communist. Lukàcs's writing accentuated Hegel's thesis on the importance of human consciousness; as such, he dismissed **Friedrich Engels's** claims that Marx had identified some eternal laws of nature. Thus, for Lukàcs, human action is not predetermined: Marxists must fight and win the war of ideas. In this sense, Lukàcs hoped to drain orthodox Marxism of the deterministic claims that "objective historical forces" moved humanity (Miller 1991, 296).

Lukàcs drew several conclusions from this analysis that would prove to be influential for mid-20th-century Marxist theory. Inspired by Marx's **fetishism of commodities**, he argued that **reification** was one of capitalism's most harmful effects. He posited that human productions transform into animate entities that oppress and "**commodify**" workers. The oppression of workers through specialization and the **detailed division of labor** reduces them to **machine**-like status, merely subsisting in a fragmented, chaotic, and essentially meaningless world. Lukàcs also deployed reification as a way of understanding how **bourgeois** ideology penetrated the structure of knowledge, erecting a formidable barrier to the **proletariat's** achievement of **revolutionary class consciousness**.

Lukàcs invoked the idea of a "totality" to encapsulate his attempts to refurbish Marx's analysis of **historical materialism**. He appears to draw on fellow Hungarian philosopher Karl Manheim's contrast between "particular" and "total" ideologies, the former being the kinds of justifications for existing power structures and an **exploitative** status quo, while the latter reflected a sort of comprehensive perspective of an entire historical period. For Lukàcs, the proletariat could achieve such a privileged standpoint, although how such an oppressed class might attain that holistic perspective remained somewhat of a mystery in Lukàcs's work.

Lukàcs represented a unique position in 20th-century Marxism. Uniquely vulnerable to the coercive implications of **Stalinism** in the coldest depths of the Cold War, Lukàcs attempted to disentangle Marxism from Stalin's crudely deterministic interpretations of **dialectical materialism** without appearing to reject Stalinism *in toto* and running the risk of an all-too-certain reprisal. Despite his opacity regarding the worst aspects of Stalinism, Lukàcs exerted an extensive influence on the development of Marxist theory in western Europe, particularly among members of the Frankfurt School of critical theory.

LUMPENPROLETARIAT. The lumpenproletariat are typically characterized as criminals, the chronically **unemployed**, the mentally unstable, and the homeless. Marx originated the term to describe those "unleavened" portions of the working class lacking **revolutionary class consciousness**. Within the **Marxist** vocabulary, "lumpenproletariat" is a term of abuse as those elements of the poor insufficiently incorporated into the **proletariat** to identify their interests with their fellow **workers**. As such, Marx and **Engels** viewed them as untrustworthy and prone to manipulation. They saw their presence as obstacles that the proletariat must overcome to achieve a genuine **socialist revolution**.

Marx's and Engels's use of the term in *The German Ideology* and *The Eighteenth Brumaire of Louis Bonaparte* suggest a need to separate the proletariat "properly understood" from the significant eruptions of social and political unrest taking place in Europe throughout the middle of the 19th century. The failures of the **Revolutions of 1848** and the **Paris Commune** were not the failures of the proletariat but rather the miscarriages of a disorganized "rabble." Marx characterized those movements as first halting steps on the pathway toward the establishment of a proletarian revolutionary class consciousness, advancing but not constituting the proletarian revolution.

Later, anticolonialists such as Franz Fanon would appropriate the term, denoting the sense in which **imperialists** viewed native **populations** and attempted to use the word in a positive sense. **Vladimir Lenin** would render the need for a distinction between proletariat and lumpenproletariat moot with his call for a **vanguard party**, made necessary by the presence of such a large lumpenproletariat population in Russia. **Mao Zedong** similarly made a virtue of necessity, creating the category of "rural proletariat" to differentiate China's rural **peasantry**—on whom Mao staked his revolutionary ambitions—from Kuomintang supporters. German-born American socialist Herbert Marcuse lamented that consumer society had scourged America's working class of any sense of consciousness beyond consumerism and harnessed his aspirations for change on America's impoverished.

Within Marxist thought, the idea of a lumpenproletariat denotes an important distinction between those deemed capable of discerning their class interests from short-term calculations of gain or expressions of desperate though fruitless revolt. Over time, various iterations of **Marxism** have opportunistically expanded, contracted, or eliminated which groups are considered capable of establishing a **revolutionary consciousness**. *See also* AGRARIAN QUESTION, PAUPERISM, SURPLUS LABOR.

LUXEMBURG, ROSA (1871–1919). Rosa Luxemburg was a Polish socialist and revolutionary. Born to a Jewish family during the Russian domination of Poland, Luxemburg was a shy but intelligent scholar very much interested in liberal (and subsequently radical) politics. In 1893, Luxemburg helped found the Social Democracy of the Kingdom of Poland and Lithuania Party. Her political activity eventually compelled her to flee Poland for Switzerland, where she ultimately earned a doctorate. In 1898, Luxemburg moved to Germany, the location of most of her subsequent political and **revolutionary** activities. Among those socialists active in the period after Marx's death and until the end of World War I, Luxemburg displayed the most consistent fidelity to **Marxist** analysis and principles. She wrote extensively and made significant contributions to socialist literature, including *Social Reform and Revolution* (1899), *Organizational Question of Russian Social Democracy* (1904), *Mass Strike, Party and Trade Unions* (1906), and *The Russian Revolution* (1918).

Luxemburg was a fierce advocate for a relatively doctrinaire interpretation of **Marxism**. She bitterly denounced **Eduard Bernstein** for his criticism of Marxism in 1899, accusing him of **utopianism** for his belief in "**evolutionary socialism**." Luxemburg's position, supported by **Karl Kautsky**, prevailed within the **Social Democratic Party of Germany (SPD)**. At the same time, she critically engaged with **Vladimir Lenin** on the issue of national self-determination within the workers' movement.

Lenin believed that the **proletarian revolution** might occur in one nation. Luxemburg, on the other hand, believed that general mass strikes—properly coordinated—would topple **capitalism** and lead to proletarian-led **social democracies**. Later, she would warn against the dictatorial impulses of the newly installed **Bolsheviks** in Russia.

Luxemburg was an influential voice among those younger members of the SPD who tired of parliamentary maneuvering within a German state that was increasingly hostile to the workers' movement. Elements of the SPD became increasingly hostile to Germany's participation in World War I. Eventually, disagreements with the senior leadership of the SPD caused Luxemburg and others to form, successfully, the **Spartacus League** and then the **Communist Party of Germany**. Although both she and her fellow leader **Karl Liebknecht** believed that the **Spartacist Uprising** was doomed to failure, both felt compelled to support the effort. Armed elements of the German *Wehrmacht* (see Freikorps)

Photograph of Rosa Luxemburg.

returning from the front in the aftermath of German capitulation brutally suppressed the uprising. The Freikorps tortured and executed both Luxemburg and Liebknecht as leaders of the revolt.

Many socialists lionized Luxemburg, including Lenin, who, despite Luxemburg's criticisms, viewed her as a valuable ally. The Communist Party of Germany commemorated Luxemburg as a hero. During Germany's partition after World War II, the ruling Communist Party of East Germany named various places in Luxemburg's honor; the Polish Communist Party also named several places in Warsaw in her honor.

LUXURY GOODS. Capitalism needs economic **growth** to survive, and for this to occur, part of the **surplus value** expropriated from the workers must be reinvested in **capital** rather than consumed in the form of consumer and luxury goods. "In other words, it must be transformed into additional **constant capital** (buildings, equipment, energy, raw materials, auxiliary products, etc.) and additional **variable capital** (money capital available to hire an increased labour force). The **accumulation of capital** is nothing other than this (partial) capitalization of surplus-value, i.e., the (partial) transformation of profit into additional capital" (Mandel 1978, 17). Marx condemns the diversion of labor into the production of luxury goods if it hampers the making of the means of subsistence. However, the manufacture of such products is a necessity in the **capitalist mode of production** to provide the nonproducers an outlet to enjoy their wealth and, for those capitalists who deal in such goods, "a means of coining money, of producing surplus-value" (Marx 1867/1976, 1046).

M

MACHINES. A machine, according to Marx, consists of three different parts: (1) the motor mechanism, or the driving force of the machine—whether a hand crank, waterwheel, animal, steam power, or other; (2) the transmission mechanism (consisting of ropes, pulleys, belts, or gears); and (3) the tool, or working part, of the machine. It is this last part that is at the heart of the **Industrial Revolution,** for the tool of the machine is a modified form of the **tool** used by the craftsman, but is now fitted into a mechanism to perform "the same operations as the worker formerly did with similar **tools**" (Marx 1867/1976, 495). While a worker is limited in his use of tools that he can simultaneously use by his physical organism, the number of tools wielded by a machine in simultaneous operations is virtually limitless. "The machine, which is the starting-point of the industrial revolution, replaces the worker, who handles a single tool, by a mechanism operating with a number of similar tools and set in motion by a single motive power, whatever the form of that power" (497). Such machines—not the steam engine per se, according to Marx—represent the starting point of the Industrial Revolution. The perfection of the steam engine intensified the process; it allowed machinery to become larger, concentrated in towns and cities, instead of being scattered over the countryside and powered by waterwheels(499). As capitalists perfected machines able to execute all the movements required to transform raw materials into **commodities,** workers became tenders, giving only supplementary assistance to the machine's automatic processes that set the pace and continuity of production (502). In its most developed form, there exists an organized system of machines, "a mechanical monster whose body fills whole factories," powered from a central location with "countless working organs" (503).

Marx uses the paper industry in making distinctions between various **modes of production** based on different **means of production** as well as "the connection between the **social relations of production** and those modes of production" (503). In India and China, he writes, there are two distinct **Asiatic** forms of the paper industry. The old German papermaking trades, he writes, provide an example of **handicraft production.** Holland and **France** in the 17th century provide examples of the **manufacturing mode of production,** and the English paper industry of his day are examples of machine production (or **large-scale industry**) (503–5).

The most developed system of machine production consists of a network of machines powered by a central source that dominates a factory floor. The technical foundation of large-scale industry, Marx writes, began in manufacture production, which produced the machinery that eventually replaced "handicraft and manufacturing systems" (503). Over time, this material basis for large-scale industry grew inadequate. Large-scale industry was crippled, Marx writes, as long as artisans and specialized workers "wielding their dwarf-like implements" produced the machines (504). Apart from the matter of the cost of machines made in this way (a dominant motive for the capitalist, Marx adds), there were significant technical problems in continuing to produce them through handicrafts or even manufacturing production. Such industries required highly trained workers who could not increase their ranks fast enough to keep up with demand. The machines themselves became more substantial and more powerful, complex, and diverse in form. Increasingly made from steel, such machines were notoriously hard to manufacture with simple tools.

The technical foundations of large-scale industry necessitated machine production of the machines themselves. This gradually began to take place in the first few decades of the 19th century. "But it is only during the last few decades that the construction of railways and ocean steamers on a vast scale has called into existence the Cyclopean machines now employed in the construction of prime movers" (506). **Innovation** and transformation of the mode of production in one industry call forth similar transformations in other spheres (504). Marx gives several examples of this phenomenon. For example, machine spinning called forth machine weaving. Machine spinning and weaving called forth the cotton gin and made necessary a chemical revolution in bleaching, printing, and dyeing. All of this innovation made possible the growing of cotton on an industrial scale. Finally, the revolution in the production of industry and agriculture called forth a revolution in the **means of communication and transportation**.

When first introduced into an industry, machinery tends to replace existing **labor**, thus lowering the cost of production of a commodity. The first capitalists to employ the machines in an industry have a **monopoly** of sorts, Marx writes, and the capitalist will enjoy short-term **profits** because of the innovation. However, to sell the increased output, the capitalist will have to lower the price below that of his competitors. Moreover, to remain competitive in the market, others will have to adopt the new (or newer) **technology**. However, the general employment of more efficient technology in the production process

causes the exchange value to decline. Consistent with the concept of **socially necessary labor time**, **labor power** replaced by machines does not contribute to the **surplus value** of the capitalist; it is only the labor power employed tending these machines that lead to **profit** (530).

Marx is not against advances in machine technology; rather, he is against how capital has employed technology. Marx begins chapter 15 of *Capital: Volume I* remarking that rather than operating machinery to reduce human labor, capitalism uses machinery to minimize the cost of production, thereby reducing the part of workday where the worker reproduces his wages and increasing the share that he "gives to the capitalist for nothing. The machine is a means for producing surplus-value" (492). Machinery, automation, and production technology can be a liberator of people, freeing them from competitive labor. However, capital employs machines to enslave humanity in the name of profit and ever-accumulating wealth. Machines also produce and reproduce the **industrial reserve army**. This army of **unemployed** provides the capitalist with a supply of workers that always exceeds demand, thus keeping wages low and adding to the surplus value expropriated by the capitalist. *See also* INDUSTRIAL REVOLUTION, PREFACE, THE.

MALTHUS, T. ROBERT (1766–1834).

Thomas Robert Malthus was born on 13 February 1766. He was the second son and sixth child of Daniel Malthus, a country gentleman. Educated at Cambridge in mathematics and natural philosophy (**science**), he became an ordained minister immediately after graduating in 1788 and became a curate at Oakwood near his family home in Surrey (Winch 1987). After graduation, Robert moved in with his parents and for 10 years led a contemplative life of reading and discussion with his father. Malthus originally published the 1798 *Essay on the Principle of Population* as an anonymous pamphlet. He later revised the work in 1802 (identifying Malthus as the author). The *Essay* went through seven editions—each of them relying more heavily on empirical examples in support of the underlying theory (Appleman 1976; McNicoll 1998).

While Malthus is widely considered the founder of social demography, his more significant contribution is perhaps in ecological-evolutionary theory. His *Essay* points out that our ability to produce children will always outstrip our ability to provide energy for their survival. He asserted that the population must be kept in line with what society can produce in the way of sustenance. Further, he claimed, every method available to keep this population in check (including birth control) has negative consequences for society. Because of this simple fact, Malthus argues, we can never achieve the utopia anticipated by many of his contemporaries.

The subtitle of *Essay on the Principle of Population* is "As it affects the future improvement of society with remarks on the speculations of **Mr. Godwin**, M. Condorcet, and other writers." As the subtitle makes clear, the *Essay* was a contribution to the then-current debate on the perfectibility of man and society. Many social thinkers at the end of the 18th century had espoused the idea of "progress." The imminence of a new century, recent scientific discoveries, as well as new technological achievements made it seem to many that there were no limits to the ability of science and reason to create a better world (Price 1998). Many of these ideals were to find expression in the American and **French Revolutions** as well as in the ideologies of **capitalism** and socialism. While the particular vision varied, many saw social progress as the ultimate triumph of some principle or condition, such as equality, material wealth, freedom, science, or reason. The idea of social progress was ingrained in 19th-century Western societies. Malthus's *Essay* emphatically refuted these optimistic notions.

For Malthus, the debate over progress began with his father, a great admirer of Rousseau (Malthus's father, Daniel, is the "friend" mentioned in **The Preface** to the first *Essay*). Malthus's *Essay* addressed two essential works of the day. Marquis de Condorcet had recently published *Outline of the Intellectual Progress of Mankind* (1795), in which he claimed that societies pass through stages, each stage

representing the progressive emancipation by science of man's reason from superstition and ignorance (much of Condorcet's vision gets passed on to his French successor, Auguste Comte). In 1793, William Godwin published *Enquiry concerning Political Justice*, which made similar claims regarding the perfectibility of society. Godwin wrote that corrupt institutions repressed man's natural goodness. The spread of reason and greater social equality would gradually replace these institutions (Godwin 1820/1976). Both Godwin and de Condorcet followed Rousseau in attributing all social ills to defective institutions (Price 1998). While Malthus agreed that institutions of society exacerbated many social troubles, he also asserted that there was a fundamental social inequality based on natural law. The view that no form of social organization can create or preserve a just and equitable society permeates the *Essay*.

Critics bitterly attacked Malthus's ideas almost from the outset of publication. Samuel Coleridge railed against "the monstrous practical sophism of Malthus." Robert Southey, the poet laureate, wrote, "Mr. Malthus is cast in his action against God Almighty." Since his passing, others have joined the attacks. Charles Dickens reportedly used Malthus as the model for Scrooge (Rohe 1997). Karl Marx (1867/1976) criticizes Malthus as one of the classical economists he railed against, calling him a plagiarist (639) and an idolizer and true priest of the **ruling class**, "explaining the **growth** of **surplus population** by the eternal laws of nature, rather than the merely historical laws of the nature of capitalist production" (666).

It is perhaps due to his stand on progress that Marx is particularly hostile to Malthus's work, namely, his insistence that no form of social organization (which would include socialism) could eliminate inequality (Petersen 1979). Malthus's critique of progress also goes a long way toward explaining the hostility that Malthus's work still receives in our society. **Marxists,** of course, continue to attack Malthus as the theorist of the ruling class (e.g., see Foster, John Bellamy). True believers in progress through reform or **revolution**—and this would include socialists of every stripe—attack Malthus for his assertions that no social order can achieve lasting social equality and justice. While societies can always do better, Malthus writes, such a paradise is not in our future. *See also* POPULATION, SURPLUS POPULATION.

MANAGERIAL SKILLED LABOR. With the rise of **joint-stock companies**, Marx recognized the **growth** of another type of **skilled laborer**, that of supervision and management. These positions come into being with the growth of **large-scale industry**, and he asserts that managerial labor will continue to grow along with the growth of **capital**; joint-stock companies, especially, tend to separate management from ownership (Marx 1885/1978, 510). Such managers and commercial workers, Marx asserts, are skilled labor that receive above-average wages. The wages, he adds, tend to fall in relation to average labor for a couple of reasons: (1) the ever more **detailed division of labor** means that such skilled labor is extraordinarily narrow and easily mastered, and (2) such necessary skills and knowledge are reproduced easily through the extension of public education. Widespread education increases the supply of potential managers and commercial workers, and much of their training falls on the public sector (414).

Data from the U.S. Census Bureau (2017) indicate that the largest occupational group in the American workforce consists of management, business, science, and arts, which includes many professions as well. This group alone accounted for 41 percent of the full-time employed **population**. This group is quite diverse in terms of income, prestige, and occupational control. It is also true that they have only their labor to sell in exchange for their livelihoods. Overall, according to the 2017 census data, the broad occupational group had a median income of $47,016—putting them only slightly ahead of those working in natural resources, construction, and maintenance ($41,963); sales and office workers ($40,078); and those working in production, transportation, and material moving occupations ($37,318). The most exploited group is

the service workers, who had a median income of $29,000 in 2017. Much of the American workforce—even many of those in management, business, science, and arts—would fall well within the **proletariat**.

However, Marx may have failed to foresee the rise in the size and wealth of a professional-managerial class in advanced capitalist societies. The same Census table displays the median income for each occupation in the management category, which ranges from a low of $25,552 (preschool and kindergarten teachers) to a high of $202,908 (physicians and surgeons). Managers and professionals in the higher ranges would have the resources to invest significant capital or start private enterprises. Estimating the size of this higher-level professional-managerial class by counting those within this occupational group with a median income of $100,000 or higher yields a rough estimate, as many in this category are dependent on corporate and government employment or are subject to professional dominance by others, but many within the group enjoy not only salaries well above the average but also occupational control and special privileges not accorded to other laborers. This group is roughly 13 percent of the management, business, science, and arts census category, or about 5 percent of the total American workforce in 2017. Chief executive officers, computer systems managers, engineers of all types, lawyers, and higher-level health care workers dominate this group. *See also* ABSTRACT LABOR, BOARD OF DIRECTORS, CAPITALIST CLASS, DESKILLING, FACTORY SYSTEM, LABOR THEORY OF VALUE, PETTY BOURGEOISIE, WAGE LABOR.

MANIFESTO OF THE COMMUNIST PARTY. See *THE COMMUNIST MANIFESTO.*

MANUFACTURE MODE OF PRODUCTION. See MANUFACTURE PERIOD.

MANUFACTURE PERIOD. Marx's classification of early capitalist production before the **Industrial Revolution** that extends roughly from the middle of the 16th century to the last third of the 18th century. The transition from the feudal mode of production to early capitalism marks the transformation of handicraft labor to a process based on the detailed division of labor. During this period, machinery played a subordinate part. This period originates in two ways. First, it can arise from combining several workers with various handicrafts in a single workshop under the oversight of an individual capitalist. Each of these workers works on a small part of the product and then passes it on to others until completed. Marx uses the example of the production of a carriage to illustrate this form of simple cooperation. In the era of handicraft production, the carriage was the product of wheelwrights, harness makers, locksmiths, painters, carpenters, tailors, and other skilled artisans. "In the manufacture of carriages, however, all these different craftsmen are assembled in one building where the unfinished product passes from hand to hand" (Marx 1867/1976, 455). Gradually, the production process devolves into simple, detailed operations that become the province of a particular worker, the final product the result of a combination of these partial, detail workers. However, those occupied in the making of carriages in this manner lose the skill of carrying on their broader trade. Their activities are one sided and focused on specialized tasks.

Manufacture can also arise when a capitalist employs several artisans who all do the same work. In this case, each of these workers makes the entire commodity. Working in the traditional handicraft way, the craftsman performs all of the necessary steps in succession in the production process. However, soon, Marx asserts, external circumstances—such as a big order—demand an increased quantity of the article within a short period. The capitalist than divides the work, each craftsman assigned to perform "one, and only one" task in the production process, and the whole of them together performed simultaneously. This "accidental" division of labor develops advantages and gradually becomes the standard operating procedure (456). Regardless of how it started, however, Marx states that the manufacturing period has as its final form a productive mechanism consisting of human beings engaged in a detailed division of labor, every stage performed by hand, and all of the steps form a separate handicraft. Each step is dependent on the skill and strength of the individual worker, although this skill is technically narrow. Every worker, therefore, is consigned to a detailed task, and "his labour-power becomes transformed into the life-long organ of this partial function" (457). See also CAPITALIST MODE OF PRODUCTION, HANDICRAFT PRODUCTION, LARGE-SCALE INDUSTRY.

MANUFACTURING DIVISION OF LABOR. See DETAILED DIVISION OF LABOR.

MARCH 1850 ADDRESS TO THE COMMUNIST LEAGUE. See ADDRESS TO THE CENTRAL COMMITTEE OF THE COMMUNIST LEAGUE.

MARKET GLUT. See OVERPRODUCTION.

MARKET PRICE. See EXCHANGE VALUE.

MARX, EDGAR "MUSH" (1846–1855). Jenny and Karl's third child and first son was born in **Brussels.** Named after Karl's boyhood friend and Jenny's younger brother, by all accounts he was a precocious child and much loved by his parents. Edgar, called "Mush" within the family, developed an illness with symptoms of stomach pains, fever, and respiratory distress. He died in his father's arms at the age of eight on 6 April 1855. "The death of this son was the greatest tragedy in Marx's life. At Edgar's funeral, his friend and political associate **Wilhelm Liebknecht** attempted to console him, reminding him of his wife, daughters, and friends, but Marx, close to losing control, just groaned in reply: 'All of you cannot give me my boy back.' Edgar's death left Marx depressed and dispirited for the next two and a half years. If he did not give in entirely to despair, it was only, as he told **Engels,** because of the 'thought of you and your friendship . . . and the hope that together we can still do something sensible in the world'" (Sperber 2013, 294).

MARX, ELEANOR "TUSSY" (1855–1898). Jenny and Karl's sixth and youngest child was the only one of their children who was born in the poverty of London to survive. Eleanor, called "Tussy" within the family, was active in socialist and trade union politics throughout her life. "She was a member of the **Social Democratic Federation (SDF)**, founded the **Socialist League** as an alternative to the nationalism of SDF leader **Henry Hyndman**, attended the founding congress of the Independent Labor Party (ILP), and had involvement with the **Second International**. She was especially active as an organizer for militant **trade unions** in the late 1880s and 1890s, particularly as a committee member for the Gas workers' Union and as an activist helping to mobilize women strikers" (Johnson, Walker, and Gray 2014, 275–76). She was in love with **Edward Aveling**, who left her for another woman, returning only when struck with a fatal disease. She committed suicide shortly after by ingesting poison.

MARX-ENGELS INSTITUTE. Established in Moscow in 1919, the Institute served as a research center and publishing house for official Soviet work on **Marxist** doctrine. The Institute collected unpublished manuscripts by Marx and **Engels** and other Marxist theoreticians as well as pamphlets and periodicals related to socialist movements. In 1931, Stalin purged its leadership, and the Institute merged with the Lenin Institute to become the Marx-Engels-Lenin Institute. After the fall of the Soviet Union, the new government terminated the Institute, and its holdings are now part of the Russian State Archives. *See also* COLLECTED WORKS OF MARX AND ENGELS (MECW), MARXIST INTERNET ARCHIVE (MIA).

MARX, FRANZISKA (1851–1852). Jenny and Karl's fifth child died within a year of her birth. Poverty may well have been a contributing factor in her death, although the official cause of death was a respiratory ailment. The death of two infants within two years was a severe blow to both Jenny and Karl. *See also* DEMUTH, HENRY FREDERICK (FREDDY), MARX, HEINRICH GUIDO.

MARX, HEINRICH (1777–1838). Karl's father, Heinrich Marx, was born in Saarlouis, the third son of Marx Lewy, a rabbi who moved to **Trier** in 1788. (Marx Lewy was also known as Meier Halevi Marx; the family took the name of Marx as a surname around 1788.) Heinrich left Trier around 1811 and eventually began study at the School of Law at Koblenz, graduating just six weeks after Napoleon's defeat. Heinrich moved back to Trier in 1814 and started the practice of law. He married **Henriette Pressburg**, a member of a prosperous Jewish family from the Netherlands. Their first child, Mauritz David, was born in 1815 more than a year after the marriage but died three years later. Sophia, their second child, was born in 1816. Karl Marx was born to this middle-class Jewish family in Trier on 5 May 1818. In all, the family had nine children. Heinrich supported this large family through his law practice representing clients in both criminal and the more lucrative civil cases.

Prussia, which took over the Rhineland in 1815, had issued an Edict of Emancipation for the Jews in 1812, stating that they could not work for the government or as attorneys in private practice. For this reason, Heinrich Marx converted to the Christian Evangelical Church of Prussia, which baptized him sometime between 1816 and 1820. Perhaps another reason for the conversion was Heinrich's strong **Enlightenment** beliefs; for such a man, Protestantism was an ideal **religion**. The church baptized Karl in 1824 some years after his father, Henriette, about a year later. Biographers believe that Heinrich's Enlightenment beliefs were a strong influence on his son. Reason as the primary source of authority and legitimacy, an emphasis on science and the scientific method, as well as associated ideas of liberty, progress, and religious tolerance were all part of this Enlightenment heritage. Karl told his daughter **Eleanor** that his father was a "true eighteenth-century Frenchman" who "knew his Voltaire and Rousseau by heart" (Bottomore 1973, 4). Evidence of his father's influence on Karl consists of reports that Karl "never tired of speaking of him" and always carried a "daguerreotype of Heinrich, which the family placed with Karl Marx in his grave" (Sperber 2013, 21). *See also* JEWISH LIFE IN TRIER, SAMUEL MARX.

MARX, HEINRICH GUIDO (1849–1850). Karl and **Jenny**'s fourth child was born on 5 November 1849 and died the following year on 19 November. Jenny, who was pregnant with **Franziska** at the time, took the death of the child very hard. Marx wrote to **Engels** a few days after the death that Jenny "is in a truly dangerous condition of being worked up and upset. She had nursed the child herself and had purchased his existence with the greatest sacrifices in the most difficult of circumstances. In addition, the thought that the poor child has been a victim of our wretched conditions, although he did not lack for any care" (Sperber 2013, 261). *See also* DEMUTH, HENRY FREDERICK (FREDDY).

MARX, HENRIETTE (née PRESSBURG; 1788–1863). The mother of Karl Marx was born in 1788. She was from a Jewish family that originated in Hungary, settled in the Netherlands during the 18th century, and became successful merchants. There is no record of how she met **Heinrich Marx**, some 11 years her senior, though they married in 1814. Henriette brought a substantial dowry to the marriage, including money and household furnishing, which allowed Heinrich to establish his middle-class lifestyle as well as his law practice. On Heinrich's death in 1838, Karl began pressing his mother for his inheritance, which she was reluctant to give, giving in only a little at a time; this created much conflict between mother and son for the rest of Henriette's life. Karl "got along badly with her, seeing her as a philistine, with no interest in intellectual questions, quarreling constantly with her over his inheritance, and showing little emotion at the news of her death" (Sperber 2013, 21–22).

MARX, JENNY (NÉE WESTPHALEN; 1814–1881). The wife of Karl Marx. Karl became formally engaged to Jenny in 1837 when Jenny was 22 years old, four years older than Karl. By all accounts, Jenny was beautiful, willful, and prone to passionate outbursts and, even before marrying Karl, had a strong sense of social justice. Because of Karl's university studies and lack of financial prospects, the engagement lasted some seven years, during which Karl wrote love poetry; while his letters to her did not survive (thanks to **Eleanor** and **Laura Marx**), their relationship was reportedly one of passion and lifelong love. They married in 1843. Shortly after they married, they moved to **Paris**, the second-largest city in Europe at the time. When the French government expelled Karl from Paris at the behest of the Prussian government, he left Jenny behind to sell the furniture to pay for the move to **Brussels**. Jenny shared her husband's passion for socialist politics, often serving as an interpreter of his terrible handwriting. While in Brussels, she became involved in the German Workers' Education Association. While living in Brussels, friction occurred between Jenny and **Mary Burns**, **Engels**'s longtime companion. This friction caused some tension between Karl and Engels for many years.

During the **Revolutions of 1848**, Jenny and her children stayed with her mother in **Trier** while Karl moved to **Cologne**. When he relocated to **England** in August 1849, Jenny and the children moved there in September. Biographers note a long-standing love affair between the two, with occasional fights—usually centered on money—and one major crisis that almost ended the marriage. This crisis involved the birth of **Henry Frederick (Freddy) Demuth**, Karl's illegitimate son. Engels averted the disaster by claiming paternity, and Jenny went along with the fiction. Through most of their married life, the family lived in genteel poverty. Although Karl had some intermittent work as a **journalist**, their primary source of support appears to be short-term loans, money from Engels, and eventual inheritance from their families. Jenny became gravely ill with smallpox in 1860 and had chronic health problems, at least partly due to their living conditions. They had six children, three living to adulthood. The deaths of their children deeply affected them. In declining health for several years, she died of cancer in December 1881. *See also* DEATH OF KARL MARX, ILL HEALTH OF KARL MARX, MARX'S CHILDREN, DEMUTH, HELENA (LENCHEN).

MARX, JENNY CAROLINE (1844–1883). Karl and Jenny Marx's first child, named after her mother. The family raised the child, along with her little sister, **Laura**, in middle-class style, with private schools, language lessons, as well as lessons in art and music. Raised as a freethinker, the girls took on the politics and outlook of their parents. Jenny married **Charles Longuet**, a French refugee, in 1872, and they had six children together. The marriage was cut short by her premature death in 1883, probably from cancer.

MARX, LAURA (1845–1911). The second daughter of Karl and Jenny. Although they lived in genteel poverty for most of their adult lives, they managed to give their two eldest daughters, **Jenny Caroline** and Laura, private school lessons as well as lessons in Italian and French, art, and music. It was their intention of raising them in a middle-class lifestyle, with some uncommon exceptions. Karl and Jenny raised their daughters as freethinkers and outspoken atheists and immersed in the politics of their father (Sperber 2013, 470).

In 1866, Laura became involved with **Paul Lafargue**, an exiled French student and member of the General Council of the **International Working Men's Association**. Karl made it clear in letters to Lafargue that he expected the two to remain chaste and that his primary concern with the impending marriage was over financial matters: he feared that the couple would live in poverty (Sperber 2013, 471–72). The couple married in 1868 and remained married for over 45 years and had several children—none of whom survived infancy. Like the Marx family, **Engels** subsidized them over the years, even leaving them much of his estate when he died. On Karl's death, Laura, along with **Eleanor**, destroyed much of their father's correspondence that they thought critical of Engels and other figures that might prove embarrassing to their father as well as personal letters between their father and mother. Both Laura and her husband Paul were active in French working-class movements. The couple committed suicide together in November 1911.

MARX, SAMUEL (1775–1827). Samuel Marx was **Heinrich Marx**'s elder brother and uncle to Karl. The family moved to **Trier** in 1788 when their father, Mordechai, or Marx Lewy (also known as Meier Halevi Marx), became the rabbi for the Jewish community. Mordechai died in 1804, and Samuel succeeded his father as rabbi of Trier until his death in 1827. In 1807, **Napoleon Bonaparte** convened the "Grand Sanhedrin" to address the status of Jews in the empire. Samuel, along with other rabbis and prominent Jews, attended the assembly. As a result, rabbis became state employees like Protestant and Catholic pastors. Also, like Protestants, the Sanhedrin mandated a General Consistory to govern the Jewish **religion**—all measures designed to bring the faith under closer supervision of the state. Yet another Napoleonic decree, the "infamous decree," mandated a host of discriminatory practices against Jews. Samuel urged his congregation to abide by these decrees, railing against usury and calling youth to trades in agriculture or the sciences. *See also* JEWISH LIFE IN TRIER.

MARXIAN MYTHOLOGY. The mythology surrounding Marx, as well as much that has come to be known as **Marxism**, began shortly after his death through the writings of **Engels** and then elaborated by the leaders of the **Social Democratic Party of Germany**, particularly **August Bebel**, **Karl Kautsky**, **Eduard Bernstein**, and **Franz Mehring**. "The German Social Democratic Party in the years before 1914 was the largest socialist party in the world and exercised a dominant influence upon the development of socialism elsewhere. Partly out of conviction, but mainly to buttress the authority of the Party, its leaders found it opportune to protect and to advance Marx's reputation as the revolutionary founder of a science of history" (Stedman-Jones 2016, 2). As the guardians of Marx's and Engels's papers, they promoted an image of Marx's personal life as exemplary and that he had conclusively demonstrated that the **contradictions of capitalism** would bring **crisis** and inevitable collapse. It is only with the widespread publication and translation of many of their papers as well as the research of modern biographers that a more accurate understanding of his life and works becomes possible. *See also* ZUSAMMENBRUCHSTHEORIE.

MARXISM. Johnson, Walker, and Gray (2014) trace the origins of Marxism and related terms. They report that, initially, opponents of Marx and his followers used the word pejoratively. Both **Wilhelm Weitling** and **Mikhail Bakunin** used the terms "Marxian" and "Marxist" to disparage supporters of Marx as well as their ideas. By the 1880s, the label was beginning to be used more positively by groups and organizations inspired by Marx's standing among European radicals. "Marx's intellect, strong personality, and tactical maneuvering within the **First International** made him dominant within the European labor movement of the time, and he achieved wider fame through the aligning of **the International** with the **Paris Uprising** and the **Paris Commune** in 1871. Marx was identified by the press of the time as the head of the dangerous **International**, giving him a wider reputation" (2).

Marx's theories, concepts, and ideas spread more slowly. During his lifetime, there were popular tracts that he wrote that received a broad audience. *The Communist Manifesto* and *The Civil War in France* sold thousands of copies in his lifetime. However, the acceptance of Marxism as a distinct ideology of a significant number of people develops after his death with the work of **Friedrich Engels** and the publication of *Anti-Dühring* as well as the more popular pamphlet based on this work: *Socialism: Utopian and Scientific*. Taking their cue from Engels, the leaders of the **Social Democratic Party of Germany (SPD)**, particularly **August Bebel, Karl Kautsky, Karl Liebknecht, Eduard Bernstein**, and **Franz Mehring**, elaborated and mythologized Marx perhaps out of sincere conviction. As the largest socialist party in the world prior to 1914, the party had an enormous influence on the development of socialist theory; spreading Marx's theory of history and the inevitability of socialism was a way of advancing the party. "By the new century, *Marxism* and *Marxist* were in common usage, being particularly strongly identified with the SPD and organizations of a similar outlook. The Russian Marxists,

especially **Vladimir Lenin**, commonly used the term as well, although others, such as **Rosa Luxemburg**, still favored labels such as *scientific socialism* or *social democracy*" (Johnson et al. 2014, 2).

MARXIST. *See* MARXISM.

MARXIST INTERNET ARCHIVE (MIA). This website at https://www.marxists.org is a public library maintained by an all-volunteer staff. In addition to many of the original works of Marx as well as Marxists, anarchists, socialists, and others, the site contains extensive encyclopedic entries on biographies, history, events, and ideas of the movement. *See also* MARX-ENGELS INSTITUTE.

MARX'S CHARACTER. Much has been written about Marx's personal life and his character in terms of his relationships with family and friends, his personality, and his work ethic. Major biographies—of which more than a dozen have been published since the latter half of the 20th century—detail a complex portrait of Marx's character driven in many ways by the dialectical contrast of Marx's materialist middle-class lifestyle and his revolutionary theory and persona.

Marx often struggled financially to maintain the middle-class lifestyle expected by his family. Karl and his wife **Jenny Marx** were by all accounts devoted parents, and the surviving **Marx children** were well educated and supported. Marx's devotion to Jenny, however, did not prevent him from having an affair with their live-in maid **Helene Demuth (Lenchen)**. The relationship produced an illegitimate son (**Henry or "Freddy" Demuth**). The Marx family's desire to keep up appearances led to **Friedrich Engels** claiming the son as his own, sparing the Marx family the public embarrassment. Although their marriage survived, the family was often in serious debt. Karl wrote to Engels in 1865 that, while living in London in 1865, the family had "been living purely out of the pawn house" (Seigel 1978) and was under almost constant threat of eviction. Meager earnings from **Marx's journalistic career**, the occasional inheritance, and

Karl Marx ("The Moor").

only after much procrastination in only six or seven weeks. The bulk of the document was written in a period of days after the Central Committee sent him an ultimatum on 24 or 25 January 1848, demanding a 1 February deadline for the manuscript (Wheen 2001).

Throughout his life, Karl suffered a host of health issues (Rühle 2011), and his **ill health**, combined with the health problems (including mental health) of Jenny and the death of several of their children, may be at least partly to blame for Karl's reputation as aggressive and domineering toward his friends, acquaintances, and colleagues. He often used crude and degrading language to insult those with whom he disagreed (Seigel 1978), and it is notable that after his **death**, only 11 people attended his funeral.

MARX'S CHILDREN. Jenny and Karl Marx had six children, three of whom lived to adulthood. Karl doted on his children and grandchildren. "Visitors to his house as well as his own children, commented on his love and affection for them. They noted the way he played with them, told them stories, and read to them. The desolate moods that followed his children's deaths bespoke a paternal love that was anything but distant. Marx profoundly enjoyed the presence of children—not just his own but all children" (Sperber 2013, 469). *See also* MARX, EDGAR ("MUSH"), MARX, ELEANOR ("TUSSY"), MARX, FRANZISKA, MARX, HEINRICH GUIDO, MARX, JENNY CAROLINE, MARX, LAURA.

MARX'S JOURNALISTIC CAREER. Marx's journalism included work on the *Rheinische Zeitung* (*Rhineland News*) shortly after receiving his doctorate and the *New Rhineland Newspaper* during the **Revolutions of 1848** and the *New York Tribune* in the 1850s. In addition, Marx placed items in left-wing newspapers throughout the 1850s and into the early 1860s. It was through his journalism that he was able to earn a semidecent living for his family, although the income was somewhat sporadic, and **Engels** had to supplement it when he could. Sperber (2013) details the work that went into these articles, going to the

the generous and frequent monetary gifts from his friends and supporters (most notably Engels) were barely enough to keep the debt collectors at bay. The Marx family's poor financial situation was, in many ways, a result of Karl's devotion to his theoretical and revolutionary writings and work—work that did not produce significant income.

Marx's approach to his work was manic. On Karl's work habits, **Arnold Ruge** writes, "He has a peculiar personality—perfect as a scholar and author but completely ruinous as a journalist. He reads a lot; he works with unusual intensity and has a critical talent that occasionally degenerates into a wanton dialectic. But he finishes nothing, breaks off everything and plunges himself ever afresh into an endless sea of books. . . . He is irritable and hot-tempered, particularly when he has worked himself sick and not gone to bed for three, even four nights on end" (quoted in Stedman-Jones 2016, 156). Marx completed the writing of *The Communist Manifesto*, for example,

Library of the **British Museum** for hours at a time, reading English, German, and French newspapers and reports of British parliamentary investigative committees and parliamentary debates as well as doing some personal reporting on these debates and demonstrations. In today's terms, he was more of a columnist than a reporter, writing about 500 such pieces in the course of his life. "His substantial essays (which occupy five to ten pages when reprinted in the collections of his works) contained extensive commentary, shot through with typical ironic and satirical invective. The sheer volume of his newspaper work is impressive. Although the journalism is sparsely examined in most biographies, the extent of the newspaper articles written by Marx between 1853 and 1862 was greater than everything else he published during his lifetime put together. In the **eulogy** summing up the life of his friend, Engels emphasized—quite rightly—the intellectual and political significance of Marx's journalism" (296).

MATERIALIST CONCEPTION OF HISTORY. *See* ECONOMIC THEORY OF HISTORY; PREFACE, THE.

MEANS OF COMMUNICATION AND TRANSPORTATION. The means of communication and transportation that accompanied the small-scale production of **agricultural** goods and **handicrafts** were inadequate for the needs of **capitalist** production with its mass production, extended **division of labor,** and expanding **world markets. Large-scale industry** needed speed, communication systems that could help in coordinating global activities, and transportation systems that could connect to world markets to transport vast masses of timber, coal, and iron as well as finished products (Marx 1867/1976, 506). The **capitalist revolution** in the **mode of production**, Marx writes, necessitated a **revolution** in the means of transportation and communication, hence the revolution in shipping, railways, and telegraphs in Marx's day and further revolutions in **transportation and communications technology** as the **laws of capitalist production** intensified. Marx also points out that it

was the prime mover of the factory, the steam engine, which was adapted for land and ocean transportation as well as revolutionizing the building of locomotives and ships. The combination of transport and communications technology and large-scale industry allowed Europe to exploit world markets. "By ruining **handicraft production** of finished articles in other countries, machinery forcibly converts them into fields for the production of its raw material" (579).

Like the **systems of credit** made available to capitalists through **joint-stock companies** and **banks,** the means of transportation and communications significantly sped up the circulation time of capital. "And the last fifty years have brought a revolution in this respect that is comparable only with the **industrial revolution** of the second half of the last century" (Marx 1894/1991, 164). Marx writes of the railways, steamer lines, the Suez Canal, and telegraph cables. More recent **innovations**, of course, have a more dramatic impact on the pace of trade and thus the accumulation of **surplus value.** However, even in Marx's day, he estimates that the turnover rate in commerce "has been increased two or three times and more" through improvements in transportation and communication, all of which have a significant effect on the rate of **capital** growth (164). *See also* PRODUCTIVE LABOR.

MEANS OF PRODUCTION. The means of production is Marx's term for the inanimate part of the **forces of production.** This part includes land, raw materials, **tools, machinery, factories,** bridges, canals, railroads, and ships—everything within the forces of production except **labor power,** the animate part of the production process and the part necessary to produce **surplus value.** The transportation of commodities is part of the production process (and thus the labor involved as **productive labor**). Transport is an integral part of production industries in transferring resources from the mines to the factories or crops to food-processing plants and on to retail outlets. The **use value** of things, Marx argues, "is realized only in their consumption, and their consumption may make a change of location necessary";

thus, he considers such transportation expenditures as part of the cost of production (Marx 1885/1978, 226–27).

The **expropriation** of **surplus labor** and thus the system of **capitalism** itself **monopolizes** the means of production. Whenever a part of society controls the means of production, the worker must not only work to produce her maintenance but also put in an extra quantity of **labor** for the owner of the means of production. This need for the expenditure of additional work is true whether a **slave** in an **ancient society**, a **serf** under **feudalism**, or a **worker** under a capitalist (Marx 1867/1976, 344–45). *See also* CONSTANT CAPITAL, DEAD CAPITAL, MODE OF PRODUCTION, RELATIONS OF PRODUCTION, UNPRODUCTIVE LABOR.

MEHRING, FRANZ (1846–1919). A prominent leader of the **Social Democratic Party of Germany**, Mehring joined the party in 1891. He became the chief editor of the *Social Democrat* newspaper from 1902 to 1907. Most important, in 1918, he wrote the first biography of Marx, *Karl Marx: The Story of His Life*, and helped to popularize and mythologize Marx's life and theoretical contributions. In addition to the biography, he urged **August Bebel** and **Eduard Bernstein** to censor the correspondence between Marx and **Engels** before publishing them. The letters contained insulting references to many **Social Democrats** as well as some overt racism. *See also* MARXIAN MYTHOLOGY.

MENSHEVIKS. In 1903, Russian socialists were attempting to organize themselves while in exile. In the party congresses that followed, two factions emerged. The followers of **Vladimir Lenin** were characterized as "the majority" (*Bolshinvstvo*, or **Bolshevik**) and the supporters of Julius Martov as "the minority" (*Menshinstvo*) despite the fluid nature of support for both factions. There was considerable churn in the years before the **1905 Revolution** as coalitions formed and reformed. Various efforts to unify the respective factions failed as partisan differences hardened and as a corrupt czarist regime began to disintegrate,

opening up realistic possibilities for a thoroughgoing revolution.

From the outside, the differences between Bolshevik and Menshevik were minor but in practical terms revolved around the ruthlessness evidenced in the factions' pursuit of political power. The Mensheviks aspired to form a mass-based parliamentary party patterned after European social democratic parties, particularly Germany's **Social Democratic Party**. The Bolsheviks followed Lenin's thinking in *What Is to Be Done?* Published in 1901, Lenin argued for a **vanguard party**, or the formation of a small, conspiratorial, revolutionary party dedicated to the principle of **democratic centralism**, which allowed open deliberation internally but forbade public dissent. The Bolsheviks routinely engaged in criminal activities—particularly bank robberies—to support their propaganda efforts, while the Mensheviks adopted more conventional party-building tactics.

While the Mensheviks supported the **February Revolution** in 1917, they opposed the **October Revolution**, which overthrew the Russian Provisional Government. In the post-1917 environment, support for the Mensheviks sharply dissipated. During the Russian Civil War, Menshevik leaders like Julius Martov supported the **Red Army** against the royalist White Army but continued to denounce the excesses of the Bolsheviks. During Lenin's period of rapidly declining health, the state banned the Menshevik party in the early 1920s. Many Mensheviks fled into exile following Lenin's death and **Joseph Stalin**'s rapid consolidation of power. Stalin would later inaugurate his control over the Soviet state by conducting "show trials" of 14 former Mensheviks in 1931.

METABOLIC INTERACTION. Human **labor** is the process by which humankind regulates, mediates, and controls the metabolism—that is, the flow of raw materials and energy between society and nature. "He sets in motion the forces which belong to his own body, his arms, legs, head and hands in order to appropriate the materials of nature in a form adapted to his own needs" (Marx 1867/1976,

283). Through action on nature, Marx adds, he changes it, and in the process, he changes his nature. Such labor, according to Marx, is a distinctly human characteristic.

John Bellamy Foster points out that Marx uses the concept of metabolism to characterize the relationship between man and nature. Capitalist production, Marx writes, collects **population** in ever-growing **urban** centers; this disrupts the metabolic interaction between man and the earth and prevents the recycling of wastes back to the soil. All the progress in **capitalist agriculture** robs not only the worker but also the soil. All the artificial ways of increasing soil fertility for the short term ruin the long-term health of that fertility. Capitalism causes **urbanization**, Marx argues. "It disturbs the metabolic interaction between man and the earth, i.e., it prevents the return to the soil of its constituent elements consumed by man in the form of food and clothing; hence it hinders the operation of the eternal natural condition for the lasting fertility of the soil. Thus it destroys at the same time the physical health of the urban worker, and the intellectual life of the rural worker. . . . In modern agriculture, as in urban industry, the increase in the **productivity** and the mobility of labour is purchased at the cost of laying waste and debilitating **labour-power** itself" (637–38). Capitalism is an economic system in which the **exploitation** of nature as well as of labor is fundamental to the continuation and **growth** of the system itself.

The **environmental crisis** is due to the **contradiction** between **capitalism**'s need for continual growth and the limits of the natural environment. Modern-day ecologists have commented on the issue; it is somewhat surprising to many that Marx wrote of it in the 19th century. Marx calls it our "metabolic relation to nature." In modern terms, he is referring to **ecology**. The **forces of production** are essential in determining the relationship of humans to the natural world. However, the focus of Marx's analysis quickly moves to the **relations of production**. The class interests that the forces of production serve—their purpose as well as the extent of their use—are central in human ecology. The **exploitation** of the

environment and the worker is endemic to the capitalist system. Those who control the **mode of production** are profiting from this exploitation. They value the growth of capital above all else. This relationship is at the heart of the environmental crisis.

Capitalism needs **perpetual growth**, but Marx recognized that there are two ultimate limits to that growth. Once the industrial processes of agriculture, mining, commodity production, and the means of transport and communication are fully developed, it will have "no barriers but those presented by the availability of raw materials and the extent of sales outlets" (578–79). Foster suggests that Marx's theory could lead environmentalists to focus less on the industrial **means of production** and more on the **capital** that controls these means. *See also* CAPITALIST AGRICULTURE, CLASS CONFLICT, CONTRADICTIONS OF CAPITALISM, ECOLOGY, OVERPRODUCTION, UNDERCONSUMPTION.

MODE OF PRODUCTION. The mode of production is the overall term for the type of production that characterizes a sociocultural system. It consists of the **forces of production** and **relations of production**. The mode of production has a profound effect on the entire **superstructure** (such as government, **religion**, family, and ideology). Marx asserts that there is an **evolutionary** sequence of production modes: **primitive communism**, **Asiatic**, **ancient**, **feudal**, and **capital**.

It is the **contradictions** between the **forces of production** and the relations of production that lead to **class conflict**. The relation to the production process defines social classes. In **ancient society**, the two classes were **slaves** and **masters**, in feudal society **serfs** and **lords**, and in capitalist society **bourgeoisie** (capitalists) and **proletariat** (workers), in summary, the exploiter and the exploited. The material interests of the class that control the forces of production, Marx asserts, are the dominant interests within society. In feudal societies, it is the nobility that controls the forces of production, thus making them the **ruling class**; in a capitalist society, it is the capitalist (bourgeoisie).

With **capitalism**, there is a conflict of interest between the bourgeoisie and the proletariat. Eventually, Marx asserts, with the development of the forces of production, it reaches a point where the existing relations of production become a fetter on the development of the forces of production, producing a **crisis**. Under capitalism, the crisis is one of **overproduction**, as consumers cannot purchase all of the commodities that the system produces. This overproduction results in the failure of many enterprises and the consequent loss of class position and wealth of some capitalists as well as massive unemployment for the proletariat. Over time, as the cost of labor falls and inventories are cleared, recovery takes hold; surviving enterprises become more **centralized and enlarged** as well as more productive, thus creating conditions for the next crisis to become even more severe. In these times of crisis, the **revolutionary class consciousness** of the proletariat will spread. The crises will become so severe that this proletariat will revolt and successfully overthrow the **bourgeois state** and establish a socialist state under the **dictatorship of the proletariat**, which will oversee the transition to **communism**. *See also* PREFACE, THE, *WAGE LABOUR AND CAPITAL*.

MONEY. Economists tend to view money as a unit of value that serves a broad array of purposes, including acting as a unit of exchange and as a basis for preserving value. For Marx, money's capacity as a medium of exchange facilitates the "confounding and compounding" of economic relationships, which feeds the **fetishism of commodities**. In his *Economic and Philosophic Manuscripts of 1844*, Marx comments on the role that money plays in mystifying economic and human relationships:

He who can buy bravery is brave, though he be a coward. As money is not exchanged for any one specific quality, for any one specific thing, or for any particular human essential power, but for the entire objective world of man and nature, from the standpoint of its possessor it therefore serves to exchange every quality for every other, even contradictory, quality and object: it is the fraternization of impossibilities. It makes contradictions embrace. (Marx 1843, 61–62)

For Marx, money contributes to the capitalist system by rendering the concentration of wealth more efficient. That the **bourgeoisie** can use money to buy and sell **labor power** contributes to the **objectification** and **alienation** of the **proletariat**.

Marx acknowledged that the rise of merchant wealth eased the old feudal relations of production off the stage. In *Grundrisse*, he asserts that "monetary wealth helped to *strip* the **labor-power** of able-bodied individuals from these conditions; and in part this process of divorce proceeded without it" (Marx 1857–1861, 445). However, the significant critique of money is that the social bonds in a capitalist society have taken on the appearance of an impersonal relationship between things:

The reciprocal and all-sided dependence of individuals who are indifferent to one another forms their social connection. This social bond is expressed in **exchange value**, by means of which alone each individual's own activity or his product becomes an activity and a product for him; he must produce a general product— exchange value, or, the latter isolated for itself and individualized, money. On the other side, the power which each individual exercises over the activity of others or over social wealth exists in him as the owner of exchange values, of money. The individual carries his social power, as well as his bond with society, in his pocket. (95)

Money enhances human capacity (e.g., "I am ugly, but I can buy the most beautiful woman for myself") (Avineri 1968, 111), feeding the impulse to accumulate higher levels of wealth extracted from the reproduction of goods, which generally require escalating acts of **expropriation** of **labor power**. Marx's criticisms of money echo long-standing denunciations of money as the "root of all evil." However, Marx is somewhat vague on how a socialist and later a communist society with **large-scale industry** would operate in the absence of some form of currency. Likewise, Marx confidently envisaged a communist future that would produce sufficient abundance that the hoarding of money would be a kind of atavism. However, he omitted an account of how a socialist society could achieve such a state.

MONOPOLY. Monopolies destroy free markets by preventing competitors from entering a market. Monopolies and cartels regulate production, and because they control supply, they can artificially inflate the price of the **commodity**, thus making surplus profits (called differential rents) over and above the average rate of profit within a society. Marx recognized that there is a long-term tendency for monopolies to form within a given market due to competitive forces within industries. Over time, **competition** produces a few successful firms where many competitors have been absorbed or run out of business. Once monopolies form, several factors can serve to bar new competitors from entering the market and thus perpetuate the monopoly. One significant barrier is the sheer size of successful firms. **Large-scale industry** with the advantages of **economies of scale** dominate many markets and present significant obstacles. Starting a successful automobile manufacturing company, for example, would take well over a billion dollars today; this would be a substantial barrier to many. Other impediments include patents, the ability of the monopoly to lower its prices until the new competitor fails, or other forms of competitive practices to protect market shares.

However, Marx asserted that such monopoly power could also engender counter forces. It may provoke "state intervention," as the state is interested in the success of the entire **capitalist class** rather than individual capitalists (Marx 1894/1991, 569). Barriers to high initial **capital** investment may not be so formidable with the availability of **credit systems** such as **banks** and **joint-stock companies** (corporations). Potential competitors are especially encouraged to enter lucrative markets. In sum, although Marx foresaw the

centralization and enlargement of capital and the formation of monopolies, he did not see monopolies as a permanent impediment to market economies. In this, he may well have been mistaken. *See also* BOURGEOIS STATE, DICTATORSHIP OF THE BOURGEOISIE, MONOPOLY CAPITALISM.

MONOPOLY CAPITALISM. Marx, like many **classical economists** of his time, recognized that the capitalist system of his day operated primarily through **competition** among many individual capitalist businesses, each of which on its own formed only a negligible portion of the total value of the economy. Because of this, no single capitalist firm could significantly influence the overall market. However, Marx argued, this system was inherently unstable, as larger firms could more effectively limit labor costs and expand production, giving them an advantage over smaller firms. He notes that in the battle to lessen the price of **commodities**, much depends on the **productivity** of labor. Moreover, the output of labor depends in large part on the **scale of production**. "Therefore the larger capitals beat the smaller" (Marx 1867/1976, 777).

The instability of the system would lead to fewer and fewer competitive firms. Marx argued that this was one of the many **contradictions of capitalism** that lead to **crises** and, ultimately, a **revolt** of the working class and the transition to a **socialist mode of production**. By the early 20th century, however, it was apparent that the **capitalist mode of production** was still thriving. Baran and Sweezy (1966) popularized the term "monopoly **capitalism**" after their publication of *Monopoly Capital*. Their book recognized the tendency of capitalist firms to form monopolies as a stage of capitalism rather than as a fatal flaw as Marx envisioned it. The modern view of monopoly capitalism is one that focuses on the **economic stagnation** resulting from business consolidation that further reduces the political power of labor.

MOORE, SAMUEL. Moore was one of the English translators, along with **Edward Aveling** and **Friedrich Engels**, of the first volume of

Capital. A close friend of Engels, he was consulted closely in the more mathematical parts of the work. When Engels was dying of cancer, there was gossip that he had disowned his son, **Freddy Demuth**. To protect Engels's reputation, Moore told **Eleanor Marx** that Karl was Freddy's father, which Eleanor refused to believe. She went to Engels to get confirmation. Engels was dying from esophageal cancer and too weak to speak but wrote down the fact on a slate. He had told Moore, "Tussy [Eleanor] wants to make an idol of her father" (quoted in Stedman-Jones 2016, 374).

MOOR, THE. The nickname that family and close friends had for Karl Marx. It probably originated at the **University in Bonn** and given to him by friends because of his dark complexion. On the day of **Jenny Marx**'s death, for example, **Engels** remarked to **Eleanor Marx**, "The Moor has died as well" (quoted in Sperber 2013, 541).

MORGAN, LEWIS HENRY (1818–1881). Morgan was a social theorist and one of the first American anthropologists. He is best known for his book *Ancient Society* published in 1877, which presented an evolutionary framework for the development and change of human societies. In it, he traced the evolutionary relationship between **technology**, family and social relations, property relations, and social structure across the known span of human existence. His theory of **social evolution** presented three significant stages of societal development: savagery, barbarism, and civilization, where progress in technology mainly drives change in social conditions.

Marx read *Ancient Society* in 1881 and recognized it as further evidence supporting his **historical materialist** framework for the development and change of social and economic systems. Before his death, Marx began working on his book based on Morgan's work,

published posthumously as *The Ethnological Notebooks of Karl Marx*. **Engels** continued this work, further developing Marx's and Morgan's ideas in his book *The Origin of the Family, Private Property, and the State* (1884). *See also* PREFACE, THE.

MUTUALISM. Mutualism represents a kind of **anarchist** "free-market" interpretation of **socialism**. Originating in the thought of **Pierre-Joseph Proudhon**, mutualists have imagined a world in which **large-scale industry** could exist simultaneously in a world without massive government and where individuals could generate wealth but where "**private property** is theft," to follow Proudhon's famous dictum. Representing a significant fraction of the socialist movement in **France**, mutualism served a kind of "middle path" between capitalist advocacy of private property and the communist prohibition of private property. Most mutualists advocated **evolutionary** change and believed that human society would eventually transcend the need for government. Essential to the mutualist school of thought are voluntary associations and the importance of freedom of association.

Mutualism was not particularly influential in France or Spain, but French socialists advocated mutualist positions at several meetings of the **First International**. At various points, mutualism offered a significant contrast to **Marxism** as a potential alternative approach to socialism. Other anarchists, such as **Peter Kropotkin** and **Mikhail Bakunin**, ridiculed the proposition that the free market could spontaneously form an egalitarian society. Mutualists exerted some influence in international socialist organizations in the 19th century. As a 20th-century phenomenon, mutualism represents a manifestation of "libertarian-socialism," committed to the prospect of an egalitarian society organized along free-market principles and believe that state regulation is mostly superfluous.

N

NAPOLEON III (1808–1873). Born **Charles-Louis Napoleon Bonaparte**, later Louis Napoleon, and finally known as Napoleon III. He was elected president of **France** in 1848 amid the **Revolutions of 1848** and in 1852 assumed monarchical authority, becoming Emperor Napoleon III. As king, Napoleon III launched ambitious public works projects, sought to reform France's archaic financial system, and expanded France's railroad system. Among his most significant works was the extensive rebuilding of vast sections of **Paris**, demolishing medieval neighborhoods, and rebuilding the road system with broad boulevards. Napoleon III led an ill-prepared France into the **Franco-Prussian War** of 1870. France's rapid defeat culminated in Napoleon III's capture following the Battle of Sedan (1870), which effectively ended the war in humiliating fashion.

In 1851, Karl Marx wrote *The Eighteenth Brumaire of Louis Napoleon*, in which Marx interpreted a contemporaneous event through the lens of his **materialist conception of history**. For Marx, Napoleon III represented a "mediocrity" that accidents of history uplifted to dictatorial power. From a materialist perspective, Napoleon's seizure of power in France illustrated the circumstances that could pave the way for counterrevolutionary forces to seize the power of the state, reinforcing Marx's belief that a specific combination of conditions was required to bring about a **socialist revolution**. Marx, in letters to **Engels**, initially supported Germany in the Franco-Prussian War, believing that a German defeat would deal a crippling blow to the prospects of a proletarian revolution (Berlin 2013, 236).

NAPOLEON, LOUIS. *See* NAPOLEON III.

NARODNIKS. The Narodniks (Russian translation: populism) was a **Russian** intellectual movement that emerged in the 1860s and lasted into the 1870s. Encouraged by Czar Alexander II's emancipation of the **serfs** in 1861, the Narodniks conceived themselves as a progressive movement dedicated to the removal of the last vestiges of **feudalism** and to resisting the transition to **capitalism**. Narodniks like **Aleksandr Herzen** believed that capitalism could find no purchase in an agrarian society like Russia but that **socialism** could. A mostly middle-class movement, Narodnism had little practical impact on Russian politics but provided the intellectual inspiration for a more radical younger generation of Russian reformers, notably **Narodnoya Volya** (the "People's Will").

Ideologically speaking, Narodnism shared with Marxist interpretations of socialism a profound hostility toward accumulation; in the case of the Narodniks, the foci of their enmity were the Kulaks, former serfs who had become affluent landholding farmers. The Narodniks shared this antagonism toward the Kulaks with 20th-century Russian socialists. Also, like Marxian socialism, the Narodniks identified an oppressed class, but rather than the proletariat, they believed that the Russian **peasantry** had **revolutionary** potential. However, the Narodniks thought that the peasantry needed the guidance and persuasion of leaders; to that end, many Narodniks traveled into the countryside, living with and among the Russian peasantry, hoping through oratory and inspiration to form the peasantry into a revolutionary mass.

Predictably, the peasants largely distrusted the Narodniks, who found the urban, intellectual Narodniks to be odd. The Narodniks quickly drew the suspicions of czarist authorities who swiftly arrested and sent them into internal exile. The naïveté of the Narodniks likely informed the far more paranoid and militant approach of "Land and Liberty," a more secretive cabal that formed in 1876, and of its more violent splinter group, **Narodnoya Volya** (the "People's Will"), whose members advocated "direct action" to overthrow the czarist regime and successfully assassinated Czar Alexander II in 1881.

NARODNOYA VOLYA. Translated as "People's Will," Narodnoya Volya emerged as a conspiratorial **revolutionary** organization dedicated to the overthrow of the **Russian** state. In the early decades of the 19th century, czarist autocracy, a predatory nobility, and the persistence of **feudal** social arrangements conspired to produce crushing poverty and **economic stagnation**. These conditions inspired the formation of several middle-class reformist movements, including the **Narodniks**, *Zemlya i Volya* ("Land and Liberty"), and a rapidly proliferating, loose constellation of **anarchist** organizations. All of these organizations were dedicated to the proposition that the abolition of czarism precedes any meaningful reforms. In particular, the Narodniks' attempts to directly appeal to and enlist the Russian **peasantry** in the overthrow of czarism met with crushing failure.

Early in this period, Czar Nicholas I's heavy-handed oppression yielded to Alexander II's halting, indecisive mixture of reform and repression. While he emancipated all Russian **serfs** in 1861 and launched massive reforms of the Russian economy and military, he also—following an unsuccessful assassination attempt in 1866—created a secret police force known as "Okhrana" to defend and protect the regime from the mounting threat of anti-czarist dissidents. Narodnoya Volya emerged as a more radicalized splinter of those populist groups, forming out of workers' organizations in several large Russian cities, and infiltrated the Russian army and navy. In light of the czarist regime's aggressive suppression of dissident groups, its leaders adopted a highly secretive cell structure designed to prevent the exposure or arrest of one cell from compromising the rest of the organization. Fewer than 50 self-selected members sat on its executive board. Because of fear that any direct appeals to the Russian people would draw the attention of the secret police, Narodnoya Volya's nominal leadership rejected democratic organizational principles.

Narodnoya Volya's highest-profile action was the successful assassination of Czar Alexander II in 1881. Traveling along a known route in a bulletproof, Cossack-guarded carriage to a Sunday military review in St. Petersburg, three members of Narodnoya Volya staged themselves along the road with bombs. A first bomber successfully blew up the carriage and killed several guards, while a second threw a bomb at the feet of the czar, fatally wounding him. Okhrana arrested a number of the cell members responsible for plotting the assassination and subsequently executed them.

Narodnoya Volya's focus on terrorism would prove ineffective, but its successful assassination of Czar Alexander II inspired later iterations of **revolutionary socialist** organizations committed to the "propaganda of the deed." The waves of terrorist violence committed by Narodnoya Volya members would provoke further retrenchment on the part of succeeding czars, further retarding political and economic reforms and paving the way for better-organized and better-supported revolutionary organizations, including the **Bolsheviks**, who would successfully topple the Russian regime in 1917.

NEGATION OF THE NEGATION. Originating with the **dialectic** philosophy of **Georg Hegel**, the negation of the negation is a phrase that, within **Hegelian dialectics**, describes the logical process by which new ideas or forms develop through contradictions. All ideas or forms contain a thesis and an antithesis (or the negation of the thesis). New forms develop through reconciliation of the thesis and antithesis (or the negation of the negation). This process results in a return to a previous form (i.e., it does not eliminate the previous form), but the new version of the form is of a higher or more complex level. Marx incorporated this concept into **historical materialism** in his explanations of the development of new social and economic forms, introduced in *Capital: Volume I* and later thoroughly explored in **Engels's** *Anti-Dühring*. In his account of changes in property ownership, for example, Marx writes that capitalist **private property** began as the expropriation of the scattered property of the many into the hands of the few. The process was extremely violent and protracted. The process of transforming capitalist private production facilities to social property, which does not involve a change in the **forces of production**—promises to be much less violent and protracted. "In the former case, it was a matter of the expropriation of the mass of the people by a few usurpers; but in this case, we have the expropriation of a few usurpers by the mass of the people" (Marx 1867/1976, 929–30).

NEW RHINELAND NEWS (NEUE RHEIN-ISCHE ZEITUNG). Authorities in **Belgium** viewed the **Paris Uprising** and the establishment of a republic in 1848 both as a threat of foreign invasion (as occurred with the last French Republic) or as the spur for an uprising by local radicals. On 3 March, the government instructed Marx, then an officer of the **Communist League** as well as vice president of the **Brussels Democratic Association**, to leave the country within 24 hours. Authorities later arrested Marx before the deadline and arrested Jenny as well when she attempted to visit him in jail. Released the next day, Marx returned to Paris, where other members of the Communist League gathered. Within weeks, revolt had spread to **Prussia** and **Austria**, and liberal governments were appointed to quell the disturbances. Marx then proposed that members of the League return peaceably to German

soil. Marx, along with **Engels** and **Schapper** and other members of the League, returned to **Cologne** and established the *New Rhineland News*. The new government in Prussia had established freedom of the press, and Marx was now free to openly express his views to a broader though educated audience.

For a year beginning in the spring of 1848, Marx became the editor of the *New Rhineland News*, which became the largest-selling radical newspaper in the Rhineland. The subtitle of the paper was "Organ of Democracy." The newspaper reflected Marx's politics. In it, Marx attempted to organize the working class across the **German Confederation** and pushed for revolutionary action in establishing a German republic. "In all of these activities, Marx persistently promoted the **revolutionary** strategy he had first envisaged in his essay *On the Jewish Question* and would present in scintillating language in *The Communist Manifesto*. Marx pressed for a democratic **revolution** to destroy the authoritarian Prussian monarchy. At the same time, he aspired to organize the working class to carry out a communist uprising against a capitalist regime he expected such a democratic revolution to establish" (Sperber 2013, 195). While Marx may have aspired to provoke class warfare at this time, he found it politically expedient to tone down his anticapitalism and focus on anti-Prussian sentiments and the establishment of a German republic in his editorials and speeches throughout most of 1848, in effect ignoring workers' issues. This downplaying of class issues was a major point of disagreement with the **True Socialists**. However, the conservative nature of the general assembly and its approval of a "constitutional monarchy" led Marx and his followers in 1849 to put greater emphasis on a second wave of revolution led by the proletariat and to be more dismissive of the democrats.

With increasing unrest in Cologne and environs in May 1849, Prussia accused Karl of inciting insurrection and expelled Marx, who had renounced his citizenship years before, as an undesirable alien. The *New Rhineland News* soon ended. "The swan song issue, dated 19 May 1849, was printed in revolutionary red. Enormously popular, it had to be reprinted repeatedly, eventually selling 20,000 copies" (Sperber 2013, 236). *See also* MARX'S JOURNALISM.

NEW YORK TRIBUNE. Marx became a European correspondent for the *New York Tribune* in 1851, writing about the political turmoil on the continent. The original series was so successful that the paper asked Marx to write regular pieces for the *Tribune* in 1852. "Over the course of a decade, Marx was paid for 487 pieces, many appearing in the *Tribune* as lead articles. About a quarter of them were actually ghostwritten by Engels, who pitched in when Marx's health problems made it hard for him to write, but Engels also wrote articles on military matters, which were 'The General's specialty'" (Sperber 2013, 295). In February 1861, the *Tribune* suspended its European correspondents to better focus on the coming American Civil War. *See also* ILL HEALTH OF KARL MARX, MARX'S JOURNALISTIC CAREER.

19TH-CENTURY SOCIALISM. Several historical forces contributed to the emergence of **socialism** as a set of complex social, economic, and political movements in the 19th century. The **Enlightenment**'s convictions regarding human progress, combined with the industrialization and the resulting **urbanization** of Europe, were significant factors in its emergence. In addition, the somewhat haphazard diffusion of education beyond political and economic elites into the middle and working classes culminated in a broad and diverse commitment to egalitarianism, which found expression in several strands of socialist thought. By the end of the 19th century, socialism had developed into a robust and influential ideology.

There are three distinct phases of 19th-century socialist thought. Pre-Marxist socialism emerged in the early part of the century and tended to advance **utopian** agendas. **Marxism** emerged and consolidated a vision of socialism as a class-based **revolutionary movement**. Finally, following Marx's death, socialism entered a contested period where **anarcho-libertarian socialism** vied with more authoritarian

variants of **revolutionary socialism**. Among the early proponents of socialism, **Claude-Henri de Saint-Simon** (1760–1825) saw the transformational implications of industrialization and prophesied societies organized on scientific principles where the state planned and directed the production and distribution of goods and services. His predictions regarding the disappearance of the state as a vehicle of monarchical aspirations and the replacement of "rule" by "administration" exerted tremendous influence over 19th-century socialist and liberal thinkers.

Much of the early 19th-century socialist thought and activity centered on utopian socialist planning along with the parallel emergence of the **Chartist Movement**. Utopian socialists like **Charles Fourier** and **Robert Owen** believed that the reorganization of society into smaller, planned units would transform society. **Pierre-Joseph Proudhon** contributed the notion that "property is theft," advancing a **mutualist** vision of socialism that advocated the abolition of the state and **private property** and the organization of society into small, planned, autonomous communities.

Anarchism represents an influential strand of 19th-century socialism. Anarchist socialists like Proudhon, **Mikhail Bakunin**, and **Peter Kropotkin** rejected authoritarianism in all forms, placing a premium on the dignity of the individual. Anarcho-socialists advocated for the abolition of the state, though they differed over how to achieve this elimination. Some, like Bakunin, were hardened revolutionaries, while others, like Kropotkin, advanced a more quietist approach, believing that human progress would tame the competitive urges that lead to war and oppression.

The **Chartist Movement** emerged in **England** as a working-class protest of the Reform Act of 1832, electoral reforms that eliminated some corruption but retained property requirements for voting eligibility. From this protest, the labor movement took root, advocating for an eight-hour workday and improvements in wages, access to improved health care, and expansions of voting rights. Union politics in the 19th century were associated with the left but tended to be more pragmatic and tactical in their political programs.

The **Revolutions of 1848** inaugurated the second distinctive phase of 19th-century socialism. These **revolutions** demonstrated the mounting frustrations of Europeans at the increasingly illegitimate neofeudal European governments and highlighted the increasing demands for more representative forms of governance. In this hothouse environment, Karl Marx and his close collaborator **Friedrich Engels** offered the most coherent, synthetic vision of socialism to date. Combining **Left Hegelianism** with **classical economics**, Marx's **historical materialism** presented a cohesive explanation of the past, a trenchant critique of **capitalism**, and a compelling vision of the future. The Marx–Engels interpretation of socialism focused on **class conflict**. It argued that the **bourgeoisie**'s exploitation of the **proletariat** and the resulting **alienation** of the working class necessitated a **socialist revolution** and the replacement of capitalism by a **dictatorship of the proletariat**.

Internecine conflict over the direction of socialism characterized the final two decades of the 19th century. Within the Marxist factions, revisionists like **Eduard Bernstein** identified what he perceived to be critical shortcomings with the Marxist tradition, and revolutionary Marxists like **Rosa Luxemburg** attacked the revisions. The final decades of the 19th century witnessed the emergence of **Russian** revolutionary socialism, led **by Vladimir Illich Lenin**. By the end of the century, socialism had emerged as a set of vibrant and diverse intellectual and ideological movements, united in the Enlightenment conviction of the possibility of human progress through the elimination of class conflict.

NORTH GERMAN CONFEDERATION. A short-lived Confederation of German states under Prussian leadership. **Bismarck** created the confederation after the defeat of **Austria** in the **Austro-Prussian War**, annexing some German states that had supported Austria and uniting other small states into the North German Confederation. In doing this, Bismarck called for universal manhood suffrage as well as a Reichstag or parliament. Many veterans of the **Revolution of 1848** supported Bismarck in this reform, though Marx and **Engels** did not. The North German Confederation dissolved in 1871 after the **Franco-Prussian War** and became the **German Empire** under Prussia's Prince Wilhelm I.

OBJECTIFICATION. A term often used interchangeably with **reification**, objectification relates to **alienation** and the sense in which the **proletariat** is viewed solely as a means to an end (e.g., **profit**) by the **bourgeoisie**. There are many senses in which to objectify a person or class of people: the objectification of women occurs when viewed solely through the lens of their availability and utility as sexual objects rather than as beings with ends other than sexual gratification. Feminist theorists have written extensively on gender objectification. Hegel's treatment of consciousness effectively renders objectification and alienation synonymous. However, Avineri (1968) notes that Marx "distinguishes between objectification, the promise of material existence, and alienation, a state of consciousness resulting from a specific method of relationship between men and *objects*" (97).

Nussbaum (1995) notes that objectifiers may treat a person as a "thing" in seven different ways. They may treat a person "instrumentally" as a "tool" for their purposes. Second, they may "deny autonomy" to the individual, thereby depriving the person of their "self-determination." A third type of objectification of a person is to treat them as "inert," or "lacking in agency." Nussbaum terms the fourth type of objectification as one "fungibility." This is where the objectifier treats the person as "interchangeable" with other objects or even with objects of different types. The fifth type is one of "violability," where they treat the person as an object lacking in boundaries, or "something that they can break up, smash, or break into." The sixth is "Ownership." In this type, they treat the person as something "that is owned by another," one who "can be bought or sold." Finally, the seventh type of objectification occurs when the objectifier denies subjectivity to a person, treating a person as a thing "whose experience and feelings (if any) are of no account" (257). Nussbaum's discussion of Marx's interpretation of objectification focuses on workers' "spiritual violation" due to the deprivation "of the central means of their self-definition as humans" (263). For Marx, to objectify another is to **exploit** that person. To use workers—particularly within an economic system, incentivizing the exploiter to seek ever-higher levels of exploitation—starts the proletariat down the pathway toward **revolutionary class consciousness**.

OCTOBER REVOLUTION. *See* BOLSHEVIK REVOLUTION.

ODGER, GEORGE (1831–1877). George Odger was an innovative British trade unionist who worked energetically for a variety of leftist causes. A shoemaker by trade, Odger stood unsuccessfully for parliament several times and was secretary of the London Trades Council, an early umbrella organization of British **trade unions**. He was a participant in a variety of British leftist movements and wrote forcefully in opposition to **slavery** during the American Civil War. As a founding member of the **International Workingmen's Association**, Odger gave a speech at its inaugural meeting, calling for international cooperation among the diverse organizations of the European working classes.

George Odger's career is illustrative of the distinctive nature of English **socialism**, which represented a parallel development of the worker's entrance into the world of politics. Odger represented the kind of constrained trade unionism—instinctively gradualist and resistant to any hint of radicalism—that so frustrated Marx's **revolutionary** ambitions. Beloved and respected among Britain's working classes, Odger was held in contempt by British political elites as a "striver" who lacked the sophistication expected of those holding elective office. Ineluctably English, Odger never embraced violence or revolution, anticipating the **Fabian** trust in English culture that patient and persistent pressure would yield results. Unlike the Fabians, Odger did not merely sympathize or identify with workers; he was and remained a worker.

ON THE JEWISH QUESTION (1844). First published in **Paris** in 1844, the essay analyzes two studies by **Bruno Bauer**, who advocated that Jews could achieve full political freedom in a secular state only by abandoning their **religion**. In his critique, Marx argued that the "secular state" is not opposed to religion but rather considers religion as a personal affair with no prominent role in social life. Comparing the state's treatment of religion to its treatment of property, education, and occupation, Marx states,

> The state abolishes, in its own way, distinctions of birth, social rank, education, occupation, when it declares that birth, social rank, education, occupation, are nonpolitical distinctions, when it proclaims, without regard to these distinctions, that every member of the nation is an *equal* participant in national sovereignty, when it treats all elements of the real life of the nation from the standpoint of the state. Nevertheless, the state allows **private property**, education, occupation, to *act* in *their* way—*i.e.*, as private property, as education, as occupation, and to exert the influence of their *special* nature. Far

from abolishing these real distinctions, the state only exists on the presupposition of their existence; it feels itself to be a political state and asserts its universality only in opposition to these elements of its being. (Section I, para. 30)

Marx concludes that the secular state frees individuals from the constraints of religion, family, and occupation—insisting that such distinctions are of individual significance only and no longer determined the relation of the individual to the state. Rather than acting as members of a particular faith, occupational group, or class, public affairs became an individual matter, thus giving free rein to the individual's material interests. "But, the completion of the **idealism** of the state was at the same time, the completion of the materialism of civil society. Throwing off the political yoke meant at the same time throwing off the bonds that restrained the egoistic spirit of civil society. Political emancipation was, at the same time, the emancipation of civil society from politics, from having even the *semblance* of a universal content. . . . The liberty of egoistic man and the recognition of this liberty, however, is rather the recognition of the *unrestrained* movement of the spiritual and material elements which form the content of his life" (Section I, para. 77). Freeing individuals from the constraints of these groups gives them free rein to pursue their material interests, that is, to exploit their fellow man.

Political emancipation is not human emancipation! "*All* emancipation is a *reduction* of the human world and relationships to *man himself*." Political emancipation reduces man to an egoistic, independent, individual member of civil society, to a citizen subject to equal treatment under the law. However, to achieve human emancipation, man must become a **species-being** in his everyday life and work, that is, recognize his social powers and use this power to organize social life beyond the merely political.

In the second part of the essay, Marx equates Judaism with **capitalism**. Using all the stereotypes of the day, Marx compares the worldly Jew with a concern for practical need, self-interest, worship of money, and huckstering (attempting to sell something of questionable value). "Very well then! Emancipation from *huckstering* and *money*, consequently from practical, real Judaism, would be the self-emancipation of our time." There are lively debates in the literature over whether Marx is an anti-Semite, as evidenced in this quote and other writings. Without engaging in this debate, note that Marx was a creature of his times. Further, his real concern here is not the Jews but rather capitalism, and his point is that real human emancipation is contingent on freeing ourselves from this **alienating** system.

ON THE ORIGIN OF SPECIES (1859).

Charles Darwin's description and outline of the process of **evolution** by means of natural selection was, according to Marx, an "epoch-making work" (Marx 1867/1976, 461). Indeed, the book revolutionized not only biology but social science as well, introducing a mechanism (natural selection) to describe change over time in systems both natural and social. Although Marx had already developed many of the ideas behind his conception of historical change in social and economic systems (**historical materialism**) prior to the publication of *On the Origin of Species*, he nonetheless recognized its importance, writing to Engels that "this is the book which contains the basis on natural history for our view" (quoted in Foster 2000, 197). Marx cites the book in the second edition of *Capital*, arguing that the same forces of **competition**, adaptation, change, and transformation observable in the natural world are operating in the social world. "Darwin has directed attention to the history of natural technology, i.e. the formation of the organs of plants and animals, which serve as the instruments of production for sustaining their life. Does not the history of the productive organs of man in society, of organs that are the material basis of every particular organization of society, deserve equal attention? And would not such a history be easier to compile, since, as Vico says, human history differs from natural history in that we have made the former, but not the latter? Technology reveals the active relation of man to nature, the

direct process of the production of his life, and thereby it also lays bare the process of the production of the social relations of his life, and of the mental conceptions that flow from those relations" (Marx 1867/1976, 493). *See also* ECOLOGY, ENGELS'S EULOGY FOR MARX.

ORIGIN OF THE FAMILY, PRIVATE PROPERTY, AND THE STATE, THE (1884).

Considered the seminal work of **Friedrich Engels**, *The Origin of the Family, Private Property, and the State: In Light of the Researches of Lewis H. Morgan* was first published in Switzerland in 1884 (with a German version stalled from publication by **Bismarck**'s **Anti-Socialist Laws**). The book was subsequently translated into a variety of other languages in the 1880s, and an English translation first appeared in 1902.

Engels undertook the writing and completed the work in 1884, approximately a year after the death of Marx. Engels was inspired to write on the subject after reading Marx's synopsis and notes of **Lewis Henry Morgan**'s influential anthropological book *Ancient Society* (Marx's notes were later published as *The Ethnological Notebooks of Karl Marx*), as Engels believed that Marx had intended to write a full volume on the subject. He noted that Morgan's work was a "rediscovery" of the rules of **historical materialism** that Marx had first outlined decades earlier and that the patterns Morgan discovered in the **evolution** of prehistoric human societies offered further proof of the reality of Marx's materialist conception of history.

The book begins with an exhaustive discussion of the major points of *Ancient Society*, describing the evolutionary stages of human society proposed by Morgan. Whereas Morgan emphasized the role of **technology** in driving **social evolution**, Engels argued that ultimately **social relations** governed technological changes and that the two factors determined the control of resources. The changes in access to the products of nature, therefore, drive the transitions from savagery to barbarism to civilization. Engels spends significant time discussing the original domestic institution outlined by Morgan, drawing attention to the fact that it was likely a matrilineal clan (as opposed to a nuclear family) and that this type of social organization made possible a form of **primitive communism**. The rise of property, which, according to this evolutionary scheme, occurs during the barbarism stage, results in the disempowerment of women as property inheritance passes down along monogamous patrilineal lines. So, for Engels (and for Morgan), social evolution also is driven by changes in family structures. Engels goes on to argue that the monogamous patrilineal system that enables property and inheritance is, in Engels's time, enforced through the **superstructure** controlled by the **bourgeoisie**. Religious and political rules governing marriage, for example, are in place primarily to ensure the continued existence of capitalism. These rules, according to Engels, lead to moral decay and the "enslavement" of women, as domestic unions are in place to ensure proper property ownership and inheritance rather than for the natural expression of human sex-love relationships. Engels argues that the **proletariat** was the only class free from the restraints of property and the required social relations and would, therefore, be free of the moral problems inherent in the system, making them the ideal class to lead the coming social revolution. Engels predicted that after the coming revolution and abolishment of **private property** and the establishment of a **classless society**, family structure would assume its natural monogamous form where sex-love would form the basis of marital unions.

OVERPRODUCTION. The crisis of overproduction involves the capitalists' inability to sell their products. Marx writes that this inability is because there is a delay between production and exchange, or between when the capitalist produces a **commodity** and when the capitalist realizes **surplus value**. There is a tendency toward equilibrium between the production of a commodity and its consumption, but this "comes into play only as a reaction against the constant upsetting of this equilibrium" (Marx 1867/1976, 476). The adoption of ever more productive **machinery** by capitalists made compulsory for every manufacturer because of **competition** leads to ever-higher production but growing structural unemployment. Capitalists want to pay their workers low wages but need every other capitalist to pay high salaries to buy their commodities. What is rational for a single capitalist is irrational for the whole. This fallacy of composition is a fundamental contradiction in the capitalist system, leading to excess supply over demand and periodic crises. **Engels** (1877) describes the historical pattern:

> As a matter of fact, since 1825, when the first general crisis broke out, the whole **industrial** and **commercial** world, **production** and **exchange** among all civilized peoples and their more or less barbaric hangers-on, are thrown out of joint about once every ten years. Commerce is at a stand-still, the markets are glutted, products accumulate, as multitudinous as they are unsaleable, hard cash disappears, credit vanishes, factories are closed, the mass of the workers are in want of the means of subsistence, because they have produced too much of the means of subsistence; bankruptcy follows upon bankruptcy, execution upon execution. The stagnation lasts for years; **productive forces** and products are wasted and destroyed wholesale, until the accumulated mass of commodities finally filter off, more or less depreciated in value, until production and exchange gradually begin to move again. Little by little the pace quickens. It becomes a trot. The industrial trot breaks into a canter, the canter in turn grows into the headlong gallop of a perfect steeplechase of industry, commercial credit, and speculation, which finally, after breakneck leaps, ends where it began—in the ditch of a crisis. And so over and over again. We have now, since the year 1825, gone through this five times, and at the present moment (1877) we are going through it for the sixth time. And the character of these crises is so clearly defined that **Fourier** hit all of them off, when he described the first as "crise pléthorique," a crisis from plethora. (117–18)

Engels concludes that capitalist production and social well-being are incompatible because the goal of capitalist production is maximizing profit, not the satisfaction of social needs and desires. Overproduction prevents productive forces from working because the capitalist cannot sell the products and turn them into additional capital; the continuous circulation of capital essential for the system slows. Production slows, unemployment rises, and people lose their means of subsistence. The contradiction between production and exchange becomes a crisis, and when a crisis becomes severe, Marx asserts, it will become apparent that capitalists are unable to manage the society's productive forces, and the **revolution** of the **proletariat** will be at hand.

Note that Marx is not predicting that any one crisis will bring about the collapse of the system. He is saying that a series of crises will contribute to the proletariat's growing **revolutionary consciousness** and eventual revolution. Also, note that Marx failed to specify the timing of the revolution or the degree of severity that the crises would have to reach before this revolutionary action occurs. While there have been a series of economic crises experienced by capitalist countries since Marx wrote, several of them quite severe, they do not appear to have contributed to the proletariat's revolutionary consciousness. *See also* CLASS CONFLICT, PREFACE, THE, UNDERCONSUMPTION, WORKERS AS CONSUMERS, ZUSAMMENBRUCHSTHEORIE.

OWEN, ROBERT (1771–1858). Robert Owen was a successful Welsh textile manufacturer considered one of the founders of **utopian socialism**. He published several books in the first two decades of the 19th century outlining his visionary ideas and explicitly put them into practice in his textile factory, where he implemented shorter working hours, schools for the children of workers, and renovated housing. One of his primary goals was the promotion of childhood education and the provision of child care for the children of laborers. Owen established experimental utopian communities, the most famous of these in New Harmony, Indiana. Owen met with numerous U.S. political leaders (including Adams, Jefferson, and Madison) and was one of the first to introduce discussions of socialism into American politics. Marx and **Engels** were highly critical of utopian socialism, contrasting it with their view of **scientific socialism** and elaborating critiques in *Anti-Dühring* and *Socialism: Utopian and Scientific*. *See also* FOURIER, CHARLES, SAINT-SIMON, HENRI DE.

P

PARIS. Marx first came to Paris in mid-October 1843 to begin publishing the *German-French Annals*. At that time, Paris was one of the largest cities in Europe; the city had close to a million inhabitants with thousands of political émigrés from Germany and other parts of Europe. Sperber (2013) writes, "The entire left-right political spectrum—not to mention groups claiming to be in another political dimension altogether—was vigorously present in Paris, from conservatives to pro- and anti-government liberals, to radical democrats and republicans, to pacifist **Fourierist** socialists, to revolutionary communists. Supporters of all these views articulated their opinions forthrightly in the periodical press, parliamentary debates, legal and clandestine associations, public and private gatherings" (117). Karl and Jenny would be there for a year and a half as Marx wrote articles, edited the work of others, and attempted to solicit contributors to the journal. After the failure of the *Annals*, Marx worked on the *Economic and Philosophic Manuscripts of 1844*, a work that was unpublished for years. In January 1845, at the behest of the Prussian government, Marx was expelled from **France**; he and his family relocated to **Brussels**. He was to return to Paris only briefly at the beginning of the **Revolution of 1848**, laying plans with members of the **Communist League** to return to Germany.

PARIS COMMUNE (1871). At the Battle of Sedan in the **Franco-Prussian War**, Emperor **Napoleon III** surrendered on 2 September 1870. His government collapsed, a new French Republic was declared, and the war continued. **Paris** came under siege by Prussian troops by 20 September, an assault that was to last four months, during which many members of the middle and upper classes fled the city. The Prussians cut communications with the outside world, and famine and disease spread throughout the city. In early January, the Germans began shelling Paris, and by 26 January, the national government signed a cease-fire. **Bismarck** insisted that the French hold new elections, **Adolphe Thiers** became the chief executive of the French Third Republic, and the new government concluded a peace treaty with Bismarck on 24 February. The peace consisted of many concessions to Prussia, including the ceding of the French provinces of Alsace-Lorraine and the payment of war reparations. Parisians—mainly socialists and republicans—were furious over the concessions and "demanded a continuation of war and a return to the principles of the First Republic" (Johnson, Walker, and Gray 2014, 314). When the national government sent troops to seize the cannons in the forts surrounding Paris, the people resisted, and open rebellion broke out.

Demanding independence from the national government, the people elected the Paris Commune as a municipal council. Almost 230,000 Parisians, mainly working class, elected a 92-member Central Committee that included **republicans**, socialists, **Blanquists**, **anarchists**, and members of the **First International**. The Commune ruled the city from 18 March to 28 May 1871. Marx (1871) takes up the story in *The Civil War in France*:

On the dawn of March 18, Paris arose to the thunder-burst of "Vive la Commune!" What is the Commune, that sphinx so tantalizing to the bourgeois mind? "The proletarians of Paris," said the Central Committee in its manifesto of March 18, "amidst the failures and treasons of the **ruling classes**, have understood that the hour has struck for them to save the situation by taking into their own hands the direction of public affairs. . . . They have understood that it is their imperious duty, and their absolute right, to render themselves masters of their own destinies, by seizing upon the governmental power." (23)

The Commune assumed administrative and legislative power over the city, passing decrees consistent with **social democracy**, such as the separation of church and state and the establishment of worker production associations. They planned for a federation of self-governing communes throughout **France** but soon focused on military matters and the defense of Paris against the national government led by Thiers. State authorities brutally put down the Commune in the "Bloody Week," which began early on the morning of 21 May and ended on 28 May. Contemporary estimates of the massacre range from 10,000 to 25,000 people killed in the week of bloody fighting. Following the uprising, the national government imprisoned or executed some 13,000 suspected Commune supporters and deported 7,500 to New Caledonia. "Karl Marx himself claimed that the Paris Commune had represented the first step to full communist **revolution**, and in *The Civil War in France* (1871), he provided a description of events relating to the Commune that was later used by **Vladimir Lenin** to justify the **dictatorship of the proletariat** in Russia" (Johnson et al. 2014, 315). *See also* COMMUNARDS.

PARIS MANUSCRIPTS, THE. See *ECONOMIC AND PHILOSOPHIC MANUSCRIPTS OF 1844*.

PARIS UPRISING (1848). Part of widespread **revolutions** that swept through Europe in 1848, the "June Days Uprising" of Parisian workers against the increasingly reactionary monarchy of King Louis Phillippe became a focal point of long-festering grievances among French workers. Increasing demands for better working conditions and the expansion of voting rights led to rising levels of repression from the regime. When Louis Phillippe abdicated, he set off a series of actions that resulted in the bloody riots of June 1848.

Following the king's abdication, a provisional government called the Second Republic enacted a series of reforms, among the most important of which were democratic reforms, including universal male suffrage. The organizational fulcrum for the subsequent uprising was "national **workshops**," organized by the provisional government as a means of providing aid to **unemployed** workers. The workshops, funded by new taxes, were quite successful and popular but antagonized rural landowners, who refused to pay the taxes. The failure of the taxes to generate sufficient revenue provoked a financial crisis. April elections produced a legislative body dominated by moderates and conservatives, an outcome viewed as unacceptable by Parisian workers.

The Constituent Assembly issued a decree announcing the imminent closure of the workshops, and unemployed workers confronted conscription or dismissal. The order sparked four days of rioting and street battles between Parisian workers, who barricaded narrow streets, and the French National Guard was called out to put down the revolt. The uprising led to roughly 3,000 workers killed along with 1,500 National Guard troops and thousands wounded or otherwise injured. Following legal proceedings, the provisional government deported 4,000 insurgents to **France**'s colonial possessions in Algeria.

Karl Marx interpreted the Paris Uprising as evidence of **class conflict** but viewed the uprising as imbued by the motivations of the **petite bourgeoisie**, or small business owners, who, in Marx's view, outnumbered the **proletariat**. The revolt frightened those same bourgeois interests that subsequently advocated crushing the rebellion. For Marx, the Paris Uprising of 1848, along with the other revolutionary movements that punctuated the late

1840s and into the 1850s, offers a cautionary story about the need for a developed proletariat animated by **revolutionary class consciousness**. *See also CLASS STRUGGLES IN FRANCE, 1848–1850* (1895).

PAUPERISM. Part of the **surplus population**, pauperism is "the hospital of the active labour-army" and a necessary condition of capitalist production and wealth (Marx 1867/1976, 793). Marx divides paupers into four groups. The first group consists of those who are able to work but who have been **unemployed** through an economic crisis. A second group consists of orphans and pauper children. Both of these groups are candidates for the **industrial reserve army** in times of prosperity; capitalists induct them into the army of active workers when needed in large numbers. Those maimed, mutilated, or injured in the mines and the factories, as well as the demoralized, mutilated, sickly, or widowed who are unable to work, are the third category of paupers described by Marx. Finally, there is yet a fourth category, the **lumpenproletariat**, who are outside the bounds of civil society. This group consists of the vagabonds, criminals, prostitutes, and similar people who live outside the law. *See also* IMMISERATION HYPOTHESIS, SURPLUS POPULATION.

PEASANTRY. Peasantry is a general term used to describe rural, preindustrial agricultural laborers collectively. The word is most often associated with such groups living under feudalism, especially during the Middle Ages in Europe. Peasants during this period were often not owners of the land they worked and were required to pay rent, taxes, fees, or services to the (usually aristocratic) landowners or **landlords**. Marx details attention to the role of the peasantry in the *Eighteenth Brumaire of Louis Bonaparte*. In this work, he addresses the impacts of the **French Revolution** on the large **population** of French peasantry and the historical factors leading to the establishment of **capitalism** in **France**. He notes that the emancipation of the peasants from **feudal** obligations led to a system where the rural peasantry owned and managed the land

and formed an almost symbiotic relationship with the **urban bourgeoisie** that limited the impact of aristocratic reaction to the **revolution**. However, Marx notes that this relationship was ultimately one sided and that, like the **proletariat**, capitalists exploited the peasantry's labor for profit—mainly through means of debt and usury, which led to increasingly marginal ownership of their land (Katz 1992). The role of the peasantry both in the transition to capitalism and from there to socialism and their subsequent place in postcapitalist economies is a core element in Marxist arguments about the **agrarian question**. *See also* SERFS, VASSAL.

PEASANT WAR IN GERMANY, THE (1850). Shortly after settling in **England**, **Engels** wrote *The Peasant War in Germany*, an abbreviated account of the 16th-century peasant uprisings amid the Protestant Reformation. Engels used the peasant uprisings to draw parallels with the recently suppressed **Revolutions of 1848**. He suggested the nature of the two bursts of revolutionary violence were similar and that the adversary was the same.

PERMANENT REVOLUTION. This idea originated with Marx and **Engels** but is most commonly associated with **Leon Trotsky** to describe an accelerated phase of **revolutionary** activity where the **proletariat** achieves **revolutionary class consciousness** and rejects any conciliatory overtures on the part of the **bourgeoisie**, nurturing the proletariat's autonomy. Debates over the inevitability and comprehensiveness of a **socialist revolution** suggest the range of tactical differences among socialists. More **orthodox Marxists** generally adhered to a deterministic view of the inevitability of such revolutions, holding that the steady **immiseration** of large sectors of the proletariat would produce the conditions leading to a "point of no return." Marx himself was at times ambiguous on the subject, holding steadfastly to the belief that such a revolution was at once necessary and inevitable but also cautioning against the impatience of such "**alchemists of revolution**" as **Mikhail Bakunin** and **Louis-Auguste Blanqui**.

Poster advocating permanent revolution.

In Marx's various invocations of the phrase, "permanent revolution" referenced a sustained proletarian radicalism and class-dependent political perspective that would perpetuate the movement toward a "**dictatorship of the proletariat**" and culminate in the emergence of **communism**, or a **classless society** in which the state would "**wither away**." Marx considered such a permanent revolution to be necessary for the proletariat to maintain its independence. Marx envisioned a process dictated by material circumstances, likely beginning with an economic **crisis** in one of the more advanced nations of western Europe with a developed industrial **base**.

In appropriating the term "permanent revolution," Trotsky needed to overcome a significant challenge. Marx was consistently pessimistic regarding the revolutionary potential for a country like Russia (or the United States); for Marx, a period of bourgeois domination was a sine qua non ("without which not") condition that established the necessary preconditions for a socialist revolution. This argument among **revolutionary socialists** echoed the debates between Marx and the **anarcho-socialists**, such as Blanqui and Bakunin. Should a revolutionary movement always seek to precipitate confrontation? Do

continual assaults on the state risk wasting the movement's energy? Do such attacks feed **counterrevolutionary** impulses in society?

Trotsky advanced his theory in an essay written in 1924 and subsequently published as a book in 1931. His conceptualization extends **Lenin**'s notion of a **vanguard**, an ideologically and doctrinally pure party organized to lead the proletariat in the struggle to overthrow the bourgeoisie. Rather than advocate for distinctive "stages" in a revolutionary sequence, Trotsky argued that successful socialist revolutions would be impromptu and improvisational. He believed that the Russian **peasantry**, properly led, could bypass the industrialization that Marx viewed as necessary for a socialist revolution. Importantly, Trotsky believed that counterrevolutionary forces would quickly overwhelm a socialist revolution in one country unless uprisings began simultaneously in several places.

Within the **Bolshevik** Party, **Nikolai Bukharin** and **Joseph Stalin** countered Trotsky's position with the argument for "**socialism in one country**." Where Trotsky argued that the **Russian Revolution** would inspire socialist movements in the more industrialized parts of Europe and those movements required the support and collaboration of Russia, the failure of socialist revolutions in eastern Europe persuaded many Bolsheviks of the prudence of a more cautious approach. Following Lenin's death, Stalin was able to persuade leading Bolsheviks that Lenin's writings supported the "socialism in one country" line. This debate served mainly as a proxy fight for leadership of the Bolshevik Party. By the end of 1928, facing exile, Trotsky fled the **Soviet Union**. Others have subsequently articulated variants of the "permanent revolution" position within Marxist ideological doctrine, most notably **Ernesto "Che" Guevara** and **Mao Zedong**.

PERPETUAL GROWTH. Marx's economic analysis synthesized several different schools of economic thought, including the classical economists, such as **Adam Smith, T. Robert Malthus, David Ricardo**, as well as French socialists, such as **Charles Fourier, Henri de Saint-Simon**, and **Pierre-Joseph Proudhon**. Marx's achievement lay in synthesizing various strands of economics within a Hegelian philosophical system "turned upon its head" by the rejection of Hegelian **idealism** in favor of his **materialist conception of history**.

Marx's historical narrative focused on the **division of labor** producing inequality; in other words, history is replete with **class conflict**, with a small elite exploiting and oppressing the remainder of humanity. Central to Marx's historical analysis is **Hegel's dialectical** idea of **alienation**. Because **capitalism** converts **workers** into mere objects of labor, they become estranged from the activity of production, from their fellow workers, and from their very humanity; capitalism exploits and immiserates workers. The **bourgeoisie's** relentless search to increase their **capital** within a system of ever-shrinking profits generates "**contradictions**," another appropriated Hegelian term that in this context references the condition of the ever-enriching bourgeoisie existing alongside an ever-impoverished proletariat.

Marx contended that the **declining rate of profit**—an assertion borrowed from the classical English economists—feeds a cycle of exploitation; seeking to depress the wages of labor to extract its profit, the bourgeoisie

resorts to **automation, deskilling** existing labor, and creating a more "disposable" and lower-paid labor supply. Brief wage hikes do not change the inevitable logic; eventually, the logic of profit works its will, steadily tightening the noose on the **proletariat**. The resulting "**boom and bust**" **cycle** of **growth** and recession that further fuels the growing resentments of workers eventually leads to the establishment of **revolutionary class consciousness** among a large enough proportion of the proletariat to justify **revolutionary** action.

The idea of "perpetual growth" derives from how Marx envisions the transition from capitalism to **socialism** and from socialism to **communism**. A couple of considerations deserve note. First, Marx did not expect the proletariat to destroy capitalism; instead, he predicted that the workers would seize the state but retain the productive energies harnessed by capitalism. Second, Marx believed that the **dictatorship of the proletariat** would be "of, by, and for" the proletariat, with the dictatorship necessitated solely by the need to restrain the bourgeoisie from counterrevolutionary activity and to prevent the reinstitution of **private property** as a means of dividing and insinuating "bourgeois" ideology into the proletariat.

Once the proletariat has institutionalized collective ownership of the **means of production**, Marx believed that the state would "wither away" and flower into a communistic society in which the distributive principle of "from each according to his ability, to each according to his needs" would banish the "feast or famine" cycles experienced under capitalism. Greed's replacement with the fulfillment of human creative needs would eliminate the conditions that produced poverty. Marx's description of the emancipation from class divisions in *The German Ideology* is suggestive of the release of creative energies that he believed would be the source of perpetual growth:

> For as soon as the distribution of labour comes into being, each man has a particular, exclusive sphere of activity, which is forced upon him and from which he cannot escape. He is a hunter, a fisherman,

a shepherd, or a critical critic, and must remain so if he does not want to lose his means of livelihood; while in communist society, where nobody has one exclusive sphere of activity but each can become accomplished in any branch he wishes, society regulates the general production and thus makes it possible for me to do one thing today and another tomorrow, to hunt in the morning, fish in the afternoon, rear cattle in the evening, criticise after dinner, just as I have a mind, without ever becoming hunter, fisherman, shepherd or critic. (quoted in Tucker 1978, 160)

Some critics of Marx have found in his discussions regarding perpetual economic growth and the **withering away of the state** as evidence of "**utopianism.**"

PESCH, SYBILLE. Sybille was **Moses Hess's** companion; the two lived next door to the Marx family in **Brussels**. She was the subject of rumors of having met Hess in a brothel. Despite these rumors and being from a working-class background, she spent time taking care of the Marx children. Her relationship with the Marx family caused considerable strife among the couples, as **Jenny Marx** would have nothing to do with **Mary Burns**, **Engels's** partner. Jenny snubbed Mary seemingly because of her working-class background yet treated Sybille as a friend. Both Hess and Engels blamed Karl for not controlling his wife, and Marx retaliated by writing sarcastic remarks to friends about Engels's intelligence and Hess's being a dreamer sponging off his friends. Eventually, Engels and Marx settled, but neither fully reconciled with Hess.

PETITE BOURGEOISIE. "Petite bourgeoisie" is an often-derogatory term that refers to a transitional **class** falling in between the **bourgeoisie** and the **proletariat**. During Marx's time, the petite bourgeoisie consisted of small-scale capitalists, such as self-employed artisans, shopkeepers, and others, who managed production or other economic activities (but did not directly own the **means of production**). Marx argued that the petite bourgeoisie,

though they might be able to buy the labor of the proletariat, could never expect to equal the bourgeoisie in the ability to own the means of production and that the **enlargement and concentration of capital** among the bourgeoisie would ultimately push the petite bourgeoisie into the ranks of the proletariat. The persistence of the petite bourgeoisie in more modern capitalist systems has led later **Marxist** analysts to focus on the role of this class in contemporary societies. For these Marxists, the petite bourgeoisie includes managerial and professional occupations that often mirror the ideological, political, and economic interests of the authentic bourgeoisie. The term retains Marx's largely pejorative connotation, as many argue that the genuine interests of the petite bourgeoisie lie closer to those of the proletariat than to those of the authentic bourgeoisie. *See also* MANAGERIAL SKILLED LABOR.

POLITICAL ECONOMY. A branch of economics and a forerunner of sociology, the discipline originated in the 18th century with such luminaries as **Adam Smith** and continued into the 19th century with **T. Robert Malthus** and **David Ricardo**. Political economy is concerned with the study of **production**, trade, **population**, and **labor** and their relations with other social phenomena, such as the **distribution** of goods, wealth, and income; government policy; and law. In a footnote in *Capital: Volume I*, Marx (1867/1976) writes, "Let me point out once and for all that by classical political economy, I understand that economy which, since the time of W. Petty, has investigated the real **relations of production** in **bourgeois** society, in contradistinction to vulgar economy, which deals with appearances only, ruminates without ceasing on the materials long since provided by scientific economy, and there seeks plausible explanations of the most obtrusive phenomena for bourgeois daily use, but for the rest confines itself to systematizing in a pedantic way, and proclaiming for everlasting truths, trite ideas held by the self-complacent bourgeoisie with regard to their own world, to them the best of all possible worlds" (174–75). Marx's theoretical work was very much in the tradition of classical political economy.

In **The Preface** to *A Contribution to the Critique of Political Economy*, Marx (1859) writes of his work as an editor on the *Rhineland News* (*Rheinische Zeitung*) in 1842–1843. At that time, he was dealing with such material-economic issues as the theft of forest wood by **peasants**, free trade, and protective tariffs. He admits that he felt woefully unprepared by his previous studies of law, history, and philosophy to engage in these debates fully. "On the other hand, at that time when good intentions 'to push forward' often took the place of factual knowledge, an echo of French socialism and **communism**, slightly tinged by philosophy, was noticeable in the *Rheinische Zeitung*. I objected to this dilettantism, but at the same time frankly admitted in a controversy with the *Allgemeine Augsburger Zeitung* that my previous studies did not allow me to express any opinion on the content of the French theories" (1). As the publishers of the paper attempted to be more compliant with government censorship in the hopes of saving the newspaper, Marx writes, he took the opportunity to withdraw to his studies. The first work he undertook was a critical examination of the **Hegelian** philosophy of law. "My inquiry led me to the conclusion that neither legal relations nor political forms could be comprehended whether by themselves or on the basis of a so-called general development of the human mind, but that on the contrary they originate in the material conditions of life, the totality of which **Hegel**, following the example of English and French thinkers of the eighteenth century, embraces within the term 'civil society'; that the anatomy of this civil society, however, has to be sought in political economy" (1).

POPULATION. The population is not subject to natural law as posited by **T. Robert Malthus**, Marx argued. Instead, the mode of production determines population level, **growth**, and the consequent distribution of resources. According to Marx, it is the **law of capitalist production** that lies at the heart of the "supposed natural law of population." According to the laws of supply and demand, in a booming economy with low unemployment, wages rise,

and, other things being equal, **unpaid labor** becomes a smaller portion of wages, and accumulation begins to slow. Capitalists curtail production when it slows to the point that the creation of capital is no longer profitable. When this happens, capitalists lay off people, wages begin to fall, and the economy goes into recession or worse. The rise of wages can never seriously threaten the capitalist system, and, in fact, any increase will stimulate the reproduction of the working class, thus securing capitalism's expansion.

The poor, Marx asserted, are a **surplus population**, the size of which was due to the class that had control over the **mode of production**. This class had no interest in feeding or housing the poor; in fact, their interest is in maintaining or even increasing their numbers. Capitalist societies have polarized the distribution of wealth both between and within nation-states. This polarization is the cause of an extensive working class as well as an **industrial reserve army**—a surplus population that is often **unemployed** and underemployed—that lives in poverty in times of recession and depression but is readily available in boom times so that labor costs are not subject to the laws of supply and demand. Marx formulates the "absolute **general law of capitalist accumulation**" to summarize the relationships between the rule of capital and the working classes: the higher the wealth, the greater the concentration of this wealth into the hands of a few. The higher this concentration, the more extensive the mass of workers, their **productivity**, and the **surplus value** they produce. Finally, the higher this concentration of wealth, the more intensive the exploitation of the working class and the surplus population. All this is necessary, according to Marx, as it forms the foundation of the accumulation and continuing growth of capital (Marx 1867/1976, 798). *See also* ECOLOGY, MALTHUS, T. ROBERT, OVERPRODUCTION, PROLETARIAT.

POVERTY OF PHILOSOPHY, THE (1847). First published in **Paris** and **Brussels**, where Marx was living as an exile (from 1843 to 1848), Marx wrote it to address the economic arguments of the French **anarchist**

Pierre-Joseph Proudhon's *The System of Economic Contradictions, or The Philosophy of Poverty* (1846). A key passage from the work follows:

> M. Proudhon the economist understands very well that men make cloth, linen, or silk materials in definite **relations of production**. But what he has not understood is that these definite social relations are just as much produced by men as linen, flax, etc. Social relations are closely bound up with **productive forces**. In acquiring new productive forces men change their mode of production; and in changing their mode of production, in changing the way of earning their living, they change all their social relations. The hand-mill gives you society with the feudal lord; the steam-mill, society with the industrial capitalist. (Marx 1847a, Chapter 2, para. 2)

Many cite this passage as evidence that Marx is very much a **technological determinist**. Relations between people must necessarily be in line with productive forces. When men acquire new productive forces, when they change their mode of production—say, from a feudal to a capitalist mode—their social relations must necessarily change to come in line with the way by which they make a living. "The same men who establish their social relations in conformity with the material **productivity**, produce also principles, ideas, and categories, in conformity with their social relations. Thus the ideas, these categories, are as little eternal as the relations they express. They are historical and transitory products" (49).

PRAXIS. Praxis is a concept first articulated by Aristotle as one of his three necessary activities of humans: thinking (*theoria*), making (*poiesis*), and doing (*praxis*). For Marx and later Marxist thinkers, writers, and **revolutionary** leaders, their goals go beyond just theory and description of social systems to actions resulting in changes to those systems. For Marx, praxis is more than just action, however. Praxis involves *both* understanding and action; it is an intellectual as well as a practical effort. Marx viewed the goal of revolutionary activity as a continuous process in which theory and practice are more than just dual sides of the same coin. Instead, for Marx and his followers, theory inextricably links with practice such that one cannot exist without the other. Praxis, then, is the process by which the **proletariat**—with **Marxist** theory as a guide—breaks through the **bourgeoisie** ideological veil and understands the system against which they are fighting and then proceeds to change that system. Theses XI from Marx's *Theses on Feuerbach* famously summarizes the concept of praxis: "The philosophers have only interpreted the world, in various ways; the point is to change it."

PREFACE, THE. In a remarkable Preface to *A Contribution to Political Economy* (1859), Marx brilliantly summarizes his **economic theory of history**, an approach he would elaborate on for the rest of his life. Marx wrote the Preface in clear prose, and it serves as an excellent guide to Marx's **historical materialism**:

> The general conclusion at which I arrived and which, once reached, continued to serve as the leading thread in my studies, may be briefly summed up as follows: In the social production which men carry on they enter into definite relations that are indispensable and independent of their will; these **relations of production** correspond to a definite stage of development of their material powers of production. The sum total of these relations of production constitutes the economic structure of society—the real foundation, on which rise legal and political **superstructures** and to which correspond definite forms of social consciousness. The **mode of production** in material life determines the general character of the social, political and spiritual processes of life. It is not the consciousness of men that determines their existence, but, on the contrary, their social existence determines their consciousness.
>
> At a certain stage of their development, the material **forces of production** in society come in conflict with the existing

relations of production, or—what is but a legal expression for the same thing—with the property relations within which they had been at work before. From forms of development of the forces of production these relations turn into their fetters. Then comes the period of social **revolution**. With the change of the economic foundation the entire immense superstructure is more or less rapidly transformed. In considering such transformations the distinction should always be made between the material transformation of the economic conditions of production which can be determined with the precision of natural science, and the legal, political, religious, aesthetic or philosophic—in short **ideological** forms in which men become conscious of this conflict and fight it out.

Just as our opinion of an individual is not based on what he thinks of himself, so can we not judge of such a period of transformation by its own consciousness; on the contrary, this consciousness must rather be explained from the **contradictions** of material life, from the existing conflict between the social forces of production and the relations of production. No social order ever disappears before all the **productive forces**, for which there is room in it, have been developed; and new higher relations of production never appear before the material conditions of their existence have matured in the womb of the old society. Therefore, mankind always takes up only such problems as it can solve; since, looking at the matter more closely, we will always find that the problem itself arises only when the material conditions necessary for its solution already exist or are at least in the process of formation. In broad outlines we can designate the **Asiatic**, the **ancient**, the **feudal**, and the modern **bourgeois** methods of production as so many epochs in the progress of the economic formation of society. The bourgeois relations of production are the last antagonistic form of the social process of production—antagonistic not in the sense of individual antagonism, but of one aris-

ing from conditions surrounding the life of individuals in society; at the same time the productive forces developing in the womb of bourgeois society create the material conditions for the solution of that antagonism. This social formation constitutes, therefore, the closing chapter of the prehistoric stage of human society. (1–2)

The Preface is central to understanding Marx and puts much of his analysis of **capitalism**, **social evolution**, **contradictions of capitalism**, **crises**, and working-class **revolution** in the context of his overall theory. *See also CIVIL WAR IN FRANCE, THE* (1872), *CLASS STRUGGLES IN FRANCE 1848–1850* (1895), *COMMUNIST MANIFESTO, THE* (1848), *EIGHTEENTH BRUMAIRE OF LOUIS BONAPARTE* (1852).

PRESBURG, HENRIETTE. *See* MARX, HENRIETTE PRESBURG.

PRICE OF LABOR. *See* LABOR MARKET.

PRIMARY NEEDS. In the *Grundrisse* (1857–1861), Marx develops the concept of **species-being**, contending that **human nature** is characterized by "a totality of needs and drives" (the chapter on **capital**, para. 3) and that humans will always act to fulfill those needs. Of these needs, Marx notes that primary needs include such necessities as "sexual relations, food, water, clothing, shelter, rest and, more generally, for circumstances that are conducive to health rather than disease" (quoted in Geras 1983, 72). However, these needs are not the totality of primary needs, for Marx argues that among primary human needs is also the "need of people for a breadth and diversity of pursuit and hence personal development" (72). When the social order fails to meet this primary need, it leads to **alienation**. *See also* SECONDARY NEEDS.

PRIMITIVE ACCUMULATION. In *Capital: Volume I*, Marx (1867/1976) writes that "the **accumulation of capital** presupposes **surplus-value**; surplus-value presupposes capitalistic production; capitalistic production presupposes the pre-existence of considerable masses of capital and of **labour power** in the hands of producers of **commodities**. The whole movement, therefore, seems to turn in a vicious circle, out of which we can only get by supposing a primitive accumulation (the 'previous accumulation' of **Adam Smith**) preceding capitalistic accumulation; an accumulation not the result of the capitalistic mode of production, but its starting point" (873). Primitive accumulation, then, is the "seed" capital needed for the origin of the **capitalist mode of production**. Marx was highly critical of Smith's account of "previous accumulation," which held that wealth was eventually built up by those who worked the hardest, calling this explanation "insipid childishness . . . preached to us in the defence of property" (873). Instead, Marx maintained that primitive accumulation was a part of the process of the transition from the **feudal mode of production** into the capitalist mode. This accumulation was possible due to the state-sponsored forced exploitation of resources and labor inherent in **colonialism**. "The discovery of gold and silver in America, the extirpation, enslavement and entombment in mines of the indigenous **population** of that continent, the beginnings of the conquest and plunder of India, and the conversion of Africa into a preserve for the commercial hunting of blackskins, are all things which characterize the dawn of the era of capitalist production. These idyllic proceedings are the chief moments of primitive accumulation" (915). In all of this, Marx maintained, the power of the state was critical in the speed of the transition from feudalism to capitalism. "Force is the midwife of every old society which is pregnant with a new one. It is itself an economic power" (915). *See also* CAPITALIST CLASS.

PRIMITIVE COMMUNISM. Although never explicitly formulated by Marx, later interpretations of his work (most notably by **Friedrich Engels** and later Soviet scholars) suggest that he envisioned a stage-like theory of **social evolution** with a progression of forms from primitive communism, **slave societies**, **feudalism**, and **capitalism** and eventually to a **classless society** characterized by **communism**. Primitive communism, in this sense,

describes hunter-gatherer and some subsistence-agricultural societies characterized by shared ownership of property and goods and egalitarian social relations. Such communities pool and share food obtained by hunting and gathering or as the products of agriculture and, importantly, do not generate a surplus. These societies tend to be highly mobile, so there is also little accumulation of durable goods. Communities hold the durable goods that do exist, such as housing or **tools**, rather than individuals owning such assets. Likewise, the community controls land for farming (or hunting-and-gathering "territories"), with equal access for any member of the social group as needed. Although there is a lack of a standardized or official political hierarchy, there may be individuals who hold relatively more authority for group actions through seniority, experience, or other personal traits, but these individuals do not have direct power or control over others. The work of anthropologist **Lewis Henry Morgan** forms the basis of much of Marx's and Engels's notion of primitive communism. *See also* EVOLUTION, HISTORICAL MATERIALISM, *ORIGIN OF THE FAMILY, PRIVATE PROPERTY, AND THE STATE, THE*, PREFACE, THE.

PRINCIPLES OF COMMUNISM (1847). An unpublished draft authored by Engels in 1847 that served as a foundational document for the *Manifesto of the Communist Party* of 1848 (later retitled as *The Communist Manifesto*). *Principles* went through several drafts written in a "catechism" style. The manuscript is a straightforward statement of each of the major themes that appear in the *Manifesto* but lacks the rhetorical power of that work. On its completion, Engels sent it to Marx with the following note:

> Give a little thought to the Confession of Faith. I think we would do best to abandon the catechetical form and call the thing Communist Manifesto. Since a certain amount of history has to be narrated in it, the form hitherto adopted is quite unsuitable. I shall be bringing with me the one from here, which I did; it is in simple nar-

rative form, but wretchedly worded, in a tearing hurry. I start off by asking: What is communism? and then straight on to the proletariat—the history of its origins, how it differs from earlier workers, development of the antithesis between the proletariat and the bourgeoisie, crises, conclusions. In between, all kinds of secondary matter and, finally, the communists' party policy, in so far as it should be made public. The one here has not yet been submitted in its entirety for endorsement but, save for a few quite minor points, I think I can get it through in such a form that at least there is nothing in it which conflicts with our views. (quoted in Isaac 2012, 19–20).

The writing of the *Manifesto* was all Marx but based on the *Principles* manuscript written by Engels—a very complicated coauthorship.

PRIVATE PROPERTY. The concept of private property is central to many of Marx's ideas. He was quite explicit in his arguments against private property, writing in **The Communist Manifesto** that "the theory of the Communists may be summed up in a single sentence: Abolition of private property." Despite the centrality of private property to Marx's arguments, he never explicitly defined the term "private property" in any one place. In a broad sense, private property is any property—capital and consumer goods—that is not owned communally or by government or state entities. Therefore, this definition would include personal private property like durable consumer goods. Critics of Marx and **communism** often use this broad definition, arguing that communism seeks to strip individuals of their personal property. However, Marx did not intend the term "private property" to include such personal items. For Marx, the concept of private property has more to do with the **social relations of production** and **bourgeoisie** control of the **means of production**. Private property, as Marx intends, then, is the power held by owners of the means of production that allows them to exploit the labor of the **proletariat** and thus extract **surplus value**. Private property in this sense includes

ownership of things like factories, land, and **banks**, and when Marx refers to the abolition of private property, this is the type of property (along with the legally enforced power that it enables for the bourgeoisie) to which he is referring.

PRODUCTIVE FORCES. Marx can be somewhat vague in the various terms he uses to describe production variables. He uses the term **means of production** in referring to the inorganic material used in the production process. Such means would include such things as **tools**, machinery, factories, raw materials, canals, railroads, ships, and any material object used in producing **commodities**. **Labor power**, combined with these means of production, is what Marx calls the **forces of production**. The **relations of production** is a separate term referring to the relationships between the producers and the conditions under which they organize their activities in the act of producing goods and services. These social relations vary according to the character of the forces of production and include ownership relations to these forces as well as the **social division of labor**.

In his analyses of societies, Marx gives primacy to the forces of production, but he never conceived of it as a simple case of the forces determining the relations. Instead, there is an ongoing and continuous interplay between the forces and relations of production throughout the process of **social evolution**. For example, the **rise of capitalism** precedes the **Industrial Revolution** by at least a century. At first, capital production was closer to the **handicrafts** of **feudal** society than to the industrial methods of today. In the early capitalist **manufacture period**, the relations of capitalist production, with its drive toward the expansion of profits, stimulate an ever more **detailed division of labor** as well as **technological** development. With the development of **machines**, particularly the steam engine, **large-scale industry** and the **factory system** become the norm. In turn, this development of the forces of production affects the continuing development of the relations of production—that is, **capitalism** itself. Marx ties social relations directly to productive forces. In changing productive forces—that is, changing the way a society exploits its environment and labor for food and raw materials—they change all their social relations. These changes carry through to the present day under **monopoly capitalism**. "Social relations are closely bound up with productive forces. In acquiring new productive forces, men change their mode of production; and in changing their mode of production, in changing the way of earning their living, they change all their social relations. The hand-mill gives you society with the feudal lord; the steam-mill, society with the industrial capitalist" (Marx 1847a, Chapter 2, para. 2). The **social relations of production**, Marx writes, will vary according to the character of the forces of production.

Marx compares the dynamics between the forces and relations of production to the relationship between the weapons of war to armies and warfare. New weapons development changes the organization of armies as well as the character of warfare itself. So too, developments within the forces of production—be it shortages of raw materials, new technologies, and processes—have the potential to alter or even transform the relations of production, such as ownership, the detailed division of labor, or the size and character of the **surplus population**. The forces and relations of production are intimately connected, and Marx coins the concept of **mode of production** when talking about their combined impact on the rest of the system. However, the two are separate forces as well. *See also* PREFACE, THE.

PRODUCTIVE LABOR. As defined by Marx, productive labor is labor added to the **means of production** to produce a **commodity**. However, Marx adds, this is not a sufficient definition of productive labor under **capitalism**. The essence of capitalist production is not merely the production of commodities but rather the production of **surplus value**. Under the capitalist system, the worker produces not simply for himself but for **capital**. The "authentic product of capitalist production is surplus value," not the commodity itself. Productive labor, therefore, is only labor that produces surplus value for the capitalist, that is, labor that contributes

to the **valorization process** (Marx 1867/1976, 1038). *See also* CAPITALIST CLASS, MANAGERIAL SKILLED LABOR, PROLETARIAT, UNPRODUCTIVE LABOR.

PRODUCTIVITY. The **exchange value** of a **commodity**, Marx argues, changes with every variation in the productivity of labor. Increasing the productivity of work to increase **surplus value** is the goal of the capitalist. However, by increasing productivity, the capitalist gains only a short-term advantage. Producing more of a given commodity, the capitalist must set a price below the **competition** to sell the increased output. This lower selling price forces competitors to adopt the new methods—or something like them; thus, the **socially necessary labor time** congealed in the commodity declines, as does the surplus value extracted by the capitalist (Marx 1867/1976, 436). Thus, increasing the productivity of labor, according to Marx, is beneficial to the capitalist in the short term but pernicious in the long term, as it necessarily leads to a **decline in the rate of profit**.

However, Marx asserts, there is one exception to this rule. Improving the productivity of labor in industries producing **wage goods**, or "commodities that contribute towards the necessary means of subsistence," will lower the cost of these commodities and, therefore, the value of **labor power** (436). This is because the value of consumer goods necessary for the reproduction of labor power at a given standard of living determines the cost of labor power. Therefore, by its constant tendency toward increasing productivity and cheapening commodities, it also tends "to cheapen the worker himself" (436–37). *See also* ABSOLUTE SURPLUS VALUE, LAW OF VALUE, RELATIVE SURPLUS VALUE.

PROFIT. Profit is **surplus value** created in the **production** of **commodities** and **expropriated** from the labor of the **proletariat**. *See also* CAPITALIST CLASS, CAPITALIST CYCLES, CONSTANT CAPITAL, DEAD LABOR, DESKILLING, DETAILED DIVISION OF LABOR, ECONOMIES OF SCALE, FACTORY SYSTEM, JOINT-STOCK COMPANIES,

LABOR THEORY OF VALUE, LIVING LABOR, MACHINES, SURPLUS LABOR, VARIABLE CAPITAL, WAGE LABOR.

PROLETARIAT. A proletarian has nothing to bring to the market except for one's labor. Marx posited that as **capital** grows, so grows the working class (Marx 1867/1976, 762–64, 795). This relationship, Marx adds, is produced on an ever more massive scale, creating ever more concentration of wealth, encroaching on both old and new branches of production, and creating new supplies of workers (1062).

Paid labor is the amount of wages needed to provide subsistence to the worker. **Unpaid labor** is that part of the workday over and above this subsistence wage. It is only labor engaged in commodity production, Marx asserts, that produces **surplus value**, the source of all capital. There are several ways to increase surplus value (all of which have been used by capitalists): (1) by holding wages down, (2) through a more **detailed division of labor**, (3) increasing the hours of the workday, (4) increasing the intensity of work, and (5) the employment of **machines**. In *The Communist Manifesto*, Marx and **Engels** (1848/2012) write, "Of all the classes that stand face-to-face with the **bourgeoisie** today, the proletariat alone is a really **revolutionary** class. The other classes decay and finally disappear in the face of modern industry; the proletariat is its special and essential product" (10). This class, as well as the **surplus population**, will necessarily grow as **capitalism** expands.

It would be a mistake to view manual labor as being the only occupational category of the proletariat. In Marx's view, anyone with insufficient means to their livelihood without selling their **labor power** is part of the proletariat. This includes all such wage laborers whose salary level does not permit the sufficient **accumulation of capital** for ownership of the **means of production**, whether they be **productive** or **unproductive** workers. Such a definition would include many clerical workers as well as service and sales workers, categories that have increased in recent decades as operative and laborer occupations have declined in proportion to the total workforce in developed capitalist societies. In 2017, the U.S. Census Bureau estimated that service occupations accounted for 14 percent of the labor force. Sales and office occupations accounted for 22 percent of the American labor force. Those working in natural resources, construction, and maintenance occupations accounted for about 10 percent, and those working in production, transport, and materials handling accounted for about 13 percent. Thus, 59 percent of the American workforce are engaged in essentially proletarian occupations.

As **large-scale industry enlarges and centralizes**, many small capitalists lose their privileged positions, and it becomes more difficult for individuals to attain sufficient capital to enter the marketplace or to sustain their place in the face of **competition** from such behemoths. The capitalists become fewer (if not in number, at least in proportion to the overall **population**), and the proletariat continues to grow. *See also* CAPITALIST CLASS, MANAGERIAL SKILLED LABOR, PETITE BOURGEOISIE.

PROUDHON, PIERRE-JOSEPH (1809–1865). A French socialist whose **mutualist** and **anarchist** theories exerted considerable influence in the 1840s, Proudhon later served in the French Parliament and worked as a journalist. When Marx was in exile in **Paris**, he and Proudhon became friends; over the years, they engaged in a lively and, at times, warm correspondence. Their relationship would later descend into a mutual antagonism that prefaced the enduring schism between anarchist and **Marxist** interpretations of **socialism**. Proudhon believed in the power of worker cooperatives and that the abolition of **private property** could bring about a peaceful social **revolution**. Proudhon's writings continued to exert considerable influence among southern European socialists.

Proudhon demonstrated a natural gift for learning. Apprenticed as a printer, he began working as a proofreader and mastered Latin to better practice his craft. He began self-study in theology and philosophy and applied for a pension that would support his commitment to philosophy as an occupation. His first published work—*What Is Property?*—included his famous declaration that "Property is theft!" Subsequent writings in the 1850s—*General Idea of Revolution in the Nineteenth Century* (1851) and *On Justice in the Revolution and the Church* (1858)—articulated a systematic presentation of modern **anarchism**.

While Proudhon initially supported the revolutionary movements that beset **France** in 1848, his disappointment in the liberal direction of the movement's leadership provoked his withdrawal. He began working as a journalist in the opening days of the Second French Republic, advocating for the redistribution of property to worker associations. His trenchant writing style won him an audience, as he contributed to at least four leftist publications, but his writings also made him enemies. In 1853, the French government imprisoned him for three years for libeling President **Louis-Napoleon Bonaparte**, and he spent another four years exiled in **Belgium**.

Proudhon rejected **Marxism** as the replacement of one form of despotism with another. He termed his version of anarchist socialism "**mutualism**," arguing that while property is theft, shared property held the key to human emancipation. Thus, he agreed with Marx that private ownership of the **means of production** led to the **exploitation** of the **proletariat**, believing in the abolishment of all forms of property ownership. Proudhon contended that

the only legitimate property was that created through labor. Therefore, the replacement of private ownership by cooperatives would constrain any one individual's capacity to accumulate wealth. In later life, Proudhon modified his more unqualified critique of state authority, advocating a more decentralized federalism that would prevent the state from advancing toward authoritarianism. Proudhon was an advocate of revolution, understood as a social transformation rather than a violent political uprising. As a nascent libertarian, he opposed war, militarism, and imperialism.

Marx's critical reaction to Proudhon's *The Philosophy of Poverty* (1846) led him to write a vicious rejoinder titled **The Poverty of Philosophy** in 1847, which—following an initial limited-run publication—was not reprinted in Marx's lifetime. Despite the deliberate insult embedded in the title, Proudhon never formally engaged with Marx over the balance of his life. The core of Marx's criticisms of Proudhon amounted to an accusation of naïveté, a particularly poignant critique given Marx's previous acknowledgment of Proudhon's unique credibility as a member of the French working class. For Isaiah Berlin, Marx's attacks on Proudhon are rooted in his conviction of the necessity of a unified proletariat. Citing Marx, "To leave error unrefuted is to encourage intellectual immorality" (2013, 108).

R

RED ARMY. Vladimir Lenin sought to create a voluntary people's militia fused with the military to ensure continued control of the country as well as the success of the **Russian Revolution of 1917**. The Red Army (also known as the Workers' and Peasants' Red Army) formed during the **revolution** by the **Bolsheviks** and was led by **Leon Trotsky**, who leveraged resistance to the provisional government and Russia's involvement in World War I to organize and control workers' militias and soldiers. With control of these groups, the Bolsheviks allied with the **Soviets** to form the **Red Guards**, later called the Red Army, and overthrew the provisional government.

The new Soviet government established compulsory military training for all workers and peasants, overseen by an officer corps consisting mostly of former officers of the Russian Imperial Army, with politically appointed commissars overseeing units and ensuring their reliability and loyalty to the Soviets (often through propaganda campaigns among the troops). By the mid-1930s, members of the **Communist Party of the Soviet Union** made up more than half of the ranks of the Red Army, and newly established Soviet military academies were graduating officers who were reliable and loyal to the party.

In 1937 after **Joseph Stalin** took control of the state government, a purge of his political opponents from the Red Army decimated the officer corps and led to a significant drop in the efficiency of the Red Army that likely accounted for their early defeats suffered during the first year of the German invasion of Russia in 1941. The Red Army ultimately recovered and was instrumental in the defeat of Germany in World War II, providing the most massive land force in the Allied victory of the war. In 1946, the Soviet government officially changed the name of the Red Army to the "Soviet Army," though throughout the Cold War, the name "Red Army" became its nickname. The government officially disbanded the Soviet Army in 1991.

RED GUARDS. The Red Guards were composed of workers, peasants, and soldiers organized by the **Bolsheviks** before and during the **Russian Revolution of 1917** to fight for the **Soviets**. The state reorganized and centralized the Red Guard into the **Red Army** starting in 1918, which served as the primary Soviet military force until the 1990s.

RELATIONS OF PRODUCTION. For Marx, the relations of production correspond to a definite stage of development of the **forces of production**. The totality of the relations of production, Marx goes on to say, constitutes all social relations of a society at a particular stage of historical development. Each period has distinctive characteristics. "**Ancient society, feudal society, bourgeois (or capitalist) society**, are such totalities of the relations of production, each of which denotes a particular stage of development of mankind" (Marx 1847, "The Nature and Growth of Capital," para. 7). For example, capitalism, as a bourgeois relation of production, produces goods within specific social relations. Ownership of capital goods (factories, machinery, and other technologies) and **labor power**—in sum, the forces of production—determine these relations. Products and services are produced, accumulated, and distributed within definite social relations between capitalist and worker, including **ownership** and the **detailed division of labor**; the character of these relationships affects all social relationships within a society. The total of these relations of production, along with the forces of production, constitutes the economic **base** of society or the **mode of production**—the foundation on which legal, philosophical, literary, artistic, and political development rests. *See also* PREFACE, THE, SUPERSTRUCTURE, *WAGE LABOUR AND CAPITAL* (1847).

RELATIVE SURPLUS VALUE. The **socially necessary labor time** that it takes to produce a **commodity** determines the value of that commodity. The **surplus value** of a commodity, or the amount of **surplus labor** time that the capitalist expropriates from the worker, is determined by the difference in the necessary labor time that a worker labors to reproduce himself (food, shelter, and family) and the **length of the working day** itself. To maximize the surplus labor time, the capitalist must reduce the labor time necessary for the worker to reproduce himself. Barring the paying of workers below the value of their **labor power** "despite the important part which this method plays in practice," the capitalist can increase the surplus value produced by the worker by increasing the worker's **productivity** (Marx 1867/1976, 431):

> By an increase in the productivity of labour, we mean an alteration in the labour process of such a kind as to shorten the labour-time socially necessary for the production of a commodity, and to endow a given quantity of labour with the power of producing a greater quantity of **use-value**. Hitherto, in dealing with the production of surplus-value in the above form, we have assumed that the **mode of production** is given and invariable. But when surplus-value has to be produced by the con-

> version of necessary labour into surplus labour, it by no means suffices for capital to take over the labour process in its given or historically transmitted shape, and then simply to prolong its duration. The technical and social conditions of the process and consequently the mode of production itself must be revolutionized before the productivity of labour can be increased. Then, with the increase in the productivity of labour, the value of labour-power will fall, and the portion of the working day necessary for the reproduction of that value will be shortened. (431–32)

Marx labels this increase in productivity and the curtailment of necessary labor time "relative surplus-value."

Productivity gains in those industries that produce **wage goods** have the most effect on the value of labor power. By lowering the cost of these goods, the capitalist simultaneously reduces the cost of reproducing labor and thus the value of labor power. David Harvey (2010a) gives a modern-day example:

> So the value of labor-power is not a constant. It fluctuates not only because the costs of subsistence commodities vary but also because the commodity bundle needed to reproduce the laborer is affected by all these wide-ranging forces. The value of labor-power is sensitive to changes in the value of the commodities needed to support them. Cheap imports will reduce that value; the Wal-Mart phenomenon has thus had a significant impact on the value of labor-power in the United States. The hyper-exploitation of labor-power in China keeps the value of labor-power down in the United States through cheap imports. This also explains the resistance, in many quarters of the **capitalist class**, to put barriers to entry or tariffs on Chinese goods. To do so would be to raise the cost of living in the US, leading to a demand from workers for higher wages. (105)

RELIGION. Marx had a complex view of religion described as generally hostile though perhaps not to the same degree as his subsequent Marxist followers (most notably **Lenin** and **Stalin**, who were strong proponents of state-sponsored **atheism**). Within Marx's **materialist** understanding of the world, he viewed religion primarily as a social institution that is dependent on the particular material and economic **base** within a given society, writing in *Capital: Volume I* that the religious world is but the reflex of the real world (Marx 1867/1976, 172–73). In the introduction to *A Contribution to the Critique of Hegel's Philosophy of Right*, he states, "Man makes religion, religion does not make man." Marx argued that religion contributes to **false consciousness** and that just as capitalism causes **alienation** from the value produced by individual labor, religion alienates humans from their dignity and happiness by requiring that dignity and happiness be granted by an external, unknowable, and (for Marx) irrational being called a god. Perhaps most famously, Marx viewed religion as the "opium of the people," which is wielded by the ruling **bourgeoisie** as a tool to oppress and to hide the true nature of this oppression from the **proletariat**. *See also* FEUERBACH, LUDWIG, HEGEL, GEORG WILHELM FRIEDRICH.

RENT. *See* LANDLORD.

REVOLUTION. Within history and social theory, revolution means a change in the structural organization of society. Although not without exception, most social revolutions historically involved violence, as those without power often are required to remove those with power from control forcibly. Marx's historical work focused on how such revolutionary changes originated, arguing from a **dialectical materialist** position that each new socioeconomic form that arises out of revolution contains the seeds (or, in **Hegelian dialectical** terms, the contradictions) that ultimately lead to the next revolution. The **French Revolution**, for example, abolished the aristocratic monarchy and replaced it with a capitalist system that, Marx argued, would ultimately lead to a **socialist revolution**. While some of Marx's contemporaries and followers argued that the achievement of a socialist system did

not require revolution (through **evolutionary socialism**), Marx was firm in his assertion that only **revolutionary socialism** could produce the necessary changes in the social and economic **base** to bring about a socialist system.

REVOLUTIONARY CLASS CONSCIOUSNESS. Class consciousness is a general term used by Marx and **Engels** to refer to a state of awareness of the social and economic conditions and circumstances of one's **class**, including recognition of relationship to the **forces of production**. As such, different classes have different levels of class consciousness. For example, the class consciousness of the bourgeoisie includes a commitment to retain control and preserve the capitalist system. A **proletarian** class consciousness (though generally suppressed by the bourgeoisie through control of **superstructural** elements of society, such as **religion**) likewise includes awareness of the relationship of class members to the means and forces of production. Notably, a proletarian class consciousness can exist but does not necessarily go so far as to recognize the revolutionary potential of the proletariat. Revolutionary class consciousness takes this definition a step further: it not only is aware of existing social and economic relations but also has an awareness that the proletariat can overthrow capitalism through revolution. *See also* CLASS CONFLICT, CLASS STRUGGLE, DICTATORSHIP OF THE PROLETARIAT.

REVOLUTIONARY CONSCIOUSNESS. *See* REVOLUTIONARY CLASS CONSCIOUSNESS.

REVOLUTIONARY SOCIALISM. In *The Communist Manifesto*, Marx writes that the ends of the communists "can be attained only by the forcible overthrow of all existing social conditions" (Marx and Engels 1848/2012, 102). He and **Engels** argued that only through revolutionary socialism—where a class-conscious **proletariat** rises up and forcibly seizes political and economic power—would **capitalism** be destroyed and replaced by **socialism**. This view was in contrast to the **evolutionary socialism** envisioned by **Eduard Bernstein** and proposed by a variety of **Social**

Democratic political parties, which holds that a socialist, nonviolent, state-sanctioned incremental change gradually won through democratic processes can bring about a class-free society. While revolutionary socialism does not necessarily dictate that violence will drive revolutions, in Marx's early work, he maintained that capitalists would never accept socialist policies even if they arose from a democratically elected government and that the **socialist revolution** would be one characterized by violent overthrow of the capitalist **bourgeoisie** by the proletariat.

However, at **The Hague International** of 1872, he softened this insistence that **violent revolutions** are always necessary for achieving socialism. "You know that the institutions, mores, and traditions of various countries must be taken into consideration, and we do not deny that there are countries . . . where the workers can attain their goal by peaceful means. This being the case, we must also recognize the fact that in most countries on the Continent the lever of our revolution must be force; it is force to which we must some day appeal in order to erect the rule of labor" (Marx 1872, para. 9). Avineri (2019) points out that this speech was in the context of his struggles with anarchists, "as Marx viewed with great concern the tendency of Bakunin and his Russian followers to use violence, personal terrorism, and assassination in their activities" (164). In conclusion, it appears that Marx was concerned with ill-timed and excessive violence in achieving socialism, but he did not see a nonviolent path toward socialism (Marx 1867/1976, 929–30). As further evidence of his ultimate reliance on force, he continued to attack the purely evolutionary strategy of the **Social Democratic Party of Germany**'s **Gotha Program** in his *Critique of the Gotha Programme*, published in 1875.

Politically, **Marxist** movements during Marx's life and afterward took different approaches in terms of how to enact revolutionary socialism. Marx (and some later Marxist leaders, such as **Rosa Luxemburg**) was firm in his assertion that revolution and the political machinations necessary to destroy class structures required mass movements and organization of the working class as well as an eventual **dictatorship of the proletariat**. Other Marxist movements maintained that revolution needed the organization of smaller, organized, militant groups that could seize command of the state by force and enact socialist changes. Leaders in the **Vanguard Party**, **Vladimir Lenin**, and **Leon Trotsky** favored this sort of approach to revolution, also known as **Blanquism**. The **Russian Revolution** is an example of this revolutionary approach. *See also* CLASS CONSCIOUSNESS, REVOLUTIONARY CLASS CONSCIOUSNESS.

REVOLUTIONS OF 1848. Also known as the "Year of Revolution," 1848 witnessed a series of social upheavals throughout **Europe**. Occurring in both Catholic and Protestant countries, revolutionaries gave voice to frustration at the persistence of **feudal** authoritarian political systems. Elsewhere, rapid **technological** changes threatened to displace artisans and craftspeople who rose out of a spirit of the fear of loss of status and place in society and so were more **reactionary**. In parts of the **Austrian Empire**, a sort of war of all against all occurred, as nobles lashed out at imperial absolutism and the **peasantry**, in turn, revolted against the nobility. The origins of these **revolutions** were complex, and historical descriptions of these events tend to focus attention on the way they unfolded in **France**, particularly in **Paris**.

The tumult caused by these outbreaks of social and political unrest exerted considerable influence on socialist thought and practice in the mid-19th century. For professional agitators like **Louis-Auguste Blanqui**, the Revolutions of 1848 were a formative experience and provided a template for overthrowing corrupt authoritarian governments. Marx's far more nuanced evaluation of the Revolutions of 1848—offered in *The Eighteenth Brumaire of Louis Bonaparte*—offered a premonition of later Marxist thought on the rise of fascism. For Marx, the social, political, and, above all, economic forces mobilized by the Revolutions of 1848 were not genuinely **proletarian**. Instead, they were forces mobilized by the **bourgeoisie** and for bourgeois ends, namely, the final disposal of the shards of a feudal order that the **Congress of Vienna** (1815) had attempted to reestablish in the aftermath of **Napoleon**'s "continental system."

In practical terms, Marx's analysis of events in contemporary Europe suggested that the "correlation of forces" arrayed between the bourgeoisie and proletariat tilted decisively in favor of the bourgeoisie. For Marx, the lesson of the Revolutions of 1848 was that the proletariat had a long way to go in organizing and building the kind of movement of the scale and depth to overthrow **capitalism**. A genuinely proletarian **revolution** could not occur until the further consolidation of capitalism prepared the ground. Such a revolution awaited the emergence of economic "**contradictions**" and the rise of ever-higher levels of inequality, which would create the conditions that would culminate in **revolutionary** **class consciousness** among the proletariat. Until such conditions prevailed, Marx remained sympathetic yet critical of the revolutionary strivings of his more impatient fellow socialists.

RHINELAND NEWS (RHEINISCHE ZEITUNG). After the collapse of his academic prospects in 1842, Marx became a writer and, in its last four months of publication, an informal editor with the *Rhineland News*. This journalistic work would be a turning point in Marx's life. He became a crusading journalist, making a name for himself among European radicals, **Cologne** liberals, and Prussian authorities. Journalism, or, rather, writing commentary on current events for a variety of newspapers, became his primary way of making a living over the next two decades as well as an outlet for his political activism.

Painting of the 1848 revolution in Berlin.

The *Rhineland News* began in 1842 as an alternative newspaper to the *Cologne News* through the efforts of **Georg Jung**, a supporter of the **Young Hegelians**, and **Moses Hess**, a socialist or communist (the terms were used interchangeably at that time). Investors in the paper tended to be political liberals who were somewhat opposed to authoritarian Prussian rule and the nobility. They favored a constitutional monarchy, with guarantees of civil liberties and an elected legislature. Rejecting Hess as an editor, they instead eventually turned to **Adolf Rutenberg**, a Young Hegelian and brother-in-law to **Bruno Bauer**, to edit the paper. Both Hess and Jung had previously met Marx, and, being very impressed with the young man, they invited him to contribute essays to the newspaper.

Marx wrote two essays for the paper that appeared in the spring and summer of 1842. One of the two pieces was in defense of freedom of the press, harshly criticizing the Prussian state's attempts to stifle the press and linking its efforts to propping up an archaic society. He linked freedom of the press to other fundamental freedoms, including a representative legislature and a constitution guaranteeing fundamental rights. The essay struck a positive chord with radicals and liberals alike but quite the opposite chord with Prussian authorities. The paper was under increasing pressure to moderate its tone, which, under Rutenberg, was haphazard. Jung and Hess began setting editorial policy and hired Marx in October 1842 to reinforce their editorial role. Marx sought to tone down the paper—to bring its editorial policies more in line with its liberal investors as well as the Prussian state. It did not work:

As part of the new pro-free trade editorial policy, the newspaper published an attack on Russia's economic protectionism, pointing out how it harmed Prussian interests. The government perceived the articles as an attack on the Czar, the King of Prussia's friend and ally. This official unwillingness to meet the *Rhineland News* halfway only encouraged Marx's tendency not to restrain himself. His two articles on the debates in the Provincial Diet concerning a law against wood theft were so hostile to the institution of the Diet that the infuriated provincial governor demanded the subversive editor be fired; only, unaware of Marx's new editorial position, he blamed Rutenberg, who duly lost his job. (Sperber 2013, 94)

Marx's involvement with the editorial staff is when he first became involved with **class politics**, socialist ideas, and **political economy**. However, at this time, he remained a pro-capitalist, free-market 19th-century liberal with some sympathy for the plight of the poor.

Prussian authorities demanded on 21 January 1843 that the *Rhineland News* cease publication on 1 April of that year. Despite a general petition from many citizens of Cologne and promises of a change in editorship on the part of investors, the government shut down the newspaper. *See also* MARX'S JOURNALISTIC CAREER, *NEW RHINELAND NEWS*, *NEW YORK TRIBUNE*, RUGE, ARNOLD.

RICARDO, DAVID (1772–1823). Ricardo is among the most prominent British **political economists** and parliamentarian of the classical era. Ricardo was born into a Sephardic Jewish family of Portuguese ancestry that had emigrated from Holland. His father was a prosperous investment banker. At a young age, his marriage to Priscilla Ann Wilkinson and conversion to Unitarianism provoked a break with his family, and he found work as a stockbroker with a prestigious investment bank. His investments allowed him to amass a considerable fortune (due primarily to speculation regarding the outcome of the Battle of Waterloo), and he retired to a brief career in politics before his premature death resulting from an inner ear infection.

Ricardo was close friends and interlocutors with James Mill and Jeremy Bentham and engaged in vigorous debates on various economic subjects with **T. Robert Malthus**. Ricardo's reading of **Adam Smith**'s *An Inquiry into the Nature and Causes of the Wealth of Nations* sparked his interest in economic theory. He began publishing articles in economics in his thirties, and in 1817, at age 45, he published *Principles of **Political Economy** and Taxation*, in which he promulgated his **labor theory of value**, positing that the value of a good derives from the amount of labor necessary to produce it and not from either demand or scarcity. Like most classical economists, Ricardo's work included a sustained critique of mercantilist economic theory and advocacy of principles of free trade. Ricardo made significant contributions to economic theories on rent, comparative advantage, and international trade.

Socialists saw in Ricardo's analysis potentially radical implications. Ricardo's work exerted considerable influence among English utilitarians and socialists in the 1820s (although Adam Smith's concept of the labor theory of value, which differs somewhat from Ricardo's theory, also was influential among the English socialists). Marx cited Ricardo's concept of the labor theory of value; in Marx's economic theories, the labor theory of value became "**the law of value**," linking Hegelian notions of **alienation** with classical economic thinking. Avineri cites **Ferdinand Lassalle**, who reportedly remarked to Marx that he was "Ricardo turned socialist, Hegel turned economist" (Avineri 1968, 176). Avineri further described Marx's conceptualization like this:

> Political economy . . . , according to Marx, ideologically reflects alienated life, as indicated by its insistence that its concepts have objective, ontological reality and attain a validity external to the specific human relations whose organizational principles it tries to express and systematize. Alienation is created in capitalist society not by the production of commodities but by the transformation of this production, according to political economy, from objectified human activity into "objective" laws which independently regulate human activity. The human subject become the object of his own products, and the laws of political economy are only an ultimate and radical expression of this inverted consciousness that make man into a predicate of his own products and thus mystifies human reality. (107–8)

In this sense, Marx imputes normative implications to Ricardo's economic analysis and provides a way of linking Hegel's concept of alienation with an empirically oriented economic theory to create a more coherent account of exploitation within the **capitalist mode of production**. As such, Ricardo's influence on Marx's thought appears to have been significant.

RISE OF CAPITALISM. Marx's materialist conception of history posits that the "history of hitherto existing society is the history of **class struggles**" (Tucker 1978, 473). History, from this perspective, constitutes a progressive movement from one set of economic arrangements to a more efficient economic system, from **slavery** to **feudalism**, and from feudalism to **capitalism**. For Marx, the "progressive" aspect of history is decidedly amoral, referring to the greater efficiency of the **means of production** in sustaining human communities. Thus, feudalism was superior to slavery as a basis for organizing the means of production, as capitalism would prove more efficient in organizing an **industrial economy**.

Marx contends that certain conditions were required for capitalism to take hold and replace feudalism. First, sufficient **capital** accumulation gradually enabled the **bourgeoisie** to replace feudal lords as the ruling **exploiting** class. Essential to the rise of the bourgeois class is the equally gradual emergence of a **free laboring class**, made possible by the rise of market towns, where **serfs** with skills could take shelter from the lords' intent on holding them to the land. The unshackling of serfs from a system of ascribed status as a class facilitated their tradition to "**wage laborers**," setting in motion a newer and more efficient cycle of economic exploitation at the hands of the bourgeoisie. The gradual disintegration of feudalism led to massive dislocations of agrarian serfs and a considerable movement of **populations** from rural to **urban** settings.

The key to the emergence of the **proletariat** was the rise of the **factory system**, which broke the **guild** system. The guilds were associations of **skilled laborers** that often asserted near-**monopolies** over essential crafts (e.g., carpentry, butchers, bakers, and the like). The factory system facilitated **mass production** and a more **detailed division of labor** and thus a more efficient and competitive set of economic arrangements.

Marx argued that two additional factors contributed to the rise of capitalism and the demise of feudalism. First, with the expansion of the factory system came **mechanization** and **automation**; for Marx, "machinery, objectified labour itself appears not only in the form of the product or the product employed as a means of labour, but in the form of the **force of production** itself" (quoted in Tucker 1978, 280). As "**fixed capital**," machinery "appears as superfluous to the extent that his action is not determined by [capital's] requirements" (quoted in Tucker 1978, 281). Second, the expansion of **money** as a medium of exchange contributed to the forging of the proletarian class by separating laborers from their labor through the process of **alienation**. In *Grundrisse*, Marx observed, "Money wealth neither invented nor fabricated the spinning wheel and the loom. But, once unbound from their land and soil, spinner and weaver with their stools and wheels under the command of money wealth" (quoted in Tucker 1978, 271).

Marx believed that capitalism emerged slowly, over several centuries, with significant capital accumulation occurring in the 16th and 17th centuries, as international trade—facilitated by **colonialism**—intensified. Capitalism developed in conjunction with the modern nation-state, as a civil authority dedicated to the protection of **private property** and the bourgeoisie's control over the means of production. *See also* PRIMITIVE ACCUMULATION.

RUGE, ARNOLD (1802–1880). Ruge was an advocate of a free and united Germany, and he took part in the student demonstrations from 1821 to 1824, for which he was jailed from 1824 to 1830. He became a **Young Hegelian** and lecturer at the University of Halle in 1838 and founded and edited the journal the *Annals of Halle*. Like many of the Young Hegelians, he aspired to professorships at a German university. However, Prussian conservatism blocked him, like other Young Hegelians,

from attaining academic appointments. After the Prussian government suppressed the *Annals of Halle*, Ruge started the *German Yearbooks* in the Kingdom of Saxony, away from direct Prussian interference. Ruge also wrote for the *Rhineland News*. When the **Society of Free Men**, a Young Hegelian group, "advocating **atheism** and calling on supporters to leave the Christian churches," both Ruge and Marx wrote against them (Sperber 2013, 92). Seeking to separate the *Rhineland News* from the group, they wrote critical articles about the Free Men's lifestyles, rejection of conventions, excessive drinking, and romantic attitudes regarding **revolution**. This criticism led to a break with **Bruno Bauer** and other Young Hegelians. In 1842–1843, Ruge and Marx were very close both politically and socially, with Ruge serving as the younger man's mentor (Stedman-Jones 2016, 125).

When the Kingdom of Saxony—under Prussian pressure—banned Ruge's *German Yearbooks* and Prussia forced the closing of the *Rhineland News*, Ruge and Marx decided on a new venture. They founded the **German-French Annals**, devoted to publishing articles by German and French radicals. Ruge and Marx were coeditors of the journal headquartered in **Paris**. The journal failed to attract further financial backers, nor was it freely distributed in German provinces. Furthermore, the journal was unable to attract French writers; subsequently publishing only one double issue, it quickly folded. Shortly thereafter, Ruge and Marx quarreled; thus, Karl became estranged from two of his mentors. The surviving account of the split comes from Ruge, who attributes the break to Marx's newfound communist beliefs, claiming that Karl "explained to me he could no longer work together with me since I was only political, while he was a communist" (quoted in Stedman-Jones 2016, 156). Ruge remained critical of **communism** and Marx for the rest of his life. Later, he became a supporter of the Kingdom of Prussia when it began to unify Germany, supporting Prussia in the **Austro-Prussian War** as well as the **Franco-Prussian War**, and even accepted a pension from **Bismarck** (Sperber 2013, 556). *See also* MARX'S CHARACTER.

RULING CLASS. *See* CAPITALIST CLASS.

RUSSIA. Although Marx never set foot inside Russia, his ideas radically shaped the history of the country. After the **Revolution of 1917**, Russia became the world's first communist state as **Marxist** theory and **praxis** formed the basis of its political and economic systems (though there is much disagreement regarding the degree to which Russian **Soviet communism** follows **orthodox** Marxism). Several Russian revolutionary thinkers and actors, including **Mikhail Bakunin**, frequented the same European intellectual circles as Marx. However, most of the prominent actors involved in the Russian Revolution of 1905 and that of 1917, as well as the **Bolshevik Revolution** and the eventual establishment of the **Communist Party of the Soviet Union** and the founding of the **Union of Soviet Socialist Republics (USSR)** never met or worked directly with Marx.

Nonetheless, the Russian intelligentsia were supportive of Marx's work when he was alive, and, notably, the first translations from German of many of his works (including his opus *Capital*) were into Russian. During his life, Marx was sympathetic to the **Narodniks** and other **revolutionary** Russian groups, although he was skeptical of **socialist revolution** in Russia, primarily because of the agrarian, precapitalist nature of Russia's economy during the late 1800s (an issue central to the **agrarian question** concerning the precursors necessary for socialist revolution). Marx's personal opinions concerning Russia, however, are largely immaterial, as **Lenin** and later leaders of the USSR cited Marx's ideas as their inspiration. Many argue that had Soviet communism not taken root in Russia, Marx's theories may have enjoyed much less posterity than they currently enjoy. *See also* BUKHARIN, NIKOLAI, COMINTERN, COMMUNIST REVOLUTION, KROPOTKIN, PETER, MARX-ENGELS INSTITUTE, MENSHEVIKS, NARODNOYA VOLYA, RED ARMY, RED GUARDS, RUSSIAN SOCIAL DEMOCRATIC LABOR PARTY (RSDLP), STALINISM, STALIN, JOSEPH, TROTSKY, LEON, ZASULICH, VERA, ZINOVIEV, GRIGORY.

RUSSIAN REVOLUTION OF 1905. By the end of the 1800s, the Russian economy was in a deep recession, and agricultural **productivity** stagnated as the price of grain in Europe dropped. These economic problems aggravated existing social unrest, with the educated **population**, peasants/agrarian laborers, and industrial workers dissatisfied with the czarist government. Responding to a workers' strike in St. Petersburg in 1904, czarist troops opened fire on demonstrators (an event known as "Bloody Sunday"), which most historians point to as the official start of the 1905 Russian Revolution. Over the next year, there were additional worker strikes, peasant unrest, and military mutinies leading to political reforms, including the establishment of a multiparty political system, a new parliament (the "State Duma"), and ultimately the drafting and acceptance of a new constitution—the Russian Constitution of 1906. The czar, however, stayed in power. The events of the 1905 revolution set the stage for the **Russian Revolution of 1917**, and many historians suggest that it allowed the **Bolsheviks** to emerge as a leading political movement in Russia. **Vladimir Lenin**, in his later writing, pointed to the 1905 revolution as a "rehearsal" without which the **October Revolution** in 1917 would not have been possible. *See also* BOLSHEVIK REVOLUTION, RUSSIA, SOVIETS.

RUSSIAN REVOLUTION OF 1917. After the political reforms resulting from the **Russian Revolution of 1905**, social unrest continued, and various revolutionary movements and groups grew in power and influence, the most notable among them the **Bolsheviks**, led by **Vladimir Lenin**. Russia's involvement in World War I beginning in 1914 proved disastrous, with massive Russian casualties, food and fuel shortages, and cascading economic problems. The general **population** grew increasingly dissatisfied with the czarist government, and protests culminated with the "February Revolution" starting on 8 March 1917 (23 February on the Julian calendar in use in Russia at that time). The February Revolution saw massive crowds of demonstrators supported by striking industrial workers in the streets, and on 11 March, the government called in troops to quell the protests, with some opening fire on demonstrators. Protests only grew, though, and soon the soldiers began to abandon their posts. The Duma, a parliament formed as one of the reforms of the 1905 revolution, officially formed a provisional government on 12 March. Within days of this move, the czar abdicated the throne, ending centuries of autocratic czarist rule of Russia. When Lenin learned of the abdication of the czar from his exile in Switzerland, he and other Russian refugees arranged to return to Russia. The German government, recognizing that these dissidents could further throw Russia into turmoil, allowed them passage through Germany in a "sealed train," and on arrival in Petrograd, Lenin took charge of the Bolshevik Party. The continued involvement of Russia in the war led to further problems with food supply, and peasant and labor uprisings continued against the provisional government.

On 6–7 November 1917, the **Bolshevik Revolution** began (often referred to as the **October Revolution**, as it occurred on 24–25 October of the Julian calendar), with Lenin's Bolsheviks successfully overthrowing the provisional government and establishing a **Soviet** government ruled directly by organized councils of soldiers, peasants, and workers. Civil war among various factions (namely, the **Red Army**, the White Army, and various socialist factions that took up arms against the Bolsheviks) broke out, but by 1923, Lenin and the Red Army were victorious and officially established the **Union of Soviet Socialist Republics**, the world's first communist state. *See also* COMMUNIST PARTY OF THE SOVIET UNION (CPSU), STALIN, JOSEPH, TROTSKY, LEON.

RUSSIAN SOCIAL DEMOCRATIC LABOR PARTY (RSDLP). *See* BOLSHEVIK REVOLUTION.

RUTENBERG, ADOLF (1808–1869). Adolf Rutenberg was a **Berlin** member of the **Doctor's Club** and a friend of Karl during his time at the **University of Berlin**. When **Moses Hess** and **Georg Young** started the *Rhineland News* in **Cologne** in 1842, they soon offered the position of editor to Rutenberg. At the time, Rutenberg was a well-known **Young Hegelian** and was already under surveillance in Berlin, so the Prussian government insisted that he not get the position. Instead, Rutenberg worked as an editor on an informal basis, with the publishers acting as the official editors. Rutenberg did not give the paper reliable editorial guidance or direction; he was good at recruiting writers and copyediting but did not write articles himself. The government perceived the newspaper as an outlet for Young Hegelian writers, including **Bruno Bauer**, **Arnold Ruge**, **Friedrich Engels**, and Karl Marx. The Prussian government was hostile to the paper since its inception, finding the editorial policies subversive, Young Hegelian propaganda, full of French liberal ideas, and pushing **atheism**. The publishers brought on Marx in October 1842 as one of the editors, and he worked on their behalf to appease the Prussian government. While he brought direction to the editorial policy and the paper continued to grow in circulation, it continued to conflict with the government. Rutenberg received much of the blame, though, unbeknownst to the authorities, Marx was responsible for much of the later content. The editors fired Rutenberg in a move to appease the government but to no avail, and the government soon forced the paper to cease publication.

S

SAINT-SIMON, HENRI DE (1760–1825). A French social theorist and a founder of Christian socialism. Saint-Simon asserted that industrial development would solve the problems of poverty and want. He advocated that industry leaders, scientists, and engineers organize social life around the production of goods and services for all. He also argued that **religion** should work to improve the lot of the poorest classes. His ideas influenced **Pierre-Joseph Proudhon** as well as Marx and **Engels**, who identified him as one of the first **utopian socialists**.

SCHAPPER, KARL (1812–1870). Karl Schapper was a German-born socialist and revolutionary contemporary of Karl Marx. Unlike many of his comrades, Schapper came from a working-class background. He was active in revolutionary organizations as a young man and was imprisoned in Germany after a failed insurrection. He escaped and fled to Switzerland, where he was subsequently deported, making his way to **Paris**, where he joined the **League of the Just**. Again, Schapper was arrested and imprisoned after another failed insurrection led by **August Blanqui** and was subsequently expelled from **France**. He went this time to London, where he reorganized the **Communist League** and was instrumental in the organization of the **German Workers' Educational Association**. As the head of the correspondence committee for the League, Schapper oversaw the publication of *The Communist Manifesto* in 1848. Schapper returned to Germany after the **Revolution of 1848**, continuing to work closely with Marx, but the two soon split ideologically, with Schapper and **August Willich** forming the **Willich-Schapper Group** advocating a **Blanquist** approach to **revolutionary socialism**.

Schapper and Marx reconciled in 1856 with Schapper joining Marx in founding the **International Workingmen's Association** in London in 1864. His extensive connections with international socialists and groups proved invaluable to the Association. Schapper was elected to the General Council of the **International** in 1865 and was a loyal supporter of Marx in the factional disagreements within the International, though he died of tuberculosis soon after in 1870.

SCHURZ, CARL (1829–1906). Carl Schurz was a German-born revolutionary who fought for democratic reforms in Germany during the **Revolutions of 1848**. After the failed revolutions, Schurz emigrated to the United States as part of the **Forty-Eighters** political refugees. In the United States, he was an active antislavery advocate within the early Republican Party and served as a general in the American Civil War, where he fought at the Battle of Gettysburg. After the war, he won election to the U.S. Senate as the first German-born American in the body.

SCIENTIFIC SOCIALISM. In 1840, **Pierre-Joseph Proudhon** first used the term "scientific socialism" to describe a society ruled by a government in which reason is the foundation of sovereignty (rather than force or some irrational basis, such as **religion**). **Engels** subsequently used the term in his pamphlet *Socialism: Utopian and Scientific* to describe the overall theory developed by Marx to describe and analyze history, society, politics, and economy. Scientific socialism, in this sense, stands in sharp contrast to **utopian socialism**. Both views reject **capitalism** and seek to replace it with socialism. However, the latter does not attempt to understand or analyze the existing capitalist system. Utopian socialists, such as **Charles Fourier** and **Robert Owen**, reject the necessity of revolution and believe that perfectly ordered societies would naturally evolve through social reform. Marx (and Engels) had a dim view of utopianism as hopelessly naive. Unlike Proudhon's usage of the term, Engels's usage conveys an approach to understanding social and economic systems and revolutionary change in those systems that utilized Marx's **historical materialism** as an analytical (or scientific) framework.

SECONDARY NEEDS. Secondary needs are desires that arise when fundamental or **primary needs**—food, shelter, clothing, and safety— are satisfied. Secondary needs would include such things as entertainment, stylish clothes, gourmet foods, alcohol, and other commodities that satisfy a psychological need. "The **commodity** is, first of all, an external object, a thing which through its qualities satisfies human needs of whatever kind. The nature of these needs, whether they arise, for example, from the stomach, or the imagination, makes no difference" (Marx 1867/1976, 125). Advertising and marketing create or stimulate many secondary needs.

SECOND INTERNATIONAL, THE (1889–1914). The Second International was born out of the factionalized politics that destroyed the **First International**. Formed from the socialist movements of more than 20 countries, the Second International formally barred **anarchist** socialist organizations from participation. Notable for its declaration of 1 May as "International Workers Day" in 1889 and its articulation of women's rights, the Second International also agitated for an eight-hour workday. Internally, the Second International was riven by ideological divisions between more libertarian socialists and **revolutionary socialists**, whose authoritarian impulses provoked resistance from those socialists who espoused the cause of individual rights.

The Second International foundered on the shoals of pre–World War I politics, as socialist parties of the nations in the **International** failed to establish a coherent socialist response to the impending war. While some socialists responded to the socialist critique of the war as "a rich man's war but a poor man's fight" and argued for workers in warring countries to reject the call to war, other socialist parties responded to the siren song of **nationalism**. By 1920, the Second International was moribund. The subsequent **Russian Revolution** sparked the formation of the **Third International**, which was more aligned with militant versions of **Russian** socialism.

SERFS. Serfs make up a social and economic **class** that exists within systems characterized by the **feudal mode of production**. Serfs are bound to the land on which they were born and on which they practice agriculture. In many ways, serfdom was similar to **slavery**. Serfs were required to work for the landowner and, in return, were granted protection and the right to grow food. Marx considered serfdom and the role of the **peasantry** extensively in his work, examining the rise of the **capitalist mode of production**, most notably addressing the part of serfs in the **French Revolution** in his *Eighteenth Brumaire of Louis Bonaparte*. *See also* AGRARIAN QUESTION, LANDLORD, VASSALS.

SKILLED LABOR. Marx recognizes that even under **large-scale industry** with its proliferation of **machine technology**, there is a need for skilled labor and that it will be necessary to pay this labor more for their services. However, the goal of the capitalist in employing machinery is not only to reduce the quantity of labor but also to substitute "the less skilled for the more skilled" (Marx 1867/1976, 560). *See also* ABSTRACT LABOR, CHILD LABOR, DESKILLING, FACTORY SYSTEM, LABOR

THEORY OF VALUE, MANAGERIAL SKILLED LABOR, WAGE LABOR.

Next! Art Young, 1912 (Library of Congress), by pingnews.com.

SLAVERY. Slavery is a system in which humans are subject to ownership by other humans, allowing slave owners to buy, sell, or trade humans as a form of property. Unlike **serfs**, neither law nor custom ties slaves to any particular piece of land. While serfs are a **class** found within societies characterized by the **feudal mode of production**, slaves, under **capitalist modes of production**, are considered not a class but rather a form of property. In his criticisms of **capitalism**, Marx frequently cited the slavery practiced in his day, mainly that in the United States, as a particularly brutal form of oppression that, in his estimation, was a logical outcome of a capitalist system that values the production of **surplus value** above all else. He notes in *Capital: Volume I* that

> considerations of economy, moreover, which, under a natural system, afford some security for humane treatment by identifying the master's interest with the slave's preservation, when once trading in slaves is practiced, become reasons for racking to the uttermost the toil of the slave; for when his place can at once be supplied from foreign preserves, the duration of his life becomes a matter of less moment than its productiveness while it lasts. It is accordingly a maxim of slave management, in slave-importing countries, that the most effective economy is that which takes out of the human chattel in the shortest space of time the utmost amount of exertion it is capable of putting forth. (Marx 1867/1976, 377)

Given Marx's dim view of slavery (and capitalist oppression in general), it is no surprise that he was quite supportive of abolitionist movements, seeing them as potential catalysts for a more massive **socialist revolution**. Notably, there was a good representation of antislavery organizations and their working-class members in the formation of the **International Workingmen's Association**. After the U.S. Civil War, Marx continued to promote a race-free vision of the working class, noting that "labour in a white skin cannot emancipate itself where it is branded in a black skin" (414).

SLAVE SOCIETY. *See* ANCIENT MODE OF PRODUCTION.

SMITH, ADAM (1723–1790). Adam Smith was a Scottish economist and philosopher whose ideas are considered by many to lay the foundations of modern economics, especially classical free-market economic theory. In his classic work *An Inquiry into the Nature and Causes of the Wealth of Nations*, published in 1776, Smith describes the concept and perceived benefits of the "invisible hand" of the market, or the tendency (in his view) of free markets to evolve in ways that benefit their participants. He also introduces and describes the importance of the **division of labor** as a driving force in economic markets. Smith's work was incredibly influential, and virtually all significant writings concerning **political economy** in Marx's time referred to Smith's work. Smith was a frequent target of Marx's critical work, with Marx explicitly analyzing and criticizing Smith's ideas about **capitalism**, capitalist markets, and his **labor theory of value** in *A Contribution to the Critique of Political Economy, Economic and Philosophic Manuscripts of 1844, Capital,* and other works. *See also* COMPETITION, DECLINING

RATE OF PROFIT, MALTHUS, T. ROBERT, RI-
CARDO, DAVID, WAGE LABOR.

SOCIAL ANARCHISM. Social anarchism is
a broad category of theories and movements
combining aspects of **anarchism**, socialism,
and **communism**, including such ideas/theo-
ries as **mutualism**, **collectivist anarchism**,
anarcho-communism, and other approaches.
A common theme is that the end goal is a
nonstate form of socialism that sees mutual
aid and cooperation as a requirement for individual freedom within society. Unlike more
individualist strains of anarchism, social anarchist movements and theories emphasize
social equality and collectivity. Anarchists
advocate the conversion of privately held
property to communal property, though most
require such conversion only for productive
property that serves the good of the community. Social anarchism still upholds a degree of
respect for private personal property. Prominent social anarchist theories and practitioners
during Marx's lifetime include **Pierre Proudhon**,
Louis-Auguste Blanqui, **Mikhail Bakunin**, and
Peter Kropotkin. Marx was often highly critical
of both the theoretical and the practical/revo-
lutionary aspects of social anarchist doctrines.

SOCIAL DEMOCRACY. Social democracy
refers to a political regime type in which the
government and economy include significant
redistributive elements; that is, vital sectors of
both the economy and government operate in
ways calculated to encourage an equal distribution of wealth. All governments intervene in
their economies to a greater or lesser extent.
For some, the interventions are so modest
(e.g., the United States) that a designation as
"democratic socialist" would be misleading;
in the instance of other countries, although
self-described as "democratic" and "socialist"
(e.g., China, Cuba, North Korea, and so on),
the regimes do not hold free and fair elections
and are widely considered by the international
community to be authoritarian. In contrast,
states characterized as "social democratic" are
electoral democracies, where multiple political
parties—with at least one dominant party espousing a socialist platform—compete for

political offices through free and fair elections.
Examples of nations that most scholars designate as "social democracies" include **Belgium**,
Canada, Denmark, the United Kingdom, Finland, Germany, India, Ireland, the Netherlands,
New Zealand, Norway, Portugal, and Sweden,
among others.

Most social democracies have compara-
tively high rates of taxation, either through
progressive income tax, a value-added tax, a
corporate tax, or (most often) some combination thereof. The higher rates of taxation typically translate into a significantly larger public
sector footprint in the economy in the form of
government-subsidized or government-pro-
vided health care, free public education, significant degrees of economic regulation, and,
in many instances, generous unemployment
benefits. At times, the investment in the public
sector is uneven; in some countries, the provisions for health care take up a significantly
higher proportion of gross national product; in
others, the national government's commitment
to education takes up a more significant share
of the national expenditure. Consistently, public
support for government investments in health
care, education, and welfare is strong in those
nations characterized as social democratic.

Social democracies are also usually characterized by active multiparty systems, where
public discourse regarding redistributive policies is a matter of "more-less," as opposed to
countries like the United States, where the very
question of redistributive policies is profoundly
controversial. In the United Kingdom, welfare
provisions did not originate with socialists
but were instead the result of "Tory Democracy." Benjamin Disraeli–led Conservatives
appealed to working-class voters in the aftermath of the passage of the Reform Act (1867),
which significantly expanded the franchise and
compelled the Conservative Party to alter its
electoral strategy fundamentally. Similarly,
Bismarck initiated a welfare system in Germany as a conservative palliative to divide and
undermine a diverse workers' movement that
had considerable radical potential. In those instances, even such "revolutionary" figures as
the United Kingdom's Margaret Thatcher were
reluctant to advocate publicly the elimination

of the more popular social democratic elements of the British welfare state, particularly the National Health Service.

The question of what distinguishes a social democratic regime from a liberal democratic government is often one of degree. Liberal democracies generally place a somewhat higher priority on individual rights and, as a result, place significant constraints on the capacity of government to intervene in economic relationships. For example, the aforementioned fact that redistributive policies are so controversial in the United States would lend support to the proposition that the United States is a liberal rather than a social democracy. Social democratic governments, on the other hand, are committed to promoting significant levels of equality and are often more willing to engage in fiscal policies that, in liberal democracies, would be more controversial. For example, when Sweden suffered a significant banking-related financial crisis in 1991–1992, the government did not extend vast sums of taxpayer dollars to its **banks** to keep them solvent; instead, the government required the banks to "write down its losses and issued warrants to the government" (Daugherty 2008). The Swedish government seized the banks, creating one government agency to extend financial assistance and another agency to sell off real estate and other assets, in essence making the government the principal shareholder to whom the banking sector's management was answerable. Such an intrusive approach would have been highly unlikely in a **liberal democracy**.

From a **Marxist** perspective, participation in electoral politics represented a kind of temptation, inspiring the false hope that the **bourgeoisie** would be willing to allow genuine **competition** for power. In various writings, Marx contended that the choices presented to voters via the electoral process would always be empty ones. Marx's *Critique of the Gotha Programme*, written in 1875, vehemently attacked the "Eisenacher" faction of the **Social Democratic Party of Germany** for its proposed unification with the **General German Workers' Association** as "revisionism," which for Marx amounted to "capitulation." Marx's enduring commitment to a **revolutionary** remedy to the ills of **capitalism** highlighted his skepticism regarding the utility of workers' pursuit of an electoral strategy. In that light, contemporary social democracy represents a divergent path and a distinctive interpretation of socialism in practice.

SOCIAL DEMOCRATIC FEDERATION (SDF). **Henry Hyndman** organized Britain's first socialist political party in 1881. Hyndman had read both *The Communist Manifesto* and *Capital* and after meeting Marx was inspired to start the political party, formerly called the **Democratic Federation**. However, Karl became angered with Hyndman for paraphrasing *Capital* without attribution and broke off relations with him. **Engels** followed suit. The Democratic Federation adopted a socialist platform in 1884 and became the SDF. Dominated by Hyndman from the beginning, the group favored the achievement of socialism through the electoral process. Shortly after changing its name, the group splintered, with the more radical members forming the **Socialist League**. The SDF continued to be a force in socialist politics in Great Britain, splintering, building new alliances, reconstituting, and disbanding. In time, its members were gradually absorbed into other socialist parties. *See also* AVELING, EDWARD, MARX, ELEANOR (TUSSY).

SOCIAL DEMOCRATIC PARTY OF GERMANY (SOZIALDEMOKRATISCHE PARTEI DEUTSCHLANDS). The oldest electoral party in Germany, the Social Democratic Party (SPD), formed in 1875 as a merger of the **General German Workers' Association (ADAV)** and the **Social Democratic Workers' Party (SDAP)**. The SPD gained significant support within the German electorate despite the passage of the **Anti-Socialist Laws**, which effectively banned espousing socialist principles. German Chancellor **Otto von Bismarck** formulated a sophisticated approach to the SPD. He proposed the Anti-Socialist Laws on the one hand while on the other creating one of the first welfare states in Europe in the hope of creating bonds of loyalty between German workers and the newly unified German state.

The SPD's initial platform, the **Gotha Program**, adopted in 1875, reflected the compromises necessary to forge a union between the **Marxist** SDAP and the **Ferdinand Lassalle**–influenced ADAV. This platform acknowledged Marx's critique of capitalism while accepting electoral politics as the pathway to improving the lot of German workers. Among Karl Marx's last sustained written works was *Critique of the Gotha Programme*, which he viewed as a capitulation to Lassalle's embrace of **nationalism** and belief that workers could compete through the electoral process for control of the state. The **Erfurt Program**, adopted in 1891, took a more expressly trenchant rhetorical stance in terms of capitalism and the German state, which had by then sided with German capitalists against workers.

Despite principled opposition to late 19th-century German militarism under Kaiser Wilhelm II, the SPD supported Germany's decision to enter World War I in support of Austria-Hungary, a decision that proved controversial among German socialists. The support for the war led to the formation of the **Spartacus League** and the Independent Social Democratic Party, which eventually reformed as the **Communist Party of Germany**. In the aftermath of German capitulation and the resulting German Revolution, the SPD under the leadership of **Friedrich Ebert** (1871–1925) helped form the Weimar Republic and remained one of the major parties during the Weimar era. However, the Weimar regime's ineffectiveness and the economic devastation of the early 1930s brought the Nazi Party to power in 1933. The Nazi regime killed or arrested numerous SPD leaders, and the rest fled into exile, forming an exile organization, first in Prague and then, following the German occupation of Czechoslovakia, in **London**.

Following Germany's defeat in World War II, the allies permitted the return of the SPD, which, alongside the center-right **Christian Democratic Union (CDU)**, has been one of the two major political parties. The Godesberg Program, adopted in 1953, reflected an ideological moderation of the SPD and a commitment to broaden its electoral appeals. Factions within the contemporary SPD have embraced liberal Keynesian principles, while other factions continue to support **social democracy**. In 2017, the SPD joined a grand coalition with the CDU in the administration of Angela Merkel.

SOCIAL DEMOCRATIC WORKERS' PARTY OF GERMANY (SDAP) (SOZIADEMOKRATISCHE ARBEITERPARTEI DEUTSCHLANDS).

The first socialist party in **Germany** formed in 1869 in the town of Eisenach, Saxony. Alternatively known as "Eisenachers," leading German socialists like **Wilhelm Liebknecht, August Bebel**, and **Eduard Bernstein** were members. Although the party lasted only until 1875, the SDAP was significant in at least two respects. First, it was the first German socialist party to organize and demonstrate electoral strength. Second, apart from Marx and **Engels**, it formed the principal (if imperfect) vessel for orthodox interpretations of **Marxism**. In 1875, the SDAP merged with the **General German Workers' Association**, led by followers of **Ferdinand Lassalle**, once a rival of Marx for influence within the socialist movement. Much speculation circulated regarding Marx's influence over the "Eisenach Faction," but he expressly disavowed the platform that announced the merger of the two parties into the **Social Democratic Party of Germany** in what would become known as the *Critique of the Gotha Programme* (1875) as a capitulation to the **Lasallians**.

SOCIAL DEMOCRATS.

Social democracy has its ideological roots in **evolutionary socialism** of theorists and activists like **Eduard Bernstein** and **Karl Kautsky**. Social democrats during this period argued that incremental changes implemented through democratic processes could bring about a socialist system. They were opposed to the **Bolshevik Revolution** and its antagonism toward **bourgeois democracy**. In Germany, the social democrats formed the **Social Democratic Party of Germany**. In the following decades, democratic socialists further distanced themselves from **Stalinism** in the **Union of Soviet Socialist Republics** and other authoritarian state approaches to socialism. After World War II, social democrats moved toward a position of compromise between **capitalism** and socialism. They advocated the maintenance of capitalism's system of private ownership of the **means of production** (except for certain critical public utilities and services such as medical care) while promoting active state intervention and the development of a well-developed welfare state. The Nordic nations exemplify modern social democracies. *See also* FABIANISM, SOCIAL DEMOCRATIC FEDERATION.

SOCIAL DIVISION OF LABOR. The **division of labor** in society is the foundation of all **commodity** production. The social division of labor refers to such divisions as agriculture, manufacturing, services, and their various broad divisions and subdivisions. The division of labor in society develops, according to Marx, within the family and later within the tribe, where there is a natural division caused by differences in sex and age. This division intensifies with the expansion of the community, increases in **population**, and conflicts between different tribes, leading to conquest and subjugation. It is the size and density of population that is the precondition for the division of labor within society, though Marx adds that this density is relative. A well-developed **means of communication and transportation** would have a "denser population" than a more populous country with an undeveloped communication system (Marx 1867/1976, 472–73). *See also* DETAILED DIVISION OF LABOR, MANUFACTURE PERIOD, SOCIAL LABOR, SOCIALIZATION OF LABOR.

SOCIAL EVOLUTION. One of the basic underlying principles of **historical materialism** is that **superstructures** undergo predictable changes as the **mode of production** changes and that these changes were inherently predictable and unilinear. Evolutionary thought was highly influential during the 19th century, especially within the field of anthropology. **Lewis Henry Morgan** was the most well-known proponent of anthropological, social evolution. He proposed that human society proceeded through three major stages—savagery, barbarism, and civilization—and that

technological aspects primarily determined the different stages and the progress between stages. This work intrigued Marx, and toward the end of his life (between 1880 and 1882), he wrote copious notes about the evolutionary work of Morgan and others. These notes were published posthumously as *The Ethnological Notebooks of Karl Marx* in 1972 and subsequently covered by **Engels** in his book *The Origin of the Family, Private Property, and the State*.

Marx had a similar conception of socioeconomic and **technological** change across the whole of human history, though most of his work was on the transition from **feudalism** to **capitalism**. Although Marx never specifically formulated a stage-like theory of social evolution, the subsequent interpretation of his work—mostly by **Engels** and Soviet scholars (Hoogvelt 1982)—established the now well-known progression of social forms from **primitive communism**, **slave societies**, **feudalism**, **capitalism**, and eventually a **classless society** or a modern communist system. *See also* PREFACE, THE.

SOCIAL LABOR. Over time, **labor** has outgrown its distinctive forms of subsistence farming and **handicraft production**. With the **growth** of the **social division of labor**, particularly the **detailed division of labor** under the **manufacture period** of early **capitalism**, work became interdependent, productive, and social. **Large-scale industry**, which relies on machine production, "operates only by means of associated labour"; therefore, the social character of the labor process becomes a necessity (Marx 1867/1976, 508). Marx contrasts this growth of social labor with the **centralization and enlargement** of capitalist enterprises that are privately owned and employed solely to increase the capital of private individuals. *See also* ABSTRACT SOCIAL LABOR, PRODUCTIVE LABOR, SOCIALIZATION OF LABOR; UNPRODUCTIVE LABOR.

SOCIAL RELATIONS. Marx described social relations as modes of social organization designed to provide the material needs for survival. Scarcity creates a considerable incentive for coercion, and Marx's **materialist conception of history** assumes a coercive basis: societies organized around hunting benefit hunters disproportionately. In contrast, agricultural societies disproportionately benefit those who control the land. **Industrialization** creates an infinitely more complex set of social relations but continues to be coercive in its implications and produces **alienation** among the **proletariat**. Marx contended that the state existed primarily to enforce this coercive set of social relations. Further, a proletarian **revolution** is required to realize human freedom to its fullest extent. He asserted that under **communism**, social relations would be founded on mutual respect and eliminate coercion as a basis for collective action.

SOCIAL RELATIONS OF PRODUCTION. *See* RELATIONS OF PRODUCTION.

SOCIAL REPRODUCTION. Marx introduced the concept of social reproduction in *Capital: Volume I* in his discussion of production in a general sense. Although Marx was concerned primarily with economic processes, he notes that "every social process of production is at the same time a process of reproduction." In other words, any **mode of production** (including the social structures associated with it) also reproduces itself. Social reproduction, in this sense, suggests that not only the **social relations of production** constantly reproduce themselves but also the cultural forms related to any given relation of production reproduce themselves. Sociologists, in particular, have used Marx's idea of social reproduction to analyze how social inequalities (e.g., class and gender disparities) persist from one generation to the next.

SOCIALISM IN ONE COUNTRY. Vladimir **Lenin**'s death in 1924 provoked considerable confusion as to who would replace him as the titular leader. For the first seven years after the **Russian Revolution**, Lenin had rejected forming a multiparty state and holding free and fair elections, establishing a Bolshevik alliance with the socialist revolutionaries instead and governing in an increasingly autocratic

manner. During this period, Lenin had expressed growing concerns regarding the fitness of **Joseph Stalin** (1878–1953), at the time secretary of the Communist Party's Politburo, viewing him as unintelligent, crude, and excessively prone to violence. Lenin preferred that **Leon Trotsky** (1879–1940)—with Stalin, one of the four *primer inter pares* (Latin translation: "first among equals")—replace him, but his rapidly deteriorating health precluded decisive action; rendered uncommunicative by a stroke, his passing created the first great void in Bolshevik leadership a scant seven years removed from the **revolution**.

In the years before Lenin's death, Stalin had effectively populated key party positions with "New **Bolsheviks**," party members who had joined after the **October Revolution**, who were often from modest backgrounds, and who, as a result, felt a personal sense of obligation to Stalin. They began maneuvers calculated to isolate any "Old Bolsheviks," individuals whose party membership predated the October Revolution and consolidated Stalin's position within the party. Stalin also used his former editorship of *Pravda*, the Bolshevik Party's major newspaper and ideological organ, to portray himself as the most loyal of Leninists as well the most authoritative interpreter of **Marxism**.

An essential parallel to this multisided internecine struggle for leadership and power was the future direction of the Russian state: whether to promote workers' struggles in other countries or to consolidate communist control over the Russian state. While there were a large number of aspiring Bolshevik leaders of the Soviet state, two quickly emerged in the struggle for power—Stalin and Trotsky—who combined a personal antipathy with diametrically opposed visions of how to consolidate control over Russia and advance the cause of socialism in western Europe. Trotsky advocated **permanent revolution**, a term initially coined by Marx and **Engels** to suggest that the first **proletarian** revolution would have a "demonstration effect" to other (likely industrialized) nations. In contrast, Stalin argued for prudence; in the aftermath of the failure of communist revolutions in eastern Europe—inspired by the October Revolution—Stalin and fellow senior Bolshevik **Nikolai Bukharin** argued that the resources of the Russian state should be devoted to preserving socialism in Russia and acting as a symbol for proletarians throughout the world.

Trotsky and his fellow senior Bolshevik **Grigory Zinoviev** (1883–1936) harshly criticized "socialism in one country" as heretical to Marxist principles. Both factions contended that Lenin's writings supported their positions, but in the parlous mid-1920s—in the aftermath of civil wars, the failures of communist takeovers in Germany and eastern Europe, and economic devastation visited on Russia as a result of Lenin's initial moves toward collectivization—the median Bolshevik mind-set appeared to favor caution. The "New Bolsheviks" supported Stalin, and there remained plenty of internal obstacles to the Bolsheviks' consolidation of power within Russia. More important, Stalin's organizational maneuvers enabled him to win control of the Communist Party in the 1924 elections. Ultimately, Stalin and Zinoviev were able to strip Trotsky of his positions of influence successfully; recognizing the warning signs, Trotsky fled Russia in 1929.

Stalin's successful prosecution of Trotsky would provide a blueprint for the establishment of a **"cult of personality"** and Stalin's assumption of absolute control over the **Communist Party of the Soviet Union**. Throughout the 1930s and 1940s, in a series of "show trials," Stalin would purge and kill anyone who threatened his authority.

SOCIALISM: UTOPIAN AND SCIENTIFIC

(1880). Written by **Friedrich Engels**, it is one of the most popular socialist pamphlets in the world, second only to *The Communist Manifesto*. At the suggestion of **Paul Lafargue**, Engels took three chapters of *Anti-Dühring* and created the brochure. The pamphlet details the origins of socialism and **Marxism** and then describes their similarities and differences. The work then outlines **historical materialism** and, through this lens, explains how the intensification of **productive forces** leads to the establishment of a **socialist mode of production**.

In this work, Engels draws the contrast between **utopian socialism** as represented by **Henri de Saint-Simon, Charles Fourier**, and **Robert Owen** and scientific socialism as represented by Marx and Engels. In the following passage, Engels summarizes the distinction:

The Socialism of earlier days certainly criticised the existing capitalistic mode of production and its consequences. But it could not explain them, and, therefore, could not get the mastery of them. It could only simply reject them as bad. The more strongly this earlier Socialism denounced the exploitation of the working-class, inevitable under **Capitalism**, the less able was it clearly to show in what this exploitation consisted and how it arose. But for this it was necessary—(1) to present the capitalistic method of production in its historical connection and its inevitableness during a particular historical period, and therefore, also, to present its inevitable downfall; and (2) to lay bare its essential character, which was still a secret. This was done by the discovery of **surplus-value**. It was shown that the appropriation of **unpaid labor** is the basis of the **capitalist mode of production** and of the **exploitation** of the worker that occurs under it; that even if the capitalist buys the **labor-power** of his **laborer** at its full value as a **commodity** on the market, he yet extracts more value from it than he paid for; and that in the ultimate analysis this surplus-value forms those sums of value from which are heaped up the constantly increasing masses of **capital** in the hands of the possessing classes. The genesis of capitalist production and the production of capital were both explained.

These two great discoveries, the **materialistic conception of history** and the revelation of the secret of capitalistic production through surplus-value, we owe to Marx. With these discoveries Socialism became a science. The next thing was to work out all its details and relations. (Engels 1908, 94–95)

The materialist conception of history, Engels writes, begins with the production of the means to support life. These **forces of production** affect the **relations of production** and are, therefore, the basis for the rest of the social system. Changes in the mode of production cause social change and revolution, not a philosophy or a better understanding of eternal truth or social justice.

Moreover, the capitalist mode of production is continually changing. The search for ever-greater profits and staying ahead of competitors forces the capitalist to increase productive forces. "But the capacity for extension, extensive and intensive, of the markets is primarily governed by quite different laws, that work much less energetically. The extension of the markets can not keep pace with the extension of production. The collision becomes inevitable, and as this cannot produce any real solution so long as it does not break in pieces the capitalist mode of production, the collisions become periodic. Capitalist production has begotten another 'vicious circle'" (116–17). About once every 10 years, Engels writes, markets become glutted, commerce stagnates, credit vanishes, factories are closed, and many are thrown out of work. Under pressure from productive forces of its creation, the capitalist mode of production breaks down. The **technology** necessary to produce subsistence, shelter, employment, and wealth are present, but production itself has become the source of misery and want. This **crisis** can last for years, while the surplus of commodities remains. Gradually, workers return to work, and the economy slowly recovers, heating up until, finally, it goes at full speed, employing more of the **industrial reserve army** and raising the **price of labor** and thus reducing surplus value and profit until eventually crashing the system again. With each crash, the process of the **concentration and enlargement** of industry grows through the ruin of many large and small capitalists.

The only solution, Engels writes, is for the society as a whole to take control of the **means of production**; only then will the producers themselves benefit from their **social labor**. Rather than being a source of periodic collapse, productive forces will then be harnessed to the needs of the people rather than to the enrichment of a few. "Active social forces work exactly like natural forces: blindly, forcibly, destructively, so long as we do not understand, and reckon with them" (125). However, once we understand them, we can bend them to our will and purpose rather than be subject to them. It is as the difference between "a conflagration, and fire working in the service of man" (125). With the recognition of the real nature of modern productive forces, "the social anarchy of production gives place to a social regulation of production upon a definite plan, according to the needs of the community and of each individual" (125).

All this will come about, according to Engels, as the capitalist transforms the vast majority of the **population** into proletarians— creating a power that will eventually revolt. "The proletariat seizes political power and turns the means of production into State property" (126). When this happens, Engels writes, the proletariat will abolish class distinctions as well as the state. The state, he notes, is, at its essence, an organ of the exploiting class, keeping the established order and making sure the exploited stay oppressed. *See also* PREFACE, THE, SCIENTIFIC SOCIALISM, UTOPIAN SOCIALISM, WITHERING AWAY OF THE STATE.

SOCIALIST ANARCHISM. *See* SOCIAL ANARCHISM.

SOCIALIST LEAGUE. An early socialist organization begun in **England** in 1885, it originated as a splinter group from the **Social Democratic Federation (SDF)**. The reason for the fracture was that many perceived the leader of the SDF, **Henry Hyndman**, as overbearing and focused exclusively on the national politics of the United Kingdom. Hyndman argued for an electoral path to socialism through the British Parliament and, swayed by **nationalism**, favored some British **imperialism**. His opponents were staunchly anti-imperialist and argued that Parliament was both corrupt and controlled by capitalists. Among those leaving the SDF and forming the new Socialist League were **William**

Morris, **Eleanor Marx**, and **Edward Aveling**. At its height, the League included up to 6,000 members with a mix of beliefs, including **anarchists**, **Fabians**, and **Marxists**. Over time, the combination proved too fractious, and when anarchists began to dominate the organization, it disbanded in 1901.

SOCIALIST MODE OF PRODUCTION. Marx believed that a **proletarian revolution** would result in a **dictatorship of the proletariat** in which production would fulfill the needs of humanity as a whole rather than the **accumulation of capital**. In Marx's *Critique of the Gotha Programme*, he argued that in this initial phase of **communism**, the state would control the **means of production**, and individuals would be rewarded based on their contributions to the whole society. Once society advanced to a higher stage of communism, the distributive principle would naturally transition to an equal distribution. "From each according to his ability, to each according to his needs." This transition would be facilitated by the gradual dispersion of bourgeois norms and mores and the increasing **automation** that would render work more pleasurable rather than burdensome.

SOCIALIST REVOLUTION. *See* CLASS STRUGGLE.

SOCIALIZATION OF LABOR. While **labor** under **capitalism** has become **social labor**, **production** has remained in the hands of private capitalists. With the **Industrial Revolution**, the socialization of labor intensified. An ever more extensive **mode of communication and transportation** now connects capitalist enterprises to **world markets**; virtually the entire **population** of the globe is now economically dependent on capitalism for the supply of **raw materials**, agricultural products, and manufactured goods. This globalization is yet another symptom of the **contradictions of capitalism**. Capitalist production is not possible without social labor, the interdependence and cooperation of hundreds if not thousands of workers in a variety of private and public organizations. However, the private control

of the system of capitalism and its production is for the maximization of **surplus value** rather than social goods or needs. According to Marx, the increase in communication and physical contacts among a growing **proletarian class**, as well as increasing awareness of their exploitation, will lead to the development of **revolutionary class consciousness** that will eventually lead to **revolution**. *See also* CLASS STRUGGLE, EXPROPRIATION OF LABOR, TRADE UNION CONSCIOUSNESS.

SOCIALLY NECESSARY LABOR TIME. Marx's concept that encompasses the average labor time needed to produce a **commodity** under widespread conditions of labor **productivity** in a given society. Socially necessary labor time would vary with the **technology** (**machinery** and the **division of labor**) prevalent in a given society at a given time. Socially necessary labor time determines the **exchange value** of a commodity. Note that it is not the specific amount of labor invested in the production of a product, as an inefficient firm that produces pins by hand will have far more labor time invested in a single pin than a factory that produces thousands of pins per hour through machines. However, the pins will sell for the same amount, and the pin maker that continues to rely on such **handicraft** will soon go out of business. Instead, exchange value is dependent on the socially necessary labor time in the production of a commodity that has **use value** to others. *See also* ABSTRACT SOCIAL LABOR, ECONOMIC SURPLUS, PRODUCTIVE LABOR, SURPLUS LABOR, SURPLUS VALUE.

SOCIETY OF FREE MEN. A **Young Hegelian** faction in **Berlin** in the 1840s that focused on a radical lifestyle rather than **political economy**. **Engels**, before he collaborated with Marx, belonged to the group, although he always maintained his allegiance to political action. Other members included **Bruno Bauer**. The group advocated **atheism** and advocated that their supporters leave Christian churches. Marx and **Arnold Ruge** attacked the group in the pages of the *Rhineland News*. Sperber (2016, 93) asserts that it was a split among radicals. For the Free Men, radicalism was about lifestyle and a rebellion against social convention, thus their support of atheism and heavy drinking. For Marx, radicalism was about political and economic change. This split between Marx and the Free Men was one of the first among many schisms of 19th-century radicalism.

SOVIETS. Derived from a Russian word meaning "council," Soviets were coalition groups formed by mostly industrial workers beginning with the **Russian Revolution of 1905**. In the lead-up to the **Russian Revolution of 1917**, the Soviets joined with military groups and committees to form the **Red Guard** and subsequently the **Red Army**, eventually coming under the control of **Vladimir Lenin** and the **Bolsheviks**. After the success of the **Bolshevik Revolution**, the soviet groups were instrumental in the formation of the **Communist Party of the Soviet Union (CPSU)**. They established the **Union of Soviet Socialist Republics (USSR)**, the world's first socialist state. Under the USSR, the term "soviet" took on a broad meaning, referring to any body or assembly with authority in the new government. Soviets, then, were part of the federal structure of the USSR charged with implementing the policy of the CPSU at the local level. *See also* STALIN, JOSEPH, TROTSKY, LEON.

SPARTACIST UPRISING (SPARTAKUSAUF-STAND). Members of the **Communist Party of Germany (KPD)** led the Spartacist Uprising as part of the rising political instability resulting from Germany's defeat in World War I. This truncated rebellion, brutally suppressed by returning German troops, represented an overly optimistic and largely spontaneous uprising of elements of the German left. It was driven alternatively by aspirational hopes of repeating the example of the **Bolshevik** seizure of power in Russia and the sheer desperation of a splintered and increasingly radical trade unionist movement that had been enervated by the German state's arbitrary and capricious treatment since **Bismarck's** rule.

Germany's flagging fortunes in World War I caused rising tensions between the German army's Supreme Command (the Oberste Heersleitung) and the Imperial Navy. The Supreme Command had effectively acted independently of the Kaiser's direction for much of the latter portion of the war; as the German army's hopes of landing a decisive blow on the Allies dwindled, the legitimacy of the Supreme Command's conduct of the war came under increasing question. A series of naval mutinies spread civil unrest throughout portions of Germany and led the German Supreme Command to open negotiations with the Allies to end the war.

One by-product of this uncertain period was the fragmentation of the **Social Democratic Party (SPD)**. While the SPD, led by **Friedrich Ebert**, established a caretaker government in the hopes of transitioning to a postwar government, younger, activist members of the SPD rejected any conciliatory gestures regarding **capitalism** and advocated radical measures. Members of this splinter group wanted to emulate the **Russian Revolution** that had occurred 14 months earlier. The SPD resisted the formation of these radicalized groups into local "**Soviets**." As a result, **Karl Liebknecht** and **Rosa Luxemburg** initially formed the "**Spartacus League**," so named for the famed first-century slave rebellion against Republican Rome led by the Thracian slave Spartacus, who emerged as an important symbolic figure in the 19th century. This organization was shortly after renamed the KPD.

On 5 January 1919, the KPD called a general strike in **Berlin**, some within the movement took to the streets, and rioting took place. Liebknecht and Luxemburg found themselves riding a wave not of their making and supporting an ill-fated revolution. Some within the movement expressed the intention of overthrowing the moderate caretaker government and installing a communist state. KPD negotiations with naval units that had previously mutinied against the German Supreme Command failed. Likewise, talks between the strike leaders and the government broke down when it became apparent to KPD members that the government was engaged in hiring soldiers returning from the war to form militia groups (e.g., **Freikorps** ["Free Corps"]) with the intent of suppressing the uprising.

On 8 January, street-to-street fighting broke out in Berlin between strikers and members of the Freikorps, many units of which retained their weapons issued during the just-ended war. By 15 January 1919, fighting had ended, and the striking KPD members dispersed with heavy casualties. A division of the Freikorps captured Karl Liebknecht and Rosa Luxemburg in a Berlin apartment and questioned, tortured, and executed them.

The Weimar Republic emerged from this violent background but failed to provide a foundation for an enduring government. With governing elites riven by mutual suspicion, a populace untutored in democratic norms, and crushed by the burden of postwar reparations, a succession of narrowly supported governments collapsed in the face of mounting economic difficulties. In the end, the Weimar Republic legislated itself out of existence in favor of Nazism in 1933. *See also* SPARTACUS LEAGUE.

SPARTACUS LEAGUE (SPARTAKUSBUND). The Spartacus League was a group formed during World War I by **Karl Liebknecht**, **Rosa Luxemburg**, and other members of the **Social Democratic Party (SPD)** that opposed any capitulation by the SPD toward **capitalism**. Instead, the League favored radical **revolutionary socialism** in an approach inspired by the **Bolshevik Revolution**. In 1918, the League changed its name to the **Communist Party of Germany** and launched the **Spartacist Uprising**, consisting of massive demonstrations and a general strike designed to destabilize the German government and bring about a revolution in Germany. With the aid of the **Freikorps**, the government quickly crushed the uprising, and Liebknecht and Luxemburg were captured and killed in custody.

SPECIES-BEING. Marx derived the term "species-being" (Gattungswesen) from **Feuerbach**'s philosophy to describe certain aspects of his concept of **human nature**. He notes in the *Economic and Philosophic Manuscripts of 1844* that "man is directly a natural being" and that "the objects of his instincts exist outside him, as objects independent of him; yet these objects are objects that he needs—essential objects, indispensable to the manifestation and confirmation of his essential powers." According to Marx, humans are the same as animals in their **primary needs**. However, Marx also argues, "free conscious activity constitutes the species-character of man" (327–28). The concept of species-being leads Marx to define human nature as a combination of our physical relations to nature as well as our social relationships with one another. The interplay of these relations defines humans at any given point in history. Contrary to Feuerbach's conception of species-being, then, Marx's conception gives special attention to the context of specific social and historical formations.

STAGES OF HISTORICAL DEVELOPMENT. The concept of **evolution** in historical progression grew out of **Enlightenment** thinking and was prevalent during Marx's time, with essential works published dealing with biological evolution (from **Darwin**) as well as **social evolution** (e.g., **Morgan**'s most famous work, *Ancient Society*). Marx's analytical framework of **historical materialism** also proposed a stage-like evolutionary scheme for social forms, with stages determined primarily by the dominant material **forces of production** and associated **relations of production**. These stages are **primitive communism, feudalism, capitalism**, and finally **communism**. *See also ETHNOLOGICAL NOTEBOOKS OF KARL MARX, THE, ORIGIN OF THE FAMILY, PRIVATE PROPERTY, AND THE STATE, THE (1884).*

STAGNATION. *See* ECONOMIC STAGNATION.

STALINISM. **Joseph Stalin** emerged within the **Soviet** leadership by wrapping himself in the mantle of **Lenin**'s reputation; allying with key Politburo members **Nikolai Bukharin**, Lev Kamenev, and **Grigory Zinoviev** against **Leon Trotsky**, Stalin used his power as general secretary to replace "Old **Bolsheviks**" with new Communist Party members dependent on and loyal to himself. Stalin's success in ruthlessly negotiating for a "Transcaucasian Socialist Federative Soviet Republic" of the southern nations of Armenia, Azerbaijan, and Georgia and in advancing the theory of "**socialism in one country**" enabled Stalin to outmaneuver Trotsky, who fled the Soviet Union in 1929. By 1927, Stalin wielded extensive influence over the Russian Communist Party but had not yet established totalitarian control of the state.

Over the period 1927–1939, Stalin engaged in a series of ruthless purges of all real and potential opposition to totalitarian rule. Exploiting grain shortages, Stalin instituted "forced collectivization" of Soviet agriculture, which was inaugurated by the suppression of the "kulaks," enterprising former peasants who had benefited under Lenin's moderate "New Economic Policy." Confronting stagnating industrial **growth**, Stalin promoted the "Stakhanovite movement," centered on the dubious exploits of Alexei Stakhanov, a miner who allegedly mined 102 tons of coal in less than six hours. As agricultural yields continued to decline during state seizures of the agrarian sector, Stalin promoted the ideologically informed pseudoscience of Trofim Lysenko, who rejected genetics and the heritability of traits in the belief that "natural cooperation" had the remarkable capacity to transmute grains—from rye to wheat and from wheat to barley—and unleash plants' natural "proletarian" potentiality. Stalin endorsed Lysenko's pseudoscience, advanced Lysenko within the Communist Party, and purged scientists who criticized "Lysenkoism."

Throughout the 1930s, Stalin became increasingly intolerant of any sense of opposition, engaging in increasingly comprehensive purges, culminating in the "Great Terror," replete with "show trials," dramatic confessions, and the execution or internal exile of millions of Russians. Stalin dramatically expanded the system of labor camps in Siberia, begun by Lenin, creating an extensive network of "gulags," where millions of Russian dissidents, criminals, and the merely misfortunate, were consigned. Millions died in those labor camps, which Alexander Solzhenitsyn, in *The Gulag Archipelago* (1973), brought to the world's attention. By the late 1930s, Stalin had established totalitarian control over the Soviet state.

In the late 1930s, fearing attack from both the Nazis to the west and Japan to the east, Stalin forged a nonaggression pact with Germany. Both countries then invaded Poland in September 1939 and later agreed to partition the Baltic states of Estonia, Latvia, and Lithuania into spheres of influence. Stalin had begun a massive rearmament of the **Red Army** but also savagely purged its leadership following the Red Army's disastrous performance in the attempted invasion of Finland in 1939, creating an enormous leadership deficit in the Red Army that left the Soviet Union vulnerable.

The Nazi invasion of the Soviet Union initially shocked Stalin, but he quickly recovered and appealed to Russian patriotism to mobilize the Soviet state in its defense. He also ordered the NKVD to execute Ukrainian political prisoners before retreating from advancing Nazi troops. Stalin moved much of the Soviet Union's industrial capacity to the east of the Ural Mountains and accepted Allied aid. The Red Army gradually ground down the Wehrmacht's military capability. At Allied meetings in Tehran, Iran, in 1943 and at Yalta, Crimea, in 1945, Stalin negotiated with Britain's Winston Churchill and U.S. President Franklin Roosevelt regarding the shape of the postwar world, arguing forcefully for a "spheres of influence" approach to the division of power. Stalin's literal interpretations of those agreements set the stage for the Cold War, which began in 1947 following U.S. and western European leaders' protests over the Soviet Union's military occupations of eastern European countries, and the establishment of pro-Soviet governments in what would become known as the "Warsaw Pact" countries. His attempt to seize control of **Berlin** via a blockade of Allied-controlled portions of the city and the resulting "Berlin Airlift" is one of the first instances where tensions between former allies nearly erupted into conflict.

By 1945, Stalin had built up a formidable "cult of personality" and spent his remaining years in declining health, growing increasingly reclusive and paranoid regarding potential (and in some instances real) threats to his absolute authority within the Soviet Union and the so-called Second World (countries allied with the Soviet Union with socialist regimes).

Stalin joined Chinese Communist leader **Mao Zedong** in supporting North Korea's attempted conquest of South Korea, calculating that the United States would accept a *fait accompli*, and subsequently encouraged Chinese intervention when U.S. General Douglas MacArthur invaded North Korea and approached the North Korean–Chinese border at the Yalu River. Stalin's death in 1953 raised suspicions of poisoning.

Stalin's contributions to **Marxism** were mixed. He publicly claimed to be a committed Marxist and anticapitalist and remained convinced throughout his adult life that **class conflict** was inevitable. His argument for "socialism in one country" bought time for the Russian Communist Party to consolidate control over the Russian state and its vast empire. He respected Lenin and appeared instinctively to understand that his pathway to power lay in his ability to seize Lenin's mantle as principal "Commissar" (a designation of authority within the Russian Communist Party) of Russian Marxism. At the same time, Stalin's depredations led to the deaths by execution and starvation of millions of Russians deemed by Stalin to be "enemies of the revolution." "Stalinism," as an interpretation of Marxism, pushed the deterministic elements of Marxism to its logical extremity and as such proved to be unworkable as a political approach to economic organization.

STALIN, JOSEPH (1878–1953). Joseph Stalin was a Georgian Marxist whose "Stalinist" interpretation of **Marxism** dominated in the Eastern bloc during the early years of the Cold War. A crude theorist but an energetic organizer, Stalin outmaneuvered would-be rivals for leadership of the **Union of Soviet Socialist Republics (USSR)** following the death of **Vladimir Lenin** (1870–1924). Stalin successfully harnessed the **Soviet** state to his will through a serious of violent internal purges of actual and potential rival ethnic groups and institutions and purges of the Communist Party and military leadership. Forging an alliance of convenience with the United States and the United Kingdom, Stalin successfully led the USSR through World War II. His ruthless interpretation of Churchill's notion of "spheres of influence" resulted in Soviet military occupation of eastern Europe, the decades-long partition of Germany, and the ignition of an ideological "Cold War" between the United States and its allies and the USSR and its **vassal** states.

Stalin was born Yosef Dzhugashvili in eastern Georgia. His family lived in relative poverty, and his mother took him to live with a family friend who was a member of the Eastern Orthodox Church. In his early years, his mother hoped that Stalin could obtain an education and prepared for a life in the clergy. An injury at age 12 left him with diminished use of his left arm. At age 16, he received a scholarship to study at a seminary in Tbilisi, the Georgian capital. Initially considered a gifted student, over time, he lost interest in religious subjects and joined a secret book club where he read the works of Karl Marx. He left the seminary at age 21 and found work as a meteorologist.

While still in his twenties, Stalin began demonstrating organizational and leadership potential, recruiting a relatively large group of followers in secret workers meetings in Tbilisi. At the time, the Georgian capital was a hotbed of political ferment. Stalin exploited the situation; working secretly, he argued for strikes and demonstrations and rose to a leadership position within the **Russian Social Democratic Labor Party (RSDLP)**. Police arrested party officials for holding a mass demonstration after a funeral for protestors who were shot by the police. The Okhrana arrested Stalin for planning to break them out of jail. In 1903, the court sentenced him to internal exile in Siberia for three years. He escaped and made his way back to Tbilisi, where the RSDLP had split into "**Bolshevik**" and "**Menshevik**" factions. Stalin quickly rose to a leadership position within the Bolshevik faction and in 1905 met Lenin at a conference of regional Bolshevik leaders in Finland.

Stalin developed a reputation as a brash and direct leader in the years leading up to the Russian Revolution. He organized a gang, labeled "the Outfit," and conducted bank robberies and other large-scale heists to help

Painting of Joseph Stalin with Vladimir Lenin painting in the background.

fund Bolshevik revolutionary activities. Stalin recognized the importance of revolutionary theory and became a crude yet effective writer and theorist. Perhaps more important, at various points, he assumed the editorship of Bolshevik newspapers. After another arrest and internal exile, the newly elected Bolshevik Central Committee invited Stalin to join. He agreed and on his escape from exile moved to the Russian capital of St. Petersburg in 1912, writing articles for *Pravda*. He began using the pseudonym "Stalin"—which was loosely translated as "man of steel"—during this period. In 1913, Stalin authored "Marxism and Nationalism," which established his reputation as an expert on how to treat issues of nationalism in socialist doctrine, a sensitive subject in an empire of many nationalities.

Stalin's rapid advancement to the Bolshevik senior leadership owed much to his relationship with Lenin. Stalin treated Lenin with elaborate courtesy and respect; in those instances where Stalin's brashness led to differences between himself and Lenin, he adjusted his views with alacrity. In the opinion of Lenin and his closest advisers, Stalin's presence in the leadership was useful; as a Georgian, Stalin was a minority untroubled at the prospects of continued Russian cultural dominance. Stalin's arguments regarding nationalism suggested that "cultural self-determination" would work to the detriment of minority cultures and that the correct pathway was to make their contributions within the framework of a unified, "higher" culture.

Stalin was in yet another internal exile when Russia entered World War I. Conscripted into the Russian army, he was determined to be medically unfit for service and returned to internal exile. However, when the Russian army's disastrous performance against German troops forced Czar Nicholas II's abdication, leading Bolsheviks, such as Lenin and Stalin, began organizing for a putsch against the Provisional Government, a fragile and narrowly supported coalition that included royalist, industrialist, and moderate factions. Stalin played a significant role in both planning and executing the Bolsheviks' subsequent *coup d'état* and supported Lenin's determination to negotiate a withdrawal from World War I, culminating in the Treaty of Brest-Litovsk in March 1918.

Confronting a multisided civil war in the aftermath of withdrawal, Stalin served in military commands in southern Russia, where his military acumen came under question, as did his penchant for mass executions, reinforcing Stalin's reputation for ruthlessness. In 1919–1920, Stalin participated in mop-up operations against "White" forces and participated in the Soviet Union's abbreviated war with Poland. While Lenin had believed that the Polish proletariat would rebel against the fledgling Second Polish Republic, Stalin's skepticism regarding the revolutionary potential of Polish workers proved more realistic. Stalin and **Trotsky** blamed each other for the failure.

In the years 1921–1924, the Soviet political leaders struggled to manage the inheritance of the czarist empire while managing a transition in leadership. Lenin, his health compromised by multiple assassination attempts, increasingly withdrew from an active role in governance. Stalin filled that void, taking charge as general secretary of the Central Committee of the Russian Communist Party in 1922. Lenin took his concerns regarding Stalin's "crudeness" and penchant for violence to his grave. *See also* STALINISM.

STATE. *See* CAPITALIST STATE.

STIRNER, MAX (1806–1856). Max Stirner was a German philosopher and contemporary of Marx and **Engels**. He attended the **University of Berlin**, where he was a student of **Georg W. F. Hegel**, who exerted significant influence over Stirner's subsequent work. While in **Berlin**, in 1841, Stirner began participating in discussions with the **Young Hegelians**, meeting and interacting with Engels, **Bruno Bauer, Arnold Ruge**, and other prominent philosophers of the time. It is unclear if Marx ever had direct interaction with Stirner, though certainly Engels did. In letters to Marx, Engels is enthusiastic about Stirner's most famous work, titled *The Ego and Its Own*, noting to Marx that among the Young Hegelians, Stirner was one of the most talented and independent. Ultimately, though, Marx and Engels came to be highly critical of Stirner's work, criticizing it extensively (along with the **idealism** of other Young Hegelians) in *The German Ideology* and *The Holy Family*.

Stirner's philosophical ideology can best be described as "egoist **anarchism**." He argues that truth (and concepts such as law and morality) are artificial concepts and that the only reality is power. Power, for Stirner, is best exemplified through the ownership of property (an idea vehemently criticized by Marx). Social institutions, likewise, are artificial concepts or illusions, and Stirner promotes an amoral view of the world where the rights of individuals exist only insofar as that person has the power to enforce them. Scholars often cite Stirner's

work as a precursor to nihilism, existentialism, and postmodernism.

STRUCTURE. *See* BASE.

SUPERSTRUCTURE. In Marx's theory of **historical materialism**, he inverts Hegel's **idealism**, arguing that the **mode of production** fundamentally shapes the way that society is structured and evolves, or the superstructure of a sociocultural system. Marx characterizes the superstructure as consisting of **religion**, ideology, art, culture, law, politics, and philosophy. The purpose of superstructures is to "normalize" the relations of production and the resulting inequality. Marxists historically viewed the relationship between the **base** (e.g., **forces of production** and the **relations of production**) and the superstructure as interactive and mutually reinforcing. Rather than relying exclusively on coercion, the superstructure of **capitalism** consists of rituals, ideologies, and social arrangements that support the status quo. Such superstructural elements predispose both the oppressors and the oppressed to accept capitalism as at best a just order or, at worst, "the way it has always been."

Marx and **Engels** appeared at times dismissive of the role of the superstructure as anything but an obstacle to the advancement of history (Tucker 1978, 172). Marx's famous characterization of religion as the "**opiate of the masses**" in his critique of Hegelian philosophy illustrated his tendency to minimize widespread ideologies as merely reflecting the settled convictions of an unjust status quo. This disdain is evident in Marx's famous declaration that the "ideas of the **ruling class** are in every epoch the ruling ideas." This statement exemplifies Marx's convictions regarding superstructure as a manifestation of **false consciousness** and, as such, devoid of philosophical merit (172).

Revisionists, such as **Eduard Bernstein**, criticized Marx for ignoring the significance of moral principles. Bernstein considered himself a Marxist and largely accepted **Marxism** as an economic and philosophical system. However, he believed that events in the world had raised doubts about aspects of Marxism, leading him to call for revisions to Marxism. His principal complaint was with the deterministic elements of the theory. As a Kantian, Bernstein believed in free will, arguing that Marx's commitment to **revolution** rendered him systemically indifferent to moral considerations. For Bernstein, the ends of socialism did not justify taking any means to that end; some methods would so taint the end as to render it indistinguishable from the injustices of **capitalism**.

Advancing into the 20th century, Marxists became more aware of the significance and durability of superstructures. In particular, **Western Marxists**, such as **Antonio Gramsci**, argued that **cultural hegemony** presented a more significant obstacle to the achievement of **revolutionary class consciousness** than Marx had supposed. Gramsci argued that Marx's use of superstructure lacked nuance and required further elaboration. In his distinction between "political" and "civil" society, political society occupied a similar role to the superstructure's justifications of the status quo, while civil society contributed to capitalists' class domination. For Gramsci, civil society was the arena within which Marxists could battle for control over the superstructure. It is there that Marxists should strive to replace capitalist propaganda masquerading as "good sense" with ideas and ideologies promoting proletarian interests.

SURPLUS LABOR. Marx illustrates the concept of surplus labor by contrasting the corvée system with "free" labor under **capitalism**. The corvée is an obligation to perform **unpaid labor** for **landlords** on private estates that were widespread in Europe under the **feudal mode of production**. Marx remarks that contrary to capitalism, in which the wages disguise the amount of surplus labor, "every serf knows that what he expends in the service of his lord is a specific quantity of his own **labour-power**" (Marx 1867/1976, 170). The amount of surplus labor given to the landlord was marked off from necessary labor— typically, a number of days' work each year—and perceptible to all.

With the free worker, however, working for a wage disguises surplus labor given to the capitalist. The goal of the capitalist is to expand his capital; to do this, he invests in the **means of production** (factories, machinery, and **tools**) and labor power to make commodities for exchange in the marketplace. As the goal is to expand capital, the capitalist must sell the commodity for more than the amount he has invested in its production. Capitalists accomplish this by getting more value from this labor than he pays in wages. Marx divides the working day into necessary labor (the labor necessary to produce enough product to cover the workers' wages) and surplus labor (the labor that produces **surplus value** that goes to the capitalist). For example, the standard working day in America today is eight hours. Suppose that in that eight-hour day, a steelworker works five hours of necessary labor and three hours of surplus labor. In a five-day workweek, the steelworker has given 15 hours of labor to the capitalist (or almost two days). "But this fact is not directly visible. Surplus labour and necessary labour are mingled together" (345–46).

Under the system of **slavery**, Marx writes, all labor—even the labor that goes into his own subsistence— appears as labor for the master. Under serfdom, there is a clear distinction in time and space between the labor of the serf for himself and the labor for the landlord. The wages of capitalism, however, obscure every trace of the division of the working day into necessary labor and surplus labor—all labor appears to be paid (360). In capitalist societies, the extraction of **economic surplus** from labor disguises itself from the working class (and often from the capitalist). Capitalist **ideology** legitimates the extraction as wages rather than **expropriation**. In addition, the extraction of surplus value becomes the overriding goal of production rather than production for social needs. Capitalism produces **commodities** for surplus value, a value realized only in the market. Moreover, this leads to a significant **contradiction** within the capitalist system. *See also* CAPITALIST CLASS, MANAGERIAL SKILLED LABOR, PROLETARIAT, SOCIALLY NECESSARY LABOR TIME.

SURPLUS POPULATION. *See* LUMPENPROLETARIAT, POPULATION.

SURPLUS VALUE. In feudal societies, the appropriation of surplus from peasants was a straightforward and transparent process. In return for access to the land, peasants would give over a large part of their surplus to the lord of the manor or be obligated to work the lord's land a certain number of days in exchange for this access. With **capital**, the appropriation of the surplus is opaque, hidden from the **proletariat** and often from the capitalist as well. It all begins with **labor power**, specifically the purchase and selling of labor power. This underlying transaction, according to Marx, is fraught with consequences for the entire social system. Human labor creates the value of all goods and services (all **exchange value**). Capitalism is a system built around the drive to increase capital. To expand his capital, the capitalist invests some in the purchase of **tools, machinery**, and **labor** to make **commodities** for exchange in the market. To expand his capital, he has to sell his commodity at a price more than the amount he has invested in making it. The capitalist can achieve this by getting more value out of this labor than he has invested in it. The more **surplus labor** he can **expropriate** from his workforce, the higher the profitability and the higher the **capital accumulation**.

Under the system of capitalism, of course, the capitalist has a great incentive to increase the amount of surplus value she can extract from her workers and thus increase her profit. Assuming a constant demand for the commodity, the capitalist can increase surplus value in two primary ways. Extending the **length of the working day** beyond the number of hours needed to maintain the worker creates **absolute surplus value**. This lengthening was the favored method of early capitalists in which men, women, and children worked 12- to 16-hour days. The capitalist produces **relative surplus value** by getting workers to work more efficiently and decreasing the number of hours it takes the worker to reproduce his wage while holding the hours of the workday constant. The capitalist does this by dividing and simplifying the tasks that go into making the commodity—that is, intensifying the **detailed division of labor**. Alternatively, with the coming of the **Industrial Revolution**, relative surplus value increases by introducing ever more efficient tools and machinery to raise the output of each worker.

However, Marx points out a problem. There is a gap between the production of a commodity and its realization sometime later in the market. "The division of labour converts the product of labour into a commodity and thereby makes necessary its conversion into money. At the same time, it makes it a matter of chance whether this transubstantiation succeeds or not" (Marx 1867/1976, 203). As there are potentially thousands of capitalists competing for a share of the market, all employing the techniques of increasing surplus value to its maximum, this conversion to profit (surplus) becomes more of a gamble. *See also* CONSTANT CAPITAL, ECONOMIC SURPLUS, LAW OF VALUE, SOCIALLY NECESSARY LABOR TIME, VARIABLE CAPITAL.

T

TECHNOLOGICAL DETERMINISM. A term first introduced by American sociologist Thorstein Veblen, technological determinism is used to refer to any theory that maintains that **technology** and technological change is the primary determining factor in the **base** (and, by extension, the **superstructure**) of society. Technology is a frequent theme in Marx's work, as it is a critically important variable in the definition of the **forces of production**, human **labor power**, and any given system of **means of production**. As "the material basis of all social organization," **productive forces** are intricately linked with the various forms of technology that allow humans to extract resources and ultimately to produce value (Marx 1867/1976, 372). The importance of technology in this scheme leads many analysts of Marx to conclude that his theory of **historical materialism** is one of technological determinism. Scholars disagree on the degree to which Marx intended his materialist conception of history to be one of technological determinism. It is noted, for example, that it is easy to find evidence in Marx's writing that he firmly believed in technology as a driving force for social structure (Shaw 1979). In *The Poverty of Philosophy*, for example, Marx notes that "the hand-mill gives you society with the feudal lord; the steam-mill society with the industrial capitalist" (Marx 1847a, 49). Despite such statements, many argue that Marx did not *intend* his theory to be one of pure technological determinism—at least not what some term as "*vulgar* determinism" (a derogatory charge levied by some critics of **Marxism**).

There are various "degrees" of technological determinism. While technology is considered a critical variable, for Marx, the social processes and their relation to technology are more important in the analysis of social and economic structure and change (Bimber 1990). In other words, Marx's "forces of production" cannot be directly equated with technology. For Marx, technology is always something that is associated with economic activities and, therefore, one cannot ignore the **social relations of production** as a critical variable. *See also* ALIENATION, *ANCIENT SOCIETY*, DESKILLING, ECONOMIES OF SCALE, FACTORY SYSTEM, INDUSTRIALIZATION OF AGRICULTURE, INDUSTRIAL REVOLUTION, LARGE-SCALE INDUSTRY, MACHINES, MACHINE TECHNOLOGY, MORGAN, LEWIS HENRY, SKILLED LABOR.

TECHNOLOGY. Marx makes frequent reference to technology in his work. Technology is a critically important variable in the definition of any given **means of production**, as almost all extractive activities utilize some form of technology. Marx argues that the means of production primarily determines the **superstructure** of society such that technological changes in the means of production can produce societal changes—a line of thought that causes some analysts to charge Marx as a **technological determinist** (Mishra 1979). With the rise of capitalist systems and the **growth** in the importance of technology (starting primarily with the **Industrial Revolution**), technological forces make it possible to increase the **productivity** of labor significantly, thereby increasing **relative surplus value**. This can lead to the ability of the **bourgeoisie** to increase the **exploitation** of the **proletariat**. Marx notes this effect within the **factory system**, where technological advances often led to the displacement of workers, increases in the **length of the working day**, intensification of work, and **exploitation** of **child labor** (Roth 2010).

Furthermore, as the role of technology in production becomes increasingly important, it leads to **deskilling** and higher levels of **alienation** of the **labor** force. Firms that employ technology that advances the productivity of labor will enjoy a temporary boost in profit over its competitors. However, this advantage will generally disappear when the new technology becomes standard in the industry and the value of the commodity comes in line with the higher productivity of labor. Marx was also interested in technological advances, such as improved **means of communication and transportation**, that made it possible for capitalists to reach **world markets** and enable **economies of scale**. *See also* FORCES OF PRODUCTION, MACHINES, MONOPOLY, PRODUCTIVE FORCES.

***THEORIES OF SURPLUS-VALUE* (1905).** Written by Marx between 1862 and 1863, *Theories of Surplus-Value* was a series of 23 draft handwritten notebooks intended by Marx to be the fourth and concluding volume of *Capital*. Marx intended it to be less theoretical than the first three volumes and focused it on a critique of the existing ideas concerning wealth creation, with particular emphasis placed on the exploration of Marx's concept of **surplus value** through examination of historical examples of economic systems relying on **wage labor**. After Marx's death, **Friedrich Engels** hired **Karl Kautsky** to edit and publish the notebooks, and the first published volume appeared in 1905, with two other volumes published over the next five years. Kautsky's version, however, was highly modified and rearranged and deleted portions of Marx's text. Additional translations of Kautsky's version followed over the next several decades, with

a complete three-volume version published in East Germany in 1956–1962. *See also CONTRIBUTION TO THE CRITIQUE OF POLITICAL ECONOMY, A, ECONOMIC AND PHILOSOPHIC MANUSCRIPTS OF 1844*, PREFACE, THE.

THEORY OF VALUE. *See* LAW OF VALUE.

***THESES ON FEUERBACH* (1845).** Written in **Brussels** in the spring of 1845, the original text was not published until 1924. It was not until 1938 that the English translation was published as part of *The German Ideology*. In this short work, Marx asserts that the individual is above all a social being embedded in a particular human society and that "all social life is essentially practical. All mysteries which lead theory to mysticism find their rational solution in human practice and in the comprehension of this practice" (9). He famously concludes, "Philosophers have hitherto only interpreted the world in various ways; the point is to change it" (11).

THIERS, ADOLPHE (1797–1877). Thiers was very active in French politics from the Revolution of 1830, which overthrew the Bourbon monarchy, and the **Revolution of 1848**, which established the Second French Republic. When **Louis-Napoleon** staged his coup, he had Thiers arrested and exiled. The government allowed Thiers to return to **France** in 1852, and for a time, he stayed out of politics, writing histories. Friends encouraged his political return in 1862, and he became a vocal opponent of the government, including fierce opposition to the **Franco-Prussian War**. Following the defeat of the French army, he played a crucial role in the Government of National Defense. On 8 February, elections for a new National Assembly elected Thiers to that body. On 14 February, the National Assembly named him president of the Third Republic, and he formed a government shortly after. The first order of business of the new government was to negotiate an end to the war. Soon after the armistice, on 18 March, the people of **Paris** rose in revolt. Thiers ordered the army to suppress the **Paris Commune**, which crushed the rebellion in the action known as "Bloody Week" from 21 to 29 May. *See also* BISMARCK, OTTO VON, *CIVIL WAR IN FRANCE, THE,* COMMUNARDS, *EIGHTEENTH BRUMAIRE OF LOUIS NAPOLEON,* WARS OF GERMAN UNIFICATION.

THIRD INTERNATIONAL. *See* COMINTERN.

THOMPSON, WILLIAM (1775–1833). William Thompson was an Irish political philosopher and social reformer. His writing on **political economy** exerted some influence over mid-19th-century socialists, including Karl Marx. He was influenced by continental **Enlightenment** philosophers like Marquis de Condorcet, leading him to advocate feminism and Catholic emancipation, which was far in advance of most English social reformers and established for Thompson a reputation as a radical. Influenced by Jeremy Bentham and other utilitarian ideas, Thompson's **Ricardian** socialist interpretation of the **exploitation** of labor appeared to exert considerable influence on Marx and contributed to the English **trade union** and **Chartist** movements.

Much of Thompson's philosophical engagements were notable for their originality. He appears among the first to coin the term "social science," treading a middle path between **William Godwin**'s **idealism** and **T. Robert Malthus**'s empiricism. While critical of Malthus's dire predictions regarding the expansion of the human **population**, he became concerned about the high population **growth** and rates of poverty in Ireland. As a result, he advocated political rights for women to protect women's autonomy better. With **Anna Wheeler** (1780–1848), Thompson wrote one of the most extended and informative book titles on record: *Appeal of One Half of the Human Race, Women, against the Pretensions of the Other Half, Men, to Retain Them in Political, and Hence Civil and Domestic Slavery.* This tome was in response to **James Mill**'s advocacy of the expansion of voting rights to working-class men but not women. Although Thompson believed in the power of cooperative communities, he was critical of **Robert Owen**'s various **utopian** projects. Thompson was dubious of Owen's sources of backing and more skeptical of Owen's despotic impulses. While Marx

did not cite Thompson's writings often, he was among the English social and economic theorists with whom Marx began intensive study in the mid-1840s and that influenced his synthetic approach to economic analysis.

TOOLS. In the **manufacture period**, not only does the worker become highly specialized, but the tools that she uses also become more suited to the performance of specific tasks. For Marx, a tool is not a simple **machine**, nor is a machine only a complex tool. The worker is physically limited in the number of tools he can use at one time, while the machine has no such organic limitations. The machine does not replace the tool; instead, it expands and multiplies it in a complex mechanism.

TRADE UNION CONSCIOUSNESS. Marx predicted that the **growth** of industry would begin the process of expanding and concentrating the **proletariat** and thus **socializing labor**. In their prerevolutionary stage of consciousness, the working classes would start to form associations in reaction to the capitalist's remorseless pursuit of profit:

> The unceasing improvement of machinery, ever more rapidly developing, makes their [workers] livelihood more and more precarious; the collisions between individual workmen and individual **bourgeois** take more and more the character of collisions between two **classes**. Thereupon the workers begin to form combinations (**Trade Unions**) against the bourgeois; they club together in order to keep up the rate of wages; they found permanent association in order to make provision beforehand for these occasional revolts. Here and there the contest breaks out into riots. (Tucker 1978, 480)

For Marx, trade unions represented a necessary step in the evolution of **revolutionary class consciousness**. However, Marx was not definitive in his reference to such a stage as "trade union consciousness," which was a somewhat sneering pejorative label that **Vladimir Lenin** placed on socialists like **Eduard Bernstein**, who eschewed **revolution** as a pathway to a more just political order. For Lenin and other, more revolutionary-minded socialists, trade union consciousness represented a threat to the formation of revolutionary class consciousness and became part of the more substantial justification for the **vanguard party** of committed socialists to lead the way through the **dictatorship of the proletariat** toward **communism**.

TRADE UNIONS. Associations of wage earners that emerged in 18th-century **England**, the site of the initial **Industrial Revolution**, trade unions were a culmination of two historical trends. On the one hand, the medieval history of **guilds**, artisans, and merchants often enjoyed **monopolies** on specific trades (e.g., carpentry, bakers, saddle makers, leather workers, and the like). These trades exerted considerable influence over membership and practices and laid a predicate for collective bargaining. While the guilds did not survive the transition from the medieval agrarian economy to **capitalism**, they did establish norms of cooperation and collective action among workers that influenced the formation of trade unions. On the other hand, capitalism itself produced a concentrated workforce where factory existence built powerful incentives toward collective bargaining to maintain wage levels and improve worker conditions.

An additional factor contributing to the formation of trade unions was the tendency of capitalists to minimize the costs of labor and to seek ways of constraining wage **growth**. In *The Wealth of Nations* (1776), **Adam Smith** noted the asymmetrical relationship between factory workers and manufacturers. He observed that economic elites were not shy in calling on the power of the state to prevent trade union formation, and indeed trade unions were illegal for much of the 18th century. However, over time, the persistence of organizing efforts and the success of worker organizations in large urban areas like London led to the legalization of trade unions in the latter half of the 19th century. Worker organizations figured prominently in the **Revolutions of 1848** as workers' discontent over their lot boiled over. As other

countries industrialized, trade unions emerged, in some instances quite robust and influential (e.g., Scandinavian countries) and in others relatively weak (**Russia** and the United States).

Over time, trade unions (particularly in Europe) organized nationally and took on more explicitly political orientations. In England and Germany, union legalization served expressly political purposes. In England, the Conservative Party espoused the cause of workers as a means of dividing workers from the Whig Party; in Germany, **Otto von Bismarck**—after an initial phase of repression—adopted an explicit strategy of reaching out to unions, notably the **General German Workers' Association**. In both instances, these efforts involved acknowledging the worker's right to organize as a means of enticing trade unions to move away from **socialism** and toward acceptance of the legitimacy of the state. As a result, while trade unions tended to gravitate toward the progressive end of the ideological spectrum, an essential division existed between those more inclined to accept the legitimacy of the **capitalist state** and those more prone to adopt intractably **revolutionary** platforms.

Karl Marx saw trade unions as a means to an end. Avineri (1968) notes that Marx was not as interested in the improvement of the worker's standard of living as he was concerned about "the quality of life of the human being epitomized in the worker" (121). For Marx, the activities of trade unions were primarily valuable only inasmuch as they contributed to the formation of **revolutionary class consciousness**. In his (voluminous) writings on trade unions, Marx consistently expressed support for but little interest in what he viewed as the transitory successes or failures of strikes or other labor actions. Marx tended to adopt a dim view of mass workers' movements, seeing them as too easily swayed by palliatives.

Nevertheless, he believed that trade unions would eventually provide the organizational infrastructure for a viable, unified, revolutionary **proletarian** movement. **Vladimir Lenin**, in contrast, would later contend that **trade union consciousness** was nothing more than a manifestation of **false consciousness**, a blind trail on the path toward revolutionary class consciousness. He argued instead for his **vanguard theory** of the proletariat led by a disciplined intellectual elite properly steeped in revolutionary method.

TRANSPORTATION AND COMMUNICATION. *See* MEANS OF TRANSPORTATION AND COMMUNICATION.

TRIBAL MODE OF PRODUCTION. *See* ASIATIC MODE OF PRODUCTION.

TRIER. Karl Marx's birthplace, the city of Trier, was part of the **Holy Roman Empire** until 1797, when the **French Republic** annexed it. Under the Republic, Jews were to be free and equal citizens, abolishing restrictions on occupations and residence as well as special taxes. The revolutionary government had limited success in Triers, a staunchly Catholic city, giving some resistance to its anticlericalism and festivals celebrating the Republic's patriotic **religion**. Under **Napoleon Bonaparte**, however, Jews would need to conform to the norms of their society, take family names rather than a name derived from their father's name, organize their religious practices in a system of councils patterned after Protestant religions, and not observe dietary laws when serving in the armed forces. "Most controversially, in 1808, Napoleon issued his 'infamous decree,' which required Jewish businessmen to obtain a 'certificate of morality,' with the authorities testifying to the legitimacy of their business practices, particularly that they lent money in honest and above-board fashion, in order to engage in commerce" (Sperber 2013, 10–11). After the defeat of Napoleon's armies in 1813 at the Battle of Nations in Leipzig and with the **Congress of Vienna**, Trier became a province of the Kingdom of Prussia. *See also* JEWISH LIFE IN TRIER, MARX, HEINRICH, MARX, SAMUEL.

TRIER GYMNASIUM. Instead of attending elementary school, it is likely that Marx was tutored at home. He entered the Trier Gymnasium in 1830. The Gymnasium is Germany's version of a university preparatory school. The school had a heavy emphasis on classics, with the study of Latin and Greek very much a part of the curriculum. Sperber (2013) reports that Marx's frequent allusions to the classics, as well as sprinkling his writings with Latin and Greek phrases throughout his life, testify that his classical education had a lasting impression on him (25). *See also* MARX, HEINRICH, WYTTENBACH, JOHANN HEINRICH.

TROTSKY, LEON (1879–1940). Leon Trotsky was a Russian socialist, organizer, and political theorist. His organizational skills helped facilitate the **Red Army**'s success in the Russian Civil War (1917–1919). He also made distinctive contributions to Marxist theory, dubbed "Trotskyism," which exerted considerable influence in Latin America and Asia. Outmaneuvered by **Joseph Stalin** in a leadership struggle following the death of **Vladimir Lenin**, Trotsky fled the **Soviet Union** in 1928, seeking refuge in Turkey, **France**, Norway, and ultimately Mexico, where the NKVD (a forerunner of the KGB) assassinated him in 1940.

Trotsky was born Lev Davidovich Bronstein to a Ukrainian Jewish family of affluent farmers in southern Ukraine. He was educated in Odessa and was initially attracted to the platforms of the **Narodniks**, but he later became an adherent of **Marxism**, reading some of Lenin's works and joining the **Russian Social Democratic Labor Party (RSDLP)** in 1898 at the age of 19. A gifted writer, he wrote and distributed revolutionary pamphlets among Ukrainian workers, drawing the interest of the czarist secret police, who arrested him in 1898. In 1900, the government exiled him and his wife to Siberia for four years; halfway through his sentence, Trotsky escaped and fled **Russia**. Making his way to London, Trotsky joined other Russian dissidents, becoming a writer and editor of a Russian-language magazine. Around that time, he adopted the pseudonym of "Leon Trotsky."

In 1903, Trotsky sided with the **"Mensheviks"**—Russian socialists who advocated organizing as a mass movement—over the **"Bolshevik"** faction, which included Lenin, who advocated the organization of a smaller, **vanguard** approach. Trotsky subsequently returned to Russia and began editing a Russian newspaper, significantly expanding its readership and promoting support for the newly established worker councils, or "**Soviets**," organized by Menshevik followers. He joined and was elected vice-chair of the St. Petersburg Soviet. In the aftermath of czarist Russia's disastrous military performance in the Sino-Russian War (1904–1905), mass demonstrations and strikes paralyzed the country, which included mutinies at the major naval bases at Sevastopol and Vladivostok. During this period before and after the revolution, the Bolshevik and Menshevik factions made halting efforts at coordinating and unifying, including an abortive attempt by Trotsky to fund a socialist newspaper, *Pravda* (Russian for "Truth"). Arrested for his activities during the 1905 revolution, the czarist regime again sentenced him to internal exile in Siberia. He escaped and fled to Vienna, where he worked with various socialist organizations.

In the period following the failed 1905 revolution, Trotsky frequently acted as an intermediary figure in the contentious Bolshevik–Menshevik rivalry. At the outset of World War I, the factions again split between an "internationalist" stance, exemplified in the socialist phrase that it was a "rich man's war but a working man's fight," and nationalist expressions of sympathy for the Russian state. At the time, Trotsky was in New York City editing a Russian-language newspaper at the onset of the revolution. After some delay, he was able to return to Russia later in 1917, where his organizational skills proved indispensable both in the Bolshevik seizure of power and in the subsequent multisided civil war that followed.

Trotsky quickly came to support the Bolshevik position and supported Lenin's call for the violent overthrow of the Provisional Government, then led by Alexander Kerensky. Trotsky organized and led the armed overthrow of the Provisional Government on 7–8 November 1917, adroitly using cajolery, threats, and force in the seizure of power. Trotsky supported Lenin's agreement to German terms in signing and ratifying the Treaty of Brest-Litovsk in March 1918, and he backed Lenin's rejection of a coalition government of the myriad socialist factions then roiling Russian politics.

In the Russian Civil War that followed the revolution, Trotsky organized and enforced a military draft and collaborated with former czarist officers in his successful attempt to raise the number of troops serving in the "Red Army" from roughly 800,000 to more than 3 million. He ruthlessly stationed troops immediately behind the front lines with orders to arrest or summarily execute deserters. His military organization succeeded in overwhelming the "White Army" forces as well as rival socialist factions that took up arms against the Bolsheviks.

Trotsky also supported the institution of the "Red Terror" in the aftermath of a wave of murders of Bolshevik leaders—including the attempted assassination of Lenin—in late 1918. The first significant domestic conflict in the Soviet Union centered on the status of **trade unions**. Trotsky advocated direct state control of worker's organizations, while Lenin rejected Trotsky's approach as excessively bureaucratic. The debate factionalized the Bolsheviks and the Politburo, which Stalin exploited by siding with Lenin. Trotsky ultimately lost the debate, and the Politburo removed key members of Trotsky's supporters from positions of authority and awarded Stalin a significant leadership position within the Politburo. This rift significantly weakened Trotsky's position within the government.

Trotsky supported Lenin's **New Economic Policy (NEP)**, which loosened the government's hold over the economy, allowing a certain amount of market interactions to take place to improve production, although he ultimately believed that the state would eventually have to control all aspects of the economy for socialism to take hold. From 1921 until his death in 1924, Lenin struggled to keep the Bolsheviks united and establish a succession of leadership that would survive his death. Lenin appeared to respect Trotsky's competence and unquestioned organizational talents but distrusted his judgment on matters of doctrine. In contrast, Lenin seemed to be fearful of leaving Stalin positioned to assume overall leadership of the country and made halting efforts to weaken Stalin; however, a series of strokes incapacitated Lenin, and his death in

1924 created a yawning leadership vacuum, which Stalin was in a strong position to fill.

In the years immediately following Lenin's passing, Trotsky and Stalin struggled for the leadership of the party. A major proxy for that struggle was the question of whether the Soviet Union should support socialist movements in other countries. Trotsky advanced the case for **permanent revolution**, arguing that a revolution in one country was symptomatic of broader "**contradictions**" globally and that only a world revolution would provide the conditions to enable the Soviet Union to develop into a socialist society. Stalin, in contrast, threw his support behind **Nikolai Bukharin**'s concept of "**socialism in one country**," arguing that the Soviet Union needed to consolidate its rule and defend against a counterrevolution. Connected to this argument was the question of whether to allow the market mechanisms of the NEP that had helped improve the Soviet economy to continue. Trotsky supported a faction called the "Left Opposition," which advocated for a rapid elimination of the NEP and a program of state-led industrialization. Stalin used both issues tactically to wrap himself in the mantle of Lenin's legacy and used the intramural debate—often described as the "literary discussion"—to highlight Trotsky's numerous differences with Lenin. Stalin's position prevailed in both instances, and he began quietly replacing Trotsky's allies in the Politburo and posts within the Russian Communist Party with Stalin loyalists. Stalin continued to strengthen his hold on the party and the organs of propaganda, enabling him to remove Trotsky from the Politburo (1926), expel him from the Communist Party (1927), and exile him from the Soviet Union (1929).

Trotsky spent the remainder of his life in exile and on the run just ahead of members of Stalin's secret police. Stalin attempted to write Trotsky out of the history of the Russian Revolution and the early years of the Soviet Union but failed. Trotsky's contribution to Marxism-Leninism—particularly his writing on uneven economic development and his advocacy of "permanent revolution"—continued to influence Marxist thought after his assassination. *See also* STALINISM.

TRUE SOCIALISTS. Moses Hess was one of the leaders of the True Socialists, a group of German intellectuals that included **Karl Grün** and **Andreas Gottschalk**. Hess introduced both Marx and **Engels** to socialism, and their initial ideas on socialism were similar to the True Socialists. However, Marx's studies in **political economy** rooted his predictions of the inevitability of socialism in the changing **material** conditions of **production** as well as **class conflict**. In *The German Ideology* as well as in *The Communist Manifesto*, Marx and Engels criticized the True Socialists for not basing their politics on the **material** conditions of production. Instead, they based their politics on the **idealistic** view that it is possible to reform **capitalism** and establish socialism without struggle or violence. Marx would be in continuing conflict with other versions of socialism or **communism** for all of his adult life. *See also* CRITIQUE OF THE GOTHA PROGRAMME.

U

UNDERCONSUMPTION. The disconnection between production and consumption causes underconsumption. In a capitalist society, the purpose of production is producing **commodities** for profit, not products to meet human needs. **Expropriating surplus value** from **labor power** is the means of maximizing profit. Thus, the commodity taken to **market** must always have a higher value than the amount paid for its production. Thus, where does the money come from to purchase all of the commodities produced? Capitalism's tendency to hold wages down by replacing workers with **machinery** or, should this prove too expensive, outsourcing or offshoring to the lowest bidder to save labor costs makes the problem worse. "The **factory system**'s tremendous capacity for expanding with sudden immense leaps, and its dependence on the **world market**, necessarily give rise to the following cycle: feverish production, a consequent glut on the market, then a contraction of the market, which causes production to be crippled" (Marx 1867/1976, 581). The sheer power of capitalist production thus leads to periodic crises of **overproduction** (the other side of underconsumption), most notably in recent times during the Great Depression of the 1930s and the recession of 2008. "The ultimate reason for all real crises always remains the poverty and restricted consumption of the masses, in the face of the drive of capitalist production to develop the **productive forces** as if only the absolute consumption capacity of society set a limit to them" (Marx 1894/1991, 615).

The government can address the problem of underconsumption through deficit spending for social welfare programs, preparations for defense, or actual war. Alternatively, capitalist enterprises can deal with the crisis of underconsumption by increasing consumer credit, but all such solutions can only be temporary and often lead to other crises as well. The resulting economic contraction destroys many capitalists, and **exchange value** plummets but eventually recovers. As a result, capital now becomes more **centralized and enlarged**. "Like regurgitation, the crisis brings relief to a distressed system: the shackles on the productive forces are loosened, and they again enjoy fuller employment and swift expansion. Nonetheless, relief is but temporary since the system remains unchanged, and the productive forces are continually vulnerable to dysfunctional work relations" (Shaw 1978, 102). *See also* CLASS CONFLICT, CONTRADICTIONS OF CAPITALISM, ECONOMIC EXPANSION AND CONTRACTION, ENVIRONMENTAL CRISIS, PREFACE, THE.

UNEMPLOYED. *See* INDUSTRIAL RESERVE ARMY.

UNION OF SOVIET SOCIALIST REPUBLICS (USSR). The Union of Soviet Socialist Republics (USSR), also known as the Soviet Union, was officially formed in 1922 and lasted until its dissolution in 1991. The USSR has its origin in the **Russian Revolution of 1917** that led to the overthrow of the Russian Provisional Government. The Provisional Government took over after the overthrow of the czar during World War I. By 1922, the **Bolsheviks** had leveraged control of the **Red Army** to end the civil war and established the **Communist Party of the Soviet Union (CPSU)**, which formed the government of the USSR and the world's first socialist state. After **Lenin**'s death, **Joseph Stalin** rose to power. He formalized the CPSU's Marxist-Leninist communist ideology, referred to as "**socialism in one country**," with the state assuming centralized control over all existing economic enterprises. The results of the system were rapid industrialization, leading to improved standards of living in urban areas but also significant famines and social upheaval, with Stalin maintaining control through increasingly forcible, authoritarian means, eventually leading to Stalin's "great purge" of the **Old Bolsheviks**.

The Red Army was crucial in the Allies' defeat of Germany in World War II. In the post–World War II era, the USSR was the primary driving force behind the coalition of communist states that entered the Cold War against the Western bloc countries. After the death of Stalin, a succession of communist dictators, including Nikita Khrushchev, Leonid Brezhnev, and Mikhail Gorbachev, led the country. Over this timeframe, the USSR went through significant restructuring economically and politically, abandoning many of the more orthodox **Marxist** philosophies that guided the founders of the USSR, leading ultimately to the collapse of the USSR and dissolving of the union on Gorbachev's resignation in 1991. *See also* BUKHARIN, NIKOLAI, RED GUARD, RUSSIA, RUSSIAN REVOLUTION OF 1905, SOVIETS, STALINISM, TROTSKY, LEON, ZINOVIEV, GRIGORY.

UNIVERSITY OF BERLIN (UNIVERSITÄT BERLIN). At the time of his transfer to the University of **Berlin** (1836), Karl was engaged to **Jenny Westphalen** and was somewhat distracted with love letters and poetry (to his great embarrassment in later life). It was at this time that Marx began his study of the philosophy of **Georg Hegel**. When his father died in 1838, Karl continued his studies in Berlin, although it was a financial struggle

to borrow money from his mother, friends, and acquaintances. He abandoned the study of law and gradually focused on the study of ancient philosophy through Hegelian methods. **Eduard Gans,** as well as the **Young Hegelians**, particularly **Bruno Bauer**, the leader of the **Doctors' Club**, influenced his scholarship. Bauer became a mentor to the young Marx. His dissertation was on Greek philosophy and titled "Difference between the Democritean and Epicurean Philosophy of Nature." However, Gans died, and Bauer left the university for a (short-lived) position at the **University of Bonn**. Young Hegelianism had fallen out of fashion at the University of Berlin, and Marx had exceeded the four-year maximum. While Marx had completed his studies and his dissertation at the University of Berlin, he submitted his dissertation to the faculty at the **University of Jena** for political reasons.

UNIVERSITY OF BONN (UNIVERSITÄT BONN). Marx received his university preparatory education at the **Trier Gymnasium**, leaving **Trier** for his university studies at the University of Bonn in November 1835. While he attended lectures regularly, his principal extracurricular activity was focused on tavern life and drinking with other Rhineland students. There were also brawls between the students from the Rhineland and those from Prussia's eastern provinces. "Marx was elected one of the leaders of the group of Trier students, and his role in the physical disputes culminated, during the summer of 1836, in his participation in a duel with sabers—an old German university tradition, still occasionally practiced today—defending the honor of the middle-class Rhinelanders against the eastern aristocrats" (Sperber 2013, 38–39). It is among these friends that he acquired the nickname "**The Moor.**" Because of his extracurricular activities, his father, **Heinrich Marx**, insisted that he apply himself more fully and transfer to the **University of Berlin** to continue his study of law in the fall of 1836. *See also* UNIVERSITY OF JENA.

UNIVERSITY OF JENA (UNIVERSITÄT JENA). Marx chose to submit his dissertation to the University of Jena, a reputable university that did not have a residency requirement or unreasonable fees. Marx received his doctorate from the University of Jena on 15 April 1841. While sometimes attacked by hostile biographers as a second-rate university, the school, while poorly financed, had an excellent academic reputation. Because of its precarious financial situation, the school relied on fees for supplementing its operating expenses (much like American universities today). In addition to the dissertation, the university required Karl to submit a detailed curriculum vitae, a compendium of all university courses attended, certificates of competence in Latin, and ethical behavior as well as the fee. *See also* UNIVERSITY OF BERLIN; UNIVERSITY OF BONN.

UNPAID LABOR. In simple terms, unpaid labor is work completed but uncompensated. Within **Marxist** theory, Marx himself tended to concentrate on the idea of **surplus labor**, which Marx identified as the source of the **profits** necessary for the **bourgeoisie**'s accumulation of wealth. In *Capital*, Marx contended that the extraction of excess labor was an essential source of class divisions. Marx also noted in *Grundrisse* that trade extended the possibility (or likelihood) for unequal exchanges, providing the foundation for **exploitation**. Later, socialists such as **Immanuel Wallerstein** would use the concept of exploitation in the elaboration of world-systems theory. In his view, "core" industrialized nations would engage in fundamentally inequitable trade with "periphery" developing nations, offering manufactured goods for raw materials in exchanges that inevitably worked to the disadvantage of developing countries.

Friedrich Engels developed a feminist interpretation of unpaid labor, noting the extent to which women perform much of the work associated with the establishment and maintenance of families on an uncompensated basis. In *The Origin of the Family, Private Property, and the State* (1884), Engels argued that this additional work heaped on women created a "double burden" that places women in a reliably disadvantaged position. Implicit

in Engels's analysis is that to break the inherently coercive social institutions of the monogamous family and the state to establish gender equality, a thoroughgoing social revolution was required.

UNPRODUCTIVE LABOR. Marx classifies certain forms of labor as productive and unproductive. As **productive labor** is directly involved in the production of **surplus value**, unproductive labor—while it may be socially useful and address human needs—does not directly contribute to the **growth** of the **economic surplus**. Mandel (1978, 41) gives the example of a doctor whose labor is beneficial for the health and well-being of members of society but is unproductive in terms of directly expanding capital (surplus value). While it may be "productive" for the capitalists who control the medical facility, it is "unproductive" for the **capitalist class** as a whole. Such labor serves only to redistribute the surplus value created by laborers in **commodity** production. However, Mandel continues, productive labor produces such socially harmful products as dum-dum bullets, drugs, and cigarettes, all of which do add to the creation of surplus value. Marx's definition of productive and unproductive labor thus is a value judgment not on the social usefulness of the work but rather on its functions within the capitalist system. While unproductive labor does not contribute directly to the creation of surplus value, it does speed up the **circulation of capital**, thus indirectly contributing to growth. *See also* MANAGERIAL SKILLED LABOR.

URBANIZATION. Urbanization refers to the process of **population** shift from rural areas to urban areas through either population movements or gradual changes in the proportion of populations in rural and urban areas resulting from demographic changes. More generally, the term also refers to the processes by which societies and economies change and adapt to such demographic processes.

Just prior to and during Marx's lifetime, most of western Europe was undergoing rapid urbanization that had its origin in the **Industrial Revolution**. Much of the **growth** of urban populations was a result of the improved agricultural **productivity** resulting from industrialization and advances in the productivity of agricultural **technology**. These advances freed up labor and allowed the continued growth of urban industrial production as well as decreases in the death rate as public health policies steadily improved, especially in urban areas. Marx viewed urbanization as a product of the **capitalist mode of production**, writing in *The Communist Manifesto* that "the bourgeoisie has subjected the country to the rule of the towns. It has created enormous cities, has greatly increased the urban population compared with the rural, and has thus rescued a considerable part of the population from the idiocy of rural life. Just as it has made the country dependent on the towns, so it has made barbarian and semi-barbarian countries dependent on the civilized ones, nations of peasants on nations of bourgeoisies, the East on the West" (Marx and Engels 1848/1969).

Here Marx is arguing not that rural populations are necessarily intellectually inferior but rather that capitalism has produced a system that pulled people together in urban areas and compelled them to interact in ways not possible in less populated rural areas. This increased interaction led to more progressive intellectual and cultural development. This development, combined with a **factory system** that characterized the type of labor available to the **proletariat** in urban centers, was, in Marx's estimation, a necessary precursor to a proletariat-led **socialist revolution**.

Further, Marx was skeptical that rural agricultural populations could or would drive a socialist revolution, a belief central to the debate concerning the **agrarian problem**. Later, economists and sociologists influenced by Marx, such as Max Weber, spent considerable time and effort further elaborating on the process of urbanization and its impacts on human social and economic systems. *See also* CAPITALIST AGRICULTURE, ECOLOGY, METABOLIC INTERACTION, OVERPRODUCTION.

USE VALUE. Use value is simply something that is useful to society. The use values of commodities are dependent on their physical properties. "It is, therefore, a physical body of the commodity itself, for instance, iron, corn, a diamond, which is the use-value or useful thing" (Marx 1867/1976, 126). Marx goes on to say that the use value of a commodity is unrelated to the amount of labor required to produce it. Every successful **commodity** produced under **capitalism** has a use value, or it would not be produced for any significant length of time. As use values, commodities differ in quality and by their physical properties and have no existence apart from the product itself. Use values are realized only when the product is used or consumed; they are material wealth. However, in a capitalist society, they are also the material bearers of **exchange value**. The use values of commodities vary in terms of their quality, while their exchange values vary only in quantity—exchange values "therefore do not contain an atom of use-value. If then we disregard the use-value of commodities, only one property remains that of being products of labour" (128). *See also* LABOR THEORY OF VALUE, LAW OF VALUE.

UTOPIAN SOCIALISM. The status of utopianism within the broader scope of socialism was somewhat muddled in the mid-19th century. Many early socialists and protosocialists, such as **Claude Henri de Saint-Simon**, **Charles Fourier**, and **Robert Owen**, were explicitly utopian in their aspirations; they believed that a perfectly ordered and just society could evolve on earth. Utopian socialists believed that if they got the rules of a community (or, in Fourier's case, the number of people within the community) right, then the demonstrated virtues of this community would recommend themselves to the world and take transformative effect. Marx took a dim view of the utopian socialists, viewing them as hopelessly naive. "Utopianism" in Marx's writing became an insult, and the word within socialist discourse took on a dismissive meaning.

Critics of Marx and **Marxism**, however, have noted deep currents of utopianism flowing through Marxist theory. For example, Marx appeared to believe that in the final stage of human development, several secular features of **human nature** would simply disappear. Elster (1985) suggests that the utopian "character of his views is due to his reluctance to admit that even under **communism** some hard choices might have to be made and that conflicts between values might persist" (91). The notion that material want would disappear and that human beings in a communist stage of economic development would be in a sense neutered from the kinds of impulses that motivate human energies strike many thinkers as exemplary of the sort of wishful thinking that he so excoriated in others. *See also GERMAN IDEOLOGY, THE, SOCIALISM: UTOPIAN AND SCIENTIFIC.*

V

VALORIZATION PROCESS. Valorization is the process of adding value to **capital** through the **labor process**. The process begins when the capitalist purchases at market value the **means of production** (workplace, **tools**, machinery, parts, and raw materials) and **labor power**. The capitalist then uses these inputs to produce a **commodity** to sell on the market for **money**. However, this money represents more value than the inputs—the means of production and labor power. If the essence of exchange, Marx asks, is equality of exchange, from where does profit come? He answers that labor power is capable of producing more than its exchange value (Marx 1867/1976, 300). **Capitalist production** must produce **surplus value**. The value of the commodities the worker needs to reproduce his labor at a given standard of living (this standard varies across societies, across regions within societies, and through time) determines the value of labor power. As labor power is the only commodity that the laborer possesses, he sells this power at its **exchange value**. This exchange allows the capitalist to use the labor power to produce more value than the capitalist expended in wages. The amount of surplus value created by the worker can increase through extending the **length the working day** (**absolute surplus value**), employing **machinery** or further **detailing the division of labor** to increase the **productivity** of the worker (**relative surplus value**), or lowering the cost of **wage goods**, or the commodities the worker needs to reproduce his labor (shelter, food, and reproduction).

VANGUARD PARTY. The role of intellectuals within the socialist movement has often been a point of contention. Throughout the 19th century, socialists debated whether the **proletariat** required guidance. For example, **Blanquism** favored a small, conspiratorial, and tightly disciplined group that would seize the commanding heights of the state and subsequently use the power of the state in a forced conversion to socialism. Marx was harshly critical of Blanquism, believing that the role of the socialist intellectuals was to guide the proletariat in a far more thoroughgoing **revolution** that would ultimately replace **capitalism** with **socialism** through a **revolutionary sequence**. In western Europe, **Marxist orthodoxy** largely prevailed, and intellectuals like Marx harnessed themselves (however discontentedly) to workers' parties, such as the **Social Democratic Workers' Party of Germany**, or alternatively adhered to the more anarchist–libertarian–oriented machinations advocated by **Mikhail Bakunin**. In **Russia**, the failures of various liberal movements like the **Narodniks** and the more conspiratorial terrorism of *Narodnoya Volya* (the "People's Will") presented Russian socialists with a dilemma. *See also* KAUTSKY, KARL, LENIN, VLADIMIR.

VARIABLE CAPITAL. Marx divides capital into **constant capital** and variable capital. Fixed, or constant, capital is the part of wealth used to acquire and maintain the material **means of production**—that is, the **tools** and **machinery**, factories, and **workshops**. While it is a necessary condition for producing **surplus value**, it does not produce surplus value itself. Variable capital is that part of capital used to purchase **labor power**. Labor power creates value in the production process by reproducing the equivalent of its value as well as producing excess or surplus value for the capitalist (Marx 1867/1976, 317). Only variable capital—that is, the labor power of workers—produces surplus value. The amount of surplus value **expropriated** from workers increases through a variety of stratagems to improve worker **productivity**. First, the capitalist may extend the **length of the working day**. Another method is to employ machinery or devise a more **detailed division of labor**. A third method of improving the productivity of the workforce is to increase the supervision and monitoring of worker performance. A final strategy is to cut wages in tandem with lowering the cost of **wage goods**. The **profit motive**, as well as **competition** with other firms, gives the capitalists a great incentive to take any or all of these steps to increase surplus value. The worker, of course, has interests and therefore incentives to minimize their expenditure of energy and effort and to maximize rewards (in other words, to reduce **exploitation**). Therein lies a conflict. "Marx, therefore, logically integrates the development of the **class struggle** between capital and labour into his analysis of the production of surplus-value, inasmuch as he sees that class struggle is originating in that process of production" (Mandel 1976, 35).

VASSAL. A vassal is an individual who is subordinate to or has an obligation to a higher-level noble within a system characterized by the **feudal mode of production**. Obligations might include military service or payment in agricultural goods, and usually, in return, the vassal serves as the **landlord** over land occupied by **serfs**. *See also* AGRARIAN QUESTION, *EIGHTEENTH BRUMAIRE OF LOUIS BONAPARTE* (1852), PEASANTRY.

VIOLENT REVOLUTION. *See* REVOLUTIONARY SOCIALISM.

W

WAGE GOODS. These are goods required by workers to survive and reproduce themselves and their families—food, shelter, clothing, entertainment, and the like. The prevailing standard of living determines the quantity and quality of these goods and partially determines the value of **labor power**. Keeping these goods cheap through imports or technological advance lowers the value of labor power or the share of **capital** that goes to wages (**variable capital**) and increases the percentage that goes to the capitalists (**surplus value**). Harvey (2013) asserts that wage goods can become so cheap through imports and technological advance that declining or stagnant wages to workers "can be compatible with a rising material standard of living. This has been a key feature of recent capitalist history" (13). *See also* COMPETITION, MACHINES, TECHNOLOGY, VALORIZATION, WAGE LABOR.

WAGE LABOR. For capitalism to exist, there has to be a class of people who are denied access to the **means of production** and who, therefore, must sell their **labor power** to survive and thrive. Forcibly removing peasants from the land through privatization and enclosure was an early means of separating people from this necessary means of production. Wages are for the use of labor power for a fixed period. The value of labor power varies across societies and through time. The cost of **wage goods** required by workers to reproduce themselves at the prevailing standard of living partly determines the value of labor power. A second factor that determines the value of

labor power is the service sector of society, as this sector has "been a major factor in developing the needs and living conditions of the proletariat far beyond the purely physiological bedrock" (Mandel 1978, 52). A third factor determining the value of labor power is the state of the **class struggle**. "Labour may improve its wages and living conditions through class struggles. Conversely, counter-attacks by an organised **capitalist class** may reduce the value of labor-power" (Harvey 2013, 13). *See also* COMPETITION, MACHINES, PRIMITIVE ACCUMULATION, PROLETARIAT, TECHNOLOGY, VALORIZATION.

WAGE LABOUR AND CAPITAL (1847). An essay on **political economy** first published in a series of articles in the *New Rhineland Newspaper: Organ of Democracy*, a German daily newspaper edited by Marx in 1848–1849. According to **Engels**, the text consists of a series of lectures given by Marx to the **German Workingmen's Club** of Brussels in 1847. Marx never finished the series, as the government suppressed the paper on 19 May 1849 and exiled Marx from **Prussia**. It contains many topics that he more fully develops in *Capital*, including **alienation**, **commodity**, and the **labor theory of value**. Marx's analysis of political economy continued well into his writing of Capital's three volumes.

It is in *Wage Labour and Capital* that Marx details the distinction between the **forces of production** and the **relations of production**. The two concepts are distinct and yet interrelated and reactive to one another:

In the process of production, human beings work not only upon nature but also upon one another. They produce only by working together in a specified manner and reciprocally exchanging their activities. To produce, they enter into definite connections and relations to one another, and only within these social connections and relations does their influence upon nature operate—i.e., does production take place.

These social relations between the producers, and the conditions under which they exchange their activities and share in the total act of production, will naturally vary according to the character of the **means of production**. With the discovery of a new instrument of warfare, the firearm, the whole internal organization of the army was necessarily altered, the relations within which individuals compose an army and can work as an army were transformed, and the relation of different armies to another was likewise changed.

We thus see that the **social relations** *within which individuals produce, the* **social relations of production**, *are altered, transformed, with the change and development of the material means of production, of the forces of production.* The relations of production in their totality constitute what is called the social relations, society, and, moreover, a society at a definite stage of historical development, a society with peculiar, distinctive characteristics. **Ancient society**, **feudal society**, **bourgeois** (or capitalist) society, are such totalities of relations of production, each of which denotes a particular stage of development in the history of mankind.

Capital also is a social relation of production. It is a bourgeois relation of production, a relation of production of bourgeois society. The means of subsistence, the instruments of labor, the raw materials, of which capital consists—have they not been produced and accumulated under given social conditions, within definite special relations? Are they not employed for new production, under given special conditions, within definite social relations? And does not just the definite social character stamp the products which serve for new production as capital? (emphasis added). (Marx 1847b, 13–14)

Marx gives center stage to the forces of production. However, he never conceived of it as a simple case of the forces of production determining relations. Instead, there is an ongoing and continuous interplay between the forces of production and the relations of production throughout **social evolution**. The close interactions of the means and the relations of production are especially apparent in Marx's analysis of the transition between economic systems. Such transformations are a subject of critical importance to Marx because his prediction of the inevitability of socialism depended on the full development of industrialism under **capitalism**. The **Russian Revolution of 1917** was not widely seen as a fulfillment of Marx's prediction because it was mainly a revolution in a feudal society.

The **rise of capitalism** precedes the **Industrial Revolution** by at least a century. At first, capital production was closer to the **handicrafts** of feudal society than to industrial methods. The structure of the capitalist system, with its drive toward **profit** and expansion, stimulates **technological** development, the **factory system**, and a more **detailed division of labor**. In turn, this industrial development affects the continuing development of capitalism itself. The forces of production and the relations of production are intimately connected. However, they are theoretically separate and have independent as well as combined effects on the rest of the sociocultural system. For Marx, the forces and relations of production are the foundation of all sociocultural systems. Combined, they have a profound impact on the rest of the system, strongly influencing all other aspects of the society and thus affecting the very social character, values, beliefs, and **ideologies** of the people who are members of that sociocultural system. *See also* PREFACE, THE, TECHNOLOGICAL DETERMINISM.

WAGE SLAVERY. "Wage slavery" is a term used to describe situations in which an individual's livelihood is entirely and imme-diately dependent on their ability to earn a wage through **paid labor**. Many use the term to equate the status of **wage laborers** with that of chattel **slavery**, indicating that the wage laborer has only the illusion of freedom. Marx extensively discusses the wage labor system in many of his works, most notably in *Capital: Volume I* and in the *Economic and Philosophic Manuscripts of 1844* (as well as in the posthumously published *Theories of Surplus Value*), detailing how the **bourgeoisie** owners of the **means of production** appropriate **surplus value** from the labor of the **proletariat**, permanently reducing the working class to complete dependence on the wage system. The meaning of the term is perhaps best illustrated by **Engels** in *The Condition of the Working Class in England*, where he notes that "the only difference as compared with the old, outspoken slavery is this, that the worker of today seems to be free because he is not sold once for all, but piece-meal by the day, the week, the year, and be-cause no one owner sells him to another, but he is forced to sell himself in this way instead, being the slave of no particular person, but of the whole property-holding class" (Engels 1845/1969, 91).

WALLERSTEIN, IMMANUEL (1930–2019).

Immanuel Wallerstein was an American soci-ologist who used Marx's theory to explore the history of the origins and **growth** of the world system of capitalism. According to Wallerstein, the capitalist world system began in 15th-cen-tury Europe and, pushed by an imperative to accumulate capital, by the late 19th century covered the globe. The increasing dominance of this world system defines modernity itself. It is a fundamental change that has transformed the world (Wallerstein 1974, 3). A single capi-talist world economy defines modern times, he asserts, and forms the context in which the struggles between nations, classes, races, ethnic groups, and political movements are de-cided. *See also* BRAVERMAN, HARRY, CRISES OF CAPITALISM, FOSTER, JOHN BELLAMY, ECOLOGY, WESTERN MARXISM, WORLD MARKETS, ZUSAMMENBRUCHSTHEORIE.

WARS OF GERMAN UNIFICATION. *See* AUSTRO-PRUSSIAN WAR, FRANCO-PRUS-SIAN WAR.

WEITLING, WILHELM (1808–1871).

Wilhelm Weitling was a rival to Marx for leadership in the early German communist movement. Weitling, a journeyman tailor and émigré, belonged to several radical secret societies on the conti-nent. He gained notoriety among German émi-grés for writing two books on socialism as well as for the government of Switzerland jailing him for six months in 1843 for his beliefs. Along with **Karl Schapper**, he was one of the leaders of the **League of the Just** in **Paris** and **London**. Weitling, however, favored immediate **revolution**, while Schapper favored a program of education and propaganda to prepare the people for revolt. The League debated the two views on several occasions, but by early 1846, the League rejected Weitling's views as being too militant. However, this same disagreement was to boil over in a confrontation with Marx.

While visiting Marx in **Brussels** in March 1846, Weitling attended a meeting of the **Communist Correspondence Committee** where Marx proceeded to attack him for his ideas. The crux of the argument was that Marx insisted that **communism** could happen only after capitalists fully developed the **means of production**. Weitling insisted that communism was always possible and fa-vored immediate revolution. Marx countered, claiming that Weitling's ideas gave workers false hope and would lead to repression. Marx got steadily angrier during this attack, pounding the table and shouting, "Ignorance has never yet helped anyone!" As a result of the political infighting, Weitling and his sup-porters were marginalized in the movement that spring, and Karl and his followers com-mitted against "primitive insurrectionism" (Stedman-Jones 2016, 241). Weitling re-turned to Germany during the **Revolutions of 1848** and continued to preach his brand of communism to little effect. After the failure of the revolution, he immigrated to the United States, becoming one of the **Forty-Eighters**. In his later years, he received several pat-ents for attachments to sewing **machines**. He died in New York City. *See also* COMMUNIST LEAGUE.

WESTERN MARXISM. The turn of the 20th century was a period of intellectual and theoretical drift for **Marxism**. With both Marx and **Engels** dead and with no clear inheritor to adapt Marxist doctrine to events in the world, several distinctive interpretations of "orthodox" Marxism vied for influence. The ferocious critical response to **Eduard Bernstein**'s revisionism set the tone for the debate among future generations of Marxism over its direction. As Marxism-Leninism emerged as the dominant ideology of the **Soviet Union** and as this ideology yielded to **Stalinism** throughout the 1920s, alternative interpretations of Marxism began to emerge in eastern and western Europe. Western Marxism appeared as a revolutionary alternative to Stalinism, evolving in (at least) two separate strands: one concerned with **"praxis,"** or the application of Marxist principles into workable plans of action, and the other becoming more of an academic venture (see ACADEMIC MARXISM).

The unifying theme of this doctrinally diverse movement were critical concerns over the more deterministic aspects of doctrinaire Marxism. Beginning with Bernstein, Western Marxists acknowledged the power of Marx's analysis of capitalism but expressed concerns regarding the predictive power of the Marxian analysis. In particular, Engels and his immediate intellectual heirs, such as **Karl Kautsky** and Georgi Plekhanov, adopted "naturalistic" postures concerning the inevitability of **capitalism**'s demise. Specifically, Western Marxists denied the existence of "mechanical 'laws of history,'" arguing instead that objective economic conditions establish "a range of historical possibilities" (Gottlieb 1989, 6).

Early expressions of this branch of Marxism, whose more influential members included **Antonio Gramsci** and **Georg Lukács**, contended that Marx's materialism ignored the extent to which the ideological **superstructure** of capitalism penetrated human consciousness. Capitalist ideologies erected formidable structures of domination within the language that rendered the coalescence of a universal revolutionary **class consciousness** deeply problematic if not impossible. Gramsci's conceptualization of **cultural hegemony** exerted considerable influence among Western Marxists and illustrated the seriousness with which Western Marxists approached cultural domination as a barrier to consciousness raising. Extending Marx's notion that the "ideas of the **ruling class** are the ruling ideas," Gramsci contended that cultural hegemony created a network of mutually exclusive realities that separated the **proletariat** from the **bourgeoisie** but that also erected conceptual obstacles to cooperation among **workers**. For Gramsci, the key to unlocking the revolutionary consciousness of the proletariat lay in the creation and defense of an alternative working-class culture, guided by proletarian intellectuals.

Western Marxism was doctrinally diverse in its views on the necessity of **revolution**, with some arguing for the violent overthrow of capitalism and others advocating participation in democratic elections. In the post–World War II era, as the costs of doctrinal opposition to **Stalin**'s brutal determinism rose, the number of intellectuals espousing Western Marxism within the Soviet sphere of interest shrank to the Balkan regions, where Yugoslavia's Josip Broz Tito's steadfast rejection of Soviet hegemony afforded an uncertain shelter.

The brutal suppression of the **Prague Spring** in 1968 was a clarifying event for the European left. Some western European communist parties (e.g., **France**) openly criticized the **Soviet Union** for the first time, while some communist parties' intraparty squabbling (e.g., Greece) led to factionalization. Many European communist parties began espousing a variant of Western Marxism known as Eurocommunism in the 1970s and 1980s, rejecting the Brezhnev Doctrine and signaling a turn away from Soviet hegemony. Romanian leader Nicolae Ceauşescu's (1918–1989) condemnation of the Soviet intervention illustrated the willingness of Eastern bloc leaders to criticize Soviet leadership and signaled the growing erosion of **Russian** ideological hegemony in matters related to the interpretation of Marxism.

Western Marxism continues to exert influence among left-oriented political parties in

Europe and elsewhere. Several socialist and communist parties of Europe continue to espouse platforms that echo the political and ideological concerns of Western Marxism. Similarly, Western Marxist analysis and intellectual interests continue to exert significant influence in institutions of higher education in Europe, the United States, and Latin America. *See also* BRAVERMAN, HARRY, FOSTER, JOHN BELLAMY, TECHNOLOGICAL DETERMINISM, WALLERSTEIN, IMMANUEL.

WESTPHALEN, EDGAR VON (1819–1890). Son of **Johann Ludwig von Westphalen**, younger brother of **Jenny von Westphalen**, and boyhood friend and classmate of Karl Marx in the **Trier Gymnasium**. Karl and Jenny named their oldest son, **Edgar**, after him. He studied law at the **University of Berlin** at the same time as Karl, became a lawyer, and held several posts around **Trier**. In 1847, he spent time with Jenny and Karl in **Brussels**, becoming a member of the Brussels **Communist Correspondence Committee** for a short time. By all accounts, Edgar was a hopeless romantic, believing in the possibility of a communist utopia. Seeking this better society, he moved to Sisterdale, Texas, in 1851, a community established by German freethinkers and **Forty-Eighters**. Returning to **Berlin** in 1865 broke and in despair, Edgar eventually found employment in the Prussian judicial system. Terrible at managing money, he died penniless in a charity hospital in Berlin. *See also* WESTPHALEN, FERDINAND VON.

WESTPHALEN, FERDINAND VON (1799–1876). Ferdinand was the son of **Johann Ludwig von Westphalen** and half brother to **Jenny** and **Edgar**. Johann Ludwig was married twice, and his first wife, Elizabeth von Veltheim, was from the Prussian nobility. She had four children and died in childbirth in 1807 with the last. Ludwig remarried in 1812 to Caroline Heubel, the daughter of a minor Prussian official, and had two children. Consequently, Elizabeth's family strongly influenced the four children she bore; they became quite conservative and religious in contrast to

their half siblings. Ludwig and Caroline raised Jenny and Edgar modestly. Their half brother, Ferdinand, trained as a lawyer and worked for the Prussian government first in **Trier** and then in **Berlin**. He became the Prussian minister of the interior (1850–1858) and was noted for his reactionary views regarding divine-right monarchy, Evangelical Christianity, and reestablishing a society of estates. Ferdinand was "known as the strongman of the government ministry in the age of reaction" (Sperber 2013, 44). Ferdinand's life was in stark contrast to the life led by Jenny and Karl as political refugees in **London** at that time.

WESTPHALEN, JENNY VON. *See* MARX, JENNY.

WESTPHALEN, JOHANN LUDWIG VON (1770–1842). Johann Ludwig, a widower since 1807, had married Caroline Heubel, the daughter of a minor Prussian official, in 1812. Prussia posted Ludwig to the regional government in **Trier** in 1816, and he became a close friend of **Heinrich Marx**, Karl's father. Ludwig had four children by his first wife and two who survived childhood with Caroline: **Jenny**, who became close friends of Karl's older sister, Sophie, and **Edgar**, who became a friend and classmate of Karl.

Ludwig was the official in charge of prisons for the district and a registered aristocrat, though his nobility was based on state service rather than genealogy and was thus of lower rank. Ludwig's family had no real wealth, living off the salary of a state official. Karl had great respect for Ludwig, telling his daughter **Eleanor** that they had frequently strolled together and spoken of Shakespeare, Homer, and other great literature. Ludwig was perhaps more radical than Karl's father, introducing him to **Saint-Simonian** doctrines (Bottomore 1973, 4–5). In 1841, Marx even dedicated his doctoral dissertation to his future father-in-law: "You, my fatherly friend, have always been for me the living proof that **idealism** is no illusion, but the true reality." Karl was present when Ludwig died in 1842 and married Jenny the following year. *See also* WESTPHALEN, FERDINAND VON.

WILLICH, AUGUST (1810–1878). One of the earlier German proponents of socialism, August Willich, was born into a military family. Orphaned at age three, Friedrich Schleiermacher, the influential philosopher and theologian, raised him in his household. He received an education matching a son of a Prussian officer and joined the Prussian army, where he served in an artillery unit. However, he soon resigned, writing a letter of resignation in support of a fellow republican officer, and the tenor of the letter led to his subsequent court-martial. Although the court acquitted him and allowed him to resign his commission, his participation shortly after that in one of the **Revolutions of 1848** necessitated his exile, first to Switzerland and subsequently to **London**, where he learned carpentry and found work.

In London, Willich continued to espouse increasingly radical causes and met Karl Marx, whom he viewed as excessively conservative. He may have publicly accused Marx of lying to induce Marx into fighting a duel, an inducement that Marx ignored, and he subsequently fought a duel with one of Marx's younger supporters (Stedman-Jones 2016, 301). He then immigrated to the United States in 1853 and found work first in the Brooklyn Navy Yard as a carpenter and later as a coastal surveyor, where he discovered his mathematical talents. Just before the American Civil War, he moved to Cincinnati, where he edited a socialist German-language newspaper.

Willich was one of many radical former Prussian military officers to serve in the Union army during the American Civil War, rising from the rank of first lieutenant to major general by war's end. He served competently and at times spectacularly. He played a critical role in ordering the charge of Missionary Ridge during the Siege of Chattanooga, which was crucial to lifting the Confederate siege and paving the way for Sherman's invasion of Georgia. He commanded troops in combat on numerous occasions and received a severe wound in the Battle of Resaca. Assigned to various administrative positions following his return to active duty, he retired in late 1865. Willich was among the early German converts to socialism, and he was notable primarily for

his opposition to Marx in the formative period of the **Communist League** in 1849 and his subsequent military service in the Union army during the Civil War. *See also* ALCHEMISTS OF REVOLUTION, BLANQUI, LOUIS-AUGUSTE, COMMUNIST LEAGUE, FORTY-EIGHTERS, LEAGUE OF THE JUST, SCHAPPER, KARL, WILLICH-SCHAPPER GROUP.

WILLICH-SCHAPPER GROUP. After the **1848 revolution**, two members of the **Communist League**, **Karl Schapper** and **August Willich**, became convinced that Marx was too conservative. In 1850, the two advocated continued **revolutionary** activity, whereas Marx and **Engels** advocated first building a mass workers' movement, building **revolutionary consciousness** for eventual revolution. The acrimony between the two camps became so severe that Willich reportedly plotted to kill Marx, publicly insulting him and challenging him to a duel. Marx refused. The two then formed their own group, but it proved ineffective. Willich soon immigrated to the United States in 1853, eventually becoming a general in the Union army. Schapper later reconciled with Marx, becoming one of the founders of the **International Workingmen's Association** in 1864.

WISSENSCHAFT. A German term for the systematic study of an area, be it science, humanities, history, **religion**, art, or any other area suitable to academic research. It was a part of Karl's early education in the **Trier Gymnasium** as well as the universities where he studied. Sperber (2013) characterizes Marx's philosophical and social theories—his Wissenschaft—as halfway between **Hegel** (albeit with Marx's materialist order) and positivism with its emphasis on empiricism and scientific form. "The understanding of Wissenschaft he had absorbed in his study of Hegel during his youth never left him. Marx insisted that true knowledge emerged from understanding the hidden inner logic of empirically observable phenomena, rather than simply from empirical observations themselves, even when those observations were carried out using the methods of the natural sciences" (414). **Engels**, who served primarily as an interpreter of Marx for those that followed, was far more influenced by empirical science and gave to **Marxism** a more scientific bent, as is readily apparent in the pamphlet *Socialism: Utopian and Scientific*. See also MARX, HEINRICH, MARXIAN MYTHOLOGY, TRIER, WYTTENBACH, JOHANN HEINRICH.

WITHERING AWAY OF THE STATE. The idea behind the phrase is that the state is merely the machine for oppressing one class by another—whether it be in the form of a democratic republic (**bourgeois democracy**) or a monarchy. Once the **proletariat** is successful in overthrowing the rule of the capitalist, they will rule in the name of all, and the state itself will no longer be necessary. As political power is simply a means of class domination, the disappearance of class leads to the abolition of the state. Engels writes in his introduction to the 20th anniversary of Marx's *Civil War in France* that, at best, the state is "an evil inherited by the proletariat after its victorious struggle for class supremacy." When the new society raises a generation under free conditions, they "will be able to throw the entire lumber of the state on the scrap-heap" (para. 4).

When a state truly becomes representative of the whole society, with no one to oppress, it becomes unnecessary and withers away. Engels (1908) writes, "The first act by virtue of which the State really constitutes itself the representative of the whole of society—the taking possession of the **means of production** in the name of society—this is, at the same time, its last independent act as a State. State interference in social relations becomes, in one domain after another, superfluous, and then dies out of itself; the government of persons is replaced by the administration of things, and by the conduct of processes of production" (128–29). Exploiting and exploited classes were necessary as long as production could barely create a surplus for some, but this was a temporary condition based on the "insufficiency of production." Modern **productive forces** will remove the necessity. "It is the ascent of man from the kingdom of necessity to the kingdom of freedom" (134). *See*

also CAPITALIST STATE, DICTATORSHIP OF THE PROLETARIAT, PARIS COMMUNE, *SOCIALISM: UTOPIAN AND SCIENTIFIC*.

WORKERS AS CONSUMERS. According to the **laws of capitalist production**, the working class must grow impoverished as wealth accumulates on one pole and low wages, ignorance, and the immiseration of the proletariat grow at the other. To maximize **surplus value**, Marx argues, the capitalist will pay the minimum wage the market will bear. When Marx considers the realization of value in the market in *Capital: Volume II*, he points out a fundamental **contradiction**:

> The workers are important for the market as buyers of commodities. But as sellers of their commodity—**labour-power**—capitalist society has the tendency to restrict them to their minimum price. Further contradiction: the periods in which capitalist production exerts all its forces regularly show themselves to be periods of **over-production**; because the limit to the application of the productive powers is not simply the production of value, but also its realization. However the sale of commodities, the realization of commodity capital, and thus of surplus-value as well, is restricted not by the consumer needs of society in general, but by the consumer needs of a society in which the great majority are always poor and must always remain poor. (Marx 1885/1978, 391n)

Illustrating the contradiction today is the tendency of American corporations to offshore production to low-wage nations, locating their plants in low-wage states, downsizing, contingent employment, outsourcing, union busting, holding down the wages of production workers and middle management, incorporating **technology** to replace workers, and overworking those who remain. These actions are successful in maximizing the surplus value of the particular corporation but are devastating to the overall American economy as well as to the working class. The workers in low-wage countries often work in extreme sweatshop conditions and have limited funds to purchase the products they create. The American consumer economy, which in 2019 was 68 percent of the overall economy, has been propped up through liberal extension of consumer credit to stimulate spending, government tax policies, cheap **wage goods** mainly from foreign sources, and government deficit spending to stimulate the economy. Nevertheless, these can be only temporary fixes, as they cause additional problems of their own, and the fundamental contradictions grow.

WORKERS' COOPERATIVE FACTORY. Like the **joint-stock companies**, the wages of management in a workers' cooperative factory are separate from the profit of the enterprise. In a workers' cooperative, Marx asserts, the antagonistic character of management disappears "since the manager is paid by the workers instead of representing capital in opposition to them" (Marx, 1894/1991, 512). Marx sees workers' cooperatives as a new mode of production though, because it is within the system of **capitalism**, suffering all the defects of that system. Consistent with his **materialist view of history**, Marx asserts that

> these factories show how, at a certain stage of development of the **material forces of production**, and of the social forms of production corresponding to them, a new mode of production develops and is formed naturally out of the old. Without the **factory system** that arises from the **capitalist mode of production, cooperative factories** could not develop. Nor could they do so without the **credit system** that develops from the same mode of production. This credit system, since it forms the principal basis for the gradual transformation of capitalist private enterprises into capitalist joint-stock companies, presents in the same way the means for the gradual extension of cooperative enterprises on a more or less national scale. Capitalist joint-stock companies as much as cooperative factories should be viewed as transition forms from the capitalist mode of produc-

tion to the associated one, simply that in the one case the opposition is abolished in a negative way, and in the other in a positive way. (571–72)

These two forms of production—workers' cooperatives and joint-stock companies—are a transitional phase, replacing the industrial capitalist with an associational form and thus in a form that can more easily be absorbed into a proletarian-ruled socialist state. *See also* DICTATORSHIP OF THE PROLETARIAT.

WORKING DAY, LENGTH OF THE. In the early days of **capitalism**, the primary source of **surplus value** was through lengthening the working day or through hiring women and children at a lower rate. These methods of increasing **absolute surplus value** became more and more difficult with successive passages of the **British Factory Acts**, which became more restrictive of labor abuse, as well as the increasing enforcement of these acts over time. As a result, capitalists began employing more **machine technology** to enhance the **productivity** of the workforce to increase the **relative surplus value** that they could expropriate from their labor. *See also* CHILD LABOR, CONSTANT CAPITAL, DEAD LABOR, VARIABLE CAPITAL.

WORKSHOPS. An **instrument of labor** that initially appears as the province of master craftsmen and **guilds** with strict rules on the **division of labor** and the number of journeymen and apprentices. Capitalist production begins with **manufacture** in workshops in which the capitalist employs large numbers of workers and a **detailed division of labor** to increase **productivity**. With the **Industrial Revolution**, the **centralization and enlargement of capital**, **growth** of **credit systems**, and increases in the **scale of production**, with the **factory system** largely replacing workshops.

WORLD MARKETS. Marx used the term "world markets" to refer to all non-European markets that had economic interaction with Europe. During Marx's time, this was primarily the United States, but he used the term in a general sense. Marx argued that world markets would play an increasingly important role in capitalist systems. Such systems were continually looking for new markets for sourcing raw materials and for selling goods. Further, he argued that improvements in **technology** and the **means of communication and transportation** drove the **growth** of world markets.

This exploitation of world markets was, in Marx's estimation, a natural outcome of **capitalism**. Like the division between the **bourgeoisie** and the **proletariat**, Marx saw an unequal **international division of labor**, with the European **capitalist states** engaging in imperialist activities to maintain the economic superiority of Europe. In *The Communist Manifesto*, he writes, "Modern industry has established the world market, for which the discovery of America paved the way. This market has given an immense development to commerce, to navigation, to communication by land. This development has, in its turn, reacted on the extension of industry; and in proportion as industry, commerce, navigation, railways extended, in the same proportion the bourgeoisie developed, increased its capital, and pushed into the background every class handed down from the Middle Ages" (Marx and Engels 1848/2012, 221). This enforced inequality would, Marx argued, ultimately result in a global **crisis** that would mirror the types of crises predicted within capitalist nations. **Revolution**, then, would not be contained within a single state but would be worldwide. As globalization of markets continued and expanded, the role that world markets play has become an intense focus of Marxist sociologists and economists like **Immanuel Wallerstein**. *See also* BANKS, CENTRALIZATION AND ENLARGEMENT OF CAPITAL, COMPETITION, FACTORY SYSTEM, WORKSHOPS, ZUSAMMENBRUCHSTHEORIE.

WYTTENBACH, JOHANN HEINRICH. Director of the **Trier Gymnasium** and a significant influence on young Karl Marx, who attended secondary school here. Wyttenbach was the principal of **Trier**'s secondary school under Napoleonic rule in the 1790s, and when Prussia incorporated the Rhineland, they employed him as director of the Friedrich-Wilhelm Gymnasium as well as a history teacher, probably as a conciliating gesture to aid in integrating the province into the kingdom. "The ethos of the Gymnasium in Trier, shaped by its long-term headmaster, Johann Hugo Wyttenbach, was that of the late eighteenth-century Aufklärung, the German **Enlightenment**. It consisted of a strong belief in a benign God, and a rational morality uncluttered by dogma. In his youth, Wyttenbach had been a committed Jacobin and during the period of French rule had argued that the future of the republic depended upon the education of its youth; and so in 1799 he had composed *A Handbook for the Instruction in the Duties and Rights of Man and the Citizen*" (Stedman-Jones 2016, 36). He was a member of Trier's reading club, steeped in Enlightenment ideas, and an adherent to Kant's philosophy. Sperber (2013) claims that Karl's graduation essay—the first of his preserved writings—reflected both the ideas of his mentors as well as "glimmerings of Marx's own ideas and aspirations" (29). Chief among these influences was Wyttenbach, as Karl extolled the virtues of scholar, sage, and poet (33–34).

As a former official under Napoleon's rule, Wyttenbach was under some suspicion by the Prussian government for his supposed radical sympathies and his inability to keep some of his faculty under political control. The government appointed a codirector toward the end of Karl's time at the gymnasium, a man whom Karl snubbed. *See also* JEWISH LIFE IN TRIER, MARX, HEINRICH.

Y

YOUNG HEGELIANS. The Young Hegelians (also known as the Hegelian Left or the Left Hegelians) were a loose school of disciples of **Georg Wilhelm Friedrich Hegel**. The group drew on Hegel's notions of **dialectics** to argue for radical change in society. The Young Hegelians argued that change would occur as the result of the **negation** of existing social structures that restricted freedom and reason. The school was mainly idealist and mounted their efforts at social transformation through radical critiques of existing religious and political systems, often in an overtly anti-Christian or atheistic manner.

Some of the prominent members of the Young Hegelians included **Arnold Ruge** (who edited the primary journal of the Young Hegelians—*Hallische Jahrbücher*), David Strauss, **Bruno Bauer, Ludwig Feuerbach,** and **Max Stirner**. Marx and **Engels** were members of the Young Hegelians in their youth but soon became critical of the idealist approach taken by the members of the group. Through texts such as *The Holy Family, The German Ideology,* and *Theses on Feuerbach,* Marx and Engels broke with the Young Hegelian idea that **religion** was the basis of the state's power. They argued instead for a materialist perspective that held that the **means of production** and the **relations of production** are the basis for the state's power (and the power of the **bourgeoisie**). Religion, for Marx, was a component of the **superstructure** that the bourgeoisie could wield as a means to maintain their political control. Marx's primary critique of the Young Hegelians was against their belief that ideological changes could result in revolutionary changes. *See also CONTRIBUTION TO THE CRITIQUE OF HEGEL'S PHILOSOPHY OF RIGHT,* DIALECTICAL MATERIALISM, HEGELIAN DIALECTICS.

Z

ZASULICH, VERA (1851–1919). A Russian revolutionary born into a family of impoverished minor nobility. Zasulich was well educated and fell into Russian anarchist politics, where her contacts with the Russian anarchist revolutionary Sergei Nechaev led to her arrest and a four-year term in prison. Following her release, she settled in Kyiv, where she joined another anarchist group formed by **Mikhail Bakunin**. In reprisal for the brutality of the czarist regime, Zasulich successfully shot Colonel Fyodor Trepov, the governor of St. Petersburg. In a famous act of "jury nullification," Zasulich was acquitted and fled into exile in Switzerland before the regime could retry her. While in exile, she converted from **anarchism** to **Marxism** and worked with fellow Russian Marxists like Georgi Plekhanov. When the Russian Marxist factions split into **Bolshevik** and **Menshevik** factions, Zasulich followed the Menshevik line. She returned to Russia following the **1905 revolution** but increasingly receded from revolutionary politics and activism, supporting Russian involvement in World War I and opposing the **October Revolution** of 1917.

ZEDONG, MAO (1893–1976). Sometimes known as "Chairman Mao," Mao Zedong was a Chinese revolutionary socialist who was the founding member of the Communist Party of China (CPC) and the founding father of the People's Republic of China (PRC). Born to a prosperous **peasant** family, he became interested in **Marxism** while at Peking University as a young man. As head of the CPC, Mao's

forces overthrew the nationalist Chinese government and established the PRC in 1949. Mao implemented a Marxist-Leninist style of system with nationalized ownership of industry and, in 1958, launched the "Great Leap Forward" in an attempt to rapidly transform the Chinese economy from agrarian to industrial. The program was largely a failure and led to the deadliest famine in recorded history, with 20 million to 45 million deaths between 1958 and 1962, though ultimately it led to the rise of China as a major world power. Despite the failure, Mao and the CPC maintained control and throughout the 1960s implemented a "Cultural Revolution" program in an attempt to remove opposition to Mao and the CPC. Mao maintained totalitarian control of China largely through his significant cult of personality. During his reign, he involved China in the Korean War and the Vietnamese War, and in 1972, Mao met with U.S. President Richard Nixon, signaling a start to a more open relationship between China and the West.

ZETKIN, CLARA (1857–1933). Clara Zetkin was a German Marxist, theorist, feminist activist, and elected member of the Reichstag. Educated to become a teacher, Zetkin developed strong feminist and socialist beliefs, joining the Socialist Workers' Party, a predecessor of the **Social Democratic Party** (SPD), in 1875. While a member of the SPD, she met and befriended **Rosa Luxemburg** and along with her attacked the revisionist **Marxism** of **Eduard Bernstein**. She opposed World War I and, like many young SPD members, split from the SPD to form the **Spartacus League** and later the **Communist Party of Germany**. A fierce critic of fascism, following Nazi seizure of power in 1933, Zetkin went into exile in the Soviet Union but died shortly after leaving Germany. The Soviet Union and East Germany revered her and interred her ashes in the Kremlin Wall Necropolis.

ZINOVIEV, GRIGORY (1883–1936). Zinoviev was among the "Old **Bolsheviks**," an original member of the Bolshevik Party that seized power in **Russia** and won the **Russian Civil War**. Zinoviev was born into a family of Jewish dairy farmers. Self-educated, at age 20, he joined the **Russian Social Democratic Labor Party** and attached himself to **Vladimir Lenin** when the party split between "Bolshevik" and "**Menshevik**" factions. Zinoviev's closeness to Lenin lent him considerable influence both inside of Russia and abroad. Zinoviev was with Lenin in Switzerland at the outbreak of World War I and returned to Moscow with Lenin in early 1917 following the overthrow of Czar Nicholas II. Zinoviev was one of several Central Committee members to oppose Lenin's call for armed revolt against the Provisional Government, a break with Lenin that severely damaged this relationship.

In 1918, during the Russian Civil War, Lenin allowed Zinoviev to return to the Central Committee and assigned him control of the "Petrograd Soviet," the workers' council of the second-largest city in Russia. He took charge of the defense of Petrograd against attacks by "White" military forces throughout 1919 and clashed with **Leon Trotsky** on military affairs. He also became chairman of the executive committee of the **Comintern** on its establishment in 1919. Lenin rewarded Zinoviev for his support during the Bolshevik infighting with a position on the "Politburo," the principal policymaking committee of the Communist Party. However, as Lenin's rapidly declining health impaired his leadership, Zinoviev allied with **Joseph Stalin** and Lev Kamenev, a close associate of Zinoviev.

Zinoviev and Kamenev supported Stalin during his power struggle with Leon Trotsky but subsequently found themselves in dangerous circumstances. They held enough power and popularity among fellow Bolsheviks to hold leadership positions but lacked sufficient influence to defeat Stalin in intramural conflicts. Stalin, increasingly intolerant of rivals, viewed both men and the entire body of Old Bolsheviks as potential threats. While Trotsky recognized the likely end game of his lost power struggle and fled Russia, Zinoviev and Kamenev submitted to Stalin in hopes of forgiveness. By 1928, Stalin expelled both Zinoviev and Kamenev from the Communist Party. Stalin then trumped up charges in the famed "Trial of the Sixteen." Both Zinoviev and Kamenev agreed to confess their guilt on charges of forming a terrorist conspiracy to assassinate Stalin in exchange for lifting any threat of the death penalty. The very night they were convicted, Stalin reneged and ordered their executions. These executions ushered in the far more general and thoroughgoing purges of the Bolshevik Party and the **Red Army** in 1938–1939. Zinoviev, Kamenev, and other Old Bolsheviks who were condemned in the 1936 "show trials" were the inspiration for Arthur Koestler's *Darkness at Noon*.

ZUSAMMENBRUCHSTHEORIE. The German word for "theories of collapse" often mistakenly attributed to Karl Marx. From about 1890 to the 1930s, some **Second Internationalists** asserted that Marx's theory predicted that **capitalism** would collapse not so much because of a **proletarian revolution** but because of its internal **contradictions** bringing about **crises** and, eventually, systemic failure. Stedman-Jones (2016) attributes the popularity of the theory to **Engels's** *Anti-Dühring* as well as his editing of *Capital: Volumes II and III* rather than to Marx himself. He also points to **August Bebel** and the 1891 **Erfurt Program** as asserting the inevitability of collapse. **Eduard Bernstein** attributed theories of collapse to Marx in order to argue that (1) Marx was wrong, capitalism would not collapse, and that (2) reform in response to the periodic crises would eventually establish socialism without the need for **violent revolution**.

Rosa Luxemburg asserted that the contradiction between capitalist production for the

Statue of Karl Marx.

maximization of **surplus value** rather than **use value**, the limitations on the internal consumer market brought about by limits on wages, and the conversion of **variable capital** to **constant capital** mean that capitalism must always seek new markets to sell its goods. Once the capitalist system integrates the whole world, there will be a final crisis of **overproduction**, she predicts, and capitalism would necessarily collapse. Calling the theory of capitalist collapse the "corner-stone of **scientific socialism**," Luxemburg asserted that without the collapse, the **"expropriation of the capitalist class** is impossible."

Marx did write of the contradictions inherent within capitalism and of periodic crises that would become more severe as time passed, but there is little evidence that he foresaw the inevitable **collapse of capitalism** and that socialism would rise from its ashes. Instead, Marx asserted that crises would eventually become so severe that, over time, the **proletariat** would attain **revolutionary consciousness**, revolt, and overthrow the capitalist system, establishing socialism to solve the inherent contradictions of the system. Reform of capitalism is not possible, he argued, for **exploitation** is the foundation of the system itself.

Interestingly, *zusammenbruchstheorie* has been making a comeback in recent years. **Immanuel Wallerstein**, a Marxist sociologist, posits that internal contradictions within

capitalism will eventually bring on the collapse of the capitalist **world system**. There are four interrelated contradictions identified by Wallerstein: first, a shrinking pool of exploitable labor as more countries integrate into the world system and more people concentrate in **urban** settings that lead to higher expectations and greater bargaining power; second, a growing **ecological** crisis that runs counter to the **accumulation of capital** as corporations are forced to absorb these costs at the expense of **surplus value**; third, the growing spread of democracy that brings demands of the masses for decent jobs, medical care, education, and consumer goods ("Ultimately, these moneys can only come at the cost of accumulating capital" [Wallerstein 1999, 32]); and, finally, the decline in the power of the state. State power has been critical for capitalism, serving to keep internal order, sponsoring national and international **monopolies**, and taking other steps to promote and protect the accumulation of capital. Wallerstein believes that as government reform of these conditions has proven to be ineffective, the power of the state to control the populace is in decline.

As the disorder mounts, Wallerstein expects that the world system will continue to operate as it has done in the past. "Capitalists will seek support from state structures as they have in the past. States will compete with other states to be the major loci of the accumulation of capital" (Wallerstein 2000, 431). The system will continue to expand; **commodifying** more and more activities, **populations** will become further polarized in terms of wealth and power. However, the states will gradually lose legitimacy and find it increasingly difficult to maintain order both internally and internationally. An increasingly wealthy North will confront a frequently exploited and desperate South but one with increasing military power (Wallerstein 2000, 414–15). The capitalist world system will slip into chaos, and a new order will eventually emerge (431).

Unlike Marx, Wallerstein does not predict what this new world order will be. There is no inevitability of something better or worse. What emerges very much depends on the on-going struggle. Like Marx, Wallerstein believes that the major fault of capitalism is the need for ever-greater accumulation of capital. Until recently, it has effectively minimized forces that attempted to impose constraints on this accumulation. As a result, it has created unprecedented wealth for a substantial number of the world's population and high levels of poverty for everyone else. The outcome of the struggle between the capitalists and the rest of humanity will determine whether the world system will move toward a repressive or an egalitarian restructuring. *See also* CLASS CONFLICT, REVOLUTION.

Appendix:
Extracts from Marx

In this section, we present quotes from some of Marx's seminal works. We begin with the 1848 *Communist Manifesto*, coauthored by Friedrich Engels. We follow that with the preface to *A Contribution to Political Economy* (1859), in which Marx laid out his theory of history. Finally, we conclude with quotes from his masterwork: *Capital*. All of these works appear in PDF format on the Marxist Internet Archive and are part of the public domain. The Marxists Internet Archive (MIA; http://www.marxists.org) is an all-volunteer, nonprofit public library established in its present form in 1998. MIA contains the writings of around 850 authors representing a complete spectrum of political, philosophical, and scientific thought, generally spanning the past 200 years.

Das Kapital was originally published in German in 1867; the third German edition was published in 1883 and was the source of the first English translation (1887) by Samuel Moore and Edward Aveling and edited by Engels. Moore, the primary translator, was for many years a friend of both Marx and Engels. Aveling, the secondary translator who was responsible for several chapters, was Eleanor Marx's friend and lover. Engels, Marx's longtime friend and collaborator, closely supervised and edited the work. The MIA manuscript is from this first English translation. This edition of the text is widely available online as well as in a relatively inexpensive e-book format and thus is a boon to readers who wish to explore the text further. We urge you to do so.

EXTRACTS FROM MANIFESTO OF THE COMMUNIST PARTY

Written: Late 1847
First Published: February 1848
Source: *Marx/Engels Selected Works, Vol. 1,* Progress Publishers, Moscow, 1969, 98–137
Translated: Samuel Moore in cooperation with Friedrich Engels, 1888
Transcribed: Zodiac and Brian Baggins
Proofed: and corrected against the 1888 English edition by Andy Blunden 2004
Copyleft [sic]: Marxists Internet Archive (marxists.org) 1987, 2000, 2010. Permission is granted to distribute this document under the terms of the Creative Commons Attribution-Share-Alike License.

INTRODUCTION (MANIFESTO OF THE COMMUNIST PARTY).

A spectre is haunting Europe—the spectre of communism. All the powers of old Europe have entered into a holy alliance to exorcise this spectre: Pope and Tsar, Metternich and Guizot, French Radicals and German police-spies.

Where is the party in opposition that has not been decried as communistic by its opponents in power? Where is the opposition that has not hurled back the branding reproach of communism, against the more advanced opposition parties, as well as against its reactionary adversaries?

Two things result from this fact: I. Communism is already acknowledged by all European powers to be itself a power. II. It is high time that Communists should openly, in the face of the whole world, publish their views, their aims, their tendencies, and meet this nursery tale of the Spectre of Communism with a manifesto of the party itself.

To this end, Communists of various nationalities have assembled in London and sketched the following manifesto, to be published in the English, French, German, Italian, Flemish and Danish languages (14).

SECTION I. BOURGEOIS AND PROLETARIANS

The history of all hitherto existing society is the history of class struggles. Freeman and slave, patrician and plebeian, lord and serf, guild-master and journeyman, in a word, oppressor and oppressed, stood in constant opposition to one another, carried on an uninterrupted, now hidden, now open fight, a fight that each time ended, either in a revolutionary reconstitution of society at large, or in the common ruin of the contending classes (14).

The need of a constantly expanding market for its products chases the bourgeoisie over the entire surface of the globe. It must nestle everywhere, settle everywhere, establish connexions everywhere (16).

The bourgeoisie, during its rule of scarce one hundred years, has created more massive and more colossal productive forces than have all preceding generations together. Subjection of Nature's forces to man, machinery, application of chemistry to industry and agriculture, steam-navigation, railways, electric telegraphs, clearing of whole continents for cultivation, canalisation of rivers, whole populations conjured out of the ground—what earlier century had even a presentiment that such productive forces slumbered in the lap of social labour? (17).

The weapons with which the bourgeoisie felled feudalism to the ground are now turned against the bourgeoisie itself. But not only has the bourgeoisie forged the weapons that bring death to itself; it has also called into existence the men who are to wield those weapons—the modern working class—the proletarians (18).

The essential conditions for the existence and for the sway of the bourgeois class is the formation and augmentation of capital; the condition for capital is wage-labour. Wage-labour rests exclusively on competition between the labourers. The advance of industry, whose involuntary promoter is the bourgeoisie, replaces the isolation of the labourers, due to competition, by the revolutionary combination, due to association. The development of Modern Industry, therefore, cuts from under its feet the very foundation on which the bourgeoisie produces and appropriates products. What the bourgeoisie therefore produces, above all, are its own grave-diggers. Its fall and the victory of the proletariat are equally inevitable (21).

SECTION II. PROLETARIANS AND COMMUNISTS

The immediate aim of the Communists is the same as that of all other proletarian parties: formation of the proletariat into a class, overthrow of the bourgeois supremacy, conquest of political power by the proletariat (22).

The distinguishing feature of Communism is not the abolition of property generally, but the abolition of bourgeois property. But modern bourgeois private property is the final and most complete expression of the system of producing and appropriating products, that is based on class antagonisms, on the exploitation of the many by the few. In this sense, the theory of the Communists may be summed up in the single sentence: Abolition of private property (22).

In place of the old bourgeois society, with its classes and class antagonisms, we shall have an association, in which the free development of each is the condition for the free development of all (27).

PART IV. POSITION OF THE COMMUNISTS IN RELATION TO THE VARIOUS EXISTING OPPOSITION PARTIES

In short, the Communists everywhere support every revolutionary movement against the existing social and political order of things. In all these movements, they bring to the front, as the leading question in each, the property question, no matter what its degree of development at the time. Finally, they labour everywhere for the union and agreement of the democratic parties of all countries. The Communists disdain to conceal their views and aims. They openly declare that their ends can be attained only by the forcible overthrow of all existing social conditions. Let the ruling classes tremble at a Communistic revolution. The proletarians have nothing to lose but their chains. They have a world to win. Working Men of All Countries, Unite! (34).

PREFACE TO A CONTRIBUTION TO THE CRITIQUE OF POLITICAL ECONOMY

Written: 1859
Publisher: Progress Publishers, Moscow
First Published: 1859
Translated: S. W. Ryazanskaya
Online Version: Marx.org, 1993 (Preface, 1993); Marxists.org, 1999
Transcribed: Tim Delaney, Zodiac
Proofed: and corrected by Matthew Carmody 2009

The general conclusion at which I arrived and which, once reached, continued to serve as the leading thread in my studies, may be briefly summed up as follows: In the social production which men carry on they enter into definite relations that are indispensable and independent of their will; these relations of production correspond to a definite stage of development of their material powers of production. The sum total of these relations of production constitutes the economic structure of society—the real foundation, on which rise legal and political superstructures and to which correspond definite forms of social consciousness. The mode of production in material life determines the general character of the social, political and spiritual processes of life. It is not the consciousness of men that determines their existence, but, on the contrary, their social existence determines their consciousness.

At a certain stage of their development, the material forces of production in society come in conflict with the existing relations of production, or—what is but a legal expression for the same thing—with the property relations within which they had been at work before. From forms of development of the forces of production these relations turn into their fetters. Then comes the period of social revolution. With the change of the economic foundation the entire immense superstructure is more or less rapidly transformed. In considering such transformations the distinction should always be made between the material transformation of the economic conditions of production which can be determined with the precision of natural science, and the legal, political, religious, aesthetic or philosophic—in short ideological forms in which men become conscious of this conflict and fight it out. . . .

No social order ever disappears before all the productive forces, for which there is room in it, have been developed; and new higher relations of production never appear before the material conditions of their existence have matured in the womb of the old society. . . .

In broad outlines we can designate the Asiatic, the ancient, the feudal, and the modern bourgeois methods of production as so many epochs in the progress of the economic formation of society. The bourgeois relations of production are the last antagonistic form of the social process of production—antagonistic not in the sense of individual antagonism, but of one arising from conditions surrounding the life of individuals in society; at the same time the productive forces developing in the womb of bourgeois society create the material conditions for the solution of that antagonism.

This social formation constitutes, therefore, the closing chapter of the prehistoric stage of human society (1–2).

EXTRACTS FROM CAPITAL: A CRITIQUE OF POLITICAL ECONOMY

First Published: in German 1867; English edition first published in 1887
Publisher: Progress Publishers, Moscow
Translated: Samuel Moore and Edward Aveling, edited by Friedrich Engels
Online Version: Marx.org, 1993
Transcribed: Hinrich Kuhls, Allan Thurrott, Bill McDorman, Bert Schultz, and Martha Gimenez (1995–1996)
Proofed: by Andy Blunden and Chris Clayton (2008), Mark Harris (2010), and Dave Allinson (2015)

THE PREFACE TO THE FIRST GERMAN EDITION (MARX 1867)

The country that is more developed industrially only shows, to the less developed, the image of its own future (6–7).

And even when a society has got upon the right track for the discovery of the natural laws of its movement—and it is the ultimate aim of this work, to lay bare the economic law of motion of modern society—it can neither clear by bold leaps, nor remove by legal enactments, the obstacles offered by the successive phases of its normal development. But it can shorten and lessen the birth-pangs (7).

To prevent possible misunderstanding, a word. I paint the capitalist and the landlord in no sense couleur de rose [i.e., seen through rose-tinted glasses]. But here individuals are dealt with only in so far as they are the personifications of economic categories, embodiments of particular class-relations and class-interests. My standpoint, from which the evolution of the economic formation of society is viewed as a process of natural history, can less than any other make the individual responsible for relations whose creature he socially remains,

however much he may subjectively raise himself above them (7).

In the domain of Political Economy, free scientific inquiry meets not merely the same enemies as in all other domains. The peculiar nature of the materials it deals with, summons as foes into the field of battle the most violent, mean and malignant passions of the human breast, the Furies of private interest (7).
—Karl Marx, London, July 25, 1867

FROM THE SECOND EDITION

My dialectic method is not only different from the Hegelian, but is its direct opposite. To Hegel, the life process of the human brain, i.e., the process of thinking, which, under the name of "the Idea," he even transforms into an independent subject, is the demiurgos of the real world, and the real world is only the external, phenomenal form of "the Idea." With me, on the contrary, the ideal is nothing else than the material world reflected by the human mind, and translated into forms of thought (15).

The contradictions inherent in the movement of capitalist society impress themselves upon the practical bourgeois most strikingly in the changes of the periodic cycle, through which modern industry runs, and whose crowning point is the universal crisis. That crisis is once again approaching, although as yet but in its preliminary stage; and by the universality of its theatre and the intensity of its action it will drum dialectics even into the heads of the mushroom-upstarts of the new, holy Prusso-German empire (15)
—Karl Marx, London, January 24, 1873

CHAPTER 1: THE COMMODITY

The wealth of those societies in which the capitalist mode of production prevails, presents itself as "an immense accumulation of commodities," its unit being a single commodity. Our investigation must therefore begin with the analysis of a commodity (22).

A commodity is, in the first place, an object outside us, a thing that by its properties satisfies human wants of some sort or another. The nature of such wants, whether, for instance, they spring from the stomach or from fancy, makes no difference. Neither are we here concerned to know how the object satisfies these wants, whether directly as means of subsistence, or indirectly as means of production (27).

The utility of a thing makes it a use value. But this utility is not a thing of air. Being limited by the physical properties of the commodity, it has no existence apart from that commodity. A commodity, such as iron, corn, or a diamond, is therefore, so far as it is a material thing, a use value, something useful. This property of a commodity is independent of the amount of labour required to appropriate its useful qualities (27).

Exchange value, at first sight, presents itself as a quantitative relation, as the proportion in which values in use of one sort are exchanged for those of another sort, a relation constantly changing with time and place. Hence exchange value appears to be something accidental and purely relative, and consequently an intrinsic value, i.e., an exchange value that is inseparably connected with, inherent in commodities, seems a contradiction in terms (27).

As use values, commodities are, above all, of different qualities, but as exchange values they are merely different quantities, and consequently do not contain an atom of use value (28).

We have seen that when commodities are exchanged, their exchange value manifests itself as something totally independent of their use value. But if we abstract from their use value, there remains their Value as defined above. Therefore, the common substance that manifests itself in the exchange value of commodities, whenever they are exchanged, is their value. The progress of our investigation will show that exchange value is the only form in which the value of commodities can manifest itself or be expressed (28).

The labour time socially necessary is that required to produce an article under the normal conditions of production, and with the average degree of skill and intensity prevalent at the time. The introduction of power-looms into England probably reduced by one-half the labour required to weave a given quantity of yarn into cloth. The handloom weavers, as a matter of fact, continued to require the same time as before; but for all that, the product of one hour of their labour represented after the change only half an hour's social labour, and consequently fell to one-half its former value (29).

We see then that that which determines the magnitude of the value of any article is the amount of labour socially necessary, or the labour time socially necessary for its production. Each individual commodity, in this connexion, is to be considered as an average sample of its class. Commodities, therefore, in which equal quantities of labour are embodied, or which can be produced in the same time, have the same value. The value of one commodity is to the value of any other, as the labour time necessary for the production of the one is to that necessary for the production of the other. "As values, all commodities are only definite masses of congealed labour time" (29).

The value of a commodity would therefore remain constant, if the labour time required for its production also remained constant. But the latter changes with every variation in the productiveness of labour. This productiveness is determined by various circumstances, amongst others, by the average amount of skill of the workmen, the state of science, and the degree of its practical application, the social organisation of production, the extent and capabilities of the means of production, and by physical conditions (29).

In general, the greater the productiveness of labour, the less is the labour time required for the production of an article, the less is the amount of labour crystallised in that article, and the less is its value; and vice versâ, the less the productiveness of labour, the greater is the labour time required for the production of an article, and the greater is its value. The value of a commodity, therefore, varies directly as the quantity, and inversely as the productiveness, of the labour incorporated in it (29–30).

We see, then, that labour is not the only source of material wealth, of use values produced by labour. As William Petty puts it, labour is its father and the earth its mother (31).

CHAPTER 4: THE GENERAL FORMULA FOR CAPITAL

The restless never-ending process of profit-making alone is what he aims at. This boundless greed after riches, this passionate chase after exchange-value, is common to the capitalist and the miser; but while the miser is merely a capitalist gone mad, the capitalist is a rational miser. The never-ending augmentation of exchange-value, which the miser strives after, by seeking to save his money from circulation, is attained by the more acute capitalist, by constantly throwing it afresh into circulation (107).

CHAPTER 7: THE LABOUR-PROCESS AND THE PROCESS OF PRODUCING SURPLUS-VALUE

Labour is, in the first place, a process in which both man and Nature participate, and in which man of his own accord starts, regulates, and controls the material re-actions between himself and Nature. He opposes himself to Nature as one of her own forces, setting in motion arms and legs, head and hands, the natural forces of his body, in order to appropriate Nature's productions in a form adapted to his own wants. By thus acting on the external world and changing it, he at the same time changes his own nature (127).

A spider conducts operations that resemble those of a weaver, and a bee puts to shame many an architect in the construction of her cells. But what distinguishes the worst architect from the best of bees is this, that the architect raises his structure in imagination before he erects it in reality. At the end of every

labour-process, we get a result that already existed in the imagination of the labourer at its commencement. He not only effects a change of form in the material on which he works, but he also realises a purpose of his own that gives the law to his modus operandi, and to which he must subordinate his will. And this subordination is no mere momentary act. Besides the exertion of the bodily organs, the process demands that, during the whole operation, the workman's will be steadily in consonance with his purpose. This means close attention. The less he is attracted by the nature of the work, and the mode in which it is carried on, and the less, therefore, he enjoys it as something which gives play to his bodily and mental powers, the more close his attention is forced to be (127).

CHAPTER 9: THE RATE OF SURPLUS-VALUE

The rate of surplus-value is therefore an exact expression for the degree of exploitation of labour-power by capital, or of the labourer by the capitalist (153).

CHAPTER 10: THE WORKING DAY

As capitalist, he is only capital personified. His soul is the soul of capital. But capital has one single life impulse, the tendency to create value and surplus-value, to make its constant factor, the means of production, absorb the greatest possible amount of surplus labour (163).

Capital is dead labour, that, vampire-like, only lives by sucking living labour, and lives the more, the more labour it sucks. The time during which the labourer works, is the time during which the capitalist consumes the labour-power he has purchased of him (163).

In every stockjobbing swindle every one knows that some time or other the crash must come, but every one hopes that it may fall on the head of his neighbour, after he himself has caught the shower of gold and placed it in safety. Après moi le déluge! [After me, the flood] is the watchword of every capitalist and of every capitalist nation. Hence Capital is reckless of the health or length of life of the labourer, unless under compulsion from society (181).

The establishment of a normal working day is the result of centuries of struggle between capitalist and labourer (181).

It takes centuries ere the "free" labourer, thanks to the development of capitalistic production, agrees, i.e., is compelled by social conditions, to sell the whole of his active life. His very capacity for work, for the price of the necessaries of life, his birth-right for a mess of pottage (181).

In the United States of North America, every independent movement of the workers was paralysed so long as slavery disfigured a part of the Republic. Labour cannot emancipate itself in the white skin where in the black it is branded. But out of the death of slavery a new life at once arose (195).

An industrial army of workmen, under the command of a capitalist, requires, like a real army, officers (managers), and sergeants (foremen, overlookers), who, while the work is being done, command in the name of the capitalist. The work of supervision becomes their established and exclusive function (232).

CHAPTER 14: DIVISION OF LABOUR AND MANUFACTURE

That co-operation which is based on division of labour, assumes its typical form in manufacture, and is the prevalent characteristic form of the capitalist process of production throughout the manufacturing period properly so called. That period, roughly speaking, extends from the middle of the 16th to the last third of the 18th century (237).

The work is therefore re-distributed. Instead of each man being allowed to perform all the various operations in succession, these operations are changed into disconnected, isolated ones, carried on side by side; each is assigned to a different artificer, and the whole of them together are performed simultaneously by the co-operating workmen. This accidental repartition gets repeated, develops advantages of its own, and gradually ossifies into a systematic division of labour. The commodity, from being the individual product of an independent artificer, becomes the social product of a union of artificers, each of whom performs one, and only one, of the constituent partial operations (237).

On the one hand, therefore, manufacture either introduces division of labour into a process of production, or further develops that division; on the other hand, it unites together handicrafts that were formerly separate. But whatever may have been its particular starting-point, its final form is invariably the same—a productive mechanism whose parts are human beings (238).

The manufacturing period simplifies, improves, and multiplies the implements of labour, by adapting them to the exclusively special functions of each detail labourer. It thus creates at the same time one of the material conditions for the existence of machinery, which consists of a combination of simple instruments (240).

The second kind of manufacture, its perfected form, produces articles that go through connected phases of development, through a series of processes step by step, like the wire in the manufacture of needles, which passes through the hands of 72 and sometimes even 92 different detail workmen (241).

Early in the manufacturing period, the principle of lessening the necessary labour-time in the production of commodities, was accepted and formulated: and the use of machines, especially for certain simple first processes that have to be conducted on a very large scale, and with the application of great force, sprang up here and there. Thus, at an early period in paper manufacture, the tearing up of the rags was done by paper-mills; and in metal works, the pounding of the ores was effected by stamping mills. The Roman Empire had handed down the elementary form of all machinery in the water-wheel (243).

The handicraft period bequeathed to us the great inventions of the compass, of gunpowder, of type-printing, and of the automatic clock. But, on the whole, machinery played that subordinate part which Adam Smith assigns to it in comparison with division of labour. The sporadic use of machinery in the 17th century was of the greatest importance, because it supplied the great mathematicians of that time with a practical basis and stimulant to the creation of the science of mechanics (243).

Since the collective labourer has functions, both simple and complex, both high and low, his members, the individual labour-powers, require different degrees of training, and must therefore have different values. Manufacture, therefore, develops a hierarchy of labour-powers, to which there corresponds a scale of wages (243–44).

Hence, Manufacture begets, in every handicraft that it seizes upon, a class of so-called unskilled labourers, a class which handicraft industry strictly excluded. If it develops a one-sided speciality into a perfection, at the expense of the whole of a man's working capacity, it also begins to make a speciality of the absence of all development. Alongside of the hierarchic gradation there steps the simple separation of the labourers into skilled and unskilled (244).

Different communities find different means of production, and different means of subsistence in their natural environment. Hence, their modes of production, and of living, and their products are different. It is this spontaneously developed difference which, when different communities come in contact, calls forth the mutual exchange of products, and the consequent gradual conversion of those products into commodities (244).

The foundation of every division of labour that is well developed, and brought about by the exchange of commodities, is the separation between town and country. It may be said, that the whole economic history of society is summed up in the movement of this antithesis. We pass it over, however, for the present (245).

Just as a certain number of simultaneously employed labourers are the material pre-requisites for division of labour in manufacture, so are the number and density of the population, which here correspond to the agglomeration in one workshop, a necessary condition for the division of labour in society. Nevertheless, this density is more or less relative. A relatively thinly populated country, with well-developed means of communication, has a denser population than a more numerously populated country, with badly-developed means of communication; and in this sense the Northern States of the American Union, for instance, are more thickly populated than India (245).

The Colonial system and the opening out of the markets of the world, both of which are included in the general conditions of existence of the manufacturing period, furnish rich material for developing the division of labour in society (246).

The rules of the guilds, as I have said before, by limiting most strictly the number of apprentices and journeymen that a single master could employ, prevented him from becoming a capitalist. Moreover, he could not employ his journeymen in many other handicrafts than the one in which he was a master. The guilds zealously repelled every encroachment by the capital of merchants, the only form of free capital with which they came in contact. A merchant could buy every kind of commodity, but labour as a commodity he could not buy. He existed only on sufferance, as a dealer in the products of the handicrafts. If circumstances called for a further division of labour, the existing guilds split themselves up into varieties, or founded new guilds by the side of the old ones; all this, however, without concentrating various handicrafts in a single workshop (248).

While division of labour in society at large, whether such division be brought about or not by exchange of commodities, is common to economic formations of society the most diverse, division of labour in the workshop, as practised by manufacture, is a special creation of the capitalist mode of production alone (248).

In manufacture, as well as in simple co-operation, the collective working organism is a form of existence of capital. The mechanism that is made up of numerous individual detail labourers belongs to the capitalist. Hence, the productive power resulting from a combination of labours appears to be the productive power of capital (248).

Manufacture proper not only subjects the previously independent workman to the discipline and command of capital, but, in addition, creates a hierarchic gradation of the workmen themselves. While simple co-operation leaves the mode of working by the individual for the most part unchanged, manufacture thoroughly revolutionises it, and seizes labour-power by its very roots. It converts the labourer into a crippled monstrosity, by forcing his detail dexterity at the expense of a world of productive capabilities and instincts; just as in the States of La Plata they butcher a whole beast for the sake of his hide or his tallow. Not only is the detail work distributed to the different individuals, but the individual himself is made the automatic motor of a fractional operation, and the absurd fable of Menenius Agrippa, which makes man a mere fragment of his own body, becomes realised. If, at first, the workman sells his labour-power to capital, because the material means of producing a commodity fail him, now his very labour-power refuses its services unless it has been sold to capital. Its functions can be exercised only in an environment that exists in the workshop of the capitalist after the sale. By nature unfitted to make anything independently, the manufacturing labourer develops productive activity as a mere appendage of the capitalist's workshop. As the chosen people bore in their features the sign manual of Jehovah, so division of labour brands the manufacturing workman as the property of capital (248–49).

Some crippling of body and mind is inseparable even from division of labour in society as a whole. Since, however, manufacture carries this social separation of branches of labour much further, and also, by its peculiar division, attacks the individual at the very roots of his life, it is the first to afford the materials for, and to give a start to, industrial pathology. "To subdivide a man is to execute him, if he deserves the sentence, to assassinate him if he does not... The subdivision of labour is the assassination of a people." (250).

In its specific capitalist form—and under the given conditions, it could take no other form than a capitalistic one—manufacture is but a particular method of begetting relative surplus-value, or of augmenting at the expense of the labourer the self-expansion of capital—usually called social wealth, "Wealth of Nations," &c. It increases the social productive power of labour, not only for the benefit of the capitalist instead of for that of the labourer, but it does this by crippling the individual labourers. It creates new conditions for the lordship of capital over labour. If, therefore, on the one hand, it presents itself historically as a progress and as a necessary phase in the economic development of society, on the other hand, it is a refined and civilised method of exploitation (250–51).

This workshop, the product of the division of labour in manufacture, produced in its turn—machines. It is they that sweep away the handicraftsman's work as the regulating principle of social production. Thus, on the one hand, the technical reason for the life-long annexation of the workman to a detail function is removed. On the other hand, the fetters that this same principle laid on the dominion of capital, fall away (252).

CHAPTER 15: MACHINERY AND MODERN INDUSTRY

John Stuart Mill says in his "Principles of Political Economy": "It is questionable if all the mechanical inventions yet made have lightened the day's toil of any human being." That is, however, by no means the aim of the capitalistic application of machinery. Like every other increase in the productiveness of labour, machinery is intended to cheapen commodities, and, by shortening that portion of the working day, in which the labourer works for himself, to lengthen the other portion that he gives, without an equivalent, to the capitalist. In short, it is a means for producing surplus-value (261).

In manufacture, the revolution in the mode of production begins with the labour-power, in modern industry it begins with the instruments of labour. Our first inquiry then is, how the instruments of labour are converted from tools into machines, or what is the difference between a machine and the implements of a handicraft? We are only concerned here with striking and general characteristics; for epochs in the history of society are no more separated from each other by hard and fast lines of demarcation, than are geological epochs (261).

All fully developed machinery consists of three essentially different parts, the motor mechanism, the transmitting mechanism, and finally the tool or working machine (261).

These two first parts of the whole mechanism are there, solely for putting the working machines in motion, by means of which motion the subject of labour is seized upon and modified as desired. The tool or working machine is that part of the machinery with which the industrial revolution of the 18th century started. And to this day it constantly serves as such a starting-point, whenever a handicraft, or a manufacture, is turned into an industry carried on by machinery (261–62).

The machine proper is therefore a mechanism that, after being set in motion, performs with its tools the same operations that were formerly done by the workman with similar tools. Whether the motive power is derived from man, or from some other machine, makes no difference in this respect. From the moment that the tool proper is taken from man, and fitted into a mechanism, a machine takes the place of a mere implement (262).

The number of implements that he himself can use simultaneously, is limited by the number of his own natural instruments of production, by the number of his bodily organs. . . . The number of tools that a machine can bring into play simultaneously, is from the very first emancipated from the organic limits that hedge in the tools of a handicraftsman (262).

The steam-engine itself, such as it was at its invention, during the manufacturing period at the close of the 17th century, and such as it continued to be down to 1780, did not give rise to any industrial revolution. It was, on the contrary, the invention of machines that made a revolution in the form of steam-engines necessary (263).

The machine, which is the starting-point of the industrial revolution, supersedes the workman, who handles a single tool, by a mechanism operating with a number of similar tools, and set in motion by a single motive power, whatever the form of that power may be. Here we have the machine, but only as an elementary factor of production by machinery (263).

Not till the invention of Watt's second and so-called double-acting steam engine, was a prime mover found, that begot its own force by the consumption of coal and water, whose power was entirely under man's control, that was mobile and a means of locomotion, that was urban and not, like the waterwheel, rural, that permitted production to be concentrated in towns instead of, like the water-wheels, being scattered up and down the country, that was of universal technical application, and, relatively speaking, little affected in its choice of residence by local circumstances. The greatness of Watt's genius showed itself in the specification of the patent that he took out in April, 1784. In that specification his steam-engine is described, not as an invention for a specific purpose, but as an agent universally applicable in Mechanical Industry (263–64).

The special tools of the various detail workmen, such as those of the beaters, combers, spinners, &c., in the woollen manufacture, are now transformed into the tools of specialised machines, each machine constituting a special organ, with a special function, in the system (264).

As soon as a machine executes, without man's help, all the movements requisite to elaborate the raw material, needing only attendance from him, we have an automatic system of machinery, and one that is susceptible of constant improvement in its details (265).

An organised system of machines, to which motion is communicated by the transmitting mechanism from a central automaton, is the most developed form of production by machinery. Here we have, in the place of the isolated machine, a mechanical monster whose body fills whole factories, and whose demon power, at first veiled under the slow and measured motions of his giant limbs, at length breaks out into the fast and furious whirl of his countless working organs (265–66).

A radical change in the mode of production in one sphere of industry involves a similar change in other spheres. This happens at first in such branches of industry as are connected together by being separate phases of a process, and yet are isolated by the social division of labour, in such a way, that each of them produces an independent commodity. Thus spinning by machinery made weaving by machinery a necessity, and both together made the mechanical and chemical revolution that took place in bleaching, printing, and dyeing, imperative. So too, on the other hand, the revolution in cotton-spinning called forth the invention of the gin, for separating the seeds from the cotton fibre; it was only by means of this invention, that the production of cotton became possible on the enormous scale at present required. But more especially, the revolution in the modes of production of industry and agriculture made necessary a revolution in the general conditions of the social process of production, i.e., in the means of communication and of transport (266–67).

In the same way the means of communication and transport handed down from the manufacturing period soon became unbearable trammels on modern industry, with its feverish haste of production, its enormous extent, its constant flinging of capital and labour from one sphere of production into another, and its newly-created connexions with the markets of the whole world. Hence, apart from the radical changes introduced in the construction of sailing vessels, the means of communication and transport became gradually adapted to the modes of production of mechanical industry, by the creation of a system of river steamers, railways, ocean steamers, and telegraphs. But the huge masses of iron that had now to be forged, to be welded, to be cut, to be bored, and to be shaped, demanded, on their part, cyclopean machines, for the construction of which the methods of the manufacturing period were utterly inadequate (267).

Modern Industry had therefore itself to take in hand the machine, its characteristic instrument of production, and to construct machines by machines. It was not till it did this, that it built up for itself a fitting technical foundation, and stood on its own feet. Machinery, simultaneously with the increasing use of it, in the first decades of this century, appropriated, by degrees, the fabrication of machines proper. But it was only during the decade preceding 1866, that the construction of railways and ocean steamers on a stupendous scale called into existence the cyclopean machines now employed in the construction of prime movers (267).

The implements of labour, in the form of machinery, necessitate the substitution of natural forces for human force, and the conscious application of science, instead of rule of thumb. In Manufacture, the organisation of the social labour-process is purely subjective; it is a combination of detail labourers; in its machinery system, modern industry has a productive organism that is purely objective, in which the labourer becomes a mere appendage to an already existing material condition of production. In simple co-operation, and even in that founded on division of labour, the suppression of the isolated, by the collective, workman still appears to be more or less accidental. Machinery, with a few exceptions to be mentioned later, operates only by means of associated labour, or labour in common. Hence the co-operative character of the labour-process is, in the latter case, a technical necessity dictated by the instrument of labour itself (268).

The tool, as we have seen, is not exterminated by the machine. From being a dwarf implement of the human organism, it expands and multiplies into the implement of a mechanism created by man. Capital now sets the labourer to work, not with a manual tool, but with a machine which itself handles the tools. Although, therefore, it is clear at the first glance that, by incorporating both stupendous physical forces, and the natural sciences, with the process of production, modern industry raises the productiveness of labour to an extraordinary degree, it is by no means equally clear, that this increased productive force is not, on the other hand, purchased by an increased expenditure of labour. Machinery, like every other component of constant capital, creates no new value, but yields up its own value to the product that it serves to beget. In so far as the machine has value, and, in consequence, parts with value to the product, it forms an element in the value of that product (268).

The greater the productive power of the machinery compared with that of the tool, the greater is the extent of its gratuitous service compared with that of the tool. In modern industry man succeeded for the first time in making the product of his past labour work on a large scale gratuitously, like the forces of Nature (269).

The starting-point of modern industry is, as we have shown, the revolution in the instruments of labour, and this revolution attains its most highly developed form in the organised system of machinery in a factory. Before we inquire how human material is incorporated with this objective organism, let us consider some general effects of this revolution on the labourer himself (271).

In so far as machinery dispenses with muscular power, it becomes a means of employing labourers of slight muscular strength, and those whose bodily development is incomplete, but whose limbs are all the more supple. The labour of women and children was, therefore, the first thing sought for by capitalists who used machinery. That mighty substitute for labour and labourers was forthwith changed into a means for increasing the number of wage-labourers by enrolling, under the direct sway of capital, every member of the workman's family, without distinction of age or sex. Compulsory work for the capitalist usurped the place, not only of the children's play, but also of free labour at home within moderate limits for the support of the family (272).

The moral degradation caused by the capitalistic exploitation of women and children has been so exhaustively depicted by F. Engels in his "Lage der Arbeitenden Klasse Englands," and other writers, that I need only mention the subject in this place (274).

If machinery be the most powerful means for increasing the productiveness of labour—i.e., for shortening the working-time required in the production of a commodity, it becomes in the hands of capital the most powerful means, in those industries first invaded by it, for lengthening the working day beyond all bounds set by human nature. It creates, on the one hand, new conditions by which capital is enabled to give free scope to this its constant tendency, and on the other hand, new motives with which to whet capital's appetite for the labour of others (276).

The automaton, as capital, and because it is capital, is endowed, in the person of the capitalist, with intelligence and will; it is therefore animated by the longing to reduce to a minimum the resistance offered by that repellent yet elastic natural barrier, man. This resistance is moreover lessened by the apparent lightness of machine work, and by the more pliant and docile character of the women and children employed on it (276).

The development of the factory system fixes a constantly increasing portion of the capital in a form, in which, on the one hand, its value is capable of continual self-expansion, and in which, on the other hand, it loses both use-value and exchange-value whenever it loses contact with living labour (277).

Machinery produces relative surplus-value; not only by directly depreciating the value of labour power, and by indirectly cheapening the same through cheapening the commodities that enter into its reproduction, but also, when it is first introduced sporadically into an industry, by converting the labour employed by the owner of that machinery, into labour of a higher degree and greater efficacy, by raising the social value of the article produced above its individual value, and thus enabling the capitalist to replace the value of a day's labour-power by a smaller portion of the value of a day's product. During this transition period, when the use of machinery is a sort of monopoly, the profits are therefore exceptional, and the capitalist endeavours to exploit thoroughly "the sunny time of this his first love," by prolonging the working day as much as possible. The magnitude of the profit whets his appetite for more profit (277).

As the use of machinery becomes more general in a particular industry, the social value of the product sinks down to its individual value, and the law that surplus-value does not arise from the labour-power that has been replaced by the machinery, but from the labour-power actually employed in working with the machinery, asserts itself (277).

Hence, the application of machinery to the production of surplus-value implies a contradiction which is immanent in it, since of the two factors of the surplus-value created by a given amount of capital, one, the rate of surplus-value, cannot be increased, except by diminishing the other, the number of workmen. This contradiction comes to light, as soon as by the general employment of machinery in a given industry, the value of the machine-produced commodity regulates the value of all commodities of the same sort; and it is this contradiction, that in its turn, drives the capitalist, without his being conscious of the fact, to excessive lengthening of the working day, in order that he may compensate the decrease in the relative number of labourers exploited, by an increase not only of the relative, but of the absolute surplus labour (278).

Hence, too, the economic paradox, that the most powerful instrument for shortening labour-time, becomes the most unfailing means for placing every moment of the labourer's time and that of his family, at the disposal of the capitalist for the purpose of expanding the value of his capital (278).

The immoderate lengthening of the working day, produced by machinery in the hands of capital, leads to a reaction on the part of society, the very sources of whose life are menaced; and, thence, to a normal working day whose length is fixed by law (279).

It is self-evident, that in proportion as the use of machinery spreads, and the experience of a special class of workmen habituated to machinery accumulates, the rapidity and intensity of labour increase as a natural consequence. Thus in England, during half a century, lengthening of the working day went hand in hand with increasing intensity of factory labour (279).

So soon as the gradually surging revolt of the working-class compelled Parliament to shorten compulsorily the hours of labour, and to begin by imposing a normal working day on factories proper, so soon consequently as an increased production of surplus-value by the prolongation of the working day was once for all put a stop to, from that moment capital threw itself with all its might into the production of relative surplus-value, by hastening on the further improvement of machinery (279).

The life-long speciality of handling one and the same tool, now becomes the life-long speciality of serving one and the same machine. Machinery is put to a wrong use, with the object of transforming the workman, from his very childhood, into a part of a detail-machine. In this way, not only are the expenses of his reproduction considerably lessened, but at the same time his helpless dependence upon the factory as a whole, and therefore upon the capitalist, is rendered complete (285).

In handicrafts and manufacture, the workman makes use of a tool, in the factory, the machine makes use of him. There the movements of the instrument of labour proceed from him, here it is the movements of the machine that he must follow. In manufacture the workmen are parts of a living mechanism. In the factory we have a lifeless mechanism independent of the workman, who becomes its mere living appendage (285).

At the same time that factory work exhausts the nervous system to the uttermost, it does away with the many-sided play of the muscles, and confiscates every atom of freedom, both in bodily and intellectual activity. The lightening of the labour, even, becomes a sort of torture, since the machine does not free the labourer from work, but deprives the work of all interest. Every kind of capitalist production, in so far as it is not only a labour-process, but also a process of creating surplus-value, has this in common, that it is not the workman that employs the instruments of labour, but the instruments of labour that employ the workman (285).

The technical subordination of the workman to the uniform motion of the instruments of labour, and the peculiar composition of the body of workpeople, consisting as it does of individuals of both sexes and of all ages, give rise to a barrack discipline, which is elaborated into a complete system in the factory, and which fully develops the before mentioned labour of overlooking, thereby dividing the workpeople into operatives and overlookers, into private soldiers and sergeants of an industrial army (286).

The place of the slave-driver's lash is taken by the overlooker's book of penalties. All punishments naturally resolve themselves into fines and deductions from wages, and the law-giving talent of the factory Lycurgus so arranges matters, that a violation of his laws is, if possible, more profitable to him than the keeping of them. We shall here merely allude to the material conditions under which factory labour is carried on. Every organ of sense is injured in an equal degree by artificial elevation of the temperature, by the dustladen atmosphere, by the deafening noise, not to mention danger to life and limb among the thickly crowded machinery, which, with the regularity of the seasons, issues its list of the killed and wounded in the industrial battle (286–87).

Economy of the social means of production, matured and forced as in a hothouse by the factory system, is turned, in the hands of capital, into systematic robbery of what is necessary for the life of the workman while he is at work, robbery of space, light, air, and of protection to his person against the dangerous and unwholesome accompaniments of the productive process, not to mention the robbery of appliances for the comfort of the workman (287).

The contest between the capitalist and the wage-labourer dates back to the very origin of capital. It raged on throughout the whole manufacturing period. But only since the introduction of machinery has the workman fought against the instrument of labour itself, the material embodiment of capital. He revolts against this particular form of the means of production, as being the material basis of the capitalist mode of production (287).

The enormous destruction of machinery that occurred in the English manufacturing districts during the first 15 years of this century, chiefly caused by the employment of the power-loom, and known as the Luddite movement, gave the anti-Jacobin governments of a Sidmouth, a Castlereagh, and the like, a pretext for the most reactionary and forcible measures. It took both time and experience before the workpeople learnt to distinguish between machinery and its employment by capital, and to direct their attacks, not against the material instruments of production, but against the mode in which they are used (288).

The instrument of labour, when it takes the form of a machine, immediately becomes a competitor of the workman himself. The self-expansion of capital by means of machinery is thenceforward directly proportional to the number of the workpeople, whose means of livelihood have been destroyed by that machinery (288).

The whole system of capitalist production is based on the fact that the workman sells his labour-power as a commodity. Division of labour specialises this labour-power, by reducing it to skill in handling a particular tool. So soon as the handling of this tool becomes the work of a machine, then, with the use-value, the exchange-value too, of the workman's labour-power vanishes; the workman becomes unsaleable, like paper money thrown out of currency by legal enactment. That portion of the working-class, thus by machinery rendered superfluous, i.e., no longer immediately necessary for the self-expansion of capital, either goes to the wall in the unequal contest of the old handicrafts and manufactures with machinery, or else floods all the more easily accessible branches of industry, swamps the labour-market, and sinks the price of labour-power below its value. It is impressed upon the workpeople, as a great consolation, first, that their sufferings are only temporary ("a temporary inconvenience"), secondly, that machinery acquires the mastery over the whole of a given field of production, only by degrees, so that the extent and intensity of its destructive effect is diminished (288–89).

No doubt, in turning them out of this "temporal" world, the machinery caused them no more than "a temporary inconvenience." For the rest, since machinery is continually seizing upon new fields of production, its temporary effect is really permanent. Hence, the character of independence and estrangement which the capitalist mode of production as a whole gives to the instruments of labour and to the product, as against the workman, is developed by means of machinery into a thorough antagonism (289).

But machinery not only acts as a competitor who gets the better of the workman, and is constantly on the point of making him superfluous. It is also a power inimical to him, and as such capital proclaims it from the roof tops and as such makes use of it. It is the most powerful weapon for repressing strikes, those periodical revolts of the working-class against the autocracy of capital (291).

The real facts, which are travestied by the optimism of economists, are as follows: The labourers, when driven out of the workshop by the machinery, are thrown upon the labour market, and there add to the number of workmen at the disposal of the capitalists (294).

And this is the point relied on by our apologists! The contradictions and antagonisms inseparable from the capitalist employment of machinery, do not exist, they say, since they do not arise out of machinery, as such, but out of its capitalist employment! (295).

The immediate result of machinery is to augment surplus-value and the mass of products in which surplus-value is embodied. And, as the substances consumed by the capitalists and their dependents become more plentiful, so too do these orders of society. Their growing wealth, and the relatively diminished number of workmen required to produce the necessaries of life beget, simultaneously with the rise of new and luxurious wants, the means of satisfying those wants. A larger portion of the produce of society is changed into surplus-produce, and a larger part of the surplus-produce is supplied for consumption in a multiplicity of refined shapes. In other words, the production of luxuries increases (296).

Nevertheless, in spite of the mass of hands actually displaced and virtually replaced by machinery, we can understand how the factory operatives, through the building of more mills and the extension of old ones in a given industry, may become more numerous than the manufacturing workmen and handicraftsman that have been displaced (299).

On the one hand, the immediate effect of machinery is to increase the supply of raw material in the same way, for example, as the cotton gin augmented the production of cotton. On the other hand, the cheapness of the articles produced by machinery, and the improved means of transport and communication furnish the weapons for conquering foreign markets (300).

By constantly making a part of the hands "supernumerary," modern industry, in all countries where it has taken root, gives a spur to emigration and to the colonisation of foreign lands, which are thereby converted into settlements for growing the raw material of the mother country; just as Australia, for example, was converted into a colony for growing wool. A new and international division of labour, a division suited to the requirements of the chief centres of modern industry springs up, and converts one part of the globe into a chiefly agricultural field of production, for supplying the other part which remains a chiefly industrial field. This revolution hangs together with radical changes in agriculture which we need not here further inquire into (300).

The enormous power, inherent in the factory system, of expanding by jumps, and the dependence of that system on the markets of the world, necessarily beget feverish production, followed by over-filling of the markets, whereupon contraction of the markets brings on crippling of production. The life of modern industry becomes a series of periods of moderate activity, prosperity, over-production, crisis and stagnation. The uncertainty and instability to which machinery subjects the employment, and consequently the conditions of existence, of the operatives become normal, owing to these periodic changes of the industrial cycle (301).

Except in the periods of prosperity, there rages between the capitalists the most furious combat for the share of each in the markets. This share is directly proportional to the cheapness of the product. Besides the rivalry that this struggle begets in the application of improved machinery for replacing labour-power, and of new methods of production, there also comes a time in every industrial cycle, when a forcible reduction of wages beneath the value of labour-power, is attempted for the purpose of cheapening commodities (301).

According to Adam Smith, 10 men, in his day, made in cooperation, over 48,000 needles a-day. On the other hand, a single needle-machine makes 145,000 in a working day of 11 hours. One woman or one girl superintends four such machines, and so produces near upon 600,000 needles in a day, and upwards of 3,000,000 in a week. A single machine, when it takes the place of co-operation or of manufacture, may itself serve as the basis of an industry of a handicraft character (304).

Along with the development of the factory system and of the revolution in agriculture that accompanies it, production in all the other branches of industry not only extends, but alters its character. The principle, carried out in the factory system, of analysing the process of production into its constituent phases, and of solving the problems thus proposed by the application of mechanics, of chemistry, and of the whole range of the natural sciences, becomes the determining principle everywhere (305).

Factory legislation, that first conscious and methodical reaction of society against the spontaneously developed form of the process of production, is, as we have seen, just as much the necessary product of modern industry as cotton yarn, self-actors, and the electric telegraph (315).

Apart from their wording, which makes it easy for the capitalist to evade them, the sanitary clauses are extremely meagre, and, in fact, limited to provisions for whitewashing the walls, for insuring cleanliness in some other matters, for ventilation, and for protection against dangerous machinery (315–16).

What could possibly show better the character of the capitalist mode of production, than the necessity that exists for forcing upon it, by Acts of Parliament, the simplest appliances for maintaining cleanliness and health? (316).

Modern industry, as we have seen, sweeps away by technical means the manufacturing division of labour, under which each man is bound hand and foot for life to a single detail-operation. At the same time, the capitalistic form of that industry reproduces this same division of labour in a still more monstrous shape; in the factory proper, by converting the workman into a living appendage of the machine (317).

Modern industry rent the veil that concealed from men their own social process of production, and that turned the various, spontaneously divided branches of production into so many riddles, not only to outsiders, but even to the initiated (318).

Modern industry never looks upon and treats the existing form of a process as final. The technical basis of that industry is therefore revolutionary, while all earlier modes of production were essentially conservative. By means of machinery, chemical processes and other methods, it is continually causing changes not only in the technical basis of production, but also in the functions of the labourer, and in the social combinations of the labour-process. At the same time, it thereby also revolutionises the division of labour within the society, and incessantly launches masses of capital and of workpeople from one branch of production to another (318).

It is, of course, just as absurd to hold the Teutonic-Christian form of the family to be absolute and final as it would be to apply that character to the ancient Roman, the ancient Greek, or the Eastern forms which, moreover, taken together form a series in historical development (320).

What strikes us, then, in the English legislation of 1867, is, on the one hand, the necessity imposed on the parliament of the ruling classes, of adopting in principle measures so extraordinary, and on so great a scale, against the excesses of capitalistic exploitation; and on the other hand, the hesitation, the repugnance, and the bad faith, with which it lent itself to the task of carrying those measures into practice (322).

If the use of machinery in agriculture is for the most part free from the injurious physical effect it has on the factory operative, its action in superseding the labourers is more intense, and finds less resistance, as we shall see later in detail (329).

In the sphere of agriculture, modern industry has a more revolutionary effect than elsewhere, for this reason, that it annihilates the peasant, that bulwark of the old society, and replaces him by the wage-labourer. Thus the desire for social changes, and the class antagonisms are brought to the same level in the country as in the towns (329).

Capitalist production, by collecting the population in great centres, and causing an ever-increasing preponderance of town population, on the one hand concentrates the historical motive power of society; on the other hand, it disturbs the circulation of matter between man and the soil, i.e., prevents the return to the soil of its elements consumed by man in the form of food and clothing; it therefore violates the conditions necessary to lasting fertility of the soil. By this action it destroys at the same time the health of the town labourer and the intellectual life of the rural labourer (329–30).

Moreover, all progress in capitalistic agriculture is a progress in the art, not only of robbing the labourer, but of robbing the soil; all progress in increasing the fertility of the soil for a given time, is a progress towards ruining the lasting sources of that fertility. The more a country starts its development on the foundation of modern industry, like the United States, for example, the more rapid is this process of destruction. Capitalist production, therefore, develops technology, and the combining together of various processes into a social whole, only by sapping the original sources of all wealth-the soil and the labourer (330).

CHAPTER 16: ABSOLUTE AND RELATIVE SURPLUS-VALUE

Capitalist production is not merely the production of commodities, it is essentially the production of surplus-value. The labourer produces, not for himself, but for capital. It no longer suffices, therefore, that he should simply produce. He must produce surplus-value. That labourer alone is productive, who produces surplus-value for the capitalist, and thus works for the self-expansion of capital. If we may take an example from outside the sphere of production of material objects, a schoolmaster is a productive labourer when, in addition to belabouring the heads of his scholars, he works like a horse to enrich the school proprietor. That the latter has laid out his capital in a teaching factory, instead of in a sausage factory, does not alter the relation. . . . Accumulate, accumulate! That is Moses and the prophets! "Industry furnishes the material which saving accumulates." Therefore, save, save, *i.e.*, reconvert the greatest possible portion of surplus-value, or surplus-product into capital! Accumulation for accumulation's sake, production for production's sake: by this formula classical economy expressed the historical mission of the bourgeoisie, and did not for a single instant deceive itself over the birth-throes of wealth. (418)

CHAPTER 25: THE GENERAL LAW OF CAPITALIST ACCUMULATION

As, in religion, man is governed by the products of his own brain, so in capitalistic production, he is governed by the products of his own hand (438).

But if a surplus labouring population is a necessary product of accumulation or of the development of wealth on a capitalist basis, this surplus population becomes, conversely,

the lever of capitalistic accumulation, nay, a condition of existence of the capitalist mode of production. It forms a disposable industrial reserve army, that belongs to capital quite as absolutely as if the latter had bred it at its own cost. Independently of the limits of the actual increase of population, it creates, for the changing needs of the self-expansion of capital, a mass of human material always ready for exploitation (444).

The mass of social wealth, overflowing with the advance of accumulation, and transformable into additional capital, thrusts itself frantically into old branches of production, whose market suddenly expands, or into newly formed branches, such as railways, &c., the need for which grows out of the development of the old ones. In all such cases, there must be the possibility of throwing great masses of men suddenly on the decisive points without injury to the scale of production in other spheres (444).

Overpopulation supplies these masses. The course characteristic of modern industry, viz., a decennial cycle (interrupted by smaller oscillations), of periods of average activity, production at high pressure, crisis and stagnation, depends on the constant formation, the greater or less absorption, and the re-formation of the industrial reserve army or surplus population. In their turn, the varying phases of the industrial cycle recruit the surplus population, and become one of the most energetic agents of its reproduction (444).

The expansion by fits and starts of the scale of production is the preliminary to its equally sudden contraction; the latter again evokes the former, but the former is impossible without disposable human material, without an increase, in the number of labourers independently of the absolute growth of the population. This increase is effected by the simple process that constantly "sets free" a part of the labourers; by methods which lessen the number of labourers employed in proportion to the increased production. The whole form of the movement of modern industry depends, therefore, upon the constant transformation of a part of the labouring population into unemployed or half-employed hands (444).

Capitalist production can by no means content itself with the quantity of disposable labour power which the natural increase of population yields. It requires for its free play an industrial reserve army independent of these natural limits (445).

The industrial reserve army, during the periods of stagnation and average prosperity, weighs down the active labour-army; during the periods of over-production and paroxysm, it holds its pretensions in check. Relative surplus population is therefore the pivot upon which the law of demand and supply of labour works. It confines the field of action of this law within the limits absolutely convenient to the activity of exploitation and to the domination of capital (447–48).

The greater the social wealth, the functioning capital, the extent and energy of its growth, and, therefore, also the absolute mass of the proletariat and the productiveness of its labour, the greater is the industrial reserve army. The same causes which develop the expansive power of capital, develop also the labour power at its disposal. The relative mass of the industrial reserve army increases therefore with the potential energy of wealth. But the greater this reserve army in proportion to the active labour army, the greater is the mass of a consolidated surplus population, whose misery is in inverse ratio to its torment of labour. The more extensive, finally, the lazarus layers of the working class, and the industrial reserve army, the greater is official pauperism. This is the absolute general law of capitalist accumulation. Like all other laws it is modified in its working by many circumstances, the analysis of which does not concern us here (450–51).

CHAPTER 31: THE GENESIS OF THE INDUSTRIAL CAPITALIST

The discovery of gold and silver in America, the extirpation, enslavement and entombment in mines of the aboriginal population, the beginning of the conquest and looting of the East Indies, the turning of Africa into a warren for the commercial hunting of black-skins, signalised the rosy dawn of the era of capitalist production. These idyllic proceedings are the chief momenta of primitive accumulation. On their heels treads the commercial war of the European nations, with the globe for a theatre (533).

These methods depend in part on brute force, *e.g.*, the colonial system. But, they all employ the power of the State, the concentrated and organised force of society, to hasten, hothouse fashion, the process of transformation of the feudal mode of production into the capitalist mode, and to shorten the transition. Force is the midwife of every old society pregnant with a new one. It is itself an economic power (534).

CHAPTER 32: HISTORICAL TENDENCY OF CAPITALIST ACCUMULATION

From that moment new forces and new passions spring up in the bosom of society; but the old social organisation fetters them and keeps them down. It must be annihilated; it is annihilated. Its annihilation, the transformation of the individualised and scattered means of production into socially concentrated ones, of the pigmy property of the many into the huge property of the few, the expropriation of the great mass of the people from the soil, from the means of subsistence, and from the means of labour, this fearful and painful expropriation of the mass of the people forms the prelude to the history of capital. It comprises a series of forcible methods, of which we have passed in review only those that have been epoch making as methods of the primitive accumulation of capital (541).

As soon as this process of transformation has sufficiently decomposed the old society from top to bottom, as soon as the labourers are turned into proletarians, their means of labour into capital, as soon as the capitalist mode of production stands on its own feet, then the further socialisation of labour and further transformation of the land and other means of production into socially exploited and, therefore, common means of production, as well as the further expropriation of private proprietors, takes a new form. That which is now to be expropriated is no longer the labourer working for himself, but the capitalist exploiting many labourers. This expropriation is accomplished by the action of the immanent laws of capitalistic production itself, by the centralisation of capital. One capitalist always kills many (541–42).

Hand in hand with this centralisation, or this expropriation of many capitalists by few, develop, on an ever-extending scale, the cooperative form of the labour process, the conscious technical application of science, the methodical cultivation of the soil, the transformation of the instruments of labour into instruments of labour only usable in common, the economising of all means of production by their use as means of production of combined, socialised labour, the entanglement of all peoples in the net of the world market, and with this, the international character of the capitalistic regime (542).

Along with the constantly diminishing number of the magnates of capital, who usurp and monopolise all advantages of this process of transformation, grows the mass of misery, oppression, slavery, degradation, exploitation; but with this too grows the revolt of the working class, a class always increasing in numbers, and disciplined, united, organised by the very mechanism of the process of capitalist production itself. The monopoly of capital becomes a fetter upon the mode of production, which has sprung up and flourished along with, and under it. Centralisation of the means of production and socialisation of labour at last reach a point where they become incompatible with their capitalist integument. This integument is burst asunder. The knell of capitalist private property sounds. The expropriators are expropriated (542).

The transformation of scattered private property, arising from individual labour, into capitalist private property is, naturally, a process, incomparably more protracted, violent, and difficult, than the transformation of capitalistic private property, already practically resting on socialised production, into socialised property. In the former case, we had the expropriation of the mass of the people by a few usurpers; in the latter, we have the expropriation of a few usurpers by the mass of the people (542).

Bibliography

CONTENTS

INTRODUCTION

The sheer volume of writings on Karl Marx and his collaborator, Friedrich Engels, is overwhelming. Here we list the most relevant and accessible sources for their lives, times, philosophy, and social theory. The first few sections deal with the works of Marx and Engels. We relied heavily on the Marxist Internet Archive in accessing these original works. The Archive has thousands of documents on Marx and Engels as well as writers in the Marxist tradition and critics of that tradition. The Archive is a nonprofit, and many of the works are in the public domain. It is a tremendous resource for those interested in Marx and Marxism. In addition to the Archive's versions of *Capital*, we have included references to the Penguin editions of the three volumes of *Capital*. This version is widely available in inexpensive paperback, and it is to this translation that we reference in the encyclopedic entries.

For those who are coming to Marx fresh, we recommend beginning with the *Communist Manifesto*—a work written in clear prose and for a broad audience. Next, a close reading of the *Preface to A Critique of Political Economy* would give the novice a comprehensive overview of Marx's historical materialism as well as his theory of history. Finally, once acclimated to his Germanic style of writing, one should read Marx's masterwork, the first volume of *Capital*. We have included a selection of quotes from these three key works by Marx that can serve as an excellent introduction to his analysis of capitalism in his own words.

The biography sections include a selection of early and more contemporary biographies of both Marx and Engels, including both hagiographies as well as some disparaging work. We found Isaiah Berlin's *Karl Marx* particularly useful as well as Jonathan Sperber's *Karl Marx: A Nineteenth-Century Life* and Gareth Stedman-Jones's *Karl Marx: Greatness and Illusion*. These biographies focus on the life and times of Marx and Engels but do not go into great detail on his political-economic analyses.

The historical works in the 19th and early 20th centuries were essential in detailing the historical context in which Marx, Engels, and the socialist movements around them operated. For most of the 20th century, the Soviet Union, Germany, China, and their Warsaw Pact Communist allies dominated the practice of Marxist-inspired socialism and communism. Their Cold War conflict with Western capitalist democracies led by the United States and their NATO allies (and the various proxy wars of that century) shaped global politics. The "Historical Era" section of the bibliography assembles major works that describe the significance of the establishment of socialist and Communist systems of government, both from those directly involved (e.g., work by Vladimir Lenin) and from an historical perspective. Notably, the body of literature dealing with world history as it relates to the politics and economy of socialism and communism is vast. Here we focus bibliographic entries primarily on the history of Marxist-inspired political and economic systems in Germany and the former Soviet Union.

Anarchism and related political movements in the 20th century failed to achieve the large-scale success of socialism and communism as seen in the Soviet Union, Germany, and China, though anarchist movements and organizations maintained persistent and sometimes influential presence on the global scene, especially in the early part of the 20th century when anarchists such as Antonio Gramsci attained some success in marshaling modest public support. Reviews of the writing and revolutionary work of these early 20th-century anarchists are included in the bibliography. Anarchism enjoyed a resurgence of sorts in the late 20th century, often associated with the U.S. counterculture movement. Daniel Guerin wrote several influential works in the early 1970s advocating the methods of anarchism for establishing independent communal living with the goal of ultimately abolishing the state apparatus. More recent popular writings (such as by David Priestland) seek to revive these principles of anarchism to solve contemporary problems, such as environmental crises, poverty, and inequality.

Marx's philosophical writings were also very influential within the broader field of philosophy, though notably his brand of philosophy is often interwoven with social and economic themes. As he notes in *Theses on Feuerbach*, "Philosophers have hitherto only interpreted the world in various ways; the point is to change it." This concern with social change was of primary interest to one of the most prominent and influential 20th-century

schools of thought, known as the Frankfurt School. Members of this school blended the interest in social change evident in Marx's philosophy with Freudian psychoanalysis and the core elements of ideological philosophies of Kant, Hegel, Weber, Simmel, and Lukács into a philosophical approach known as "critical theory." We included several prominent critical theorists in the "Philosophy" section of the bibliography, including Erich Fromm and Herbert Marcuse, who explicitly integrate Marx's philosophical ideas into their work. Marx's materialist explanations of the world were also highly influential in many other areas of investigation beyond those traditionally associated with Marx (e.g., politics, economy, and history). Marxist analyses of art, literature, and religion, as well as the more general philosophical questions of the concept of nature and the place of humanity in the natural world, all saw significant influence from Marx throughout the 20th century and into the 21st century, and we include a representative sample of these types of works in the bibliography.

There are a variety of interpretations of Marx's overall social theory. The works we found most useful—those that reinforced mainstream arguments as well as our readings of the original texts—included Shlomo Avineri and the writings of Jon Elster, David Harvey, and William Shaw. Each presents a realistic assessment of Marx's theory and analyses without attempting to overstate his contributions. The last section of the bibliography, "Marx's Social Science Legacy," references significant works in contemporary social theory and analyses that rely heavily on Marx's insights. In this section, we did not restrict ourselves to doctrinaire Marxism but rather theories significantly influenced by their work. The selection was difficult to limit, as Marx's influence on the social sciences of anthropology, political science, and sociology is pervasive. Of special mention in this section are Harry Braverman, John Bellamy Foster, Marvin Harris, C. Wright Mills, and Immanuel Wallerstein. While Marx's analysis has strongly influenced the modern theorists covered in this bibliography, the nature and strength of this influence vary widely. Most contemporary social scientists combine Marxian analysis with their own insights and those from other theorists to arrive at a distinctive analytical perspective. Braverman, however, is much closer to Marx's theory; that is, his overall approach is directly from Karl Marx. His problem—a study of the objective conditions of the working class—is identical to the task Marx set for himself in the first volume of *Capital*. The value of Braverman's work is not in extending Marx's analyses or in combining Marx's insights with others. Instead, the value of his work is that it applies Marx's analyses to American workers in the latter half of the 20th century and, further, renders Marx's analyses genuinely accessible to a modern audience. It is a very successful work on both counts.

MARX'S WRITINGS

Marx, Karl. 1844/1883. *A Contribution to the Critique of Hegel's Philosophy of Right.* https://www.marxists.org/archive/marx /works/1843/critique-hpr/intro.htm.

———. 1884. *On the Jewish Question.* https://www.marxists.org/archive/marx /works/1844/jewish-question.

———. 1845. *A Critique of the German Ideology.* https://www.marxists.org/archive /marx/works/download/Marx_The_German _Ideology.pdf.

———. 1847a. *The Poverty of Philosophy.* https://www.marxists.org/archive/marx /works/download/pdf/Poverty-Philosophy .pdf.

———. 1847b. *Wage Labour and Capital.* https://www.marxists.org/archive/marx /works/download/pdf/wage-labour-capital .pdf.

———. 1850. *The Class Struggles in France, 1848–1850.* https://www.marxists.org /archive/marx/works/download/pdf/Class _Struggles_in_France.pdf.

———. 1853. *The British Rule in India.* https://www.marxists.org/archive/marx /works/1853/06/25.htm.

———. 1857–1861. *Grundrisse.* https://www .marxists.org/archive/marx/works/down load/pdf/grundrisse.pdf.

———. 1859. *A Contribution to the Critique of Political Economy.* https://www.marxists .org/archive/marx/works/download/Marx _Contribution_to_the_Critique_of_Political _Economy.pdf.

———. 1860. "Herr Vogt: A Spy in the Worker's Movement." https://www.marxists.org /history/etol/newspape/ni/vol10/no08 /marx.htm.

———. 1867/1976. *Capital: Volume I.* Trans. Ben Fowkes. London: Clays.

———. 1871. *The Civil War in France.* https://www.marxists.org/archive/marx /works/1871/civil-war-france/index.htm.

———. 1872. "La Liberté Speech." https:// www.marxists.org/archive/marx/works /1872/09/08.htm.

———. 1874–1875. *Conspectus of Bakunin's* Statism and Anarchy [Extract]. https://www.marxists.org/archive/marx /works/1874/04/bakunin-notes.htm.

———. 1875. *Critique of the Gotha Programme.* https://www.marxists.org/archive /marx/works/download/Marx_Critque_of _the_Gotha_Programme.pdf.

———. 1880–1882/1974. *The Ethnological Notebooks of Karl Marx.* https://www.marx ists.org/archive/marx/works/1881/ethno graphical-notebooks/notebooks.pdf.

———. 1885/1978. *Capital: Volume II.* Trans. David Fernbach. London: Clays.

———. 1894/1991. *Capital: Volume III.* Trans. David Fernbach. London: Clays.

ENGELS'S WRITINGS

Engels, Friedrich. 1845/1969. *The Condition of the Working Class in England.* New York: Oxford University Press.

———. 1847. *The Principles of Communism.* http://www.marxists.org/archive/marx /works/1847/11/prin-com.htm.

———. 1877. "Anti-Dühring: Herr Eugen Dühring's Revolution in Science." https://www .marxists.org/archive/marx/works/1877 /anti-duhring/index.htm.

———. 1883. *Eulogy for Marx.* http://www .marxists.org/archive/marx/works/1883 /death/dersoz1.htm.

———. 1894. *Engels to Borgius.* https://www.marxists.org/archive/marx/works/1894/letters/94_01_25.htm.

———. 1895. *Introduction to The Class Struggles in France, 1848–1850.* https://www.marxists.org/archive/marx/works/download/pdf/Class_Struggles_in_France.pdf.

———. 1908. *Socialism: Utopian and Scientific.* Trans. Edward Aveling. Chicago: Charles H. Kerr & Company.

MARX'S AND ENGELS'S WRITINGS

Marx, Karl, and Friedrich Engels. 1848/1969. "The Communist Manifesto." In *Marx/Engels Selected Works, Vol. 1*, by Karl Marx and Friedrich Engels, 98–137. Moscow: Progress Publishers.

———. 1848/2012. *The Communist Manifesto.* Edited by Jeffrey C. Isaac. New Haven, CT: Yale University Press,.

———. 1975a. *Marx-Engels Collected Works (Vol. 24).* Moscow: Progress Publishers.

———. 1975b. *Selected Correspondence 1846–1895.* New York: International Publishers.

MARX'S BIOGRAPHY

Berlin, Isaiah. 1939. *Karl Marx. His Life and Environment.* London: Thornton Butterworth.

———. 2013. *Karl Marx.* Princeton, NJ: Princeton University Press.

Biography.com. 2018. *Karl Marx Biography.* https://www.biography.com/people/karl-marx-9401219.

Blumenberg, Werner. 1972a. *Karl Marx.* London: Verso.

———. 1972b. *Portrait of Marx: An Illustrated Biography.* Trans. Douglass Scott. New York: Herder and Herder.

Carr, Edward H. 1934. *Karl Marx: A Study in Fanaticism.* London: J. M. Dent and Sons.

Evans, Michael. 1975. *Karl Marx.* London: George Allen and Unwin.

Felix, David. 1983. *Marx as Politician.* Carbondale: Southern Illinois University Press.

Foner, Philip, ed. 1973. *When Karl Marx Died: Comments in 1883.* New York: International Publishers.

Gabriel, Mary. 2011. *Love and Capital: Karl Marx and Jenny Marx and the Birth of a Revolution.* Boston: Little, Brown.

Hammen, Oscar J. 1969. *The Red 48'ers: Karl Marx and Friedrich Engels.* New York: Scribner.

Holmes, Rachel. 2014. *Eleanor Marx: A Life.* London: Bloomsbury.

Kapp, Yvonne. 1972. *Eleanor Marx.* 2 vols. London: Lawrence and Wishart.

Lewis, John. 1965. *The Life and Teaching of Karl Marx.* London: Lawrence and Wishart.

Liebknecht, Wilhelm. 1901. *Karl Marx: Biographical Memoirs.* Chicago: C. H. Kerr.

McLellan, David. 1973. *Karl Marx: His Life and Thought.* London: Macmillan.

———. 1981. *Karl Marx: Interviews and Recollections.* Ed. David McLellan. London: Macmillan.

———. 1983. *Marx: The First Hundred Years.* Ed. David McLellan. London: Frances Printer Publishers.

———. 2006. *Karl Marx: A Biography.* 4th ed. Houndmills: Palgrave Macmillan.

Mehring, Franz. 1918. *Karl Marx.* London: John Lane.

———. 1981. *Karl Marx: The Story of His Life.* Trans. Edward Fitzgerald. Atlantic Highlands, NJ: Humanities Press.

Meier, Olga, ed. 1982. *The Daughters of Karl Marx: Family Correspondence 1866–1898.* Harmondsworth: Penguin.

Nikolaevsky, Boris. 1936. *Karl Marx: Man and Fighter.* Trans. G. David Mosbacher and E. Mosbacher. London: Methuen.

Padover, Saul. 1980. *Karl Marx: An Intimate Biography.* New York: New American Library.

Payne, Robert. 1968. *Marx: A Biography.* London: W. H. Allen.

Riazanov, David. 1927. *Karl Marx: Man, Thinker and Revolutionist.* New York: International Publishers.

———. 1973. *Karl Marx and Friedrich Engels: An Introduction to Their Lives and Work.* Trans. Joshua Kunitz. London: Monthly Review Press.

Rubel, Maximilien. 1980. *Marx: Life and Works.* London: Macmillan.

Rubel, Maximilien, and Margaret Manale. 1975. *Marx without Myth*. New York: Harper and Row.

Rühle, Otto. 2011. *Karl Marx: His Life and Works*. New York: Routledge.

Schwarzschild, Leopold. 1947. *The Red Prussian: The Life and Legend of Karl Marx*. New York: Charles Scribner's Sons.

Seigel, Jerrold. 1978. *Marx's Fate: The Shape of a Life*. University Park, PA: Penn State University Press.

Shuster, Sam. 2007. "The Nature and Consequence of Karl Marx's Skin Disease." *British Journal of Dermatology* 158, no. 1: 1–3.

Sperber, Jonathan. 2013. *Karl Marx: A Nineteenth-Century Life*. New York: Liveright Publishing Corporation.

Stedman-Jones, Gareth. 2016. *Karl Marx: Greatness and Illusion*. Cambridge, MA: The Belknap Press of Harvard University Press.

Thomas, Paul. 1980. *Karl Marx and the Anarchists*. London: Routledge and Kegan Paul.

Tsuzuki, Chushichi. 1967. *The Life of Eleanor Marx, 1855–1898: A Socialist Tragedy*. Oxford: Clarendon Press.

Wheen, Francis. 1999. *Karl Marx*. London: Fourth Estate.

———. 2001. *Karl Marx: A Life*. New York: Norton.

Wolfson, Murray. 1971. *Karl Marx (Columbian Essays on Great Economists, No. 3)*. New York: Columbia University Press.

Wood, Allen W. 2004. *Karl Marx*. 2nd ed. Abingdon: Routledge.

ENGELS'S BIOGRAPHY

Arthur, Christopher J. 1996. *Engels Today: A Centenary Appreciation*. Ed. Christopher J. Arthur. Basingstoke: Macmillan.

Carver, Terrell, and Manfred B. Steger. 1999. *Engels after Marx*. Ed. Terrell Carver and Manfred B. Steger. Manchester: Manchester University Press.

Carver, Terrell. 1983. *Marx and Engels: The Intellectual Relationship*. Brighton: Harvester.

———. 1989. *Friedrich Engels: His Life and Thought*. London: Macmillan.

———. 2003. *Engels*. Oxford: Oxford University Press.

Green, John. 2009. *Friedrich Engels Was Not a Hypocrite*. https://www.theguardian.com/commentisfree/2009/may/07/friedrich-engels-feminism-socialism-marx.

Henderson, William O. 1976. *The Life of Friedrich Engels*. 2 vols. London: Frank Cass.

Hunley, J. H. 1991. *The Life and Thought of Friedrich Engels: A Reinterpretation*. New Haven, CT: Yale University Press.

Hunt, Tristram. 2009. *The Frock-Coated Communist: The Revolutionary Life of Friedrich Engels*. London: Allen Lane.

———. 2010. *Marx's General: The Revolutionary Life of Friedrich Engels*. New York: Henry Holt.

Mayer, Gustav. 1936. *Friedrich Engels: A Biography*. Ed. R. H. S. Crossman. Trans. Gilbert Highet and Helen Highnet. London: Chapman and Hall.

McLellan, David. 1977. *Engels*. London: Collins.

Riazanov, David. 1973. *Karl Marx and Friedrich Engels: An Introduction to Their Lives and Work*. Trans. Joshua Kunitz. London: Monthly Review Press.

Sayers, Janet, Mary Evans, and Nanneke Redclift. 1987. *Engels Revisited: New Feminist Essays*. London: Tavistock.

THE HISTORICAL ERA

Appleman, Phillip, ed. 1976. "Introduction." In *An Essay on the Principle of Population: Text, Sources and Background Criticism*, xi–xxvii. New York: Norton.

Archer, Julian P. W. 1997. *The First International in France 1864–1872: Its Origins, Theories and Impact*. Lanham, MD: University Press of America.

Ball, Terrence, Richard Dagger, and Daniel O'Neil. 2019. *Political Ideologies and the Democratic Ideal*. 11th ed.. New York: Routledge.

Barclay, David E., and Eric D. Weitz. 1998. "Between Reform and Revolution: German Socialism and Communism from 1840 to 1990." New York: Berghahn.

Berlin, Isaiah. 1998. "Herzen and His Memoirs." In *The Proper Study of Mankind*. New York: Farrar, Straus and Giroux.

Braunthal, Julius. 1980. *History of the International*. 3 vols. Trans. Henry Collins and Kenneth Mitchell. London: Gollancz.

Bresler, Fenton. 1999. *Napoleon III: A Life*. New York: Caroll & Graf.

Carmichael, Joel. 1976. *Stalin's Masterpiece: The Show Trials and Purges of the Thirties, the Consolidation of the Bolshevik Dictatorship*. New York: St. Martin's Press.

Carr, Edward H. 1982. *The Twilight of the Comintern*. New York: Pantheon Books.

Chalmers, Douglass. 1964. *The Social Democratic Party of Germany*. New Haven, CT: Yale University Press.

Collins, Henry, and Chimen Abramsky. 1965. *Karl Marx and the British Labour Movement: Years of the First International*. London: Macmillan.

Conquest, Robert. 1990. *The Great Terror: A Reassessment*. New York: Oxford University Press.

———. 1991. *Stalin: Breaker of Nations*. New York: Penguin.

Daughtery, Carter. 2008. *Stopping a Financial Crisis the Swedish Way*. https://www.nytimes.com/2008/09/23/business/worldbusiness/23krona.html.

Dominick, Raymond. 1982. *Wilhelm Liebknecht and the Founding of the German Social Democratic Party*. Chapel Hill: University of North Carolina Press.

Dutte, R. Palme. 1964. *The Internationale*. London: Lawrence and Wishart.

Duveau, Georges. 1967. *1848: The Making of a Revolution*. London: Routledge and Kegan Paul.

Edmonds, Thomas R. 1828. *Practical, Moral, and Political Economy*. London: Effingham Wilson, Royal Exchange.

Frankel, Jonathan. 1981. *Prophecy and Politics: Socialism, Nationalism and the Russian Jews, 1862–1917*. Cambridge: Cambridge University Press.

Frolich, Paul. 1972. *Rosa Luxemburg*. Trans. Johanna Hoornweg. Chicago: Haymarket Books.

German History in Documents. 2003. *Anti-Socialist Law (October 1, 1878)*. http://germanhistorydocs.ghi-dc.org/about.cfm.

———. 2003–2012. *Anti-Socialist Law (October 21, 1878)*. http://ghdi.ghi-dc.org/sub_document.cfm?document_id=1843.

Germino, Dante. 1986. "Review Essay: Antonio Gramsci Scholarship." *American Political Science Review* 80, no. 1: 291–96.

Godwin, William. 1820/1976. "Preface to OF Population." In *An Essay on the Principle of Population: Text, Sources and Background Criticism*, edited by Philip Appleman, 143–56. New York: Norton.

Gomelsky, Victoria. 2014. *How Switzerland Came to Dominate Watchmaking*. https://www.nytimes.com/2014/11/21/style/international/what-enabled-switzerland-to-dominate-watchmaking.html.

Gramsci, Antonio. 2973. *Prison Notebooks*. London: Lawrence and Wishart.

Grimmer-Solem, Erik. 2003. *The Rise of Historical Economics and Social Reform in Germany 1864–1894*. Oxford: Clarendon Press.

Hallas, Duncan. 2008. *The Comintern*. Chicago: Haymarket Books.

Heller, Henry. 2011. *The Birth of Capitalism: A 21st Century Perspective*. London: Pluto Press.

Hobsbawm, Eric. 1996. *The Age of Revolution: 1789–1848*. New York: Vintage Books.

Horn, Jeff, Leonard Rosenband, and Merrit Roe Smith. 2010. *Reconceptualizing the Industrial Revolution*. Cambridge MA: MIT Press.

Howell, George. 1878. "The History of the International Association." *Nineteenth-Century* 4 (July): 19–39.

International, The. 1963–1968. *Documents of the First International*. 5 vols. London: Lawrence and Wishart.

Johnson, Christopher. 1974. *Utopian Communism in France: Cabet and the Icarians 1839–1851*. Ithaca, NY: Cornell University Press.

Joll, James. 1975. *The Second International, 1889–1914*. London: Routledge and Kegan Paul.

Katz, Henryk. 1991. *The Emancipation of Labor: A History of the First International*. Westport, CT: Greenwood Press.

Kennan, George. 1961. *Russia and the West Under Lenin and Stalin*. Boston: Little, Brown.

Kissinger, Henry. 2017. *A World Restored: Metternich, Castlereagh, and the Problems of Peace, 1812–1822*. N.p.: Friedland Books.

Koestler, Arthur. 2019. *Darkness at Noon*. New York: Palgrave Macmillan.

Kramer, Lloyd S. 1988. *Threshold of a New World: Intellectuals and the Exile Experience in Paris, 1830–1848*. Ithaca, NY: Cornell University Press.

Landes, David. 1969. *The Unbound Prometheus: Technological Change and Industrial Development in Western Europe from 1750 to the Present*. Cambridge: Cambridge University Press.

Laqueur, Walter. 1977. *Terrorism: A Study of National and International Violence*. Boston: Little, Brown.

Lattek, Christine. 2006. *Revolutionary Refugees: German Socialism in Britain, 1840–1860*. London: Routledge.

Lenin, Vladimir. 1919. *Capitalist "Democracy": Dictatorship of the Bourgeoisie*. https://www.icl-fi.org/english/wv/864/qotw.html.

———. 1972. "The Agrarian Question in Russia." In *Lenin: Collected Works*, by Vladimir Lenin. Trans. B. Issacs and J. Fineberg, 375–77. Moscow: Progress Publishers.

———. 1987. *"What Is to Be Done?" The Essential Works of Lenin: What Is to Be Done? and Other Writings*. Mineola, NY: Dover Publications.

Levi, Paul, and David Fernbach. 2012. *In the Steps of Rosa Luxemburg*. Ed. Paul Levi and David Fernbach. Chicago: Haymarket Books.

Levine, Bruce. 1992. *The Spirit of 1848: German Immigrants, Labor Conflict and the Coming of the Civil War*. Urbana: University of Illinois Press.

Lewis, John. 1972. *The Marxism of Marx*. London: Lawrence and Wishart.

Lich, Glen E. 2010. "Forty-Eighters." http://www.tshaonline.org/handbook/online/articles/pnf01.

Lukàcs, Georg. 1971. *History and Consciousness*. Trans. Rodney Livingstone. London: Merlin Press.

Luxemburg, Rosa. 1954. *What Is Economics?* New York: Pioneer.

Malthus, T. Robert. 1798/2001. "An Essay on the Principle of Population." In *A Commentary on Malthus' 1798 Essay on the Principle of Population as Social Theory*, by Frank W. Elwell, 127–294. Lewiston, NY: Edwin Mellen Press.

McDermott, Kevin, and Jeremy Agnew. 1996. *The Comintern: A History of International Communism from Lenin to Stalin*. New York: Palgrave Macmillan.

McNicoll, Geoffrey. 1998. "Malthus for the Twenty-First Century." *Population and Development Review* 24, no. 2: 309–17.

Merriman, John M. 2014. *The Life and Death of the Pris Commune of 1871*. New Haven, CT: Yale University Press.

Miller, David, et al. 1991. "Georg Lukàcs." In *The Blackwell Encyclopaedia of Political Thought*. Hoboken, NJ: Blackwell.

Morgan, Roger. 1965. *The German Social Democrats and the First International 1864–1872*. Cambridge: Cambridge University Press.

Namier, Lewis Bernstein. 1944/1971. *1848: The Revolution of the Intellectuals*. London: Oxford University Press.

Pankhurst, Richard. 1954. *William Thompson (1775–1833): Britain's Pioneer Socialist, Feminist, and Co-operator*. London: Watts & Company.

Petersen, William. 1979. *Malthus*. Cambridge, MA: Harvard University Press.

———. 1990. "Malthus, the Reactionary Reformer." *American Scholar* 59, no. 2: 275–83.

Price, David. 1998. "Of Population and False Hopes: Malthus and His Legacy." *Population and Environment* 19, no. 3: 205–19.

Proudhon, Pierre-Joseph. 2011. *Property Is Theft: A Pierre-Joseph Proudhon Reader*. Ed. Ian McKay. Chico, CA: AK Press.

———. 2012. *Essential Proudhon*. CreateSpace Independent Publishing Platform.

Rae, John. 1881a. "Ferdinand Lassalle and German Socialism." *The Contemporary Review* 39: 232–48.

———. 1881b. "The Socialism of Karl Marx and the Young Hegelians." *The Contemporary Review* 40: 585–607.

Raphael, Max. 1933. *Proudhon, Marx, Picasso: Three Studies in the Sociology of Art*. London: Lawrence and Wishart.

Rappoport, Mike. 2009. *1848: Year of Revolution*. New York: Basic Books.

Rohe, John F. 1997. *A Bicentenial Malthusian Essay*. 20 December 1999. http://www.trmalthus.com/reface.htm.

Schorske, Carl. 1983. *German Social Democracy, 1905–1917*. Cambridge, MA: Harvard University Press.

Service, Robert. 2004. *Stalin: A Biography*. London: Macmillan.

Shanin, Teodor. 1983. *Late Marx and the Russian Road: Marx and the Peripheries of Capitalism*. Ed. Teodor Shanin. London: Routledge and Kegan Paul.

Smith, Adam. 1776/1977. *An Inquiry into the Nature and Causes of the Wealth of Nations*. Chicago: University of Chicago Press.

Socialist International. 1969. *The Socialist International: A Short History*. London: Socialist International.

Sperber, Jonathan. 1991. *Rhineland Radicals: The Democratic Movement and the Revolution of 1848–1849*. Princeton, NJ: Princeton University Press.

———. 1995. "'The Persecutor of Evil' in the German Revolution of 1848–1849." In *Media and Revolution: Comparative Perspective*, edited by Jeremy D. Popkin. Lexington: University Press of Kentucky.

Stearns, Peter N. 1974. *The Revolutions of 1848*. London: Weidenfeld and Nicolson.

Stedman-Jones, Gareth. 1983. "The Mid-Century Crisis and the 1848 Revolutions." *Theory and Society* 12, no. 4.

———. 1984. "Some Notes on Karl Marx and the English Labour Movement." *History Workshop* 18 (Autumn).

Steenson, Gary. 1991. *After Marx, before Lenin: Marxism and Socialist Working-Class Parties in Europe, 1884–1914*. Pittsburgh, PA: University of Pittsburgh Press.

Steinberg, Jonathan. 2011. *Bismarck: A Life*. Oxford: Oxford University Press.

Stekloff, G. M. 1928. *History of the First International*. London: M. Lawrence.

Tombs, Robert. 1999. *The Paris Commune, 1871*. London: Longman.

Trotnow, Helmut. 1984. *Karl Liebknecht: A Political Biography*. Hamden, CT: Archon Books.

Tuchinsky, Adam. 2009. *Horace Greeley's New York Tribune: Civil War Era Socialism and the Crisis of Free Labour*. Ithaca, NY: Cornell University Press.

Tucker, Robert C. 1988. *Stalin as Revolutionary*. New York: Norton.

Ulam, Adam Bruno. 1998. *The Bolsheviks: The Intellectual and Political History of the Triumph of Communism in Russia*. Cambridge, MA: Harvard University Press.

Winch, Donald. 1987. *Malthus*. Oxford: Oxford University Press.

Zamoyski, Adam. 2012. *Rites of Peace: The Fall of Napoleon and the Congress of Vienna*. New York: HarperCollins.

Zetkin, Clara. 2015. *Clara Zetkin: Selected Writings*. 2nd ed. Ed. Philip Foner. Chicago: Haymarket Books.

ANARCHISM

Adamson, Walter L. 1979. "Toward the Prison Notebooks: The Evolution of Gramsci's Thinking on Political Organization, 1918–1926." *Polity* 12, no. 1: 38–64.

Bergman, Jay. 1983. *Vera Zasulich: A Biography*. Stanford, CA: Stanford University Press.

Courtois, Stephane, et al. 1999. *The Black Book of Communism: Crimes, Terror, Repression*. Trans. Jonathan Murphy and Mark Kramer. Cambridge, MA: Harvard University Press.

Cummins, Ian. 1980. *Marx, Engels and National Movements*. London: Croom Helm.

Davis, Horace Bancroft, ed. 1976. *The National Question: Selected Writings by Rosa Luxemburg*. New York: Monthly Review Press.

Djilas, Milovan. 1957. *The New Class: An Analysis of the Communist System*. London: Thames and Hudson.

Guérin, Daniel. 1970. *Anarchism: From Theory to Practice*. New York: Monthly Review Press.

Priestland, David. 2015. *Anarchism Could Help Save the World*. https://www.theguard

ian.com/books/2015/jul/03/anarchism-could-help-save-the-world.

Rubinstein, Richard E. 1987. *Alchemists of Revolution: Terrorism in the Modern World.* New York: Basic Books.

MARX'S PHILOSOPHY

Aaron, Raymond. 1968. "Karl Marx." In *Main Currents in Sociological Thought I,* trans. Richard Howard and Hellen Weaver, 145–236. Garden City, NY: Doubleday.

Arneson, Richard. 1991. "What's Wrong with Exploitation?" *Ethics* 91: 202–27.

Avineri, Shlomo. 2019. *Karl Marx: Philosophy and Revolution.* New Haven, CT: Yale University Press.

Balibar, Etienne. 1995. *The Philosophy of Marx.* London: Verso.

Baxandall, Lee, and Stefan Morawski. 1973. *Marx & Engels on Literature & Art.* New York: International General.

Bhaskar, Roy. 1992. *Dialectics.* London: Verso.

Bologh, Roslyn W. 1979. *Dialectical Phenomenology: Marx's Method.* London: Routledge and Kegan Paul.

Breckman, Warren. 1999. *Marx, the Young Hegelians and the Origins of Radical Social Theory: Dethroning the Self.* Cambridge: Cambridge University Press.

Brenkert, George. 1983. *Marx's Ethics of Freedom.* London: Routledge and Kegan Paul.

Buchanan, Allen E. 1982. *Marx and Justice: The Radical Critique of Liberalism.* Totowa, NJ: Rowman & Littlefield.

Cain, Maureen, and Alan Hunt. 1979. *Marx and Engels on Law.* Ed. Maureen Cain and Alan Hunt. London: Academic Press.

Callinicos, Alex. 1983. *Marxism and Philosophy.* London: Oxford University Press.

———. 1995. *The Revolutionary Ideas of Karl Marx.* London: Bookmarks.

Carlebach, Julius. 1978. *Karl Marx and the Radical Critique of Judaism.* London: Routledge and Kegan Paul.

Carver, Terrell, and Daniel Blank. 2014. *Marx and Engels's "German Ideology" Manuscripts: Presentation and Analysis of the "Feuerbach Chapter."* New York: Macmillan.

Cohen, Gerry A. 1988. *Labour and Freedom: Themes from Marx.* Oxford: Oxford University Press.

Cohen, Marshal, Thomas Nagel, and Thomas Scanlon, eds. 1980. *Marx, Justice and History.* Princeton, NJ: Princeton University Press.

Cowling, Mark. 2006. "Alienation in the Older Marx." *Contemporary Political Theory* 5, no. 3: 319–39.

Demetz, Peter. 1967. *Marx, Engels and the Poets: Origins of Marxist Literary Criticism.* Chicago: University of Chicago Press.

Fay, Margaret. 1983. "The Influence of Adam Smith on Marx's Theory of Alienation." *Science and Society* 47, no. 2: 462–71.

Fenves, Peter. 1986. "Marx's Doctoral Thesis on Two Greek Atomists and the Post-Kantian Interpretation." *Journal of the History of Ideas* 47: 433–52.

Forbes, Ian. 1990. *Marx and the New Individual.* London: Unwin Hyman.

Fromm, Erich. 1956. *The Sane Society.* New York: Rinehart & Company.

———. 1961. *Marx's Concept of Man.* New York: Frederick Ungar.

———. 1965. *Socialist Humanism.* New York: Doubleday.

Geras, Norman. 1983. *Marx and Human Nature: Refutation of a Legend.* London: Verso.

———. 1986. *Literature of Revolution: Essays on Marxism.* London: Verso.

Gollobin, Ira. 1986. *Dialectical Materialism: Its Laws, Categories, and Practice.* New York: Petras Press.

Gottlieb, Roger S. 1989. *An Anthology of Western Marxism: From Lukacs and Gramsci to Socialist-Feminism.* Oxford: Oxford University Press.

Gould, Carol C. 1978. *Marx's Social Ontology.* Cambridge, MA: MIT Press.

Holt, Justin P. 2009. *Karl Marx's Philosophy of Nature, Action and Society: A New Analysis.* Newcastle: Cambridge Scholars Publishing.

Lifshitz, Mikhail. 1973. *The Philosophy of Art of Karl Marx.* London: Pluto Press.

Marcuse, Herbert. 1960. *Reason and Revolution.* Boston: Beacon Press.

———. 1964. *One-Dimensional Man*. Boston: Beacon Press.

Meaney, Mark. 2002. *Capital as Organic Unity: The Role of Hegel's Science of Logic in Marx's Grundrisse*. Dordrecht: Kluwer Academic Publishers.

Meszaros, Istvan. 1972. *Marx's Theory of Alienation*. 3rd ed. London: Merlin.

Moore, Stanley. 1971. "Marx and the Origin of Dialectical Materialism." *Inquiry* 16: 421–29.

Murray, Patrick. 1988. *Marx's Theory of Scientific Knowledge*. New York: Humanities Press International.

Nussbaum, Martha C. 1995. "Objectification." *Philosophy & Public Affairs* 24, no. 4: 249–91.

Ollman, Bertell. 1980. *Alienation: Marx's Conception of Man in Capitalist Society*. New York: Cambridge University Press.

Pike, Jon. 1998. *From Aristotle to Marx*. Aldershot: Avebury.

Pilling, Geoffrey. 1980. *Marx's Capital: Philosophy and Political Economy*. London: Routledge and Kegan Paul.

Pines, Christopher L. 1993. *Ideology and False Consciousness: Marx and His Historical Progenitors*. Albany: State University of New York Press.

Plamenatz, John. 1975. *Karl Marx's Philosophy of Man*. Oxford: Oxford University Press.

———. 1992. *Hegel, Marx and Engels, and the Idea of Progress*. London: Longman.

Prawer, S. S. 1976. *Karl Marx and World Literature*. Oxford: Oxford University Press.

Regula, Qureshi. 2002. *Music and Marx: Ideas, Practice and Politics*. New York: Routledge.

Rockmore, Tom. 2002. *Marx after Marxism: The Philosophy of Karl Marx*. Oxford: Blackwell.

Rose, Margaret. 1984. *Marx's Lost Aesthetic: Karl Marx and the Visual Arts*. Cambridge: Cambridge University Press.

Rosen, Zvi. 1977. *Bruno Bauer and Karl Marx: The Influence of Bruno Bauer on Marx's Thought*. The Hague: Martinus Nijhoff.

Rotenstreich, Nathan. 1959. "For and against Emancipation: The Bruno Bauer Controversy." *Leo Baeck Institute Yearbook* 4: 3–36.

Sayer, Derek. 1979. *Marx's Method*. Brighton: Harvester.

———. 1983. *Marx's Method: Ideology, Science and Critique in Capital*. Hassocks: Harvester.

Sayers, Sean. 1998. *Marxism and Human Nature*. London: Routledge.

———. 2011. *Marx and Alienation: Essays on Hegelian Themes*. Basingstoke: Palgrave Macmillan.

Schacht, Richard. 1970. *Alienation*. New York: Doubleday.

Schmidt, Alfred. 1971. *The Concept of Nature in Marx*. Trans. B. Fowkes. London: New Left Books.

Schuller, Peter M. 1975. "Karl Marx's Atheism." *Science & Society* 39, no. 3: 331–45.

Toews, John Edward. 1980. *The Path toward Dialectical Humanism, 1805–1848*. Cambridge: Cambridge University Press.

Torrance, John. 1977. *Estrangement, Alienation and Exploitation: A Sociological Approach to Historical Materialism*. London: Macmillan.

———. 1995. *Karl Marx's Theory of Ideas*. Cambridge: Cambridge University Press.

Tucker, Robert C. 1986. *Philosophy and Myth in Karl Marx*. New York: Cambridge University Press.

Venable, Vernon. 1966. *Human Nature: The Marxian View*. Cleveland, OH: Meridian.

Walton, Paul, and Andrew Gamble. 1972. *From Alienation to Surplus Value*. London: Sheed and Ward.

White, James D. 1996. *Karl Marx and the Intellectual Origins of Dialectical Materialism*. London: Macmillan.

Wilson, H. T. 1991. *Marx's Critical/Dialectical Procedure*. London: Routledge.

MARX'S SOCIAL THEORY

Aaron, Raymond. 1968. "Karl Marx." In *Main Currents in Sociological Thought I*. Trans. Richard Howard and Hellen Weaver, 145–236. Garden City, NY: Doubleday & Company.

Acton, Harry B. 1967. *What Marx Really Said.* New York: Schocken Books.

Akram-Lodhi, A. Haroon, and Cristobal Kay. 2010. "Surveying the Agrarian Question (Part 1): Unearthing Foundations, Exploring Diversity." *Journal of Peasant Studies* 37, no. 1: 177–202.

Althusser, Louis. 1969. *For Marx.* Trans. Ben Brewster. New York: Pantheon Books.

Amin, Samir. 2006. "Globalization and the Agrarian Question: Peasants' Conflicts in Africa and Asia." In *Globalization and the Third World*, edited by B. Gosh and H. M. Guven, 165–81. London: Palgrave Macmillan.

Anderson, Kevin B. 2010. *Marx at the Margins: On Nationalism, Ethnicity, and Non-Western Societies.* Chicago: University of Chicago Press.

Avineri, Shlomo. 1968. *The Social and Political Thought of Karl Marx.* Cambridge: Cambridge University Press.

Baran, Paul, and Paul Sweezy. 1966. *Monopoly Capitalism.* New York: Monthly Review Press.

Barzun, Jacques. 1941. *Darwin, Marx, Wagner: Critique of a Heritage.* Boston: Little, Brown.

Bellofiore, Ricardo. 1998. *Marxian Economics: A Reappraisal. Essays on Volume III of Capital.* 2 vols. Ed. Ricardo Bellofiore. Houndmills: Macmillan.

Benner, Erica. 1995. *Really Existing Nationalisms: A Post-Communist View from Marx and Engels.* Oxford: Clarendon Press.

Bimber, B. 1990. "Karl Marx and the Three Faces of Technological Determinism." *Social Studies of Science* 20, no. 2: 333–51.

Bleaney, Michael F. 1976. *Underconsumption Theories: A History and Critical Analysis.* New York: International Publishers.

Bloom, Solomon F. 1941. *The World of Nations: A Study of the National Implications in the Work of Marx.* New York: Columbia University Press.

Bober, M. M. 1965. *Karl Marx's Interpretation of History.* New York: Norton.

Bohm-Bawerk, Eugen von. 1949. *Karl Marx and the Close of His System.* Ed. Paul Sweezey. Trans. Alice McDonald. New York: H. Wolf.

Bottomore, Thomas B. 1973. *Makers of Modern Social Science: Karl Marx.* Englewood Cliffs, NJ: Prentice Hall.

———. 1979. *Karl Marx.* Ed. Thomas B. Bottomore. Oxford: Blackwell.

Bradley, I., and M. Howard. 1982. *Classical and Marxian Political Economy.* London: Macmillan.

Burns, Emile. 1966. *Introduction to Marxism.* London: Lawrence and Wishart.

Carver, Terrell. 1982. *Marx's Social Theory.* Oxford: Oxford University Press.

———. 1991. *The Cambridge Companion to Marx.* Cambridge: Cambridge University Press.

Cohen, Gerry A. 1978. *Karl Marx's Theory of History: A Defence.* Oxford: Clarendon Press.

Cole, G. D. H. 1934. *What Marx Really Meant.* New York: Knopf.

Cowling, Mark. 1998. *The Communist Manifesto: New Interpretations.* Edinburgh: Edinburgh University Press.

Cullenberg, Stephen. 1994. *The Falling Rate of Profit: Recasting the Marxian Debate.* London: Pluto Press.

Cutler, Anthony, et al. 1977. *Marx's Capital and Capitalism Today, Volume One.* London: Routledge and Kegan Paul.

de Brunoff, Suzanne. 1976. *Marx on Money.* London: Pluto Press.

Draper, Hal. 1987. *"The Dictatorship of the Proletariat" from Marx to Lenin.* New York: Monthly Review Press.

———. 1990. *Karl Marx's Theory of Revolution.* 4 vols. New York: Monthly Review Press.

———. 1994. *The Adventures of the Communist Manifesto.* Berkeley, CA: Centre for Socialist History.

Dussel, Enrique. 2001. *Towards an Unknown Marx: A Commentary on the Manuscripts of 1861–63.* Trans. Yolanda Angulo. London: Routledge.

Elster, Jon. 1985. *Making Sense of Marx.* Cambridge: Cambridge University Press.

———. 1986. *An Introduction to Marx.* Cambridge: Cambridge University Press.

Elwell, Frank W. 2003. *Karl Marx: 1818–1883.* http://www.faculty.rsu.edu/users/f/felwell/www/Theorists/Marx/index.htm.

Fine, Ben, and L. Harris. 1979. *Rereading "Capital."* New York: Columbia University Press.

Fine, Ben. 1975. *Marx's "Capital."* London: Macmillan.

Fischer, Ernst. 1970. *Marx in His Own Words.* London: Allen Lane.

Fleischer, Helmut. 1971. *Marx and Marxism.* New York: Herder and Herder.

———. 1973. *Marxism and History.* Trans. Eric Mosbacher. London: Allen Lane.

Gandy, Roger. 1979. *Marx and History: From Primitive Society to the Communist Future.* Austin: University of Texas Press.

Gilbert, Alan. 1981. *Marx's Politics: Communists and Citizens.* Oxford: Robertson.

Gillman, Joseph M. 1957. *The Falling Rate of Profit: Marx's Law and its Significance to 20th Century Capitalism.* New York: Cameron Associates.

Graham, Keith. 1992. *Karl Marx: Our Contemporary: Social Theory for a Post-Leninist World.* London: Harvester Wheatsheaf.

Hammen, Oscar J. 1972. "Marx and the Agrarian Question." *American Historical Review* 77, no. 3: 679–704.

Harris, Richard. L. 1978. "Marxism and the Agrarian Question in Latin America." *Latin American Perspectives* 5, no. 4: 2–26.

Harvey, David. 1982. *The Limits to Capital.* Oxford: Blackwell.

———. 2003. *The New Imperialism.* Oxford: Oxford University Press.

———. 2010a. *A Companion to Marx's Capital.* London: Verso.

———. 2010b. *The Enigma of Capital: And the Crisis of Capitalism.* Oxford: Oxford University Press.

———. 2013. *A Companion to Marx's Capital: Volume 2.* London: Verso.

Heller, Agnes. 1976. *The Theory of Need in Marx.* London: Allison and Busby.

Hobsbawm, Eric. 1998. *The Communist Manifesto: A Modern Edition.* Ed. Eric Hobsbawm. London: Verso.

Hoffman, John. 1975. *Marxism and the Theory of Praxis.* London: Lawrence and Wishart.

Hoogvelt, Ankie M. 1982. *The Third World in Global Development.* London: Macmillan.

Horowitz, David. 1968. *Marx and Modern Economics.* London: MacGibbon and Kee.

Hughes, Jonathan. 2000. *Ecology and Historical Materialism.* Cambridge: Cambridge University Press.

Hunt, Richard. 1974. *The Political Ideas of Marx and Engels.* London: Macmillan.

Isaac, Jeffrey C., ed. 2012. *The Communist Manifesto (Rethinking the Western Tradition).* New Haven, CT: Yale University Press.

Jakubowski, Franz. 1936. *Ideology and Superstructure in Historical Materialism.* https://www.marxists.org/archive/jakubowski/1936/Ideology-Superstructure.pdf.

Jay, Martin. 1982. *Marxism and Totality.* Berkeley: University of California Press.

Jessop, Bob, and Malcolm Brown. 1990. *Karl Marx: Social and Political Thought, Critical Assessments.* 4 vols. Ed. Bob Jessop and Malcolm-Brown. London: Routledge.

Jessop, Bob, and Russell Wheatly. 1999. *Karl Marx: Social and Political Thought, Critical Assessments.* 4 vols. Ed. Bob Jessop and Russell Wheatly. London: Routledge.

Katz, Claudio J. 1992. "Marx on the Peasantry: Class in Itself or Class in Struggle?" *Review of Politics* 54, no. 1: 50–71.

Kelley, Donald. 1978. "The Metaphysics of Law: An Essay on the Very Young Marx." *American Historical Review* 83, no. 2: 350–67.

———. 1984. "The Science of Anthropology: An Essay on the Very Old Marx." *Journal of the History of Ideas* 83, no. 2: 245–63.

Kitching, Gavin. 1988. *Karl Marx and the Philosophy of Praxis.* London: Routledge.

Koren, Henry. 1967. *Marx and the Authentic Man: A First Introduction to the Philosophy of Karl Marx.* Pittsburgh, PA: Duquesne University Press.

Korsch, Karl. 1936. *Karl Marx.* New York: Wiley.

Krader, Lawrence. 1975. *The Asiatic Mode of Production: Sources, Development and Critique of the Writings of Karl Marx.* Assen: Van Gorcum.

Labriola, Antonio. 1895. *Essays on the Materialist Conception of History.* Chicago: C. H. Kerr.

Laclau, Ernesto. 1977. *Politics and Ideology in Marxist Theory*. London: New Left Books.

Lallier, Adalbert G. 1989. *The Economics of Marx's "Grundrisse."* Basingstoke: Macmillan.

Laski, Harold J. 1948. *The Communist Manifesto: A Socialist Landmark*. London: George Allen and Unwin.

Leopold, David. 2007. *The Young Karl Marx: German Philosophy, Modern Politics, and Human Flourishing*. Cambridge: Cambridge University Press.

Levin, Michael. 1989. *Marx and Engels and Liberal Democracy*. Basingstoke: Macmillan.

Levine, Norman. 1975. *The Tragic Deception: Marx Contra Engels*. Santa Barbara, CA: ABC-CLIO.

Lewis, Gordon K. 1952. "Fabian Socialism: Some Aspects of Theory and Practice." *Journal of Politics* 14, no. 3: 442–70.

Little, Daniel. 1986. *The Scientific Marx*. Minneapolis: University of Minnesota Press.

Lovell, David. 1988. *Marx's Proletariat: The Making of a Myth*. London: Routledge.

Löwy, Michael. 2003. *The Theory of Revolution in the Young Karl Marx*. London: Brill.

Luxemburg, Rosa. 1954. *What Is Economics?* New York: Pioneer.

Maarek, Gerard. 1979. *An Introduction to Marx's Das Kapital: A Study in Formalisation*. London: Martin Robertson.

Maguire, John M. 1978. *Marx's Theory of Politics*. Cambridge: Cambridge University Press.

Mandel, Ernest. 1971. *The Formation of Marx's Economic Thought*. London: New Left Books.

———. 1976. "Introduction to Capital Volume 1." In *Capital*, by Karl Marx, 11–86. London: Pelican Books.

———. 1978. "Introduction to Capital Volume 2." In *Capital Volume II*, by Karl Marx, 11–79. London: Clays.

———. 1981. "Introduction to Capital Volume 3." In *Capital Volume III*, by Karl Marx, 9–90. London: Clays.

Marković, Mihailo. 1974. *The Contemporary Marx: Essays on Humanist Communism*. Nottingham: Spokesman Books.

Mazlish, Bruce. 1984. *The Meaning of Karl Marx*. New York: Oxford University Press.

McCarthy, George E. 1988. *Marx's Critique of Science and Positivism: The Methodological Foundations*. Dordrecht: Kluwer Academic Publishers.

———. 1990. *Marx and the Ancients*. Savage, MD: Rowman & Littlefield.

———. 1992. *Marx and Aristotle: Nineteenth-Century German Social Theory and Classical Antiquity*. Ed. G. McCarthy. Savage, MD: Rowman & Littlefield.

McClellan, David. 1980a. *Introduction to "Marx's Grundrisse."* 2nd ed. London: Macmillan.

———. 1980b. *The Thought of Karl Marx*. London: Papermac.

———, ed. 1989. *Marxism: Essential Writings*. Oxford: Oxford University Press.

McMurty, John M. 1978. *The Structure of Marx's World-View*. Princeton, NJ: Princeton University Press.

Megill, Allan. 2002. *Karl Marx: The Burden of Reason*. Lanham, MD: Rowman & Littlefield.

Meikle, Scott. 1985. *Essentialism in the Thought of Karl Marx*. London: Duckworth.

Melotti, Umberto. 1977. *Marx and the Third World*. London: Macmillan.

Miller, Richard W. 1981. *Analyzing Marx: Morality, Power, and History*. Princeton, NJ: Princeton University Press.

Mishra, Ramesh. 1979. "Technology and Social Structure in Marx's Theory: An Exploratory Analysis." *Science and Society* 43, no. 2: 132–57.

Mitrany, David. 1951. *Marx against the Peasant: A Study in Social Dogmatism*. London: Weidenfeld and Nicolson.

Moore, Stanley. 1980. *Marx on the Choice between Socialism and Communism*. Cambridge, MA: Harvard University Press.

Morishima, Michio. 1973. *Marx's Economics*. Cambridge: Cambridge University Press.

Morrison, Ken. 2011. "Karl Max." In *Marx, Durkheim, Weber: Formation of Social Thought*, 35–146, 387–412. Los Angeles: Sage.

Moseley, Fred. 1993. *Marx's Method in Capital*. Atlantic Highlands, NJ: Humanities Press.

Moseley, Fred, and Martha Campbell. 1995.

"Objectification." *Philosophy and Public Affairs* 24, no. 4: 249–91.

———, eds. 1997. *New Investigations of Marx's Method.* Atlantic Highlands, NJ: Humanities Press.

Oakley, Allen. 1985. *Marx's Critique of Political Economy: Intellectual Sources and Evolution.* 2 vols. London: Routledge and Kegan Paul.

Oishi, Takahisa. 2001. *The Unknown Marx: Reconstructing a Unified Perspective.* London: Pluto Press.

Parsons, Howard L. 1977. *Marx and Engels on Ecology.* Ed. H. L. Parsons. Westport, CT: Greenwood.

Perry, Matt. 2002. *Marxism and History.* Basingstoke: Palgrave.

Philips, Paul. 1981. *Marx and Engels on Law and Laws.* Oxford: Martin Robertson.

Pierson, Chris. 1986. *Marxist Theory and Democratic Politics.* Cambridge: Polity Press.

Raddatz, Fritz. 1978. *Karl Marx: A Political Biography.* Trans. Richard Barry. London: Weidenfeld and Nicolson.

Rader, Melvin. 1979. *Marx's Interpretation of History.* Oxford: Oxford University Press.

Rosdolsky, Roman. 1977. *The Making of Marx's "Capital."* London: Pluto Press.

Roth, Regina. 2010. "Marx on Technical Change in the Critical Edition." *European Journal of the History of Economic Thought* 17, no. 5: 1223–51.

Ruben, David-Hillel. 1979. *Marxism and Materialism: A Study in Marxist Theory of Knowledge.* Brighton: Harvester Press.

Rubin, Isaak I. 1973. *Essays on Marx's Theory of Value.* Montreal: Black Rose.

Sayer, Derek. 1979. *Marx's Method.* Brighton: Harvester.

———. 1983. *Marx's Method: Ideology, Science and Critique in Capital.* Hassocks: Harvester.

Shaw, William H. 1978. *Marx's Theory of History.* Stanford, CA: Stanford University Press.

———. 1979. "'The Handmill Gives You the Feudal Lord': Marx's Technological Determinism." *History and Theory* 18, no. 2: 155–76.

Shortall, Felton. 1994. *The Incomplete Marx.* Aldershot: Avebury.

Singer, Peter. 2018. *Marx: A Very Short Introduction.* 2nd ed. Oxford: Oxford University Press.

Sloan, Pat. 1973. *Marx and the Orthodox Economists.* Oxford: Blackwell.

Smith, Cyril. 1996. *Marx at the Millenium.* London: Pluto Press.

Smith, Tony. 1990. *The Logic of Marx's Capital: Replies to Hegelian Criticisms.* Albany: State University of New York Press.

Stanley, John, and Ernest Zimmerman. 1984. "On the Alleged Differences between Marx and Engels." *Political Studies* 33: 226–48.

Stedman-Jones, Gareth. 2002. *Karl Marx and Friedrich Engels: The Communist Manifesto.* Ed. G. Stedman-Jones. London: Penguin Books.

Suchting, Wallis Arthur. 1983. *Marx: An Introduction.* Brighton: Wheatsheaf Books.

Thomas, Robert. 1997. "Enigmatic Writings: Karl Marx's *The Civil War in France* and the Paris Commune of 1871." *History of Political Thought* 18: 483–511.

Toews, John Edward, ed. 1999. *The Communist Manifesto by Karl Marx and Friedrich Engels with Related Documents.* Boston: Bedford/St. Martin's Press.

Tucker, Robert C. 1978. *The Marx-Engels Reader.* 2nd ed. New York: Norton.

Walker, Angus. 1978. *Marx: His Theory and Its Context.* London: Longman.

Walker, David M. 2001. *Marx, Methodology and Science: Marx's Science of Politics.* Aldershot: Ashgate.

Wendling, Amy E. 2011. *Karl Marx on Technology and Alienation.* Basingstoke: Palgrave Macmillan.

Wetherley, Paul. 1992. *Marx's Theory of History: The Contemporary Debate.* Aldershot: Avebury.

Wilde, Lawrence. 1989. *Marx and Contradiction.* Aldershot: Avebury.

Wolff, Jonathan. 2001. *Why Read Marx Today?* New York: Oxford University Press.

Wolff, Richard D., and Stephen A. Resnick. 1984. *Understanding Marx: A Reconstruction and Critique of "Capital."* Princeton, NJ: Princeton University Press.

———. 1987. *Economics: Marxian versus Neoclassical.* Baltimore, MD: Johns Hopkins University Press.

Zeleny, Jindrich. 1980. *The Logic of Marx.* Trans. Terrel Carver. Oxford: Basil Blackwell.

MARX'S SOCIAL SCIENCE LEGACY

Adorno, Theodore. 1950. *The Authoritarian Personality.* New York: Harper & Brothers.

Baran, Paul A., and Paul M. Sweezy. 1966. *Monopoly Capitalism.* New York: Monthly Review Press.

Barrow, Clyde W. 1993. *Critical Theories of the State: Marxist, Neo-Marxist, Post-Marxist.* Madison: University of Wisconsin Press.

Bottomore, Thomas B. 1975. *Marxist Sociology.* London: Macmillan.

———. 1981. *Modern Interpretations of Marx.* Trans. Thomas B. Bottomore. Oxford: Blackwell.

———. 1991. *A Dictionary of Marxist Thought.* Ed. Thomas B. Bottomore. Oxford: Blackwell.

Braverman, Harry. 1974. *Labor and Monopoly Capital: The Degradation of Work.* New York: Monthly Review Press.

Bronfenbrenner, Martin. 1968. "Das Kapital for Modern Man." In *Karl Marx and Modern Economic Theory,* edited by D. Horowitz, 205–26. London: MacGibbon and Kee.

Chandra, Nirmal Kumar. 1998. "Marx, Colonialism and the Market." *Economic and Political Weekly* 33, no. 23: 1375–78.

Elwell, Frank W. 1999. *Industrializing America: Understanding Contemporary Society through Classical Sociological Analysis.* Westport, CT: Praeger.

———. 2013. "Capital." In *Sociocultural Systems: Principles of Structure and Change,* by Frank W. Elwell, 155–91. Edmonton: Athabasca University Press.

Foster, John Bellamy. 1998. "Introduction to the 1998 Edition of Monopoly Capitalism." In *Monopoly Capitalism,* by Harry Braverman, ix–xxiv. New York: Monthly Review Press.

———. 1999a. *The Vulnerable Planet.* New York: Monthly Review Press.

———. 1999b. "Marx's Theory of Metabolic Rift: Classical Foundations for Environmental Sociology." *American Journal of Sociology* 105, no. 2: 366–405.

———. 2000. *Marx's Ecology: Materialism and Nature.* New York: Monthly Review Press.

———. 2002. *Ecology against Capitalism.* New York: Monthly Review Press.

———. 2006. *Naked Imperialism: The U.S. Pursuit of Global Dominance.* New York: Monthly Review Press.

Giddens, Anthony. 1981. *A Contemporary Critique of Historical Materialism.* London: Macmillan.

Gouldner, Alvin W. 1980. *The Two Marxisms: Contradictions and Anomalies in Marx's Theory of Social Reality.* London: Macmillan.

Harrington, Michael. 1976. *The Twilight of Capitalism.* New York: Touchstone.

Harris, Marvin. 1968. *The Rise of Anthropological Theory.* New York: Crowell.

———. 1979. *Cultural Materialism: The Struggle for a Science of Culture.* New York: Random House.

Heilbronner, Robert L. 1980. *Marxism: For and Against.* New York: Norton.

Herod, Charles C. 1976. *The Nation in the History of Marxian Thought.* The Hague: Martinus Nijhoff.

Johnson, Elliot, David Walker, and Daniel Gray. 2014. *Historical Dictionary of Marxism.* Lanham, MD: Rowman & Littlefield.

Johnston, Les. 1986. *Marxism, Class Analysis and Socialist Pluralism.* London: George Allen and Unwin.

Kain, Phillip J. 1993. *Marx and Modern Political Theory.* Lanham, MD: Rowman & Littlefield.

Kilroy-Silk, Robert. 1972. *Socialism since Marx.* London: Allen Lane Penguin Books.

Kornai, Janos. 1992. *The Socialist System: The Political Economy of Communism.* Oxford: Clarendon Press.

Lenski, Gerhard. 1966. *Power and Privilege: A Theory of Social Stratification.* New York: Random House.

———. 2005. *Ecological-Evolutionary Theory: Principles and Applications.* Boulder, CO: Paradigm.

Mandel, Ernest. 1975. *Late Capitalism.* Atlantic Highlands, NJ: New Left Books and Humanities Press.

Mandel, Ernest, and George Novak. 1973. *The Marxist Theory of Alienation.* New York: Pathfinder Press.

Mastellone, Salvo. 2003. *Mazzini and Marx: Thoughts upon Democracy in Europe.* London: Praeger.

Mattick, Paul. 1971. *Marx and Keynes: The Limits of the Mixed Economy.* London: Merlin Press.

McDermott, Kevin, and Jeremy Agnew. 1996. *The Comintern: A History of International Communism from Lenin to Stalin.* New York: Palgrave Macmillan.

Miller, David, Janet Coleman, William Connolly, Alan Ryan, and Joseph Femia, eds. 1991. *The Blackwell Encyclopaedia of Political Thought.* New York: Wiley/Blackwell.

Mills, C. Wright. 1951/1970. *White Collar: The American Middle Classes.* New York: Oxford University Press.

————. 1956/1970. *The Power Elite.* New York: Oxford University Press.

————. 1958. *The Causes of World War Three.* London: Secker & Warburg.

————. 1959. *The Sociological Imagination.* New York: Oxford University Press.

Petrovic, Gajo. 1967. *Marx in the Mid-Twentieth Century.* Garden City, NY: Doubleday.

Roll, Eric. 1973. *A History of Economic Thought.* 4th ed. London: Faber & Faber.

Sanderson, Stephen. 1990. *Social Evolutionism: A Critical History.* Oxford: Basil Blackwell.

————. 1999. *Social Transformations: A General Theory of Historical Development.* Lanham, MD: Rowman & Littlefield.

Steedman, Ian. 1997. *Marx after Sraffa.* London: Verso.

Sweezy, Paul. 1968. *The Theory of Capitalist Development: Principles of Marxian Political Economy.* New York: Monthly Review Press.

Swingewood, Alan. 1975. *Marx and Modern Social Theory.* London: Macmillan.

The International. 1963–1968. *Documents of the First International.* 5 vols. London: Lawrence and Wishart.

U.S. Census Bureau. 2017. *Full-Time, Year-Round Workers and Median Earnings: 2000 and 2013–2018.* https://www.census.gov/data/tables/time-series/demo/industry-occupation/median-earnings.html.

Wallerstein, Immanuel. 1974. *The Modern World-System: Capitalist Agriculture and the Origins of the European World-Economy in the Sixteenth Century.* New York: Academic Press.

————. 1980. *The Modern World-System II: Mercantilism and the Consolidation of the European World-Economy, 1600–1750.* New York: Academic Press.

————. 1989. *The Modern World-System III: The Second Era of Great Expansion of the Capitalist World-Economy, 1730–1840.* New York: Academic Press.

————. 1999. *The End of the World as We Know It.* Minneapolis: University of Minnesota Press.

————. 2000. *The Essential Wallerstein.* New York: New Press.

Wilczynski, Joseph. 1981. *An Encyclopedic Dictionary of Marxism, Socialism and Communism.* London: Macmillan.

Wood, Ellen Meiksins. 1995. *Democracy against Capitalism: Renewing Historical Materialism.* Cambridge: Cambridge University Press.

Woodin, Rupert, and Oscar Zarate. 2004. *Introducing Marxism: A Graphic Guide.* Royston: Icon Books.

Worsley, Peter. 1982. *Marx and Marxism.* London: Tavistock.

Index

64–65; IWA affiliation with, 25, 80; merger with ADAV, 101, 104, 124, 138, 205, 206; as vanguard party, 235
social division of labor, 71, 187, 207
social evolution: communism in, 49, 87, 186, 207, 213; Darwinist, 130; Engels on, 20, 173–74, 207; Enlightenment and, 213; of forces and relations of production, 47, 187–88, 238; historical materialism and, 87, 164; Morgan's stages of development, 19, 164, 173, 207; peasantry in, 15; proletariat in, 5, 7–8; technology in, 20, 173, 207
socialism: anti-imperialist, 107; Christian, 201; economic preconditions for, 63; Enlightenment and, 17, 168, 169; evolutionary, 26–27, 87, 92, 124, 146, 193–94, 206; free-market interpretation of, 164; Narodniks on, 165; in 19th-century, 104, 168–69, 223; schisms within, 23, 51, 123, 189; scientific, 19, 81, 97, 175, 201–2, 209, 251. *See also* Anti-Socialist Laws; revolutionary socialism; utopian socialism
socialism in one country, 35, 51, 180–81, 208–9, 214–15, 227, 230
Socialism: Utopian and Scientific (Engels), 19, 42, 81, 97, 157, 175, 202, 209–10, 243
Socialist League, 21, 32, 154, 205, 210–11
socialist mode of production, 163, 209, 211
socialist revolution: alienation and, 17; Blanquism on, 29; Bonapartism and, 31; collapse of capitalism and, 250; counterrevolutionary forces, 30–31, 45, 57, 165, 180–81, 227; expropriation of capitalist class in, 47; preconditions for, 1, 7–8, 15–16, 29, 45, 51, 73, 232; sequence for, 17, 29, 93, 105, 121, 180, 235; skepticism regarding, 105. *See also* class struggle; proletariat; revolutionary socialism
Socialist Workers' Party (SWP), 32, 249
socialization of labor, 42, 47, 79, 88, 211, 223
social labor, 13, 63, 92, 138, 207, 210–11
socially necessary labor time, 13, 52, 134, 150, 188, 192, 211
social relations: defined, 207–8; evolution of, 20; in primitive communism, 81–82, 186; private property and, 82, 87; of production, 105, 149, 184, 187–88, 221, 238; state interference in, 243;

technological changes and, 173. *See also* relations of production
social reproduction, 208
Society of Free Men, 82, 198, 211–12
Soviets, 30, 56, 69, 191, 212, 226
Soviet-style communism, 1, 14, 21, 53, 199
Soviet Union. *See* Union of Soviet Socialist Republics
Spartacist Uprising (1919), 75–76, 109, 141–42, 146, 212–13
Spartacus League, 56, 98, 119, 141–42, 146–47, 206, 212, 213, 250
SPD. *See* Social Democratic Party of Germany
species-being, 16, 114, 172, 185, 213
stages of historical development, 19, 53, 87, 186, 191, 207, 213, 238
stagnation. *See* economic stagnation
Stalin, Joseph: background of, 215; Bonapartism as utilized by, 31; cult of personality, 209, 214; death of, 215, 230; dialectical materialism and, 71; Great Purge (Terror) under, 35, 51, 56, 214, 230; Lenin on, 141, 208, 216–17; painting of, *216*; on social evolution, 20; on socialism in one country, 51, 180–81, 214–15, 227, 230; Trotsky and, 35, 56, 208–9, 213–14, 225, 227, 250
Stalinism, 104, 145, 206, 213–15, 240
state: anarchism on legitimacy of, 17; in Asiatic mode of production, 20; Bakunin on destruction of, 23; basis for power held by, 247; Blanquism on destruction of, 29; capitalist, 7, 11, 41–42, 65, 86, 224, 245; idealism of, 172; LaSallean view of, 27; withering away of, 49, 73, 81, 180–82, 243; in world system of capitalism, 251–52
Statism and Anarchy (Bakunin), 59
Stirner, Max, 102, 217, 247
Strauss, David, 247
structure. *See* base; superstructure
superstructure: bourgeoisie and, 24, 48, 174; capitalist mode of production and, 24, 240; durability of, 218; in historical materialism, 21, 24, 71, 112, 184, 207, 217, 247; as manifestation of false consciousness, 217; proletariat and, 24, 48, 174; religion in, 24, 48, 95, 193, 217, 247; technological determinism and, 221
surplus labor: in Asiatic mode of production, 20; in capitalist mode of production, 137,

About the Authors

Frank W. Elwell worked his way through high school and college as a dishwasher, waiter, factory operative, and ice cream man. He received a bachelor's degree from Eastern Michigan University (history/education) and became an inner-city high school teacher in New York. Going to college part-time for a few years, he received a master's degree in political science/education from the State University of New York at New Paltz. Discovering the joys of learning in that graduate program, he left his teaching job and became a full-time student at the University of Albany, earning a master's and a PhD in sociology from that institution. He has been an instructor in higher education since 1979, rising through the ranks to full professor. As a college administrator, he has served as a department chair for 12 years and a dean of liberal arts for another 12. He is currently the chair of the Faculty Senate and a full professor at Rogers State University. He is the author of six books on macrosociology, cultural ecology, and social theory. He is married to his wife Patricia, and they have four daughters and six granddaughters.

Brian N. Andrews holds a BA in anthropology from the University of Oklahoma, an MA in anthropology from the University of Wyoming, and an MA and PhD in anthropology from Southern Methodist University. His research focuses primarily on hunter-gatherer societies with an emphasis on the nature of technological evolution and change over time and its impacts on social organization, and he has active archaeological research projects in Colorado, Oklahoma, and New Mexico. His publications include papers in the journals *American Antiquity*, *Journal of Archaeological Science*, *Journal of Anthropological Archaeology*, and others. He has served as a guest editor for the journal *PaleoAmerica* and coauthored the *Oxford Bibliographies* entry for cultural materialism. As an associate professor in the Department of Psychology and Sociology at Rogers State University, he teaches a wide variety of classes in anthropology, sociology, social theory, and quantitative research methods. When not in the field or teaching, he spends time at home in Claremore, Oklahoma, with his wife Jill and their three daughters, four cats, and two dogs.

Kenneth S. Hicks (MA international relations theory, PhD political theory, University of South Carolina) is department head of history and political science at Rogers State University. He teaches courses on ideology and the discipline of political science and has taught on a wide array of issues, including political theory, national security, terrorism, and foreign policy, among others. His research interests focus on the challenges confronting the American constitutional system and the role that ideological intensification plays in contributing to the growing dysfunction of the American government.